Doctor Zero: Year One

ISBN: 1-4528-4814-9
ISBN-13: 9781452848143

Doctor Zero: Year One

John Hayward

2010

Dedication

For Marge, whose love carries me forward

Table of Contents

Introduction

I first became aware of blog writing during the primary season of the 2004 presidential campaign. A friend sent me a link to a blogger called Allahpundit. I ended up reading everything at his site, and began following his links to other writers, crawling through blogrolls well into the night. I realized I had discovered the world beyond the printing press, where writers could publish themselves without passing through editorial gatekeepers, to rise and fall largely on the merits of their work.

When Michelle Malkin launched Hot Air, it quickly became my favorite blog site. It has a lively and fast-paced mixture of news and commentary, often delivered within minutes of a major event—a dry martini of wit and information, vigorously shaken *and* stirred. I was delighted when Allahpundit, the very first blogger I followed, became a regular member of the Hot Air team. I became fascinated by the comment forums, the busiest and most engrossing I had found on the Internet. Hot Air requires comment registration, issued only once every few months. I jumped at the first registration opportunity I saw.

I never had any particular reason to be anonymous—I just wanted to come up with an interesting user name. While I was trying to think of one, my gaze fell upon a treasured gift from one of my closest friends.

During my college years, I was a fan of an obscure comic book called "Doctor Zero," published by Marvel Comics under its edgy Epic Comics imprint. The main character was an ancient, powerful being who lived secretly among humanity, until he became concerned they would devastate the Earth through nuclear war, before he was finished with it. He decided to reveal himself and pose as a super-hero, to pull humanity back from the brink of global war. His true nature was ruthless and vicious—he quickly realized that roaming around and looking for people to help was time-consuming, so it was much easier to cause accidents and disasters himself, then fly up to "save the day." As the series progressed through its short run, the writers began a subtle moral evolution for Doctor Zero, exploring the idea that an immortal, utterly amoral man might *reason* himself into becoming a true hero…one tiny, grudging step at a time. The series only lasted eight issues, so the writers never had a chance to finish the tale, but I found it very compelling.

Knowing of my fondness for this long-lost story, my artistic friend produced a unique action figure of Doctor Zero, modifying and repainting parts from existing toys. (There's a whole artistic subculture of people who practice this hobby.) This plastic treasure standing on my desk became the inspiration for my Hot Air user name. Hot Air eventually introduced a forum for guest writers called the Green Room, inviting some well-established bloggers to contribute content for their rapidly growing site. This was such a success that the administrators decided to invite some of the forum commenters to post in the Green Room as well. They set up a thread for readers to nominate the recipients of this privilege. I logged in to vote for someone else...and discovered a lot of people were voting for me. I received my formal invitation to begin writing for Hot Air a few days later, and on April 30, 2009, I wrote my first essay, "Money Versus Wealth." It's all been a happy, thrilling blur since then.

I gave up my anonymity when I launched my own Web site, www.doczero.org, on Christmas Eve of 2009. I still love writing under the name "Doctor Zero." It evokes what I've come to love about the art of blogging: starting over from zero, every single time. I have no great journalistic or professional credentials. People don't read my work because of *who I am*. To the disappointment of those who used to speculate that I was someone famous working under a pseudonym, I'm nobody—just a guy living out in flyover country who reads a lot, and discovered that people like the way I express myself. Every blog post is a fresh opportunity to take my best shot at promoting my beliefs about economics, politics, and culture. I don't have any authority or position to dazzle my readers with. I don't even have any influence over when my essays get promoted to the Hot Air main page. I start with nothing, do my best, and receive the judgment of readers within a matter of hours.

It's heaven.

What follows is a collection of essays from the first year of my blogging career. I've made some small edits, mostly to convert hyper-links into brief summaries of the material that would have been found at the link. I've also added some author's notes to provide history and context. The essays are grouped according to topic. I hope you find them to be of some value! Even if you disagree with the points I'm trying to make, I would be delighted if you at least found some entertainment in the way I make them...or, better still, discover some worthy intellectual challenge lurking in these pages.

Part One
Capitalism

Capitalism is the practical expression of freedom, and wealth allows the tangible expression of compassion.

Money Versus Wealth
April 30, 2009

Author's Note: This is the first essay I wrote for Hot Air. It touched on something I found common in media discussions of economics. I've always felt "wealth" is a very important, subtle concept, so it seemed natural to tackle it during my first time at bat. You could say this essay is the Rosetta Stone for understanding my thoughts on almost everything related to capitalism and economic freedom.

One way to measure the "transformational" power of the Obama presidency is to consider how quickly Democrats transformed from the steel-taloned deficit hawks of the Bush years, into a party very comfortable with trillion-dollar deficits, and a fifteen-trillion-plus national debt. Anyone old enough to remember the early Clinton years has seen this happen before, of course. As the shadow of the Obama deficits looms over the economy, we can expect to begin seeing the sort of breezy journalism we got in the Nineties, wondering exactly why deficits are so bad. The fact that liberals are willing to ask the question illustrates one of the fatal flaws in socialist economic policy: the confusion between money and wealth.

Money is easy to create. Obama has already stolen a trillion dollars of it from the future. All that was required was printing up a few more stacks of bills, and adding a few more zeroes to various federal balance sheets. Last night, like every other day of his presidency, Obama spoke about how much money he plans to "invest" in various government programs. Liberals in general, and the news media in particular, use the amount of money thrown at any given problem as the sole important method of measuring how much we "care" about it.

Wealth is a far more elusive, and important, part of the economy than money. Wealth is what people do with their money...and even more to the point, it's what people could do with their money. Free people in a free economy create wealth through their choices. You can run down to the grocery store and spend ten dollars buying steak to cook for dinner tonight, or you could go to a restaurant and spend two or three times that much, having the steak expertly prepared for you. Sixty bucks might seem like a lot to spend on dinner...but how much would it cost you to venture forth into the wilderness and hunt your own dinner down, or raise your own cattle and slaughter them? Suppose you make twenty dollars per hour at your job. That grocery-store steak is worth half an hour of your time, and the fine dinner at a five-star steak house cost three hours of your income. Compared to the time and effort it would take you to hunt or butcher your own meat, even assuming you knew how—and were lucky enough to have a successful hunt tonight—it's a bargain. You create wealth by giving your money to the grocer or restaurant for your dinner, and now they have money to invest or spend according to their needs and desires. Meanwhile, you also created wealth for your employer, because you were able to spend hours working at your day job, instead of fooling around in the brush with a bow and arrow, trying to bring down a deer.

Modern technology greatly amplifies wealth creation. You couldn't possibly build yourself a computer or automobile from raw materials, no matter how much time you invested. You can't perform surgery on yourself. The twenty dollars in your pocket represents vast wealth, because you can choose to spend it in so many different ways, and your employers chose to give it to you (after taxes, of course) because the hour you spent earning it was worth more than having a twenty-dollar bill sitting in their vaults. You can use that twenty dollars to buy things that the last Egyptian pharaoh could not have purchased with all the gold in his kingdom, or all the kingdoms of the world combined. The computer you're using to read these words is vastly more powerful and easy to use than it would have been a decade ago, because the pursuit of profits drove computer and software companies to compete and produce better products, and their competition created wealth. You're probably using high-speed Internet and a comfortable flat-screen monitor to read this, using a computer that can do a dozen other things at the same time, and if you wanted to share this essay with a friend, you could email a link in seconds.

The wealth built into that twenty dollar bill dissipates if you're not allowed to choose how you spend it. How wealthy are you if the grocer takes your twenty bucks and tells you that you have to eat fish instead of steak...and you're allergic to fish? How wealthy would you be if your employer paid you in company scrip, which could be spent only at the company store, on a limited selection of products the company sees fit to offer—at whatever price they decide to charge? Even though that scrip has value—you can buy stuff with it—it represents much less wealth, because you have fewer choices in how to spend it.

Socialism annihilates wealth. Government control of the economy destroys the value of the dollars circulating through its bloodstream. Every one of the trillion dollars Obama dumped on the American economy reduced the value of every dollar that was already here, because government stimulus bills create no wealth—they just force the economy to spend money in ways it didn't want to. Not a single hour of productive labor is created when a big pile of deficit dollars is sucked out of the free market and expelled from Washington. Socialism creates the illusion of prosperity by forcing money to be spent in politically favored areas, then shining the media spotlight on where the money was spent...and hoping nobody notices all the choices that weren't made, all the possibilities that were foreclosed, fading away in the darkness outside that spotlight. And deficit spending is ultimately the worst excess of socialism, because it destroys the wealth of the future, taking away their choices and options... draining the lifeblood from the America that could have been, in the arrogant knowledge that an aborted future does not have a voice to defend its interests, and the voters of today will never stumble across the corpses of murdered opportunities.

That is why deficit spending on Obama's scale is so awful: because it takes a trillion dollars from the future without asking its permission, burns away a vast amount of the wealth that money represented, replaces it with a debt that can only grow worse with every passing year, and tries to convince the American people the whole transaction was a bargain.

Who Mines the Dilithium?
May 15, 2009

Author's Note: This was a lot of fun to write. It generated a surprisingly energetic response, both from fellow sci-fi fans having a little fun, and serious students of capitalism's moral foundations. Some thought the topic was trivial, but pop culture has a powerful impact on people's expectations of the real world around them. The economics of "Star Trek," at least the latter-day revival, don't even make sense as a daydream.

One of my favorite little moments in the very entertaining new "Star Trek" movie comes when the young James T. Kirk activates the computer system of a car he swiped for a joyride, and the Nokia logo comes up. It's nice to see Nokia's still in business in the twenty-third century. Such simple touches help to humanize the Star Trek universe, which had drifted a bit too far from recognizable human experience for audiences to fully engage with its characters. The presence of a good old-fashioned corporate logo in the new movie put me in mind of a long-ago, free-wheeling, beer-fueled rant after I saw a previous "Star Trek" movie with some friends, and we asked ourselves, "Who mines the dilithium?"

In the 1996 film "Star Trek: First Contact," there is a scene in which a woman from our near future asks time-traveling twenty-fourth century Captain Jean-Luc Picard how much the Enterprise cost to build. Picard replies that money doesn't exist in his enlightened future era. "The acquisition of wealth is no longer the driving force in our lives," he assures her. "We work to better ourselves, and the rest of humanity."

Gee, that sounds swell, doesn't it? How did the Federation outgrow capitalism? Well, they have a technology called "replicators," which allows them to manufacture almost any form of matter out of energy. This might not seem like a very useful technology, since if I remember my high school physics correctly, it would take the power of a thousand exploding suns to create enough matter for a decent New York strip steak and a side order of mashed potatoes, but not to worry—they also have virtually unlimited energy in the future, thanks to a crystal called "dilithium." So, in the twenty-fourth century, they have vast amounts of cheap energy, and they can create matter with it, so nobody needs money, because all material desires are easily fulfilled.

Where does dilithium come from? You mine it from extremely unpleasant planets, where the miners live stoic lives of terrible loneliness and physical hardship, as seen in the 1960s Star Trek TV episode "Mudd's Women." The miners' lives are so wretched, they're willing to contract with a con artist to bring them mail-order brides. It would seem the mining process cannot be fully automated, since the technology of Captain Kirk's day was sufficiently advanced to have done so, if it were possible. (Of course, until the character of Lt. Data was introduced in the "Next Generation" series, the Star Trek guys seemed very squeamish about building self-aware machines—and with good reason, since they always turned into planet-destroying psychotic monsters.) So: who's working in those dilithium mines? Is the Federation lucky enough to have an adequate number of people who find self-fulfillment by volunteering to work in dingy hell-holes, digging up those precious crystals? Those guys aren't prisoners being forced to work off their sentences, are they? That didn't seem to be the case in the TV episode.

More evidence of the absurdity of the twenty-fourth century's flimsy Utopia is easy to find. In the series "Deep Space Nine", Captain Sisko's father was an expert chef who ran a restaurant in New Orleans. He might indeed have been cooking because he enjoyed it and found it fulfilling, but what about the people waiting tables in his restaurant? Is that your fate if you score poorly on the benevolent Federation's aptitude tests? A "D" grade leaves you slinging crawdaddies in Sisko's restaurant, while an "F" means it's off to the dilithium mines? That doesn't sound like a society to brag about. And what happens if you refuse to accept the menial job assigned to you by the Federation, when they determined you're a moron? Do they force you to work at gunpoint? Or is the future Earth filled with layabouts who just watch holographic game shows and replicate Hot Pockets all day? If so, perhaps they were too quick to repel the Borg invasion in "First Contact"—it would have been their best chance of reaching Bush-era unemployment lows. The Borg are always hiring.

There's an even deeper flaw in the Star Trek utopia, revealed by contemplating Sisko's restaurant: Who gets to eat there? The elder Sisko is supposed to be one of the best chefs around. How do you get a table at his restaurant? Is there a four-hundred-year waiting list, the way "free" medicine is rationed in socialist countries? All the free matter and energy in the universe can't change the fact there's only one Sisko Senior, and he's only got two hands to cook with. What about works of art? Certainly they can be copied easily enough, but what if somebody wants an original? All of the "Star Trek" shows had literary pretensions, especially regarding Shakespeare. How are theater seats doled out, when the greatest actors of the twenty-fourth century stage a production of "Hamlet?" If I get sick, I'd sure like to have a doctor as dedicated as Doctor McCoy. How are the services of the top doctors assigned? Are they exclusively assigned to take care of high-ranking military officers and Federation politicians? I'll bet that would be a feature of the twenty-fourth century that Captain Picard wouldn't employ to advertise how advanced and enlightened it is.

"Star Trek" is famous for its wonderful transporter technology, which lets people teleport instantly with planetary range. You could have breakfast in France, pop over to Alaska for a moose hunt, and be in Australia in time for dinner. Who gets to do that? How is the limited amount of transporter capacity distributed between the populace? There might be a lot of transporters, but there certainly aren't enough to allow billions of terrestrial citizens to zip around the globe at will. For that matter, who gets to ride around in starships, besides the military officers that crew the Starfleet vessels? The "Next Generation" crew were forever talking about a wonderful pleasure planet they loved to visit on vacations. Can the people waiting tables in Sisko's restaurant go there for a holiday?

It's interesting to note how quickly the futuristic utopia Captain Picard described to the woman in "First Contact" falls apart when you stop to think about the lives of the ordinary citizens—the people who don't get to boldly go on adventures in starships. Magical technologies that provide limitless resources do nothing to resolve the eternal shortage of the human resource. The kind of thinking that leads socialists to believe they can create perfect national medical systems, welfare programs, or government-controlled financial institutions doesn't even work if you have dilithium crystals to back it up...because somebody has to mine the dilithium, and somebody has to do something meaningful and valuable with all that cheap matter and energy.

Freedom, industry, and capitalism will always be the most ethical and efficient way to allocate those precious human resources. The new "Star Trek" film might have a lot of plot holes, but they've also got Nokia, which means they're living in a world that bears some resemblance to the real one.

The Instruments of Wealth
May 15, 2009

Author's Note: I received a lot of negative feedback for this article from people who despise credit-card companies and their fees. I've been on the wrong end of those fees myself, and I didn't like them either. I've had my little disputes with these companies, and I've won a few of them. I always viewed my ultimate recourse as reporting them to enforcement agencies (when they behaved in a unscrupulous manner) or taking my business elsewhere (when they did something legal I didn't like.) The credit-card reforms which prompted the writing of this piece are a classic example of opportunistic government looking for a populist issue to build its latest play for control and popularity. The results, one year later, have been about what I expected: everybody pays more, so that a targeted constituency can feel gratitude to a State that maxed out its credit cards long ago.

President Obama has lately been pushing a credit-card reform bill in the Senate, which he says is designed to curb abuses by the card issuers. Among these "abuses" are interest-rate hikes imposed on delinquent card holders, and applying payments first to lower-interest balances rolled over from other credit cards at discounted introductory rates. "Americans know that they have a responsibility to live within their means and pay what they owe. But they also have a right to not get ripped off," the President argued in his weekly radio address. "Abuses in our credit card industry have only multiplied in the midst of this recession, when Americans can least afford to bear an extra burden."

Of course, nobody who has ever been on the receiving end of a credit card rate hike likes them very much, and such increased costs are indeed tougher for consumers to bear in a recession. We might, however, ask how a company exercising its lawful right to adjust its fees—in accordance with terms clearly spelled out on the agreements signed by its customers—is "ripping Americans off." It might not be nice for credit-card companies to raise their rates on struggling clients, and it might not be a sound business practice in a down economy, but it's not fraud. Maybe someone with access to unlimited media exposure, such as the President, could use his bully pulpit to call upon these companies to exercise more compassionate policies toward their customers, and suggest the competitive advantage in being able to advertise their "kinder and gentler" credit products, instead of treating them like perps in a police lineup.

These casual accusations of criminality and deceit come easily to Obama, who has been a real bull in the china shop of the credit industry. He's threatened Chrysler's bond holders with personal destruction, and used raw government power to adjust the balances on home mortgages. Nervous banks have taken TARP funds designed to stimulate new lending, and sat on those funds instead, because they're afraid to make loans in the increasingly Venezu-elan business environment the Administration has created. U.S. Treasury bonds are losing frightening amounts of value in the face of reckless deficit spending. This Administration probably wouldn't exist if a group of fabulously corrupt senators—including Barack Hussein Obama—hadn't gotten rich by forcing the mortgage industry to make unrealistic loans to politically favored constituent groups, and fending off every attempt to correct the system before it crashed.

This is all very bad news for our future, because **credit**—in all its forms—is one of the most advanced instruments for the creation of wealth ever devised. A market filled with timid lenders and frightened borrowers is a market where wealth shrivels away.

In the most primitive type of economy, people barter goods and services directly. If you want some of the meat I brought back from my hunt, you have to give me some eggs. Besides being terribly inconvenient, the barter system makes complex financial transactions impossible, because value is so difficult to determine precisely. My hunk of venison is worth as many eggs as you're willing to give me, and the next person I trade with might be pre-pared to give me more, or less. It's hard to make trades with high values, or perform complex transactions, or carry goods over long distances to trade with distant folks. Consumers are reluctant to trade for anything they can't assess personally. How can I tell if I'm trading for good meat, or well-made shoes, or a decent clay pot, if I don't know anything about hunting, leather-working, or pottery?

The first contribution government makes to an economy is security. The government makes it safe to hunt, farm, or travel, by keeping away bandits and predators. The second contribution is a stable currency. Money gives consumers and producers a way to transport their wealth easily, and have confidence in the value of a transaction. It also makes much more complex financial arrangements possible, as people can pool their efforts in exchange for shares of value. A group of people can work together to do something, earn money, and then divide the money between themselves, much more easily than they could in a barter system. The exchange of money creates wealth. You give the shoemaker some money for a fine pair of shoes, and you are both wealthier after the exchange—you got a pair of shoes you needed more than a handful of money, and he got the money he wants, which he can spend on things he doesn't know how to make for himself.

Everyone knows the old saying that "time is money," but think about this: money lets you use your time **more efficiently.** You don't have to fool around with shoe-making tools for hours, producing a barely adequate set of footwear. You can buy those shoes from someone who knows what they're doing, and use the time you would have wasted at the workbench doing things you're better at. This creates greater overall wealth in the economy. It also creates more leisure time, which leads to even more ways for people to make money, as they use their skills to fulfill each others' desires, as well as meeting their basic needs. Moving from barter to money opens countless possibilities for people, and drives the development of technology. Nobody can organize the resources to create things like steam engines, industrial plants, or high-energy physics laboratories, if they have to trade goats and chickens to get what they need.

At the highest level of economic development is credit—the willingness of people with large amounts of money to loan it, for repayment plus interest. This is hugely important to the creation of an advanced society. Credit, in its many forms, allows enormously complex transactions, and encourages the kind of financial speculation needed for a roaring economy. It lets businessmen quickly assemble the resources to take advantage of opportunities. It encourages technology, by funding research and development—it's hard for people to make speedy technological breakthroughs if they have to save up the money before they can buy equipment and hire assistants. Credit allows young people with minimal earning power to afford higher education, repaying their loans after they acquire the skills to increase their income. Consumer loans improve the standard of living, by allowing people to buy major items like cars and houses, when it would take them years to save up the money needed. These credit purchases supercharge the economy, by making people willing to buy things they might not have the resolve to carefully save up for. Would the market for iPhones, plasma TVs, and home computers have exploded if every potential buyer had to save up the money for months and years, then bust open his piggy bank to make a purchase? Credit makes money virtual, instead of physical—you can spend tomorrow's money today.

Of course, credit can be abused. People run up loans they have difficulty repaying. Financial institutions hungry to earn interest made it easy for consumers to get in over their heads. People born in the Seventies, or earlier, can remember when credit cards were much more difficult to obtain than they are today. Consumers became addicted to buying luxuries on credit, and so has the government, which has been on a deficit spending binge. The problem with going after business and personal lending institutions and demonizing them, as Obama has been doing, is that it will reduce the supply of credit, without changing the demand. People still expect to be able to flash their charge cards and get everything they want immediately, business startups still need loans, major goods like cars and houses must still be purchased with loans, and the government shows absolutely no sign of cutting back on that massive deficit spending. However, the institutions which loan money are being frightened out of lending it, because they can no longer rely upon the value of binding contracts—the government has demonstrated a willingness to rewrite the terms by decree. Investors are wary of loaning capital to businesses that might be nationalized. Banks are a little nervous about loaning money for real estate with wildly fluctuating values. Worst of all, insane deficit spending is threatening the value of money. Lenders may wonder if risking a large sum of money to earn 6% interest is worthwhile, when the dollars repaying that loan might be worth

14

10% less. The effects of this uncertainty are making themselves felt slowly now, but they will become more obvious with increasing speed, if steps are not taken to restore confidence in the financial system.

Obamanomics is destroying the instruments of wealth in reverse order. Credit was devastated first, and money is starting to look a bit shaky. The increasing sense that politics will allocate resources, rather than financial necessity, makes money seem less important, and money pouts when it's ignored. The core of the economy is security, and ridiculous spectacles like the Pelosi waterboarding tango, the weak response to high-seas piracy, or the sad performance of Obama and Hillary Clinton during recent trips abroad, can only damage it. An actual terrorist attack or Middle East war would be catastrophic, far beyond any immediate damage inflicted (as if that wasn't bad enough.) It has become fashionable to forget the miraculous recovery of the Bush economy after 9/11. The Obama economy could never survive such a blow—it's mortgaged to the hilt, with all its credit cards maxed out, and businessmen have been learning Obama views them more as adversaries than constituents. A life-and-death crisis would irrevocably shatter what confidence they have left.

In order for the economy to recover, we need a political class that restrains itself from bullying and menacing the credit industry. We have created too much wealth in America, over the last few decades, to effectively manage and nurture it, without the vigorous use of the most sophisticated instruments of wealth.

A Modest Proposal For Real Stimulus
May 21, 2009

Author's Note: I received a great deal of complimentary feedback from home-schooling parents after I published this essay. They generally shared my belief that getting the federal government, and the absurd National Education Association, away from our schools is one of the most important reforms America can make. It occurred to me that it would also provide a tremendous opportunity for job stimulus and private-sector growth.

The Dow dropped another 150 points on Thursday, leaving it at 8292.13. It bounces around a bit, but it seems to be stuck around 600 points below where it was on the day Barack Obama was elected President. It peaked at 14908.08 in October 2007. Unemployment stands at 8.6%, after hanging around four to five percent during most of President Bush's term. When nothing came of its multi-billion dollar "stimulus" plans and bailouts, the government started pouring good money after bad, just recently announcing it will throw another $7.5 billion at General Motors Acceptance Corporation, on top of the $5 billion it has already spent. Uncle Sam is also converting $884 million in loans to GMAC into equity, which means you, the taxpayer, are being forced to buy 35% interest in a disintegrating financial company, whose stock you wouldn't normally purchase without getting drunk first. There are about 128 million taxpayers in the United States, so your share works out to a little over a hundred bucks taken out of your wallet and paid to GMAC since December. An already shaky auto industry is about to get walloped by new federally-mandated fuel efficiency increases, which is likely to depress new car sales as upper-income buyers cling to big, comfortable vehicles they won't be able to purchase any more. And California has turned into a malignant tumor that will suck billions out of productive states with sane government, as the inevitable federal bailouts begin.

It's hard to see any of the signs of renewed economic growth that Obama keeps hallucinating about in press conferences. It's time for some real economic stimulus—the fraudulent pork bill shoved down the nation's throat by Democrats didn't even pretend to "stimulate" anything until 2010. How do you stimulate an economy? Well, throwing money at favored constituencies doesn't work—if those constituencies were wealth creators, they wouldn't need infusions of pork. Bailing out failed business models is merely subsidizing failure. There are two things that would provide immediate stimulus: tax cuts, which spur positive business growth immediately, because quarterly and yearly business plans take upcoming tax rates into consideration, and the creation of new markets for businesses to exploit. Obama's corporate socialism has the needs of the economy exactly reversed—instead of having government take over failed businesses, we need failed government programs to be released into the private sector, spurring employment and spending on infrastructure. The private sector would love to gain the opportunity to bring its innovation and energy to a previously moribund government-controlled industry, and the taxes formerly collected to fund a bloated and inefficient federal department could flow directly into the pockets of taxpaying citizens, like a jolt of electricity. To rescue our economy, it's time for some of that out-of-the-box thinking we keep hearing this Administration values. Let's set partisan considerations aside and do something dramatic.

Mr. President, it's time to privatize education.

According to the U.S. Department of Education, roughly $553 billion was collected in tax revenue to fund the public school system in 2007. I couldn't find any 2008 numbers, but of course they're bound to be even higher. Can you imagine the economic stimulus of dropping a half-trillion dollar market into the private sector? The frenzy of companies forming to compete for the best teachers, build the most attractive educational infrastructure, and market their services to discerning parents would be astonishing.

The tax savings to citizens would be significant. Of course, we would need to provide educational vouchers for lower-income citizens, so some educational taxes would still need to be collected...but the federal government current spends over $9000 per year, on average, to educate each student. It's much higher than that in some areas, most notably Washington, D.C., which spends a whopping $25,000.00 per student. Does anyone doubt that competitive private schools can do better, especially when the economies of scale for handling seventy million customers kick in? Parochial schools already offer superior education at less than half the average cost of government schools.

American public education is a textbook study of a failed government program. American students lag behind the rest of the developed world in almost every category, and their performance gets worse with every passing year. As far back as the early Eighties, the Education Secretary released a report called *A Nation At Risk: The Imperative for Education Reform*, which included this infamous statement: "If an unfriendly power had attempted to impose on America the mediocre educational performance that exists today, we might well have viewed it as an act of war." Things have gotten a lot worse in the last 25 years, not least because of the tremendous amount of time wasted on foolish political indoctrination, including mandatory training in the official state religion of environmentalism—something that has gotten so out of hand that a "separation of church and state" lawsuit is just itching to be filed. The Obamas obviously had the good sense to keep their daughters far away from the awful public schools of Washington...just like every single liberal Democrat president before them.

The government has proven utterly unable to cope with the most disruptive elements of public education, a dreary litany of horrors that every parent can recite by heart: disruptive students, disconnected parents, violence in the schools, grade inflation, and the crush of immigrant students from families that refuse to assimilate. Hidebound government functionaries can't conceive of any solutions to these problems, but I'll bet highly motivated, innovative private entrepreneurs can. Parents who can shop around for the best schools will vote with their feet if private schools don't measure up. The District of Columbia was filled with parents who desperately pursued an opportunity to escape from the hell created by Congress and the teachers' unions—until Obama took it away from them.

Much of the cost of public education comes from a bloated, union-heavy bureaucracy, tangled in a cozy relationship with Jimmy Carter's Department of Education. The teachers' unions are heavy contributors to the Democrat Party, and they receive value for their money, with tired 60s radicals settled into tenured positions, and a vast army of federal officials and union apparatchiks crushing good teachers who struggle valiantly to provide a decent education in a crazy system. The flaws in government education are grown through every brick of public schools, like a vine that can't be cleared away without bringing the whole building down. Everyone familiar with the state educational system knows there is no way to reform it—its problems are built in to a system that provides such tremendous opportunities for political indoctrination, has so few mechanisms for dealing with poor teacher performance, and provides huge funds to a union that uses them to buy vast political power.

Have the courage to make a sacrifice for America, Mr. Obama—it's time for your government, your Party, and Bill Ayers to make do with less for a change. Dissolve the Department of Education, promote a right-to-work law that will shatter the teachers' union, and begin the privatization of the educational system. It would go a long way toward getting us back to the economic performance and unemployment figures of your predecessor, which so far you have only been able to regard with envy and confusion. It might get us back to a 10,000 Dow…and produce a class of 2010 that understands exactly what that means.

What We Must Do Now
June 3, 2009

*Author's Note: I started writing this as an exercise in thinking about what we **should** be doing, instead of just pointing out the mistakes our current Administration is making. Somewhere along the way, it became a battle cry. A reader told me he was printing copies of it and leaving them on the seats at airports. What we need to do now will be incredibly difficult, but not impossible…and America is the difference between difficult and impossible. The first line turned out to be sadly prophetic…*

The economy stinks, and it's going to get worse. Much worse.

What stinks about it? For starters, the Dow Jones Industrial Average has been fluctuating between eight and nine thousand, which is about five thousand points below its 2007 highs. The Dow is a calculated average of industrial stock prices, meant to measure the overall value of the American industrial sector. It includes major companies like Coca-Cola, Intel, Microsoft, Exxon-Mobil, and Wal-Mart. These companies lost a huge amount of value over the last two years, and they're not growing in value now. They represent every major sector of the economy, so when the Dow is flat, it means none of the leading companies in any industry are gaining in value. That's especially bad news, because as mediocre as it's been, today's market is probably *as good as it's going to get* for a while. Huge amounts of "stimulus" money have generated *nothing* except waste and graft. The coming wave of tax increases, along with energy shortages from Obama's insane energy policies, haven't slammed into the industrial sector yet. The Dow also maintains indexes for transportation and utilities, and they don't look so good, either. Cap-and-trade energy taxes will kill entire industries stone dead. Incidentally, one of the companies in the Dow industrial formula, since 1931, was General Motors.

What else is bad? Unemployment. Companies that are losing value don't hire people. The current unemployment rate is 8.6%. For most of the Bush years, it was around four to five percent. Nobody expects this rate to go anywhere but up, or the media wouldn't be parroting Obama's ludicrous "create or save" language about jobs—a rhetorical dodge that only someone with great faith in the boundless stupidity of the public would attempt.

Another dangerous economic indicator is the trade deficit. It's about six percent of our gross domestic product at the moment. The trade deficit means we're importing far more than we're exporting. To finance these imports, we have to borrow money from countries that are running trade surpluses. Running such a huge trade deficit means we're not supplying our own domestic needs, and foreign customers aren't buying our products. One of the major producers of a high-value product that both domestic and foreign customers *used* to be interested in was General Motors. Its transition from failing private-sector corporation to government-run disaster will not help that trade deficit any.

And of course, the fourth horseman of the economic apocalypse is our federal budget deficit, which has passed astonishing and become obscene. Endless billions plunged into pork-barrel spending, coupled with doomed attempts to keep the bloodless corporate host organisms of labor unions on life support, have threatened the bond market and the value of our currency. The current federal government debt is now over half a million dollars per American household, with plenty more reckless spending yet to come…including plans for a nationalized health care system that will suck another few trillion in imaginary money out of an utterly broke government that is mortgaged to the hilt. Among the genius ideas floated to pay for the nationalized health system is a brand-new value-added tax, a super sales tax of 10 to 25 percent, added onto the sales tax you already pay. The major immediate effect of such an idiotic scheme would be a massive reduction in spending by consumers, making an 8000 Dow look like a wistful memory of a bygone era. A significant result of nationalized health care will be a dramatic reduction of the average life expectancy, as a desperate government rations health care by declaring elderly people too expensive to treat. The elderly are generally wealthier than younger age cohorts, since they had a long lifetime to amass money and property…and since they won't be able to spend money on staying alive, they'll have more cash in the bank when they pass away, and those massive death taxes kick in. This will make one of the "unforeseen consequences" of socialized medicine an even greater wealth transfer from the private sector to the government.

These dire economic indicators are merely the prelude to the detonation of Social Security and Medicare, the Fat Man and Little Boy of financial catastrophe. These programs were going bankrupt anyway, but the doomsday clock has been greatly accelerated by a weakening economy and worse-than-broke government. Socialized medicine would relieve the pressure somewhat, by killing elderly people sooner and reducing the strain of paying their Social Security benefits, but it won't be nearly enough to stop the avalanche of entitlement spending on the aging Baby Boomers. Retirees will fight to the bitter end to collect the benefits they paid for all of their lives, and it will be absolutely impossible to pay them.

We need dramatic action to remedy the collapsing economy *now*. A state-run economy does not have the flexibility to survive sudden expenses, such as major natural disasters or terrorist attacks. Everything that's wrong with America is doubly wrong with California—what happens if they finally get that big earthquake they've always been worried is coming? Beyond the immediate physical destruction, the economic shock wave would bring the creaky American system crashing down, because we're *all* plugged into California, whether we like it or not.

So, what can be done to fix these problems? It seems to me that we need the exact opposite of what we're getting from the hapless Obama Administration. We need increased industrial activity, spurred by increased consumer demand, resulting in higher employment and more exports. None of this can come from tax-and-spend statist policies. The government does not create wealth, value, or hours of productivity when it spends money. It takes the money away from those who create those things, then skims a huge amount off the top due to bloated overhead costs, political graft, and the natural reduction of economic activity that comes from high tax rates. Major corporations and wealthy individuals have ways of avoiding high taxes, and most of them result in higher unemployment and reduced industrial output. The shriveled resources appropriated by the government are then spent inefficiently, with decisions made according to neurotic obsessions and political convenience. Digging our way out of the economic hole will require maximum productivity and efficiency. The path between employee, producer, and consumer must be as direct as possible.

We have to **shut down the government.** A great deal of it, anyway.

I wrote earlier about the enormous economic stimulus that would come from privatizing education. Many other such industries must be pried loose from the government's talons, and fed to the private sector, where they can spur employment and commerce. Laws must be passed to prevent the sickening travesty of government officials controlling, or subsidizing, private industries. Laws that enable labor unions to bleed industries dry must be repealed, and the unions broken. Unions may have begun as collective bargaining entities protecting workers from exploitation, but they have devolved into quasi-governmental agencies that exploit everyone who doesn't belong to the union—literally, in the case of the United Auto Workers, which has lifted about two hundred dollars out of your wallet over the last six months.

The only way to achieve these goals is with *massive* tax cuts. The leviathan can only be killed by starving it to death. Progressive taxation is a moral and practical atrocity that should be replaced with a flat tax or consumption-based tax (an argument for another day, but either would be better than the sheer tyranny of requiring half the country to pay 100% of the cost of bloated government.) We should flood the private sector with immediate, *real* money, broken loose from the government's vaults. Since stock prices are predictive of anticipated trends, and companies figure upcoming quarterly tax assessments into their business plans, *nothing* could stimulate the economy faster than tax cuts. Tax and spend economies are simply a collectivist instrument for directing production as the political class sees fit, as wasteful as they are immoral.

Return the freedom to create, hire, produce, and purchase to the private sector, and let the creative energy of millions of private citizens, making billions of transactions, produce results that can only astound the politically straitjacketed, manifestly incompetent minions of the Obama government. The spectacle of Treasury being run by a tax cheat, health care being administered by a lawyer with no medical training, and the fifty-billion-dollar GM boondoggle being captained by someone who appears to have been chosen randomly from a list of campaign operatives, is darkly amusing—but not at all surprising. This is the kind of garbage that happens every time politicians are given too much power. The private sector usually knows better than to hire a fraud like Turbo Tax Tim Geithner, and if it did make the mistake of hiring him, it would have fired him by now.

A revitalized, deregulated, lightly taxed private economy is the only chance we have of staving off the Social Security meltdown until private sector solutions can be applied to it. It is the only chance we have of preserving the value of the dollar, or stabilizing the bond market enough to make the Chinese stop laughing at us. Everything taken over by the government gets more expensive, but it never gets any *better*. We have to *improve*, to survive the coming storm. We need an army of screaming apparatchiks staggering out of Washington in shock, wondering what just hit them. We need the government to make sacrifices for a change. It is the largest employer, lender, borrower, and consumer in the country…or in the world. We've had enough of a blundering giant staring down at the little people and telling them to tighten their belts.

It is time to declare the utter, absolute failure of socialism, made agonizingly obvious by the expensive fumbles of this President, and the coming crash his policies are only making worse. Socialism has failed *comprehensively*, in every particular. Every single problem it asserted the power to address has gotten worse. Its acolytes have brought a mighty engine of growth and commerce crashing into ruins. Its early New Deal triumph is about to collapse into a black hole that will obliterate the wealth of future generations. The current socialist government can only pretend it's working by fudging numbers, making ridiculous excuses, and desperately trying to create distractions. We can't afford this foolishness any more. The obsessions, hatreds, and superstitions of the Left have grown too expensive. We've arrived at our last opportunity to cancel their credit cards and make them get real jobs.

The national debt is currently 80% of our gross domestic product. In ten years, it will be 100%. No one can argue that's efficient, moral, or sustainable. Bringing this bloated, spendthrift government down will not be an easy task, but we have no time to lose. We, the people, still have the power to control the destiny of the United States. We can do all the things the "smart set" tells us are impossible. We could do them in one single election. There's no reason Obama should be anything but a helpless lame duck from 2010 to 2012. Bullies are also cowards. Instead of watching the Dow Jones Industrial Average drop another couple thousand points, let's make the value of a Senate seat drop. Scare those people half to death in 2010, let them know you're ready to finish the job in 2012, and a great many things can change very quickly. The second quarter of 2009 can either be the high-water mark of the post-Bush economy…or it can be remembered as the high-water mark of the total state. The choice is ours, as it always has been, but may not be for much longer.

Big Government Versus Big Business
July 13, 2009

Author's Note: A reader who became very upset with me during the long and rowdy comment thread for "A Seemingly Very Nice Middle-Class Girl" wrote to tell me she loved this essay, and apologized for being so hard on me previously. That was very gracious of her, and it was a great moment for me. Hard-won praise has a special flavor.

Every species of liberal hates and fears big corporations. Conservatives are often amazed that liberals could place so much faith in Big Government, when it has such a horrific record of producing waste, corruption, and bloodshed, around the world and across the decades. One of the keys to understanding the Left is appreciating their conviction that either Big Business or Big Government will inevitably control American life, and they very much prefer the latter.

Both Big Government and Big Business emerged from the rapid industrialization and urbanization of the nineteenth century. Heavy industry provided irresistible economies of scale to both large businesses, and large concentrations of population. You can't manufacture heavy machinery, refine gasoline, or produce industrial-grade steel at small local mom-and-pop operations, for consumption by a purely local market. Local craftsman can't match the productivity of big manufacturing plants. The Industrial Revolution produced a huge number of factory jobs, and the population flowed into urban areas to take them. This had a profound effect on both the quality of life, and the shape of politics.

The twentieth century brought the rise of various political movements that believed industrial science could be used to shape human relations. There was a great deal of faith in the power of science to engineer an ideal society, filled with perfect citizens. All those people crammed into cities and factories were crying out to be organized, much as the factory machinery was carefully engineered to exacting specifications. The leading intellectuals of the pre-war era were almost unanimous in their belief that scientific methods should be used to create a powerful, super-intelligent central state, which would organize the citizens for maximum efficiency.

Economies of scale continue to provide incentives for corporate growth. The phenomenon of Wal-Mart, and other big-box retail operations, is based on the concept of purchasing goods in vast quantities, so they can be resold at a discount in large, no-frills stores. Huge electronics companies have created amazing devices, which they manufacture and sell at remarkably low prices. The pioneers of the personal computer may have created their first crude machines in garage laboratories, but no one could have designed and built an iPhone that way. The Left sees this inexorable movement toward large corporations as a frightening development, and feels that only an even larger and more powerful government protects them from mega-corporate greed.

Conservatives wonder how liberals could possibly be willing to sacrifice their liberties to a huge central government. The Left views many of these liberties as dead letters, or dusty antiques, in a world of huge corporations and high technology. Liberals are much more interested in "positive rights," or entitlements—the "right" to food, housing, health care, and so forth. What good is the "right" to choose your own doctor, when average folks understand nothing about medicine, and are prone to being ripped off by Big Pharma and its billion-dollar ad campaigns? How can people be held responsible for defaulting on their credit card debts, when Big Credit fooled them into accepting credit limits they couldn't sustain, at interest rates they can never repay? To the Left, ordinary citizens are helpless pawns in the schemes of immense, predatory corporate interests.

Of course, Big Government is larger, more powerful, and more destructive than any company could ever dream of being. Liberals often cite Microsoft as the ultimate example of corporate evil, falsely describing it as a monopoly. (A "monopoly" is *not* a very rich company with few serious competitors.) No matter what you think of Microsoft, it cannot actually force you to buy its products, or legally bar other companies from offering competing products. The government *can* do those things. Ford Motor Company can't apply tariffs against foreign automobiles, rearrange safety and fuel standards to make competing vehicles prohibitively expensive to the consumer, or seize money from people who aren't its customers to subsidize its business practices. The new owners of General Motors can.

Why does the Left embrace Big Government, despite its fearsome track record? Because they believe citizens have some influence over the government, but none over private industry. The act of voting for political leaders grants them a moral legitimacy that private companies can never have. The collectivist philosophies of the past century are based on the concept of government as the incarnation of the popular will. The State is the avatar of the people, and its officials are directly answerable to the voters, who can send them packing if they dislike their policies. Liberals hate big corporations because the common man is not consulted when CEOs are appointed. You'll never be more than a registration number to Microsoft, but every few years, you get to march into the voting booth and make your voice *heard* by politicians!

To accept this argument, one must ignore the role of money as a form of communication. As one of the characters in Ayn Rand's *Atlas Shrugged* puts it: "When money ceases to become the means by which men deal with one another, then men become the tools of other men. Blood, whips and guns—or dollars. Take your choice—there is no other." The private sector's response to monetary incentives is much faster, and more efficient, than government's response to elections held every few years. Barack Obama claims a mandate to restructure the entire relationship of citizens to their government, after winning the support of about 33% of eligible voters. No private company would count the support of only 33% of its potential market as a soaring success, or consider it a mandate to restructure the entire marketplace. For a national politician, 60% approval ratings are called "stratospheric." For a national corporation, 60% consumer satisfaction is a disaster.

The idealistic vision of concerned voters using their ballots to restrain incompetent or malevolent politicians is nothing but a comforting illusion. A great deal of power over your life is wielded by long-term senators and representatives from states where you have no vote. If you aren't one of the roughly 300,000 voters in Massachusetts District 4, you have absolutely no influence over Barney Frank, the man who engineered the subprime market collapse. If you hate the President's policies and want him out of your life, but 51% of the country disagrees in the next election, you're stuck. In fact, if it's a three-party race like 1992, your passionate opposition could be over-ruled even if a sizable majority of the country agrees with you. The popular fantasy of politicians as "employees" of the voters, who can "fire" them if they under-perform or misbehave, is dangerous because it has made people comfortable with giving up far too much of their freedom.

Big Government's unresponsiveness is exceeded only by its inefficiency. Government programs expand through failure. A bureaucrat only gets more funding if he can show his past year's funding was insufficient. Private companies are always hungry to increase sales and market share, which gives them a constant incentive to provide value for money. Corporate managers can't lay out failed projects and stagnant growth at a board meeting, and expect to receive big bonuses and increased funding…but that is *exactly* how Big Government works.

The liberal phobia about Big Business leads to the false premise that Americans must choose between having their lives run by either corporations or the government. Big Business isn't trying to send inspectors into your house, to make certain you're using the right kind of light bulbs. Americans should strive to ensure their government is small, transparent, and tightly focused on both enforcing and respecting the law. A vibrant, free economy gives us the wealth to attend to the needs of the poor, and take proper care of the environment. Large companies are an inevitable byproduct of that prosperity. Those companies must be policed, the same as private citizens must be policed, for no one is truly free in a state of anarchy. Learning to fight the irrational fear and hatred of Big Business is a vital endeavor, because it causes far too many people to flee into the waiting arms of Big Government…a far more powerful, predatory, and uncontrollable beast.

Capitalism Versus Racism
August 20, 2009

The political atmosphere crackles with charges of racism. President Obama's function-aries and allies make dark insinuations about the racial motives behind all opposition to his agenda. Tea party protests against Big Government are portrayed as thinly veiled Klan ral-lies. The boycott of Glenn Beck's TV show is based on the idea that calling a black liberal Democrat racist is, itself, an act of indefensible racism. The hilariously incompetent and biased MSNBC network was so desperate to portray town hall protesters as racists that it framed the image of a black man holding a rifle to obscure his face, then tried to pass him off as an armed white supremacist.

It's not surprising to see desperate Democrats throw gasoline on America's simmering racial fires, in a last-ditch effort to reverse their political fortunes. The Left believes debates are won when the other side is silenced, not when those listening to the debate are persuaded. Charges of racism would not be one of their preferred weapons, if a climate of tension didn't exist to make them effective. Racism consistently ranks near the top of issues Americans say they are concerned about. Reducing racial tensions will require building a society that is the exact opposite of the one Barack Obama favors. No system of politics and economics is more hostile to racism than classical liberalism combined with free-market capitalism…and none provides a more fertile breeding ground for tension between races, sexes, religions, and other groups than big-government socialism.

In a capitalist society, racism is both morally offensive and stupid. People might harbor some prejudices in their minds—and really, how many of us can say we go through our whole lives without having a single racist thought? However, overt expressions of racism are foolish, because they are detrimental to the success of both individuals and companies. It makes no sense to deprive your company of skilled employees by discriminating against their skin color, or drive off large numbers of prospective customers by insulting them. It's equally stupid for an individual to pass up career opportunities, or forfeit the ability to collaborate with talented peers, due to blind prejudice. Over time, those who persist in such foolishness will inevitably fall behind those who rise above it.

Legendary economist Thomas Sowell has written extensively about the pressures free markets bring to bear against discrimination, even in the absence of legal penalties for such behavior. Of course, no system is perfect, and the sun will never rise on a world that doesn't include a few blockheads scowling at each other for petty, superficial reasons…but we can aspire to build a world where the pursuit of excellence helps the human heart escape the undertow of ancient hatreds. A great nation does not require the *absence* of unjust men...only their irrelevance.

By contrast, while racism is still a moral outrage in a socialist society, it is **not stupid**. Collectivist systems reward tribal groups for maintaining their solidarity, and working as a bloc to exert pressure on the State, in exchange for rewards. Racial animosity is a brutally effective technique for maintaining solidarity—it has been proven across all the bloody centuries of human civilization. In an economy controlled by the State, the ability to deliver packages of votes, or arrange political pressure through organized demonstrations, is incredibly valuable. Barack Obama spent years baking in the furnace of Jeremiah Wright's racial hatred because it gave him vital political power in Chicago. His presence in that church, and the financial support he offered it, were morally reprehensible...but not pointless.

The racial theories of the Left state that members of preferred minority groups are immune to charges of racism, due to prior oppression. They are indulged in behaviors that would be considered totally unacceptable for less favored ethnic groups. Those behaviors allow them to organize, and maintain group discipline, far more effectively. The Democrat Party requires over eighty per cent of the black vote for its political survival. It ensures that kind of loyalty through political activities in churches, vicious insults directed at "inauthentic" blacks, and the maintenance of explicitly racial organizations like the NAACP. All of those techniques would be greeted as unspeakable hate crimes by liberals, if whites practiced them. No one should *want* to practice them. We should be more interested in national associations for the advancement of everyone...or, more to the point, anyone.

The liberal would say that concessions to preferred minority groups are necessary, to compensate for past discrimination. In the shadow of the total State, those concessions will drag on forever, because they bring too much power to those who provide them. Retributive "social justice" for the sins of the 50s and 60s is one thing "progressives" will never progress beyond. Like tobacco, state-sanctioned discrimination is too useful to be outlawed by Big Government, no matter how poisonous it is. We can only honor the ideal of a just and color-blind society by accepting it in total. The proposition that "all men are created equal" is not improved by appending a list of exceptions and qualifications.

Fortunately, we do not require the blessing of high-powered politicians to set aside our country's racial obsessions and grievances. That's the point. We can only achieve freedom and equality by changing the government, not by sitting around and waiting for it to change us. The Left would have us believe the goal of social justice requires us to cleanse every prejudiced thought from every human mind, and since that goal is impossible, their demand for power to pursue it will be endless. I believe there is no better way to conquer ignorance and resentment than to build a climate of prosperity and opportunity, where people of all backgrounds can join in the constructive pursuit of a better life. It's not a perfect, magical, universal antidote to prejudice—*nothing* is, and anyone who tells you otherwise is playing you for a fool. It doesn't have to be perfect. It only has to be good enough to whet our appetite for making it even better.

If there's one positive attribute of humanity I've never lost any faith in, it's the ability to discard useless things. The best way to make blind hatred seem useless to the vast majority of people is to make it senseless. That will never happen in a socialist nation, because tribalism is *not* senseless for people who depend on the favor of the State for prosperity, or even subsistence. One need only look at Europe to see how much ugly, murderous hatred bubbles in the state-subsidized cauldron of a permanent welfare underclass. The rise of the super-state has already divided Americans into too many warring factions…. and now the Left wants to give the State the power to dispense health care, throwing one more haunch of meat into the pit for the peasants to fight over.

Socialists like to taunt capitalists by saying the only color they care about is green. Hallelujah, and amen.

The Myth of Job Creation
September 9, 2009

Among the most unforgettable statements to come from President Obama was his repeated claim to have "saved or created" some ever-changing number of jobs. He stopped making this claim when it was greeted with roars of laughter, which in turn fell silent when unemployment numbers began threatening to set off the tilt alarm on the economic pinball machine. We were all laughing at the assumption of childlike voter stupidity in the "saved" part of this statement, but the "created" part is equally absurd.

With rare exceptions, the government does *not* "create jobs."

The government can certainly *hire* people. It has been hiring an astounding number of them, even as private-sector unemployment skyrockets. Naturally, these government jobs are among those counted as "saved or created" in the Administration's rhetoric. This kind of hiring is not what the public has in mind when it hears about *job creation*. If it were, the government could make everyone happy, and achieve full employment, by simply drafting every unemployed person into the military.

Private sector jobs are created in response to economic opportunity, while government jobs are an expense, incurred by the public in response to a specific need. Every businessman knows that expenses should be minimized, not expanded. For example, fire fighters serve a vital purpose, but if an increase in fires prompted the state to hire more of them, it would not be celebrated as an economic opportunity for the fire fighting industry. No one in a peaceful democracy applauds increased military recruitment as a positive economic indicator, heralding the creation of exciting new markets for warfare. *Nobody* wants to be first in line to get served when the United States military opens for business.

Federal "stimulus" spending is often touted as promoting job creation. That obviously wasn't the case with the Obama stimulus, which primarily affected employment by hiring people to put up signs proclaiming how wonderful the stimulus was. Federal subsidies don't "create" jobs, because they absorb tax money that could have been used for honest, economically desirable job growth. The government then converts tax dollars into "stimulus" pennies with its usual efficiency, and uses them to pay business owners to hire people they didn't think they needed. Genuine job growth requires business optimism about the future, since even in a simple job, training and payroll expenses make human resources a long-term investment. Note how the stimulus and TARP money that didn't just vanish into thin air was used mainly to pay off debt and batten down the hatches for rough times ahead, rather than increasing staff to handle future business that might never come.

There are only four ways the government can truly "create" a substantial number of jobs in the private sector, through direct actions that would immediately prompt businesses to hire people:

1. Launch an aggressive war of conquest.

2. Release additional natural resources for private industrial development.

3. Privatize an industry that was formerly controlled by the government.

4. Create a new technology the private sector finds useful.

In the United States of America today, under the Democrat Party, the first three options are equally unlikely. The fourth option, technological advance through government funding, is usually provided by the military, as in the case of research related to space travel, or the creation of the early Internet. Of course, military spending is the *last* thing most Democrats have in mind when they talk about "stimulus," and is virtually the only item in the budget they want to cut.

Broadly speaking, the government can encourage job growth by reducing taxes, lowering regulatory barriers to business creation, and taking steps to improve the confidence of consumers and investors. Hiring will also increase, and real wages will grow, when the additional costs government imposes on hiring are reduced, such as mandatory benefits and payroll taxes. Reducing the legal obstacles to terminating employees who don't live up to expectations also stimulates job growth, since common sense tells us a business is less likely to hire people when it knows they will be extremely difficult to dismiss. Organized labor is inherently hostile to job growth, since it raises the cost of labor and greatly restricts the ability of business owners to terminate unsatisfactory employees, as well as reducing the supply of labor, by restricting it to union members. Special advantages extended to unions by government, such as the Davis-Bacon Act, will therefore tend to reduce employment.

Most of the things government can do to enhance private-sector employment are more accurately described as actions it *refrains* from taking. Government can do very little to "create" jobs, but it has an unparalleled ability to destroy them, far greater than even the worst natural disaster. When it does not use its destructive powers, the economy benefits. Of course, socialist government is *defined* by the job-destroying actions it takes. A casual glance at atrocities like the cap-and-trade bill tells us that job creation is *far* from the top priority of Democrats, and they insult your intelligence by claiming otherwise. Sadly, they are much more concerned with keeping jobs "green" than keeping them filled.

Job creation is the natural tendency of capitalism, which has countless ways to take advantage of the incredible resource offered by human beings. The free market sees everyone as a producer, consumer, and investment. Socialist governments see people as problems to be solved. The choice for Americans is between free, creative, exhilarating, and occasionally messy growth, or carefully managed decay. No act of political will can conjure jobs, or prosperity, out of thin air.

A Question Of Faith
October 15, 2009

Suppose a billionaire, with extensive investments in health insurance, medical equipment, and pharmaceuticals, purchases some television time to make America a proposal: pay him five hundred billion dollars, and he will provide every American citizen with health insurance. His plan is still under development by a brilliant team of experts, working in seclusion, but he asks us not to worry about the details—he guarantees he can deliver what he promises, with no danger of cost overruns. His proposed contract with the government includes incentives for exceeding quality expectations, along with penalties for poor performance, and the government would have the right to cancel the contract at any time.

Participation in his plan would be voluntary, as the billionaire assures us we could keep our existing health insurance, if we prefer. He points out that since much of his fortune comes from medical technology and pharmaceuticals, he has every incentive to keep his end of the bargain and deliver on his promises. He certainly wouldn't want to destroy the medical industry that makes him wealthy!

What do you imagine the reaction to this astonishing offer would be? I would expect a tidal wave of ridicule and outrage. A $500 billion contract would make this wealthy businessman's operation bigger than Microsoft, which has about $50 billion in annual sales worldwide. What obscene profits this guy would collect! And how could we possibly trust some smooth-talking, greedy billionaire with our health care…especially when he says the details are still being hammered out behind closed doors? What about the massive conflicts of interest he would have, since he's already heavily invested in the medical industry? What the heck does some high-rolling entrepreneur know about medicine, anyway? He's not even a doctor!

You might have guessed what I'm going to say next: it's equally absurd to place that kind of trust in a gang of politicians. I would go even further than that. It's *more* absurd to trust the politicians. We'd be far better off trusting the billionaire.

Are you worried about the size of a business operation opening its doors with a $500 billion contract? That's nothing compared to the scale of the federal government, which has a budget of $3.6 trillion for 2009. The health care plan which cleared the Senate Finance Committee anticipates costs of nearly $900 billion, and government plans *never* come in for anywhere near their projected cost. If the government says it needs $900 billion, it will probably need at least triple that much, by the time all is said and done.. I'm more inclined to trust a proposal from a private company, especially if there are incentives for them to honor it. By contrast, the worst thing Congress has to worry about is a 5% dip in their 90% incumbency re-election rate.

What kind of people would our billionaire put in charge of that gigantic health care plan? Do you think he might choose a tax cheat, a 9/11 Troofer moron, or someone cozy with the North American Man-Boy Love Association, as President Obama has done with previous cabinet positions and czars? What percentage of large private corporations have hiring practices as lousy as this Administration?

Our billionaire's conflicts of interest are no greater than those facing Congress. The medical industry includes operations in many states and districts. Unions and other special-interest groups have enormous influence with the political class. Very few members of Congress have a medical background. What makes them any more immune to conflicts of interest, or any more knowledgeable about medicine, than a business tycoon?

Do you recoil from the idea of a billionaire raking in huge profits from this health-care contract? You must realize that corrupt Congressmen, and members of this Administration, accumulate fantastic personal fortunes during their time in office. People like Barney Frank and Chris Dodd made millions while they set the subprime crisis in motion. They defended Fannie Mae for ideological reasons, but also because it was a major cash cow. Anyone who retains a shred of belief in the superior virtue of politicians is well-advised to read Michelle Malkin's *Culture of Corruption*. Those politicians are no less greedy than the most rapacious capitalist—they're just more sanctimonious, and less efficient. Their lust for power equals, or exceeds, their financial greed. The pursuit of dollars never causes as much damage as the hunger for pages from the history books.

Some would be horrified at the prospect of gambling our health care with an eccentric businessman. The truth is that private enterprise is always less of a gamble than government programs, because it's much easier to control or terminate a private contract. Government programs are eternal—even the worst of them are extremely difficult to kill. It's hard enough to simply reduce their budgets…in fact, it can be brutally difficult to *reduce the rate of increase* in their budgets. I've always found it absurd when liberals present private-sector plans as "risky schemes," when Big Government is the real gamble, and you're chained to the card table while it deals busted flushes.

The difference in popular reaction to the hypothetical billionaire's proposal, versus the reality of the government's ambitions to take over the health-insurance industry, comes down to a question of faith. Much of the American population retains a remarkable degree of faith in the good intentions and benevolence of politicians, in defiance of the long track record of corruption and utter failure for big government programs. Perhaps some of this is due to an emotional confusion between the country and its government, as if losing faith in Congress or the White House would be equivalent to losing faith in America.

The benefit of the doubt given to politicians is a dangerous superstition. When the government exceeds its essential duties, and begins taking control of industries, the referees are leaping onto the field and tackling the players. In fact, they're taking the players down at gunpoint. The government demands you take a great deal on faith—far more than even the most eccentric businessman. The most unrealistic part of our health care thought experiment is the idea that we'd be expected to let the billionaire's people write their health-care plan behind closed doors, without worrying our little heads about the details. No contractor would pitch the biggest bid of his life with such ridiculous expectations…but that is exactly what President Obama and the Democrats expect from you. In fact, they **demand** it.

You might object that our hypothetical health-care mogul could turn out to be a fool, or a crook. He might rack up tremendous cost over-runs, discovering that his $500 billion bid was far too low…and the government might tear open that cushion full of tax dollars, and begin stuffing more billions into his hands. You'd be wise to express those concerns. I would suggest the only reliable way to address them is to place your trust in neither politicians nor billionaires, and demand the right to control your own health insurance. Make providers fight for your business, let the markets keep them efficient, insist the government keep them honest, and spare yourself the trillion-dollar betrayal of a faith you should never allow *anyone* to require from you.

The Myth Of Price Controls
October 21, 2009

Democrats are foolishly relying on price controls to manage the enormous cost of the ObamaCare plan. Price is not the same thing as cost. The Nixon Administration's love affair with price controls succeeded primarily in ruining the unfortunate industries subjected to them. If it costs you $100 to produce something, and the government tells you the maximum price you can charge is $99, your business model is doomed. After all, private industries can't make up for shortfalls by raising taxes or irresponsible deficit spending, as the government does.

I take an extremely dim view of price controls, because I maintain the entire concept is a fraud. The government cannot "control" the price of **anything.**

Most of us took some basic economics in high school or college, sandwiched between the sex education classes, environmentalist sermons, and lectures on the racist imperialism of American history. The part of Econ 101 that sticks in the mind of the average student is the law of supply and demand. Price sits at the intersection of supply and demand. If demand increases, but supply remains constant, the price will rise. This is how the market distributes a limited supply of a highly desirable product, such as health care.

Competition brings price down by increasing supply. In the case of health care, price could be most effectively reduced by increasing the supply of doctors and other medical resources, along with encouraging robust competition between medical organizations and health insurance companies. Reforms such as allowing insurance companies to compete across state lines would naturally enhance competition.

Price is also influenced by cost—every business needs to cover its costs before it can make a profit. Tort reform and similar measures would bring price down by making it possible for competitive insurance companies to charge less without compromising their profits. More lively competition within a market causes price to respond more quickly when costs are reduced, because every business is eager to attract more customers by undercutting its competitors.

The fundamental error of socialist economics—the one lesson they adamantly refuse to learn—is the absolute reality of the law of supply and demand. It is not simply one way of allocating resources, to be discarded in favor of more "compassionate" or "socially aware" systems. It is a **law,** written in iron, silver, and sweat.

Government can *distort* price, but it can never *control* it. Control implies precision, with results that bear some resemblance to objectives. No exercise in "price controls" anywhere on Earth, in all of history, could be fairly described this way. When the government tries to push prices around, it squashes that perfect "X" of supply and demand, or pulls it like taffy. Supply decreases, or demand skyrockets. Government power can never change price without twisting the rest of the economic equation out of shape.

Most forms of government intervention simply force other people to pay the price, without really changing it. Nothing is more expensive than "free" single-payer government health care—it extracts huge payments from a relatively small group of heavily burdened taxpayers, and creates a dependency class which receives benefits in excess of the minor taxes they pay into the system. This inevitably causes the overall price to increase, because it hinders competition. Consumers have little incentive to do comparison shopping when someone else is paying the bills, and the total amount of those bills is hidden within massive tax payments to fund a huge government with thousands of functions. Reckless deficit spending does the same thing, except the heavily burdened taxpayers are currently in kindergarten, unable to protest the quicksand of inflated dollars we are mixing for them.

Even if consumers *wanted* to comparison shop, they would have little ability to do so, since the government controls the market by paying the bills—and it reacts violently to any attempt by consumers to resist its authority. Consider the fines and jail terms built into the Democrats' health care proposals, for those who refuse to purchase government -approved health insurance. This kind of price shifting, and the baffling complexity of the system hiding true prices from consumers, has already inflated both the cost and price of health care—and it will get *much* worse, if the country is foolish enough to accept any version of the Obama health care proposals.

Rising costs and fixed prices equal reduced profits, which in turn will reduce supply. Who will be eager to invest heroic efforts in a system with restricted compensation, or compete for a few droplets from anemic profit margins? Even as Obama feeds Americans an endless stream of lies about how they'll be able to keep their own health insurance under his plan, the more candid Democrats tell friendly audiences that the "public option" is expressly designed to destroy private health insurance…and it will. It's easy to set a price no private industry can compete with, if you can paper over your losses with billions of tax dollars.

When the government starts jerking prices around, there are only two ways to stretch economic reality to fit: inflate supply by reducing quality, or limit demand through rationing. That's why anyone foolish enough to believe in the myth of price controls is doomed to a long wait in an understaffed office, before bored government clerks usher them in for review by the death panels.

The Mystery Of Unemployment
December 20, 2009

The Associated Press expressed confusion today over an "unexpected" rise in unemployment claims. Rising unemployment rates always seem to come as a surprise to this Administration and its media allies. Maybe I can help explain the mystery of unemployment to them.

Reducing unemployment would, of course, require the creation of more jobs. Jobs are created by businesses, right?

Wrong.

Jobs are not "created" by businesses. They are created in response to demand. Dropping a pile of money on a business does not inspire it to hire more people. Only increases in demand will do that. More specifically, the anticipation of future, steady demand prompts job creation. A business hires people in anticipation of rising demand from its customers.

Almost every business, with rare specialized exceptions, is eager to see increased demand, and therefore happy to hire people. Expansion is a joyous event. No businessman likes firing people in response to falling demand. In fact, it takes some pretty grim sales forecasts to make a business stop hiring, and bleak horizons indeed to provoke layoffs.

The purpose of a business entity is making a profit, through satisfying the demands of its customers. Jobs are a commodity the business purchases to accomplish this. Jobs are not the reason the business exists. A farm does not exist to grow corn, or hire farmhands. Its purpose is to sell corn. The land, seeds, and farmhands are all resources that help it fulfill this purpose.

Sustained job creation requires sustained demand. Temporary surges in demand produce temporary jobs. A car dealership that responded to the Cash for Clunkers program by hiring people to meet the artificial spike in demand it created would have ended up letting most of them go in the following quarter, when sales plummeted.

Government cannot create true demand. It can only create bubbles of spending, which is not the same thing…and its methods of creating these spending bubbles are horrendously inefficient, even discounting the outright theft and larceny of pork-barrel heists like the Obama "stimulus" bill. Of course it didn't produce sustained job creation. It was nothing but a transfer of over eight hundred billion dollars to favored Democrat constituencies. Handing politically favored groups piles of money to spend does not stimulate economic growth. It only stimulates politics.

Relying on stimulus spending to spur job growth is the kind of Keynesian delusion that only works with small colonies of people on desert islands. Another such growth-killing fantasy is the notion that granting tax cuts in a recession is "dangerous," because the taxpayers will just use the money to pay down debt, instead of making new purchases. Once again, this concept confuses money with demand. Money is the mechanism for expressing demand. People and corporations purchase goods and services because they want or need them. Needs generate more long-term activity than "wants." Reducing the supply of money will slow down the purchase of wants, and eventually needs.

High levels of consumer debt also reduce purchases. Businesses carefully consider the amount of interest they're paying on their debt. Some individuals keep an eye on these figures too, but even the most clueless shopaholic notices when their credit limits are exceeded, or their monthly payments become unbearable. Giving someone the means to pay down their debt does not reduce their demand for goods and services. Leaving them to wallow in debt, while the government remains lavishly funded, corrupting the money supply with its own astronomical debt, will certainly do so.

The economy is composed of countless transactions in which people and corporations create value by fulfilling each other's needs. The government also has demands, but they are inherently inefficient, because they are guided by political considerations. Obtaining the best value for the lowest price is never high on their list of priorities, although politicians occasionally find it necessary to pretend otherwise.

The money spent by government to fulfill its demands is not "earned" in transactions that produce positive value. When you hire someone, you are spending money to obtain services you cannot efficiently provide yourself. You value these services more than the money you're spending. You might need to hire a neurosurgeon to operate on you, because you can't possibly do it yourself—even if you happen to be a neurosurgeon. The surgeon, in turn, might spend a few hundred dollars hiring a maid to clean his house. He could clean the house himself, of course, but it's more efficient to hire the maid, because his time is generates far greater value performing surgery, or enjoying leisure activities. Both the maid hiring a surgeon, and the surgeon hiring a maid, are transactions that create value.

Government doesn't work that way. It seizes its money from taxpayers, who rarely choose to "hire" the government instead of a free-market alternative—certainly not on the scale of a multi-trillion dollar federal budget. Even when a government service is freely purchased, like the Post Office or Amtrak, the product is heavily subsidized by taxpayers, or enjoys legal advantages unavailable to private competitors. Government is a vacuum of healthy demand. Put simply, the primary objective of most government spending is the acquisition of votes, not the creation of value.

The Associated Press, and anyone else baffled by persistent unemployment, should ask themselves what effect draining trillions of dollars from the private sector, nationalizing industries, and running up astronomical federal debt has on the kind of healthy demand that creates value. What can a business do to enhance its sales in a command economy, other than curry favor with politicians? What future do people see when the American landscape is frozen in the wobbling shadow of a system that must, inevitably, collapse?

Your job was not created by your employer. It was created by the people who needed your employer. When the government controls everything, who *needs* anyone?

The Differences Between Government and Industry
February 1, 2010

People who support socialist programs harbor some incorrect assumptions about the nature of government agencies. Politicians and bureaucrats don't automatically become more intelligent or virtuous than private-sector business owners and employees. It's also dangerous to assume government is the *same* as the private sector—a delusion politicians like to encourage when trust in the State has cratered, and they believe they can regain some credibility by posturing as the CEOs of America, Inc.

Recent events have illustrated three vital differences between government and private industry. The first is that government does not face **consequences** the same way businesses do. The President just rolled out a budget with a deficit of $1.3 *trillion* dollars. The federal government has been running gigantic budget deficits for decades. The national debt has passed $14 trillion. Even if Enron had hired Bernie Madoff to replace Paul Krugman, it could not have endured such incredible fiscal irresponsibility for so long. Businesses faced with budget shortfalls make hard decisions in order to remain competitive. If management fails to do so, it faces bankruptcy, the wrath of shareholders, and the loss of vitally needed credit.

Government doesn't make tough decisions like that. It simply raises taxes or runs up the deficit. It does not view itself as "competitive"—it would use its power to crush private-sector competitors who threatened its interests, as the medical insurance industry will discover to our collective sorrow, if anything resembling ObamaCare is passed into law. For the State, competition ceases when legislation is signed. No matter how badly the Barack Obama People's Health Insurance Company performs, it will never go out of business…at least, not until the entire economic system has collapsed around it.

Individual politicians are likewise insulated from consequence. It's extremely rare to see a powerful politician's career end because of a single mistake. No matter how poorly Obama performs as the CEO of Government Motors, it will not be the sole, or even primary, reason he loses his job—and his job is almost absolutely secure for another three years, regardless of how unpopular he becomes.

Politicians even enjoy significant protection from outright criminal wrongdoing, which they occasionally sell to favored businessmen. No level of corruption seems capable of rousing Eric Holder's Justice Department from its long afternoon nap. Some states don't mind voting for politicians they can barely see through the ethical clouds swirling around them, as long as they bring home enough pork for key constituencies. The political class is simply *immune* to the aggressive law enforcement that purges the worst fraud from the private sector, when the hungry roots of politics are kept from digging too deeply into the soil of industry.

A second difference between the private sector and Big Government is the nature of **accountability.** When you hear someone pontificate about bringing more "accountability" to government, always remember this is a relative scale, which ends *far* below the point where it begins for private businesses. The government is the primary source of information about itself, and it feels entitled to suppress what it can't be bothered to distort, such as the SEC documents covering the AIG bailout. Much of the news we receive about the government comes from leaks and background talks, given to a media deeply sympathetic to its goals. The federal government is also entrusted with the task of policing itself, a job it feels very relaxed about performing. The government could not *begin* to pass the kind of accounting audit it requires from businesses.

Even if the government was meticulous about reporting on its performance, and the media dutifully passed along this information without filters, how could ordinary citizens hope to analyze the performance of an incomprehensibly huge super-State? If your auto mechanic consistently overcharged you for shoddy work, you'd find a new mechanic. What would you do if your auto mechanic was also your doctor, grocer, chief of police, and principal of your children's school? The idea that citizens influence government with their votes presumes a level of awareness and informed response that simply *cannot* exist, when the State becomes as bloated as ours. We seem to be on the edge of a political earthquake in 2010, but look at what it took to get us here. Voters won't display the passion and organization necessary to "fire" an immense national government until it has failed comprehensively…and *very* expensively.

The other obvious difference between government and the private sector is the government's monopoly on the use of **force.** The closest a private industry can come to compulsion are monopolistic practices, which government polices against, but is also willing to perpetrate itself. Every action taken by the government involves compulsion: the collection of taxes and the enforcement of regulations. Those little targeted tax cut ideas salted through President Obama's first State of the Union address are another form of compulsion—you have to do what the government wants, in order to enjoy those tax-cut crumbs, and everyone who refuses to comply with the designs of the State will subsidize you.

Few people would be eager to do business with a company that somehow acquired the government's combination of insulation from consequence, unaccountability, and compulsive force. Allowing the government to pretend it's a giant corporation is a terrible mistake. Those who make that mistake tend to underestimate the difficulty of running a business, and the intense competitive pressure which leads to the innovations behind our material abundance.

Ask a small business owner or corporate executive about the tough choices and risks he or she must undertake on a regular basis, then ask if they would subject themselves to such pressure if they didn't *have* to. They would laugh and tell you how much they'd like their mistakes to be subsidized, their credit to be effectively unlimited, or their competition to be held off at gunpoint.

If the State is immune to the restrictions and hardships that lead to innovation and efficiency, isn't it completely foolish to expect it to match the performance of private industry? Any politician who asks you to believe the State can do *better* deserves to be laughed off the stage.

Economics In Four Dimensions
February 10, 2010

Author's Note: One of the readers of Hot Air complained that associating time with the "fourth dimension" shows a distressing lack of respect for the current state of quantum theory. I love having an audience that points out stuff like that.

The most complex factor in the study of economics is **time.** Because liberal and statist economic theory does not properly account for the fourth dimension, it rarely predicts economic development accurately. The application of static thinking to a dynamic economy is equivalent to carving an ice sculpture out of warm water.

Take the example of the new pork bill Democrats are attempting to fry up in Congress. Even if this bill was an honest attempt to stimulate job growth, instead of the outright theft of taxpayer money to pay off favored constituencies, it would have minimal and short-term effects on job growth at best. This is because the engine of job growth is demand, particularly *anticipated demand.*

Training new employees requires a sizable investment of time and resources. Hiring comes with huge compliance costs, as well as incurring taxes and fees that workers don't usually see on their paychecks—depending on your job and the state you live in, the total cost of employing you is probably double your hourly wage. This is an investment your employer makes in the hope of *long-term* reward. Marginal reductions in the cost of labor have a minor effect on the employer's hiring decisions, because they are short-term incentives to make a long-term commitment. A foreman hiring day laborers for a short job might take on more workers, in exchange for a discount or subsidy payment, but expecting most businesses to respond to such incentives is like expecting a subsidy for wedding ring purchases to result in more marriages.

Government stimulus spending ends up doing more harm than good, because it removes money from the private sector through taxation, and when government debt reaches dizzying Obama heights, it makes corporate management nervous about the future. They understand that deficit spending jeopardizes the value of money, and they see massive tax increases lurking in its shadow. Businessmen know they're a year away from the Democrats losing power in Congress, and they've got to survive three more years of Barack Obama, whose tendencies toward populist business-bashing and socialist spending make him dangerously unpredictable.

Investment is a calculated risk, based on the investor's confidence in his ability to predict and influence future trends. In a command economy, future developments are shaped by the personality quirks of political leaders, and the demands of powerful constituencies. Political influence becomes the most valuable resource a large business can purchase…while small businessmen can only hope they aren't crushed by regulations, mandates, and policy earthquakes rippling out from Washington. No one grows into an uncertain future, especially when the ruling party makes it clear they will confiscate the "winnings" from exceptionally successful enterprises.

The Wall Street interests that supported Obama's candidacy were badly rattled when he turned on them. Obviously, they feel less confident in their ability to predict his actions, and their investment portfolios are likely to reflect this anxiety. Watching him perform an about-face under the pressure of crashing poll numbers, and begin courting them like Valentine's Day sweethearts, will not calm their nerves.

In a socialist economy, their best-case scenario is modest growth and profits, since windfall success will turn them into political targets. The worst-case scenario is economic collapse brought about by Obama's manifestly incompetent team, and his primitive wealth-destroying ideology. This vision of the future will continue to depress corporate growth, and resulting job growth, no matter what Obama says he will do *today*.

Political assaults on the banking and credit industries also do great harm to the economy, because they are the source of investment capital and consumer loans. Criticizing the profits of a bank is easy if you ignore the time factor—the previous risks and losses the bank had to endure. Banks and credit-card companies invest hard capital at a substantial risk of default, to earn money in the future through interest and fees. If they believe their ability to profit from this risk and expense is threatened, and they've been demonized to the point where they have no effective means to influence politics to their advantage, the only logical move is to reduce risk, and increase the price of the loans they feel confident in making. This hurts new businesses and low-income consumers the most, because they have the least impressive credit ratings.

Static theories of redistribution and "social justice" never account for the changes in behavior they produce. Money given or taken today produces a response tomorrow, which can be very different from the desired goal of social engineers. This is why higher tax rates never bring in anywhere near the revenue projected by greedy politicians. Redistribution schemes destroy future opportunity, for both providers and recipients.

It's significant that socialists always talk about the catastrophes that will ensue if government takes no action, but they *never* want to discuss the possibilities denied to private industry when the government passes regulations or seizes wealth. No one mourns the investments that weren't made, technologies that weren't developed, or new markets that weren't opened. The Left not only ignores the future, it proceeds as if we don't have one...or as though it's so inescapably awful that the only moral course of action is spreading the misery, so it will be easier to endure. That's why we should never stop asking who will pay off those deficits someday, or what will happen when the government can't borrow any more money from foreign interests, or the dwindling Social Security fund, to service its debt. The Left will never have an answer for those questions, because their economic theories are like a school of physics that assumes nothing in the universe will ever *move*.

The Parable Of the Bread Aisle
March 16, 2010

Author's Note: This is the first in a series of three parables, which I conceived as a way to relate my take on economic theory through familiar systems encountered in daily life. I'm happy with the way all three of them turned out, and greatly enjoyed the discussion prompted by each. This one seemed to make liberal readers most uncomfortable.

What does the bread aisle of your local grocery store look like? Chances are it's quite large, featuring shelves filled with many different types of bread. Each type of bread is also offered by different companies—you'll have several brands of wheat or rye bread to choose from. One of these options will probably be the "house brand" of the grocery store itself, and it will likely be cheaper than any of the other brands, particularly for staples such as white and wheat bread.

What purpose is served by having so many types of bread to choose from? We could all survive nicely on wheat bread. Even if we make allowances for taste, and indulge those who prefer other flavors, what's the point of having all those different brands on the shelf? And why would anyone buy a marquee brand like Wonder Bread or Pepperidge Farms, when the grocery store house brand is cheaper?

And why do we have to *pay* for bread at all? We need basic foods to survive, far more urgently than we need health insurance. Maybe it would be better if the government took over the bread industry. Think of all the money wasted on packaging and advertising, which could be saved if the State distributed Obama Bread in plain white wrappers that said RYE or WHEAT in simple block lettering. Our wise politicians could then decide if all those different varieties of bread are truly necessary.

If you have studied the history of socialism and communism around the world, you know what the inevitable results of a nationalized bread industry would be: hungry people staring at dusty shelves containing a few expensive loaves of low-quality bread. Humanity has invented few weapons that kill people more efficiently than collectivist agriculture.

Why is this always the tragic outcome of collectivism? After all, government control of goods and services is presented as a way to *control* costs. The bribes and shady backroom deals perpetrated in the service of ObamaCare are supposed to produce a system that increases "access to health insurance" and make it more "affordable." The inevitable result will be a system that reduces the quality of care, makes it harder to come by, and increases its overall cost to American citizens.

The same thing has happened across decades and around the world, *every single time* the State has taken control of a private industry. There's some grim amusement in watching a supposedly educated man like Paul Krugman make an utter fool of himself trying to pretend otherwise. ("In Britain, the government itself runs the hospitals and employs the doctors. We've all heard scare stories about how that works in practice; these stories are false.")

The reason for the failure of collectivism is revealed in the parable of the bread aisle. Why are there many different flavors of bread? Because people **demand** them. Why are those flavors provided by different companies, at various price points? Because there is **competition** to satisfy demand. These factors produce reductions in price, and increases in quality…and the burning truth every statist desperately needs you to forget is that political commandments *cannot* produce either of these things.

Why couldn't a nationalized bread industry produce higher quality bread at lower prices? A politician would simply declare bread must be healthy, delicious, and provided to Americans for fifty cents per loaf, paid by a loving government interested in the welfare of its people!

The problem is that politicians cannot redefine value, or repeal the laws of supply and demand. Ironically, given the endless invocation of the term by American liberals, the first thing sacrificed in a state-run industry is *diversity.* Political allocation of bread would see no logic in offering different brands of bread, or even different flavors…at least, not to the politically powerless average citizen, who would have no way to express his desires by spending money on the bread he prefers. The sole input available to the subjects of a state-run industry is *power.* If you don't have any, you take the bread government sees fit to provide, at the time of its choosing.

This doesn't happen because the masters of a politicized economy are heartless and cruel. One of the most dangerous, enduring illusions of the post-industrial era is the belief that collectivism has only failed in the past because nasty people were in charge of it. The elimination of diversity and choice is an inescapable requirement of command economics. Control cannot be dispersed among millions of consumers, imposing their individual preferences on the system. That's what **capitalism** does. When Pepperidge Farms tries to win your business, it caters to your demands, and it can find opportunities for profit in satisfying very specific tastes. If the State provided bread, you would need to adapt your tastes to the requirements of the State.

Reducing costs and increasing quality, to earn profits in a competitive economy, is *very difficult*. Statists think it's easy, which is why they believe an enlightened President and Congress can simply command it. Relieved of competitive pressure, the State's bread-making decisions would be guided by political considerations, at the expense of variety and efficiency. Chances would not be taken on experimental flavors that could result in wasted production, if they don't catch on with the public. The unhealthy decadence of white bread would likely be sacrificed in the name of reducing health-care costs.

Grain harvests, and the location of bakeries, would be shaped by the political power of local senators and representatives, rather than the painful demands of cost control. This is one of the reasons why government programs always cost more than the original estimates. Those estimates quickly become arbitrary limits, easily discarded when they become difficult to meet. This also makes it easy for politicians to obscure the true costs of their plans, by providing ridiculously low estimates of cost. They know they will not be held to account for those projections later, the way a private business would.

The bread aisle of your grocery store overflows with a variety of fresh, affordable options because that bread is baked in the fires of competition…where a fortune can be made by learning your tastes, and finding an inexpensive way to satisfy them. If you relied upon the government for your bread, you would accept what you were given, and you would be given what politicians think you were willing to accept. They would conceal the massive cost of its inefficient production by telling you it was free. Because this is a lie, you would soon find yourself staring at an empty shelf, remembering the days when you could choose between six different brands of honey wheat bread, while politicians explained why your nostalgia reflects a greedy and selfish desire to return to an impossible age.

The Parable Of The Satellite Dish
March 25, 2010

Author's Note: I intended this essay to provoke a specific response from readers who entertained some support for the government takeover of health insurance. I was not disappointed. On both my own blog and Hot Air, a number of them said it was impossible to compare health insurance to cable television, because health insurance is the most important product in the universe, and people will die without it. I asked in reply: "Then why are you willing to accept a bargain for health insurance that you would laugh out of the room, if someone offered it for the frivolous luxury of cable TV?" I could hear the trap door banging open beneath their feet from clear across the Internet. In case time has rendered the jest a little too obscure, the name "BFD Communications" is a play on Joe Biden's infamous declaration that signing the health-care bill was a "big effin deal."

Imagine a large condominium complex is meeting to consider a package deal with a cable TV company. Over eighty percent of the condo owners have their own satellite dishes, and are quite happy with the service. Some of them don't bother to watch television at all, preferring to rent movies from Blockbuster or Netflix for entertainment. However, the condominium Board of Directors says they're getting a lot of complaints from the residents who don't have satellite dishes, demanding the condo association purchase a cable TV package, and fold its cost into the monthly homeowner dues.

The homeowners already pay extremely high dues, and they're not happy with the quality of service they receive. They also notice that most of the people clamoring for cable television aren't even homeowners—they're renters, so they don't pay the association fees directly. The condo owners already host regular movie nights at the clubhouse, which also has a well-stocked library, so no one is truly starved for entertainment. Still, the owners feel guilty that anyone has to make do without TV service in their home, so they invite a cable company to give them a sales pitch.

The cable company, BFD Communications, produces an incredibly complicated plan for providing cable television service to the community. The plan is thousands of pages long, and no one even claims to have read the whole thing. They spend the weeks leading up to the big board meeting pestering all of the residents with relentless advertising for their services, covering doorknobs and windshields with brochures. Their presentation at the board meeting is several hours long.

BFD Communications explains that purchasing their service will require a lifetime contract, which can *never* be broken. The condo residents will be required to deal exclusively with BFD for their entertainment needs—all satellite dishes must go, and even the library will fall under their control. The contract will include funding for a large corporate security force, which will ensure compliance by issuing fines for illegal satellite dishes, or attempts to smuggle rented movies into the development. As this feature of the contract is being explained to the homeowners, a large screen behind the BFD representatives is flashing slogans like "BFD Enhances Competition!" and "BFD Saves You Money!"

The cable TV contract will be fantastically expensive. Curiously, while it is a lifetime contract, the company refuses to discuss the fee schedule beyond the first ten years. An intrepid homeowner studies the contract and discovers the costs double after ten years…and this assessment was prepared by CBO Auditing, a firm which has underestimated the cost of *every* contract it has ever reviewed. The condo Board rules that only the ten-year projections matter, and the intrepid homeowner is asked to leave the meeting.

Other homeowners announce they've been researching BFD Communications, and discovered it has *never* been able to deliver promised services at the contracted price. Every single project the company has undertaken experienced enormous cost overruns, and delivered poor quality to its customers. Every time a smaller competitor has been allowed to bid against them, the competitor's price and performance were superior—that's why BFD demands exclusive lifetime contracts. The people who make this announcement are told their input is not welcome, and asked to leave the meeting.

A resident asks what different packages BFD will offer. She has small children, so she would like educational programming, but she has no interest in premium movie channels, shopping networks, or morally offensive shows. The cable company explains that only *one* package will be offered. Its purchase will be mandatory, and the high price of its many channels will be charged to all residents. A senile old man in the audience claims the BFD executives promised him there would never be any morally offensive programming.

This prompts an angry homeowner to leap from his seat, waving a portion of the gigantic cable TV contract…which says the members of the condo Board of Directors are exempt from the restrictions, along with some of their friends! They can rent movies, purchase high quality satellite service, and avoid having the exorbitant fees for BFD tacked onto their monthly dues.

A loud argument breaks out in the meeting area, with angry residents howling that they want no part of this terrible deal. These people are told their anger disqualifies them from further participation in the meeting, and they are asked to leave.

The remaining critics of the deal suggest that other alternatives should be explored. There are less expensive entertainment options to consider, and since none of them require lifetime commitments, wouldn't it make sense to try them first?

The Board of Directors insists that the BFD contract must be signed *immediately.* It's simply appalling that anyone in the development should endure a single day without entertainment. Why, all of the surrounding condo developments have already signed up with BFD! They all have appalling service and frequent TV blackouts, they're all broke, and they borrow security officers from *our* development to keep their streets safe…but their Boards of Directors all laugh at us for refusing to provide BFD cable service to our residents, and our Board is tired of their mockery. The BFD executives mention that no one will actually receive any cable services for five years, but their fees will begin right away.

The meeting ends with the Board of Directors ignoring the demands of homeowners and voting for that lifetime contract with BFD. The residents leave the meeting hall wondering how they reached the point where a small group of Board members, up for re-election over the next couple of years, were able to ignore the clear wishes of the residents and saddle them with a lifetime contract.

Here are some lessons to ponder from the Parable of the Satellite Dish:

Never accept permanent solutions that are nearly impossible to change, when simpler and more easily modified plans are available. It's foolish to let the advocates of permanent programs dismiss flexible alternatives *before they have been tried*.

A proposal that requires you to ignore both the past and the future is a swindle, not a solution.

Free people do not accept restrictions from which their government is exempt. This is one of the differences between *leaders* and *rulers*.

A demand for commitment without a guarantee of performance is domination, not service.

When free people are told something is "inevitable," their response should be an immediate and overwhelming refusal to accept it. Inevitability is a self-fulfilling prophecy in the absence of resistance. Freedom is the never-ending quest for *alternatives*.

The people who loudly celebrate "diversity" keep coming up with universal plans. Their State is a giant who trims citizens to fit its bed, using rusty implements. The giant, the bed, and the implements were all equal sins in the eyes of our Founders. They come as a set.

When the State refuses to let you debate the terms of its plans individually, you can rest assured the whole is worse than the sum of its parts.

Freedom requires the courage to avoid being stampeded. You should ask *more* questions about something you are told is an "essential right." Sober reflection is a hallmark of maturity. A wise State would not require its citizens to act like children.

The State cannot give you anything worth having. You'll eventually find yourself guilty of the crime of wanting more. As the State fails to live up to its promises, it will be increasingly tempted to convict you of that crime...in advance.

The Parable Of The Referee
April 3, 2010

I often hear people on the Left accuse the defenders of capitalism of wanting completely unregulated markets, in which helpless citizens will be stripped of all legal protection, and placed at the mercy of rapacious bankers and businessmen. This is a straw man of such towering size that Nicholas Cage can be glimpsed inside its head, holding his broken legs and howling for his agent to land him a part in a better movie.

There are other choices besides anarchy, or a regulatory State that directly controls over half of our economy. Far from opposing all regulation, I maintain that clearly written, honestly enforced, minimally intrusive laws are both just *and* essential for wealth creation. A nation's wealth lies in transactions between its citizens, and the pace of those transactions would be greatly reduced if consumers had no confidence in providers. Shopping malls would be considerably less active, if the shoppers had to assume every food product was potentially poisonous, every piece of consumer electronics could explode, and all of the merchants were thieves.

Clearly written and honestly enforced regulation is not easy to come by, these days. To understand why, imagine that two football teams assemble for a game, under the supervision of a single referee.

As the first play begins, one of the players complains that the referee has made illegal movements across the field. The referee laughs and explains he cannot be bound by the same rules that constrain the players, or he wouldn't be able to do his job properly. He must be able to move up and down the field at will, in ways that would earn penalties for the players. Common sense supports his assertion, and the game continues.

The referee begins calling all sorts of penalties, invoking rules he has created on the fly. The players object, saying the rulebook accepted at the beginning of the game should be used without alterations. The referee mocks this notion. The field has grass, but the rulebook was written for a dirt field. It's cold outside, and there have been some snow flurries. The game will continue into the night, under electric lights. The teams include players of different sizes and fitness levels. More complex rules are needed to ensure a good game!

By the end of the first quarter, the ref announces it's too hard for him to administer such complex rules by himself. He begins pulling players off the teams, and deputizing them as assistant referees.

Early in the second quarter, the home team begins complaining of unfair calls, made in favor of the visiting team. To their astonishment, the referees actually begin tackling home team players, intercepting passes, and running touchdowns! The chief official explains that he felt the visiting team was outmatched, and had little chance of winning on its own, so he decided to make things "fair." The home team is particularly upset that the biased referees retain all their special advantages—they can move around the field at will, and ignore the play clock. The chief official dismisses these complaints, assuring everyone his actions will enhance the "competition."

The spectators are initially amused by the wild spectacle of referees tackling players, but the game quickly becomes boring. The home team becomes so confused and demoralized that their players begin to leave the field.

After the final whistle, the chief official is seen collecting money from a shady character near the locker room. It turns out the official had bet heavily on the outmatched visiting team. He had a financial interest in the outcome of the game all along...and he's the only real "winner."

Like the referees of a football game, the government *must* remain completely outside the markets it regulates. Contrary to the absurd sales pitch for ObamaCare, the State cannot enter the health insurance market as a "competitor." It shouldn't develop interests that will sour its regulatory powers into corruption.

By its very nature, government has access to power and resources which no private enterprise can equal. It can't work any other way. We can't treat the military as a business enterprise, to be shut down if it doesn't rake in sufficient profits. We must have government resources to address disasters, and most citizens would insist the government be provided with funds to care for the desperately poor and sick. Those who enforce the law must have a measure of power beyond the law: sky marshals carry guns onto airplanes, soldiers have access to heavy weapons and high explosives, government auditors can demand access to information a business would never share with its competition.

To be trusted with such power and resources, the State must practice strict adherence to a basic set of laws which constrain its behavior, and which it cannot easily disregard or change. The rulebook for the American game is her Constitution. Fidelity to those rules would produce a small State with less influence to satisfy the appetite of hyper-competitive players who wish to cheat at the game...or its own appetite for purchasing votes and imposing its ideas of "fairness." Disdain for the Constitution has led us to the present spectacle of referees who outnumber the players, unemployed players sitting dejectedly on the sidelines, and a dwindling number of investors willing to bet on a rigged game that will be decided by the whims of the officials.

The idea of a large, and yet scrupulously honest State is fraudulent to its core. As the State expands in size, it **inevitably** develops interests that lead to corruption. Its power becomes so valuable that bribery is an everyday transaction, camouflaged in sanctimonious rhetoric. Taking responsibility for errors and wrongdoing will always be less attractive than dipping into the public treasury for a few billion greenbacks to paper over the damage. As industries are first taxed, then regulated, and finally nationalized, the referees begin tackling players and running touchdowns. The **only** honest government is small government, so if you're sincerely opposed to political corruption, that's what you should insist on.

Part Two
Collectivism

Collectivist politics of any stripe require enemies, because they rely upon coercion.

The Necessary Enemy
May 2, 2009

Author's Note: This was the first time I got a really huge response to one of my posts. While reading the responses, I decided it would be best not to enter the comments area too frequently, unless one of the readers asked me a direct question. I didn't want to drive people away, including those who disagreed, and I thought it would be a little intimidating for the author of a piece to start pouncing on commenters. It seemed unfair—if I did my job well, the initial writing would stand on its own, and wouldn't need me prowling around in the forums like a pit bull to defend it. I had plenty of room to say my piece, and it was only proper to let the readers have their turn without undue interference.

The event which prompted this essay was a threat leveled against Chrysler bondholders by the Obama Administration. The bondholders were not cooperating with Administration plans to broker a deal for resolving the automaker's debts. The Administration told one of the bondholders' attorneys that they would unleash "the full force of the White House Press Corps" to "destroy their reputations." Curiously, no one in the media seemed terribly upset by the assertion that President Obama was holding their leash, and could sic them on stubborn private citizens. In the original essay, I referred to Chrysler "executives," which I intended to refer to all of the private citizens responsible for managing Chrysler's assets.

The Obama Administration's recent threats to use "public humiliation" against Chrysler bondholders, if they resist his plans to manage the company's debts, is appalling but unsurprising. Talk of turning the White House press corps into a weapon against recalcitrant executives is particularly chilling, when it comes from someone who smiles upon the kind of "public humiliation" that involves busloads of angry "activists" camping out on your front lawn. Nice life you have there, Chrysler executives. It would be a shame if something bad were to happen to it.

Obama has developed a nasty habit of using aggressive tactics against private citizens. The AIG bonus debacle, with its threats of punishment by tax laws and angry mobs…banks forced to accept TARP money and federal controls, then told they would not be allowed to return the former or escape the latter…and an election campaign that featured Democrat officials abusing their power, to destroy an inconvenient private citizen, are among the lowlights. Obama's background includes decades in a church whose pastor specialized in racist tirades, scapegoating whites for the problems of blacks, along with mentors who advocated "personalizing" political debates—and then destroying those persons. His behavior signifies more than just a young politician doing as he was taught, however, and it's going to get worse.

Collectivist politics of any stripe requires enemies, because they rely upon coercion. Socialist utopias don't come into existence spontaneously. There would be no need for confiscatory tax rates on the wealthy, if the wealthy voluntarily used their money to buy cars and houses for everyone in the lower income brackets, without requiring them to work in return. Nobody would be talking about nationalizing health care if doctors and hospital staff were happy to work eighty hour weeks for minimum wage, and pharmaceutical companies were run as giant charities that cheerfully sank billions into developing drugs they resell at cost. Few people would leave a sizable chunk of their estates to the government, if the government didn't seize the money through death taxes. No large group of people on Earth has every freely chosen to peacefully organize themselves into a socialist collective—they either slip into it through small losses of freedom that seem relatively painless as they happen, or they are forced into it at gunpoint. If Franklin Delano Roosevelt had proposed Obama's current budget and regulatory plans at the outset of the New Deal, he would have been laughed out of office, and if he had attempted to impose Obama's policies by force, he would have needed infantry platoons and tanks.

The basic premise of socialist government, as Obama famously explained to a plumber in Ohio last fall, is to take wealth away from the more successful people in society, and "spread that wealth around." This will always be a more attractive proposition to the people serving as the bread, than the people being used as the peanut butter. The creators of wealth must be forced to participate in the system, far beyond the point where a sense of civic duty or compassion for the downtrodden would keep them in line. After all, nearly half the country currently pays no income taxes, and they're not all "downtrodden" people deserving of charity. In fact, the socialist dream is to reach the point where over half the population pays no taxes, and will thus be inclined to support all expansions of government power. You can't get to the magic 51% of tax dependents just by using hungry orphans as props.

Increasing levels of coercion are necessary to expand the socialist system, and keep wealth producers trapped within it. To maintain popular support, the socialist needs voters to stay angry at designated class enemies. The Obama style of total government control over private businesses tends to turn feral with frightening speed, because it attempts to preserve the illusion of private enterprise, even as the "entrepreneurs" are enslaved to the total state. The employees and executives of Chrysler are not spoken of as government employees, and we still pretend that AIG is a "private corporation." All those banks forced to accept TARP funds are still supposedly private companies, not official branches of the Treasury Department. This has the advantage of giving politicians a measure of distance from the fate of the corporations involved. When GM announced that it would be going bankrupt anyway, after billions of dollars in bailout money, not a single person in the Obama Administration resigned in disgrace, or was even reprimanded. When the subprime mortgage industry blew up, the politicians who designed the system and controlled Fannie Mae were able to mutter that the crisis was caused by "fat cats on Wall Street." In fact, it is the official position of the

Democrat Party that not o*ne single member* of the Party did *anything* wrong in the financial-sector crisis…and to the lasting cost of the American people, the Republican presidential candidate did not dispute this position.

To keep controlling, bleeding, and blaming those private corporations, the Democrats will need to keep threatening and demonizing them. They cannot afford to allow the voters to start wondering if the corporations are being treated unfairly, or asking why no politician ever seems to be at fault for anything that goes wrong with these government-controlled industries. The Party's media allies will be happy to help them with this project. Can anyone doubt the media would have been pleased to help Obama carry out his threats to those Chrysler executives? Did you see any touching human interest stories about any of the AIG traders that had to give their bonuses back to the government? Do you think any of them was caring for a sick elder, or working to raise a family, or reaching the peak of a career they built with the help of hard-working parents who sacrificed everything to put them through school? Did we ever hear any of their *names?*

In order to keep the "partnership" between his Administration and the private sector working the way he wants it to, Obama will periodically need to remind captive corporations which side of that "partnership" has the upper hand. He can't very well afford to have Chrysler executives publicly opposing his plans for the company, or banks shoving their bail-out money back into his hands. He won't allow himself or his party to be held responsible for the damage they have done to the nation's financial system…any more than he will take responsibility for the first people to die under his national health care scheme. Businessmen will receive increasingly unpleasant reminders that their new government "partners" have nothing to bring to the arrangement except force, coupled with a highly developed instinct for escaping accountability.

The Other Side
May 5, 2009

Those of us who strongly oppose President Obama's policies often find ourselves wondering how anyone could possibly be in favor of them. It's an important question to resolve, as we work to recover from the political losses of the past few years. In a country where 51% of the popular vote is considered a landslide, and some of the worst congressmen come from districts that only cast a hundred thousand votes in each election, understanding the other side can be as important as understanding ourselves. Conservatives who hope to bring the Republican Party together on a unified message should give some thought to the audience awaiting that message.

The bulk of Democrat voters are not indentured members of the dependency class... at least, not yet. Some of them are liberals simply because they hate conservatives. They are surrounded by an academic and media culture that works hard to cast any objection to fashionable liberalism as so far beyond the pale that its enemies can only be evil, selfish, or primitive. Many liberals have a particular aversion to anything that smacks of religion, which they regard in exactly the same way that college students view the military draft. Some people fall into the liberal camp because of a single issue, because they find the conservative position on that issue to be intolerable: abortion, gay marriage, capital punishment, or similar hot-button topics. Often the liberal is misinformed about the conservative position on such an issue, which is not entirely due to media bias, since Republicans haven't done a very compelling or consistent job of explaining those positions over the last twenty years.

Republican politicians often forget that **conservatism is an argument, while liberalism is a promise.** The conservative champions both the moral and practical superiority of liberty and individualism. The liberal promises tangible rewards in exchange for votes. The conservative argument will never be over, because any free-market system will always include a certain population who fare poorly. No matter how small that population is, or how much the overall wealth of society eases the burden of their poverty, they will always be extremely receptive to the seduction of collective politics:

You're not responsible for your lot in life. You were cheated. The wealth of others is unfair. Give us the "freedom" that wasn't doing you any good anyway, and we will sharpen it into a weapon against those who took advantage of you. Give us your undying support, and you'll never have to worry about feeling confused, guilty, or inadequate again. Voting for the Democrat ticket will fully discharge your moral and intellectual duty as a citizen—we'll take it from there. In fact, we've got ACORN representatives standing by to fill that ballot out for you.

You have a "right" to housing, a job, health care, a college education, easy credit, and a host of other benefits, and the liberal promises to provide all of these things, while making nameless rich people pick up the tab.

Liberal socialism is the ongoing critique of capitalism's imperfections. To the casual center-left voter, the world seems overwhelming, confusing, and unfair. This was never more obvious than in the financial crisis that erupted last fall, when a large number of citizens became very angry and frightened about a crisis they couldn't begin to understand. They just knew something terrible was happening, and they demanded action. The Democrats stepped in with a ready-made narrative, which the Republicans suicidally left unchallenged, and offered the exact same solutions they have offered to every problem since the days of FDR: massive government spending and control. Conservatives found this dismaying and horrifying—who in their right minds would solve the problem Barney Frank created by giving Barney Frank more money and power? But Democrat voters were willing to accept this diagnosis and solution, as they always seem ready to accept liberal solutions, despite a century-long track record of absolute failure...because they need to believe that someone out there knows what they're doing, and has the answers to the overwhelming problems produced by a complex economy, and packaged by a sensationalist media in love with Big Solutions to Big Problems.

Voters who grew up in the past five decades know there are people smart enough to put men on the moon, create fantastic electronic devices, cure terrible diseases, and riddle out the secrets of the cosmos. They wonder why such intelligence can't be put to use in reducing unemployment, stimulating the stock market, and making sure everyone has a decent house to live in. When the media tells them the latest Democrat superstar has a brilliant plan to solve everything, and it won't cost "hard-working American families" a nickel, they're ready to believe the hype. Barack Obama really was the one they thought they've been waiting for...and before him it was Bill Clinton, and his wife, the smartest woman in the world.

We might ask the rank-and-file liberal why he's so willing to believe slippery, corrupt characters like politicians would be better suited to distribute the wealth of the nation, than the people who earned that wealth. The answer is the talismanic power of democratic elections. The American voter has been raised since childhood to believe voting is a sacred process that confers tremendous moral legitimacy on the winners of elections. Dollar bills are ugly instruments of crass materialism and greed in the hands of private citizens, but they acquire a luminous aura of virtue when handled by an elected official. The liberal voter believes his political leaders are entitled to control whatever portion of their constituents' wealth they require, because the voters gave them this power, voluntarily. They see ballots as an unlimited power of attorney to act on their behalf. Conservatives view their votes as a way to restrain politicians, while liberals view them as decrees of informed consent.

The liberal is comfortable with members of his Party descending from the heavens in private jets, to lecture citizens on the need to drive tiny fuel-efficient cars, and is untroubled by the spectacle of politicians who amassed vast fortunes through political corruption attacking private citizens for their greed…because those politicians were sanctified through the ritual of the popular vote. You might get a friendly liberal to admit that most politicians are crooks…but he'll hasten to add that businessmen are all crooks too, and at least the politicians gained their power and comforts through the informed consent of the voters, instead of stealing it from them with elaborate business schemes.

The gulf that divides liberal voters from conservative ideas is a crisis of faith. The liberal voter does not believe the system is fair, or that businessmen operating in a free market will provide the necessities of life that every American is entitled to. The upper class liberal doesn't have faith in the ability of the poor and downtrodden to seize the opportunities provided by capitalism, and build a better life for themselves. The dependent voter relies upon the benevolence of Big Government because he doesn't have faith in himself—he sees the competition of the free market as a rigged game he is destined to lose, rather than an exhilarating opportunity. The moralistic liberal has no faith in the judgment or compassion of ordinary people, who are products of a society forever mired in racism, sexism, phobias, and greed. The cynical young liberal thinks he knows what the ultimate goals of a wise and just society should be, and doubts that uneducated, Bible-thumping rednecks will ever arrive at those goals of their own free will. The working-class liberal is fearful that collapsing corporations will leave hordes of unemployed people who won't be able to find another decent job. High schools and colleges are filled with kids who have been taught to have no faith in the ability of free people to take proper care of their environment.

Above all, every type of liberal has been taught to have absolutely no faith in the intelligence, wisdom, or even basic humanity of Republicans. The long conservative battle against communism, in which liberals were either agnostic or actively rooting for the other side, was a psychosis. The defense of America against a vicious attack was cynically exploited to gain political influence over frightened voters, if not actually perpetrated by agents of the evil Republican hierarchy. The war in Afghanistan was a hopeless battle against the invincible Pashtun warrior, which any fool could see was a futile waste of young American lives. The war in Iraq was a brutal occupation designed to steal their oil. Tax cuts are a scheme to steal money from the Treasury, and stuff it into the pockets of rich Republicans. Social conservatives are shock troops for religious fascists. If some of the liberal conventional wisdom during the last eight years has seemed ridiculously over the top to you, remember that liberals have faith in no one except their political and cultural leadership…which they invest with the authority to renounce the blackness of Clarence Thomas, the womanhood of Sarah Palin, or the humanity of George W. Bush.

This is the challenge for conservative leadership, as it prepares for 2010 and 2012, and meanwhile rallies public opposition to the worst excesses of the Obama Administration: to address the lack of faith in enterprise, tradition, and opportunity that makes Democrat voters willing to settle for the slow, numb, bitter dissolution of the mighty nation their forefathers built through daring and industry. Republicans should remember they're offering leadership to people who wearily voted for a man they were told they needed a damn good reason to vote against, and who promised them Hope and Change, but delivered absolutely none of either. It's a mistake to think that people will easily accept painful truths about someone they were told to accept as the only worthy object for what little faith they have left.

The Power of the Collective
May 29, 2009

Much of the early opposition to Sonia Sotomayor, Obama's first Supreme Court nominee, has focused on her racialist statements concerning the superior judicial wisdom of Latin women. Sotomayor is a member of The National Council of La Raza, a Hispanic solidarity organization whose name means "The Race." La Raza is often confused with MEChA, a more openly and aggressively racist organization that advocates Hispanic racial supremacy and the reconquest of the southwestern United States by Hispanics. As recently as 2006, in response to a challenge from Georgia congressman Charlie Norwood, La Raza formally denounced MEChA and its agenda. We can take them at their word and accept the NCLR's assurances that it is entirely concerned with benevolent community outreach programs, and still marvel that someone belonging to an organization called "The National Council of The Race" is allowed to get anywhere near the Supreme Court. We most assuredly would not be debating the merits of appointing a white woman named Sonia Stephens, who belonged to a similar organization with a similar name, dedicated to "community outreach" for poor people of Anglo-Saxon descent. If her name was Sonia Sotomacher and her organization was dedicated to the advancement of German-Americans, the president who nominated her would have been impeached by now.

The president who nominated Sotomayor gained his office despite a twenty-year membership in a viciously racist church. If Jeremiah Wright had been white, and spewed comparable venom blaming all the problems of white Americans on black people, his young protégé Barry O'Bama would be an obscure fringe figure from the Chicago political underground, angrily spinning conspiracy theories to explain his crushing defeat in the state senate primaries.

Are Barack Obama and Sonia Sotomayor racists? No, but they are both proponents, and products, of **collective power.** Collective organizations are always the dominant forces in statist countries, such as America has become. Anyone who doubts this need only look at the way the American auto industry has been twisted into an incomprehensible mess for the benefit of a powerful workers' union, which relies upon money seized from taxpayers to artificially sustain a business model that should have collapsed when business managers capitulated to unreasonable union demands.

Collectives focus the political energies of their membership, becoming much more powerful and influential than disorganized majorities. This is one reason why massive social upheavals, such as gay marriage, proceed despite majority opposition to them. The proponents of gay marriage are well-organized, well-funded, media savvy, and politically connected. The opponents are a large, disorganized group of average people reading the newspaper and shaking their heads at the absurdity of two men getting married.

The formation of political collectives is natural and inevitable—the right of free association, and the effectiveness of such organizations, guarantees it. The elected representatives of a republic will always be ready to listen to someone who represents a large group of voters, particularly if they have money to donate to political campaigns. The problem is that when the state swells in size and exerts control over all aspects of the economy and culture, these political organizations become disproportionately powerful, and those who don't belong to such organizations find themselves overpowered and marginalized. In the socialist America of 2009, the entire economy has been restructured to benefit specific interest groups. If you want to buy an American-made car in 2011, your choices will be determined by environmentalists and auto workers' unions, more than by consumer demand. The mortgage industry was turned into a suicide bomb because powerful interest groups made the government over-ride the influence of the markets. Meaningful educational reform is forever blocked by the teachers' unions, which are much more influential, and brimming with political cash, than the much larger group of parents with children trapped in lousy public schools.

The state will always be more responsive to collectives with agendas that further the growth of state power. The teachers' unions didn't have to twist Jimmy Carter's arm to get the Department of Education. Barack Obama doesn't exactly look somber, humbled, or regretful as he takes over financial institutions and auto companies. Labor unions in general have gone from being collective bargaining associations that protected members from exploitation by rapacious businesses, to effectively becoming arms of the centralized state. In a practical sense, when you're talking to the head of the United Auto Workers or National Education Association, you're talking to a government official.

As the state grows larger, it increasingly becomes responsive only to large collectives, which increasingly require even more state power to accomplish their agendas. Because the Left understands this, it has always taken great pains to write the rules of American political culture to invalidate groups that oppose its agenda. ACORN and La Raza are noble community organizations, but groups the Left doesn't like are sinister "special interests." Virtually any collective organization with a conservative or libertarian agenda is swiftly discredited by declaring it hateful, racist, or fascist. There's a good reason the Left got so hysterical about the Moral Majority in the Eighties, or becomes so agitated about organized religion in general.

The problem for Americans posed by the increased power of political collectives is that all such organizations are, by necessity, coercive. Big Labor wouldn't have any power unless it could extract funds from its members and take their obedience to its agenda for granted. Nobody would pay attention to a union if half of its members could actively oppose its policies, or withhold their financial support from it. No one would pay attention to a minority association that could only claim to speak for some members of the minority. That's why groups such as the National Organization for Women or NAACP use cultural power to aggressively marginalize dissenting members of the sex or race groups they claim to speak for. There's nothing black liberal activists hate more than a successful black conservative—just ask Clarence Thomas. The last thing any collective can afford is for its members to start thinking they don't need it any more. Near-absolute obedience to the agenda of the leadership is required to produce effective political power, so collectives always resort to draconian means to suppress dissent.

It will be increasingly difficult for Americans who don't belong to collective organizations to enjoy cultural freedom or economic success, as a titanic government asserts the moral right to legislate its preferences in these areas, driven by the powerful interest groups that control the state. The power of the free market comes from vast numbers of free people making production and consumption choices in their own interest, producing an energy and vitality that dreary, plodding state-run economies can never hope to match. The economy of a free nation should be a race between millions of competitors surging forward, not a handful of clumsy, blinkered giants battling to control a rapidly shrinking arena. It's not good for harmony, prosperity, or liberty that Sonia Sotomayor proudly belongs to the type of organization that Sonia Sotomacher would be required to be ashamed of.

The Vanishing Non-Partisan
June 12, 2009

It's tough to be non-partisan these days. Lots of organizations claim to be non-partisan, of course, but it's usually just a pose, designed to cloak them in the camouflage of reason and even-handedness. A non-partisan "think tank" will be taken much more seriously than a team of political operatives, especially when their work is quoted by journalists, who are more anxious than anyone to avoid being identified as partisan. Commentators and bloggers sometimes like to pin the Medal of Free Thought, with Impartial Analysis cluster, on their chests to declare themselves above petty considerations of party, or suffocating loyalty to individual politicians. The highest praise most average folks can bestow upon themselves, during a conversation about politics or culture, is to declare themselves "moderate."

The rise of the super-state has made it increasingly difficult to remain non-partisan. A natural consequence of the growing power of central government is the unhappy movement of formerly private concerns into the realm of politics. It wasn't long ago that believing in the right of private companies and their employees to agree upon the terms of compensation, or the privacy of arrangements between mortgage holders and lenders, were "non-partisan" opinions. Now they're objectives on the ever-expanding political battlefield. Did the employees of AIG anticipate that their presidential votes in 2008 would determine whether or not they received their bonuses?

As more of the economy comes under direct government control, it becomes more essential for individuals and corporations to invest time and energy in politics. Companies like Microsoft got hard lessons in the Nineties about the importance of maintaining a well-funded lobbying operation in Washington, D.C. In the Obama era of rapacious government, every industry could be a few months away from being nationalized. Your presidential vote in past elections was based on tax rates, national security, and Supreme Court nominations. Your presidential vote in 2012 will determine the spring 2013 product line for General Motors, assuming they're still making cars by then. If socialized medicine gets pushed through, your very life will depend on your vote—as the Democrats will be happy to remind you.

Citizen participation in politics is good, but not when it's practiced for self-defense. As the stakes rise, the game becomes more bitter, and personal. People who think they're organizing to campaign for their "right" to free health care are not going to be polite or thoughtful participants in the national conversation, and they're not likely to feel themselves bound by all the fine print in our electoral laws. Someone who thinks only Barack Obama can "create or save" his job will not look at Obama's opponents as gentleman adversaries in a high-minded debate. Instead, they'll see nothing but enemies to be destroyed at all costs. The same sense of desperation is felt on the conservative side, as the last shreds of free-market capitalism go racing off into the woods, and hungry Democrats pursue with shotguns and hounds.

Every economic system ultimately boils down to a method of allocating resources. As soon as people organize beyond the level of a frontier family, hunting its own food and crafting all of its own goods, they begin devising methods of directing labor and materials to various projects. The free market is the most ethical, efficient, and productive system for allocating resources, as free people are compensated for the value of their time and goods, and a powerful engine of production and distribution is woven from the intersection of their abilities and desires. Capitalism is a simple theory that guides a massively complex system, assigning value to billions of goods and services through the chaotic brilliance of countless transactions. Obama-style statism is an ugly street brawl between two political parties to hold the knife that cuts the economic pie. It forces companies to divert valuable resources into politics, to protect themselves from predatory quasi-governmental organisms like the United Auto Workers union...and to get a share of the bailout billions. When the government is shoveling around towering piles of money, senators and congressmen become lucrative investments.

A politicized economy is an unhappy place to live, because few people are ever truly satisfied with their political leadership. How *could* they be? If the central government is limited, and performs only a dozen functions, your odds of finding candidates who agree with most of your views are pretty good. If the central government performs thousands of functions, your odds of finding candidates who agree with *any* of your positions aren't too hot. We can already see the Left growing disenchanted with Obama's inability to pay more than lip service to their many conflicting, and sometimes insane, positions. It's natural to spend a lot of time feeling disappointed by your President when he's also your banker, doctor, and car salesman. Too much of our complex economy is being stuffed into a bipolar political contest, replacing hundreds of daily free-market decisions with a single choice every few years, between a handful of candidates from a couple of parties. Binary decision-making is inadequate for guiding a digital marketplace.

In the shadow of the total state, it's difficult to believe *anyone* who claims to be nonpartisan. Those with the misfortune of living in a lawless environment of brutal anarchy often say that you have to belong to some sort of a gang, to have a chance of survival. It's funny how the same rules apply to the maximum government Barack Obama is trying to engineer.

Everything Inside the State
June 30, 2009

Author's Note: This was my first essay to receive wide linking and quotations from beyond the Hot Air community, thanks in large measure to a link from Instapundit, the all-seeing Glenn Reynolds— whose links can melt weaker servers beneath an avalanche of traffic. Reading it again, half a year later, I think its warning about the transition from "tax and spend liberalism" to command economics remains timely.

The Obama Administration has begun paving the way for the massive tax hikes that anyone capable of coherent thought knew were coming. A clumsy attempt by the White House spokesman to dodge the issue was met by laughter from the press corps, and outrage from anyone more interested in their own future than President Obama's political success. Maybe we're looking at this the wrong way. We're angry that Obama is preparing to break his pledge not to raise taxes on anyone earning less than $250k per year. However, as revealed in a recent *USA Today* analysis, each American household now carries over $550k of the national debt. That means we're all receiving over twice that $250k threshold in value from the government, so Obama can raise everyone's taxes without breaking his promise. We're all filthy rich, and we can even rely on the government to expertly balance the checkbook for us!

We're not simply looking at an increase in income taxes under Obama. The cap-and-trade monstrosity passed by the House amounts to a titanic tax increase on both consumers and virtually every sector of the economy, since almost all economic activity consumes energy. (If you like the idea of $6 per gallon gasoline, you'll *love* paying $7 per gallon for milk at your local grocery store.) A value-added tax is being considered, which would pour another layer of concrete on top of a nearly paralyzed retail sector, and likely put an end to the Internet shopping boom, at least for American companies. I doubt it would take long for the government to institute a surcharge in the VAT tax for Internet purchases, since they are currently escaping state taxes, and that's not "fair." Like all other tax increases, a Value Added Tax will produce less revenue than anticipated, because it will depress the very economic activity it was designed to feed from. New taxes *always* produce less revenue than the government predicts, spawning further tax increases to make up the difference.

The proposed health-care takeover can also be seen as a tax hike on the medical industry, to a rate of 100% if that industry is fully nationalized under a single-payer system. Every state takeover of an industry is a tax increase, because government revenue is infinitely flexible, with every dollar swept away by the massive federal bloodstream. Any profits earned by socialized medical providers will disappear into the bottomless maw of the ever-expanding super-state. The same thing will happen with General Motors, in the unlikely event it manages to turn a profit. Anyone familiar with state lotteries has seen them sold to the voters as a wonderful new source of funding for education, then watched greedy state governments pull regular funding away from education and spend it elsewhere.

In a way, the notion of "tax and spend" is becoming obsolete, because Obama's plan is to complete the re-definition of the relationship between citizens and their State. Prior to the 20th century, the American government was run something like a business, gaining its income by selling land, and services such as protection from piracy, through taxation on trade. When the direct taxation of income was made legal through the Sixteenth Amendment, the idea was to treat government as a necessary expense, borne by the wealthiest caste of Americans, to ensure the welfare of the most desperately poor. As tax rates increased, more working people were added to the tax rolls, and ever-larger benefits were paid out by the government, the relationship between citizen and state changed from welfare to socialism—which begins when the people paying for the benefits no longer control them. The modern liberal's belief that anyone who desires lower tax rates is guilty of "greed" is a deliberate expression of this altered relationship. The people paying taxes have no moral right, and increasingly no practical means, to determine how much money will be assessed or paid out. The only legitimate factor is how much money the government thinks it needs, and can get away with appropriating.

Under Obama, a final transformation is taking place: the government no longer sees itself as an expense borne by its citizens. Instead, the citizens are now seen as components of the State. If the State decides to follow the religion of global warming, the citizens will be made to pay tithe, no matter what their personal beliefs are. If the State thinks only its wise stewardship can "save" the financial industry, banks will be forced to accept government money and controls. If the State believes private health insurance is not inexpensive or comprehensive enough, it will create its own insurance program…and force everyone who does not participate to subsidize it. If the State decides an auto company must be kept in business, for the benefit of a union that has essentially become a component of the State, then all other Americans will be compelled to finance that auto company. People joke bitterly about being forced to buy cars from Government Motors someday, but the situation is far more outrageous: we all work for Government Motors already, through hundreds of dollars in subsidies extracted from our tax payments. Depending on how much you earn per hour, you've spent ten or twenty hours working for GM this year, and they'll probably conscript you again before the year is through.

We are passing through the outer boundary of the era when your contributions to the government can be described as a mere "tax." Taxes, mandates, and state-run industries all add up to one thing: control. Our destination that was made inevitable when the government was allowed to begin seizing portions of Americans' income, instead of collecting fees for essential services it provides. It's a course that was locked in when the recipients of welfare were allowed to retain the right to vote, creating the vicious cycle of an ever-expanding dependency class that accrues more political power as it demands more benefits. Now we've reached the point where simply paying "welfare," as it has traditionally been understood, is a small fraction of bloated state and federal governments. The Obama government does not even pretend to limit itself to assisting the destitute with the bare necessities of survival. It believes it has the right, and responsibility, to provide prosperity...and to trade away however much of our prosperity it thinks is necessary, to achieve other ends.

Conservatives have often taunted liberals with the infamous slogan of Marxism: "From each according to his means, to each according to his needs." The Obama concept of government is better understood through a different quote: "Everything inside the State, nothing outside the State." The author was Benito Mussolini. He meant what he said. So did the people who voted for the cap-and-trade bill.

Decomposing In A Limited World

July 9, 2009

Earlier today, Ed highlighted this interesting quote from an interview with Supreme Court Justice Ruth Bader Ginsburg, originally posted on the New York Times website:

> Frankly I had thought that at the time *Roe* was decided, there was concern about population growth and particularly growth in populations that we don't want to have too many of. So that *Roe* was going to be then set up for Medicaid funding for abortion. Which some people felt would risk coercing women into having abortions when they didn't really want them. But when the court decided *McRae*, the case came out the other way. And then I realized that my perception of it had been altogether wrong.

Justice Ginsburg's liberal and feminist credentials are impeccable, and she could fairly claim to be one of the architects of modern liberal thought, having co-founded the Women's Rights Law Reporter while a professor of law at Rutgers in the early 70s. Her candid statements on the eugenics aspects of *Roe* provide a window into the liberal mind, through one of its most enduring neuroses: population control.

Overpopulation is a constant fear of the Left, stretching back to the dire philosophy of Thomas Malthus, the nineteenth-century Anglican clergyman, who believed the wealth and technology of advanced societies would lead inevitably to exploding populations, with resulting famine and shortages of raw materials: "The power of population is indefinitely greater than the power in the earth to produce subsistence for man." Malthus was a profoundly influential writer. Not only did his writings shape the thoughts of other scholars in his century, particularly Charles Darwin, but you can see his dead hand reaching out from Barack Obama's economic policies. Malthus would have thought the soaring energy prices, and permanent economic recession, from the cap-and-trade bill are nothing more than a small step in the right direction.

Malthus used his pen to draw the outer boundaries of the liberal imagination. None of the socialists, fascists, communists, or other materialists who followed have ever been able to cross those boundaries. The grim logic of limited space and finite resources haunts the design of every collectivist utopia. The size of the world is fixed, and its natural resources are limited, so every new human born into an industrial society is one more locust nibbling away at the rotting corpse of Mother Earth. Each population increase brings a nation, and the world around it, one step closer to running out of food and living space. The Malthusian looks out his window and sees a small planet drowning in a sea of humanity. He knows that one day, the last drop of oil will be pumped from the ground, and the last forest will be cut down to build the final high-rise condominium. He believes that day is right around the corner.

This obsession with limited resources and zero-sum math runs through liberal economic theory. The amount of land and resources in the United States is fixed. The population keeps increasing. A limited pool of food, housing, medicine, and employment must be distributed among the population. Who else but a wise and benevolent state, run by highly educated and civic-minded liberals, could possibly manage that division in a fair and equitable manner? It certainly doesn't make any sense to let a bunch of greedy rich guys parcel out the nation's wealth. They'll just keep it all for themselves.

You can find this kind of thinking behind every liberal policy. It is the electric current that leaps between the neurons of the socialist mind. Rich men "steal" their wealth from the rest of us—every dollar in a millionaire's pocket is a dollar that he took from the deserving poor. The most infamous recent expression of this idea was Barack Obama's unintentionally candid admission to Joe the Plumber, during the 2008 campaign, that he thought his job as President would be to "spread the wealth around." The net worth of America is a fixed number in the minds of liberals. The only way they can imagine creating more wealth is to steal it from the future. The idea behind Obama's reckless deficit spending is to inject a pile of cash into the heart of today's moribund economy, and the only way to get the cash is to borrow it from foreign investors, and leave our children to settle the bills, plus interest, when they come due.

Justice Ginsburg's remarks on Roe vs. Wade echo a common sentiment among pro-choicers: it's wrong to bring more children into this overcrowded, cruel world. Environmentalists will occasionally refer to American babies, in particular, as larval parasites the world is better off without, since Americans consume such an outrageous share of our precious and limited natural resources. Part of the attraction of this kind of dismal thinking is that it absolves one of responsibility for the future. The machinery of prosperity is winding down anyway, and there's nothing anyone can do about it—we had to burn through our limited resources eventually. You're not being selfish by refusing to cramp your lifestyle with child-rearing—you're a noble hero, because you're leaving the next generation with a couple less mouths to feed!

Two centuries of absolute failure have not dimmed the allure of Mathusian philosophy. It's a failed idea because it overestimates the strain humanity places on the world, and underestimates the creativity and resourcefulness of free men and women. Viewing the rest of the human race as a virus flatters the liberal's sense of superiority, because he has the superior wisdom to *see* those dwindling forests and shrinking oil reserves. He's an enlightened steward of a fragile planet, not a primitive religious zealot rutting away in a trailer park, spawning the next generation of SUV drivers. He votes for politicians with detailed plans for redistributing wealth in the name of social justice…not corporate puppets selling fairy tales about opportunity and economic growth. The conservative bears witness to the wonder of human ingenuity, and the amazing possibilities that await even children born into humble circumstances. The liberal does not believe in such wonders.

Justice Ginsburg says she eventually realized her perception of abortion, as a means of controlling "growth in populations that we don't want to have too many of," was wrong. Living things grow. Dead things wither. A vital and living America can grow far beyond the limits of liberal imagination, in both prosperity and population. The dead-end social and economic theories of the Left are not concerned with encouraging growth. They believe their duty is to manage a graceful decomposition.

Zero Percent Unemployment—Now!

July 16, 2009

There are about 15 million people unemployed in the United States at the moment, and the number is rising. Barack Obama is personally responsible for every single one of them. Why? Because he could hire them all.

The wasteful, pork-encrusted "stimulus" bill rammed through Congress by the Democrats cost taxpayers $787 billion. That works out to about $52k per unemployed person. Instead of pouring all that money into the pockets of their political allies, the Democrats could have hired every single unemployed person for two years, at $26k per year, tax free. The biggest problem with Obama is his lack of vision. He's got his addled Vice President staggering around, claiming to see "workers rehired, factories reopened, cops on the street, teachers in the classroom, progress toward getting our economy back on the move" everywhere he goes. Instead of wasting everyone's time with the Joe Biden clown act, he could simply assert control over the entire American economy, and declare unemployment to be zero percent.

What would Obama do with those fifteen million new employees? Well, they've all got skills, right? Most of them are capable of working, and I would venture to say that many of them desperately *want* to work. Surely a man who can conjure the biggest, most complex medical insurance "corporation" on Earth out of thin air could find something to do with fifteen million new pairs of hands. Maybe they could write their own job descriptions, and suggest fun, productive ways to put their talents to use on behalf of America. I bet we could find "green jobs" for all of them.

Or, better yet…why not indulge in a little more deficit spending, and set up medical scholarships for those who score the highest on aptitude tests? (With the appropriate number of racial set-asides, of course. We wouldn't want newly minted Justice Sotomayor getting all *Ricci* on our brand-new program!) We'll need lots of new doctors to provide all those expanded health benefits. Don't liberals keep bleating about 47 million uninsured in this country? Well, if they're all going to suddenly have health insurance, thanks to a stroke of Obama's pen and some fat surtaxes on the wealthiest Americans, we're going to need a surge in health-care workers to take care of them all. The current ratio of doctors per 100,000 population is about 260. That means we'll need 122,000 more doctors to handle 47 million more people with health insurance. We can scrape by if about half a percent of our 15 million unemployed are doctor material.

But wait...unemployment is going to go up in the next couple of years, due to Obama's policies. Cap-and-trade will put a lot of people out of work. Come to think of it, how many people work for the medical insurance companies that Obama's new "public plan" will force out of business? Will they all go to work for Obama Insurance, Inc., or will we need to find jobs for some of them, too? Well, no problem—even if the number of unemployed doubles by 2012, we can just charge another $700 billion to Uncle Sam's deficit card, and hire them all. Zero percent unemployment forever!

Except...those two-year stimulus jobs will run out around 2012, won't they? No worries—I'm sure those people will have proven themselves highly productive assets to the economy, and America will consider it a bargain to keep them on its payroll forever. With all those new workers, the wise and brilliant Obama will have created entirely new industries. You might be shaking your head and wondering why people with guaranteed government jobs, paid in tax-free money, would feel motivated to work hard, let alone display the discipline and energy to create new industries. Let me assure you that your fears are unfounded, because... well...

Oh, hell. That's where the whole beautiful scheme falls apart.

Listening to Democrats explain their wonderful plans for universal access to free everything, you realize they have a profound misconception about the economy, which fuels many of their other delusions: *they think running a business is easy*. Being a doctor is easy. Working in a bank, a mortgage company, or an investment brokerage is a piece of cake. All of the people who do these things will continue to do them, with equal dedication...even if their taxes are raised, or their industries are nationalized. Creating a federal health insurance company of titanic size will be a snap—the Democrats will just throw a few politically reliable people into the executive slots, pour an avalanche of tax dollars into their laps, and bingo! The existing health insurance companies don't have any special knowledge about their industry, and there are no business reasons why they stubbornly refuse to provide cheap coverage for those 47 million uninsured. They only withhold that coverage because they're evil and greedy. Caring political appointees will easily succeed where they failed, on a budget fixed by next year's Congress. I'll bet they can guarantee all Americans first-rate coverage without exceeding that budget by *one red cent*.

Anyone who runs a real business knows how completely wrongheaded this is. Business ownership is **hard**. It takes entrepreneurial risk, the ability to find and exploit opportunities, discipline, and sacrifice. The owners and managers of every business, from small family operations to huge conglomerates, must make tough decisions about paying expenses, making investments, pleasing shareholders, and coping with unexpected setbacks. Sometimes these decisions are agonizing. Every business owner reading this could tell a story about sitting up late at night, staring at vendor invoices, payroll ledgers, and accounts receivable with watery eyes, trying to make them fit together and produce balanced books somehow. Even the wealthiest of them could tell you harrowing tales of lean times, when personal assets had to be put at risk, or life savings had to be tapped as investment capital. Even hearing these stories would not prepare you for the reality of owning a business of your own, if you've never tried it. You must experience it for yourself to appreciate it.

Very few Democrat politicians have ever run a business. Barack Obama certainly hasn't. I doubt he would agree with the sentiments expressed in the previous paragraph. In his heart, like every socialist, he sees business owners as nothing but rich people driving around in fancy cars…and since the federal government is richer than any of them, it will be the best business owner *ever*. The truth of the matter is that deep pockets are the government's sole advantage. It has no discipline, no entrepreneurial spirit, no reason to take its lumps when it makes a bad decision, and a very low threshold of pain. If Obama Insurance, Inc. loses money, the government will just give it more. When bondholders refuse to raise the limits on the government's deficit card any further, it will simply seize more money from taxpayers, making duly "progressive" adjustments to soak the wealthiest of them. The government will not be the best insurance company ever. It will be the worst…. and the one thing its bad decisions can never force it to do is go out of business.

Why are those 15 million people unemployed? For the most part, they're looking for jobs, but no one will hire them. Companies very much want to hire more people, and expand—no business wishes to remain stagnant. The decision to refrain from hiring people is a tough one. Business owners don't make it because they're cruel and like to laugh at people in the unemployment lines. One of the reasons the economy is contracting is because money—the avatar of time, resources, and entrepreneurship—is being forced to go where it doesn't want to go. Businesses that should fail are being propped up by reckless deficit spending. The shadow of titanic tax increases to come, including those needed to fund Obama's adventure in health insurance, looms fearfully large on the horizon—and when money is frightened, it *hides*.

Hiring people to fill job openings is not the same thing as handing them a check and announcing they're employed. The health care "crisis," to the extent one exists, cannot be solved by signing a bill and declaring everyone has health insurance now. Businessmen live at the intersection of theory and reality, while politicians angrily deny that intersection exists at all. That's one reason I much prefer dealing with businessmen.

The Engine Of Poverty
July 22, 2009

Author's note: This essay expresses an idea that I have returned to many times. If the mission of liberalism is to help the poor and downtrodden, they should take a serious look at what has made a tangible difference in the lives of the poor over the last century…and it's difficult to ignore the truth that technological advancement has made far more of a concrete difference to them than government spending programs, even before the destructive social costs of welfare are factored in.

Economic downturns make life tough on everyone. Natural disasters can cause enormous human misery, and require massive relief operations, to provide food and medical aid. To cause serious, long-term, grinding poverty, however, you need government involvement.

Big Government is the most formidable engine of poverty the industrialized world has ever seen. The worst famines to sweep the twentieth century were caused by either incompetent or malevolent government, with the Holodomor famine in Ukraine being a particularly horrifying example. Millions of Ukrainians were starved to death in the Holodomor, as a deliberate matter of Soviet policy. The infamous Ethiopian famine of the mid-80s prompted a well-meaning response from the West, including the Live Aid concerts organized by Bob Geldof…but while hundreds of millions of dollars were raised, much of the aid money and relief supplies were simply stolen by the Ethiopian military junta. Collectivist governments around the world have produced uniformly terrible standards of living.

Domestically, the Great Society's War on Poverty did nothing but waste nearly nine trillion dollars, and create more poverty. Every lower-class social pathology has grown worse since the 1960s, most of them much worse. We certainly haven't gotten much value for the money we've spent on Great Society social programs.

Of course, the meaning of "poverty" has changed a lot over the years. The poor of the United States have a higher standard of living than the middle class in much of the rest of the world. They also have a higher standard of living than the filthy rich of a hundred years ago, or the crowned royalty of the centuries before that. This improved standard of living has very little to do with the government. A poor American might get food stamps from Uncle Sam, but he will use them to buy food of incredible variety and purity from convenient local stores. Why is this high-quality food so readily available? Because people with money pay for it, and grocers compete to win their business. I challenge you to walk down any aisle of a grocery store without spotting at least a half-dozen products that are "new and improved."

The private sector is still improving this stuff long after a government-controlled grocery industry would have decided it was good enough.

If you are motivated by a humanitarian desire to help the poor—the ostensible mission of much of the modern liberal state—you must realize that nothing helps them more than the increased standard of living and economic opportunity brought about by the private sector. Every government action that shrinks the private sector hurts the poor. It hurts everyone else, too, except for the political class, and the plutocrats who find ways to shape legislation to their benefit…but it hurts the poor the most. Consider the "stimulus" travesty Obama and the Democrats shoved down the nation's throat. It stimulated nothing, and drained billions of dollars away from a private economy that could have used those resources better. It wasn't merely a waste of money. The value of every wasted government dollar must be judged by what free enterprise could have accomplished with it. The untold tragedy of the economy is the hidden story of all the things free people could do, if we started emptying out some of those fortresses in Washington and returning their money to them. The economy we have today might make you angry, but the economy we *could* have should make you furious.

Exactly what would the private sector do with its money that would be so wonderful? I don't know—and *neither does anyone else*, particularly anyone in Washington. If the six long months of this Administration serve any constructive purpose, it should be permanently dissolving the illusion that a small group of political appointees can predict what the economy will do, and control it to produce an improved outcome. There is a better plan for restoring our prosperity than anything being cooked up by Obama's brain trust. In fact, there are thousands of them—and no single person knows them all. They are scattered through the minds of people from coast to coast, formulated by small business owners behind the wheels of work trucks, as well as executives in boardrooms. People working within the incentives of the free market—operating in local markets they know personally, or national markets their companies have studied for decades—will always be able to outperform a group of academics, whose first order of business is listing all the things they won't even *consider* doing, because it would violate their ideology. You're always better off placing your bets on organizations that strive to reward their shareholders, over those dedicated to rewarding contributors.

No one benefits more from general economic strength than the poor, and no one suffers faster when the economy hits a downturn. The lowest-level jobs are the first to be filled when a company expands…and the first to go when it needs to cut labor costs. The benefits of technological progress have the most profound effect on the lower class standard of living. Even in the case of charity, the ideal results are obtained when a wealthy society has money to spend on the disadvantaged. The top private charities average about 85 cents on the dollar delivered to beneficiaries. Government welfare hits about 35 cents on the dollar, in a good year. The liberal sneers that we can't rely on private charities to take care of all the needy. Why not? If we had given $787 billion to the top 50 private charities this year, do you think it would have all vanished down a rat hole, like the "stimulus?" The liberal conceit that only the State can be trusted to address the needs of the downtrodden is one of the most dangerous threats faced by the poor in America. The true sources of liberal disdain for private charity are their lust for power, and their revulsion at the religious character of many top charitable organizations. Nothing frightens them more than the idea that dedicated volunteer and religious groups might actually *reduce poverty*, because the downtrodden cease to be useful to the Left when they cross the poverty line. What would the federal budget need to be, if it were primarily concerned with defense, law enforcement, and the welfare of the most seriously disadvantaged Americans—and that welfare was administered with 85% efficiency?

The best thing going for the poor is the increase in their standard of living brought about by the energy of free enterprise. The only way they can ever escape from poverty is by obtaining a good education, and getting a decent job. Big Government is a miserable failure at the former, and an active threat to the latter—as can be seen from the obscene cap-and-trade bill, or Obama's health care proposals. *Nothing* should be a higher priority for the poor than slashing the size of government and radically cutting taxes. The free markets are always hiring. When they slow down, it's because they aren't free.

The Aristocracy Of Intent
July 23, 2009

Author's Note: The night before this essay was written, President Obama gave the now-infamous press conference in which he accused doctors of performing unnecessary procedures, including tonsil removal, to swindle money from their patients. As a point of historic interest, Ted Kennedy died about four weeks after this was posted.

President Obama's bizarre prime-time press conference last night illustrated one of the worst aspects of socialism: the insularity of its elites. This was clearly the performance of someone who expects to be shielded from criticism, opposition, practical considerations, and the results of his actions.

People often wonder how liberals can regard themselves as such an enlightened elite, while running down every other aspect of the society they nominally belong to. If every successful person in America is greedy, cruel, and selfish, how can financially successful liberals claim to be morally superior? The answer is nothing so simple as hypocrisy, although liberals are very sensitive to that accusation, and constantly project it onto others. The truth was visible in Obama's press conference last night. What you saw was not a humble servant of the people, carrying out his duties as the executive of a constitutional republic. It wasn't even a man discussing an idea he thinks is brilliant, and trying to convince others to support it. It was a monarch who could barely conceal his anger and frustration at those who dare to question his wisdom. Liberals regard themselves as an aristocracy of intent, a privileged class made superior by their dedication to "selfless" principles.

Naturally, such an insular elite sees itself surrounded by enemies. These enemies cannot, by definition, have anything but the most vile and selfish motives—otherwise, they would be supporting the liberal program, not opposing it. That's why Obama was willing to make an utter fool of himself last night, by characterizing doctors as bloodthirsty ghouls who can't wait to dismantle our children and sell them for scrap, starting with their tonsils. It's interesting that Obama didn't have anything better prepared for his press conference, since he went in knowing the public was turning decisively against him. He really didn't think he would need to do anything other than dazzle his audience with his limitless compassion and charisma, while pointing out what soulless monsters his opponents are.

Liberal voters are always eager to excuse the failures of their leadership by emphasizing how much they "care." You can find this sort of thinking deployed on Obama's behalf today. At least he's trying to "do something" about the health-care "crisis," which we can no longer ignore! Of course, this "broken" health-care system has higher approval ratings than any politician in the country. We should be spending more time worrying about how to fix our broken government. It's especially rich to hear the architect of the "stimulus" swindle criticize anyone else for trying to rob customers by billing for unnecessary procedures. Is the total value of all extraneous medical procedures for the past six months more than $787 billion?

As it stands, government is far more responsible than any business interest for the systemic problems that do exist in the medical industry., but this idea simply does not appear on the liberal radar screen. The intent of benevolent big-government programs places their results beyond criticism. To the Left, it simply is *not possible* that "reforms" intended to increase access to health care, and make it more affordable, could result in rationing and higher prices...any more than increases in tax rates could lead to reduced revenue for the government. Since nothing could ever be improved by reducing government involvement, that option is presumptively swept off the table, leaving the Left to devise increasingly wasteful and counter-productive schemes to address the problems with its previous schemes. A sinking ship is extremely difficult to repair, if you begin by declaring the big hole in the side of the hull cannot possibly by the reason you're taking on water.

The radiant aura of their good intentions insulates liberals from even the most basic criticisms they level at others. Lots of those "greedy" health care professionals are female, but I doubt many of them are rocking $6000.00 handbags like Michele Obama. You'd have to steal a lot of tonsils to afford the kind of million-dollar night on Broadway the Obamas are known to enjoy. The moral superiority of leftist politics transcends any personal transgressions he might have committed. When Ted Kennedy finally passes away, you can expect the media to float the idea that Mary Jo Kopechne's life was a small price to pay for decades of having this magnificent liberal lion stalk the halls of the Senate.

The Left is also very selective in who it chooses to criticize for greed and selfishness. We obviously aren't meant to hate hard-working schoolteachers or auto workers for striving to provide the best for their families, but we're supposed to hate hard-working dentists so much that we'll turn their entire industry into a penitentiary. By the way, the median income for those evil tonsil-grabbing pediatricians is about $150k per year. How much is Henry Gates pulling down per year? The President seemed a lot more concerned about inconveniencing Gates than he did about disrupting the lives of the millions who are happy with their current health insurance.

The power of the free-market capitalism despised by the Democrats is that it shows far more interest in results than intentions. The free market has very little time to spare for well-meaning failures. It certainly doesn't appropriate a couple million dollars worth of prime-time television to ram them down people's throats. The profit motive, so casually impugned by desperate liberals, is the best thing going for the consumers of any product—from health care, to computers, to cat food—because it is the best way to ensure the highest level of sustained effort from the greatest number of producers. If health care is completely nationalized, there are some doctors who will continue to practice their trade with undiminished dedication, entirely out of concern for their patients…but neither health care, nor any other industry, can rely entirely on the efforts of such people.

The angry and confused man on television last night did not think he would ever find himself playing defense—and losing. He thought he only needed to announce he was giving away "free" health care, then bask in the adulation of the grateful multitudes, like any beloved king. Aristocrats rarely take criticism well, and they lack a capitalist's creative energy for dealing with setbacks. If you ever do need your tonsils out, you're better off hiring a greedy doctor than a caring bureaucrat. It looks like you might just be allowed to continue making that decision.

The War on Whatever
July 28, 2009

Heart disease is the leading cause of death in the United States. According to the Centers for Disease Control, 631,636 Americans died from it last year. Taking more steps to prevent the onset of heart disease, and developing more effective treatments, would save many lives. Therefore, I propose that every single adult in the United States dedicate themselves full-time to battling this deadly scourge. Some of this huge surge in manpower could be assigned to police the behavior of their fellow Americans, to ensure they never do anything that would increase their risk of heart disease.

Are there any objections to this bold and compassionate initiative? Well, you might say it's unfair and inhumane to ignore all the other diseases people suffer from, in a single-minded push to wipe out heart disease. Would it help if I said we'll move on to the next most common cause of death—cancer—after we eliminate heart disease? Cerebrovascular and lower respiratory diseases will be next up after we've cured cancer. Is it too much to ask for people dying of other diseases to hang tough while we devote 100% of our effort to helping the greater number of people suffering from heart disease? Well…yes, that is a bit too much to ask, isn't it?

Another flaw in my War On Heart Disease proposal is the diminishing returns we would realize, from devoting our entire working population to the task. There are only so many laboratories, and not everyone can master the skills needed to provide useful assistance to our leading heart surgeons. It's very inefficient to take master mechanics, computer programmers, or pastry chefs and turn them into mediocre lab assistants in cardiac research facilities. What sort of cold, gray world would we live in, if every single one of us worked at the same job, every single day?

You may have already skipped ahead to a related problem with my proposal: forcing everyone to work directly on the heart-disease problem would actually hinder useful research, for such research depends on contributions from many industries. The people working on cardiac research need computers, and high-quality laboratory equipment, which cannot be built by doctors who have dedicated their lives to studying medicine. They need buildings to work in, electricity to run their equipment, and food to eat. The advanced state of medicine, as with all other industries in our high-tech world, flows from specialization and diversification. Our economic and technological strength depends upon people developing many different skills, and exchanging their goods and services with each other. We have advanced far beyond the point where a doctor can be expected to blow the glass tubes for his own laboratory, or assemble and program his own computer systems.

Even if we modified our strategy for the War On Heart Disease a bit, and simply required 100% of our Gross National Product to be devoted to fighting heart disease, we would still produce inefficiencies that would hinder our quest for superior treatments—to say nothing of reducing everyone's quality of life, particularly those who suffer from other medical conditions. The same principle applies on an individual basis, because a myopic focus on devoting every aspect of your life to reducing the risk of heart disease could make you vulnerable to other conditions, as well as draining all the joy out of living.

It might also have occurred to you, while reading my original proposal, that forming up a massive volunteer Heart Cop Corps, to police everyone's behavior and force them to minimize their risk of heart disease, would be a ridiculously totalitarian approach. Even less draconian means of persuading everyone to engage in healthy behavior would become offensive to liberty if taken far enough. How much tax money should the government be able to extract from us, to fund a heart disease education program? How many public-service announcements should they be allowed to force TV and radio stations to run?

These objections to a total "war" on heart disease illustrate an important point about health care and economics. The economy is a means of allocating resources, and no amount of noble intentions can change the fact that health care exists within the framework of the economy. We can allow the economy to be shaped by the needs and desires of free people, or we can allow the political class to dictate where our resources will be invested. Government control is disastrous, because political considerations always trump efficiency and respect for individual rights. Command economies are not merely inept at allocating resources—they are inherently unable to correctly appraise the resources available to them. as you can see from the current avalanche of lunatic deficit spending.

The more complex an economy becomes, the less effectively it can be commanded by political forces. The medical industry is, all by itself, a fantastically complex economy, in which advanced resources must be assigned wisely to produce the greatest benefit for all patients. Politics have already done horrendous damage to this system: distorting the way consumers interact with providers, lumping routine and critical care together under the umbrella of "insurance," and allowing politically powerful trial lawyers to impose exaggerated malpractice costs on health care providers. We should be discussing ways to decrease political control of health care, not radically increase it. In a government-controlled health care system, pressure from organized lobbies will over-ride medical science and economic considerations, to the detriment of everyone. Groups that currently work to secure private donations for treatment and research will have no choice but to become government lobbying organizations instead.

The victims of medical conditions that don't enjoy effective lobbying organizations will find themselves on the wrong side of health care rationing. Every disease will become AIDS.

Health care is inextricably bound up in the same massive economy as all of our other needs. It's dangerous to pretend the intrinsic nobility of medicine makes it immune to economic forces, as the result of such willful blindness will be reduced quality and availability of care…which will lead to more suffering and death. Freedom produces the wealth and technology to most effectively address all of our needs. Command economies produce an endless series of "crises" that can only be fought through total "wars," because the crisis and warfare mindset is the only way politicians can motivate the population to support their agendas. Everyone who isn't enlisted in the War On Whatever ends up as collateral damage.

The Aggressor State
August 1, 2009

Some people don't like using the term "liberal" to describe the Left, since modern conservatism is the true inheritor of classical liberalism. There's certainly nothing "liberating" about the monster state Democrats are constructing, in which freeborn men and women wear chains forged from 1300-page energy bills and trillion dollar health-care takeovers. The Left is always looking for a new brand name, as each of their previous names becomes a dirty word. I'm not eager to help them with their marketing efforts, but a more accurate name than "liberals" would be "aggressors." Barack Obama may have little skill at effectively governing, but he is eminently qualified to be Commander-in-Chief of the Aggressor State.

The Left is always on the attack, because the way it requires people to live is contrary to their normal tendencies. It's debatable whether America is currently a conservative nation, but every family and community is essentially conservative by nature. The ideas we closely associate with the modern Right are the common-sense, default behavior of people left to their own devices: free enterprise, freedom of speech, freedom of association, strength in defense, respect for private property, and reverence for the value of tradition. The modern Left does not like any of those things, or at least considers them all negotiable in value. The Left obviously believes its morally superior values take priority over free enterprise. Freedom of speech and association are trumped by racial agendas. Liberal intellectuals have long viewed private property as not merely an impediment to socialist designs, but an outright evil. Defense is the only area of government spending Democrats ever feel comfortable with cutting. The Left has nothing but contempt for tradition, and often mistakes this contempt for a sign of intelligence. Ignorant of its own intellectual history, modern liberalism doesn't think anyone else's intellectual history matters, either. The tired old New Deal programs and Keynesian voodoo of the Obama Administration can seem like fresh and new ideas, provided you can convince yourself history began in November 2008.

Because liberalism defines itself as transformative, it is very comfortable with aggression. This posture serves them well with a public that believes "progress" is inherently positive. The business of building the modern super-state has been a sustained attack, using cultural pressure, legislative power, and the blunt instrument of loyal voting blocs to beat Middle America into submission. The goal of the Left is to convince the middle class to give it the power to do things they would never be depraved or dishonest enough to do themselves. Ordinary people refer to the "redistribution of wealth" as "theft." If a man wearing a tailored suit and power tie came to your door one day, and offered to take care of your health, in exchange for surrendering all control over your medical decisions to a board of faceless strangers—who also demand unlimited control over every part of your life that might conceivably impact your health—you'd slam the door in his face and call the cops. If you caught someone writing himself a $4000.00 check from your checkbook, and he explained he needs the money as tribute to his Church of Global Warming so they can save the world from an imaginary evil, you'd shoot first and call 911 later. The mission of the Left is to convince people that all of these outrages become virtuous when elected officials perpetrate them. After all, "they won."

The Left phrases everything in the most urgent terms, because offense requires initiative. Everything it does is an assault that must be launched immediately, with every moment of delay helping the enemy…and the Left has an insatiable hunger for enemies. It prefers those enemies to be faceless, because that also makes the enemy voiceless: white racists, the Evil Rich, Big Business, Wall Street fat cats…You can tell the Left is getting desperate when it starts naming its targets, as with the weird tirades Nancy Pelosi and Barack Obama launched against insurance companies and tonsil-stealing doctors, respectively.

Because it is perpetually at war, the Left is quick to turn personally vicious. No weapon was too cursed or cruel to use against Sarah Palin. An inconvenient Inspector General is declared senile, so he can be swiftly disposed of. Rush Limbaugh's patriotism is heatedly questioned. Dick Cheney is the devil. Those who oppose cap-and-trade are "traitors to the Earth," as Paul Krugman put it. The spray of vitriol would have been splashed over more targets, if Palin hadn't been around to absorb so much of it.

We have arrived at a moment when the Left has complete control over every branch of government, and the government has completed its metamorphosis into the Aggressor State, declaring war against its own citizens. It's no wonder the Obama Administration is so half-hearted and inept at foreign policy—it has little time to waste on foreign threats, because it sees too many enemies inside its own borders. Every foreign policy incident since January has seemed like an annoying distraction to Obama, whose dealings with both allies and adversaries abroad have the character of a man sighing and checking his watch, eager to get back to the important work at home. The declared enemies of this Administration include insurance companies, heavy industry, oil companies, talk radio hosts, banks, citizens who ask inconvenient questions, and everyone making over $200k per year. That's a formidable order of battle. Who's got time for oppressed Iranians when you need to defeat half of America to advance your agenda?

The Aggressor State goes berserk when its designs are frustrated. Obama is smart enough to understand the political value of his carefully manufactured aura of serene post-partisanship, so he hasn't taken to pounding his podium and screaming "no, no, no" like Bill Clinton in the early 90s. Obama is utterly finished the moment his Joe Cool mask slips, and he knows it. He looked more confused than angry in the infamous press conference that ended with his thoughtless comments on the Henry Gates arrest. He couldn't help making those comments, because racism—real or imagined—is the one thing he can get away with being nakedly angry about. The other leaders of the Aggressor State have already gone mad with rage, and the beating they're going to take from their constituents over summer recess will probably make them crazier.

Some wonder if the mounting public opposition to ObamaCare will frighten the Democrats away from it. I think they'll make a concerted push to ram it down everyone's throat, rallying faint-hearted congressional Democrats with any necessary combination of threats and rewards. Nationalized health care is the decisive battlefield for the Aggressor State's war on its citizens. If the State wins this one, there will be no further meaningful resistance, until the whole system collapses. That will be a new war for the Left, but I think its leaders will be unable to pass up on the opportunity to win a final victory in the war they've been fighting against the American republic for the last century. They only need to hold their reluctant congressional troops together for one final charge. The most urgent task awaiting every American who still values his freedom is frightening them enough to break that charge.

The Tao of the Clunker
August 2, 2009

Author's Note: If you don't recall the details, the Cash for Clunkers program was a program to subsidize new car purchases with $4500 vouchers—paid for by taxpayers, of course, as all subsidies are. The old cars traded in under this program were completely destroyed, to prevent them from causing further damage to our delicate environment. This had the effect of ruining the lower end of the used car market, and produced a short-term spike in new car sales, at the expense of sales in the following months. The total cost to the taxpayers wound up being somewhere around three billion dollars, with much of the money disappearing into thin air, as is always the case with these Big Government initiatives. Bizarrely, the administration and its media allies tried to sell this program as some kind of huge success.

The Left loves to criticize capitalism for being short-sighted, while benevolent government takes the long view, planning for the future through the brilliant designs of a command economy. Like many of the Left's beliefs, this is the exact opposite of the truth. Consider the latest example of socialist government's astonishing nearsightedness: the Cash for Clunkers program.

Originally slated to last through October, Cash for Clunkers blew through its billion-dollar funding in a week, and has received an injection of two billion additional dollars from Congress. Those are *your* dollars, by the way, assuming you are one of the 57% of Americans who pay federal income tax. You might not enjoy spending time in used-car lots, but last week, you were forced to help pay for thousands of old beaters. You might have had some unpleasant experiences at car dealerships, but I doubt any of them robbed you at gunpoint, as the Democrat Congress just did. Even more of your tax money will be appropriated to help destroy the clunkers, which aren't even being broken down for spare parts. Downturns in the free market may reduce the value of assets, but only through the magic of government can the value of a useful asset be reduced to less than zero.

If it makes you feel any better, remember that all of this is being done in the name of a religion you probably don't believe in. Oh, wait, that's going to make you feel *worse*. Good. It should. The sight of Obama's apparatchiks squealing with glee like little girls, and declaring Cash for Clunkers to be a phenomenal success, should fill you with blind rage. Maybe we could get a little value for our money by having the federal government assign the brainwashed schoolchildren trapped in its rotting educational system to fashion bits of metal from the destroyed clunkers into decorative keepsakes, and mail one to everyone who paid taxes last year. We could call them Planetary Savior Trophies, and each could come with a little prayer you recite each morning, to reduce global warming. It would be as effective as anything else Big Government forces us to do in the name of global warming.

Far from being short-sighted, the free market designed a system that generates useful value from automobiles decades after they are manufactured. New cars become "pre-owned" after their original owners decide they want a new vehicle. After the second owner gets finished with them, the cars devolve into "clunkers," affordable by the young and the poor. Even when a clunker dies, its parts become useful assets in the repair and maintenance market. Every car is an organ donor.

The genius politicians who designed Cash for Clunkers, and blew through a billion dollars of taxpayer money in five percent of the allotted time, should be laughed out of the room when they call free markets "short-sighted." What have they every produced that was still generating positive value twenty years later?

Besides transferring three billion dollars of our wealth to people who used to drive beat-up old cars, the Cash for Clunkers program also short-circuits the used car marked for the coming decade. Dealers get a short-term sales boost, but they'll pay dearly for it over the next few years. Because the program generated some positive headlines, the government pronounces it an epic success, and plows more money into it. The only criteria for the success of any Big Government program is whether it produces a short-term bump in the polls, and comes in handy as a prop, every couple of years during elections. What system could be *less* likely to produce lasting, long-term benefits and deeply rooted economic strength?

It's also worth noting that those $4500 clunker vouchers are not enough to completely pay for a new car. The people taking advantage of those vouchers will need to kick in a sizable amount of their own money. Those who would otherwise have waited to buy a new car will be diverting resources they would have invested elsewhere, if not for the voucher program—so it amounts to $3 billion spent to divert several times that much money from other industries, into new car sales. By the way, who makes those new cars? Do they have some sort of trade organization, which has a cozy relationship with the Democrats? I seem to remember reading about something along those lines.

The Left always portrays businessmen as rapacious predators who would gorge themselves on today's profits, without any thought for the future. This is a far more accurate description of socialist government. Capitalists, as a group, are not interested in destroying vast amounts of future wealth to obtain a quick infusion of immediate profit—that's just stupid. Some individual businessmen may act in such a manner, and some take it to the level of criminal activity that should be punished, but the vast majority of them are in business for the long haul. By definition, a company that destroys its own market for immediate gain is destroying itself. Individual companies rarely have the power to inflict that kind of market damage anyway—such power is the province of Big Government alone. Even if greedy new-car dealers and manufacturers wanted to increase their profits by blowing all the old cars off the road, they could never have done what Big Government did last week.

Only the government is eager to sacrifice future wealth for immediate gain. It's written into the DNA of socialism. A businessman would think you a fool for suggesting he sacrifice decades of future opportunity for immediate gain, while a politician would think you a fool for suggesting otherwise. What matters to a politician more than today's polls, and next year's elections? A businessman looks at people who aren't his customers yet, and sees the opportunity to expand his market. A politician looks at people who aren't his constituents yet, and sees enemies that need to be suppressed. Politicians think they have an infinite supply of tax money to tap into, when their schemes go wrong. The deficit can always get a little bigger, and they can always steal a little more from the vastly outnumbered top income earners. Crashing the entire financial system for political gain in the 90s was a net win for the Democrats, and they would do it again in a *heartbeat*. Destroying the auto market to provide a little economic "stimulus" they can trumpet on the Sunday talk shows is a no-brainer.

If you paid federal income tax last year, you should stop by a new-car dealership today. They're probably serving free coffee and soda to their crowds of customers. If you're lucky, they might be giving away hot dogs and pizza. Help yourself to as much as you can eat and drink, because it's the only thing you're going to get in exchange for the three billion dollars the Democrats just stole from you. When someone treats you the way Barack Obama just treated taxpayers, the least you can do is expect them to buy you a drink.

Value and Choice
August 4, 2009

Author's Note: One of the more energetic posters in the discussion forum for "The Tao of the Clunker" had a lot of trouble understanding what was wrong with a program that gave him "free money" when he went to buy a car. He had a lively discussion with the other commenters. I thought my own response merited a follow-up essay about the nature of rebates and subsidies.

I've seen some people try to defend Obama's ludicrous Cash for Clunkers program as something akin to a tax rebate or tax credit. This is rubbish, and betrays a dangerous misunderstanding of where government money comes from. A better understanding of basic economics would help Americans avoid the kind of snake oil salesmen currently running Washington. If the public school system won't provide such an education, then it falls to conservatives to explain the basics, in order to build support among the voters for the policies necessary to repair the damage Obama's madcap liberalism has wrought. We can use the Cash for Clunkers boondoggle to illustrate an important point about the relationship between freedom of choice and value. C4C doesn't just waste money—like every instrument of central economic planning, it **destroys value.**

Cash for Clunkers is not a "tax credit" or "rebate" of any sort. In order to be either of those things, it would have to be restricted to those who paid the taxes in the first place. Furthermore, it would have to be awarded progressively, just as taxes are assessed progressively. The top 1% of wage earners pay about half of all federal income taxes, so half of a true "tax credit" would have to go to them. Something tells me we'll never see a Cash for Jaguars program. Tax credits *never* work that way. When taxes are collected progressively, but credits and rebates are given in flat amounts—or weighted toward the lower tax brackets—the credits amount to more redistribution of wealth. If I pay twice as much in taxes as you do, but we both receive the same credit, the procedure amounts to a strikingly inefficient way to redistribute my money to you.

Cash for Clunkers doesn't even have the pretense of being a tax credit. It's a simple subsidy, in which taxpayers who aren't selling clunkers subsidize people who are buying new cars. Like all government subsidies, including government aid to the poor, C4C is horrendously inefficient. Various observers have pointed out that a great deal of that first billion dollars in funding disappeared into thin air. On top of the taxpayer loot being stolen and squandered, we must add the value of the cars being destroyed. The final cost of this initiative will be far more than the billions of taxpayer dollars Congress has voted to pump into it. Of course, that funding is more of Obama's reckless deficit spending, so the final total must be marked up to include the titanic interest paid to service the debt.

To properly appreciate the economic damage of such a subsidy, you must understand that even as Big Government spends these dollars, it is reducing their value. The name of the program is an insidious lie—it's not "cash" for clunkers. If it was, you'd bring in your clunker, and somebody from the IRS would hand you a pile of greenbacks, or wire the money into your account. The $4500 must be used exclusively for the purchase of a new car, which must meet the conditions set forth by the government. The value of those forty-five hundred dollars is reduced, because you have no choice in how to spend it. Imagine how much further the value of that subsidy would be reduced, if it was only good for the purchase of a specific model, designed to meet the whims of the Church of Environmentalism and sold exclusively by government-owned General Motors.

Suppose you found yourself on a deserted island, with a suitcase full of money. That money would have no value, other than as kindling for a fire, because you have no place to spend it. Now suppose the island is not deserted, but you can only spend your money at a small general store that sells a limited selection of essential supplies. Your money has value in that circumstance, but not as great as the value it would have if you were at home, able to spend it on a wide variety of goods, or invest it to generate more income for yourself.

Subsidies like Cash for Clunkers degrade the value of money by restricting the ways it can be used. All money absorbed by the government loses value this way, because the government will never have the diversity of choices available to millions of free citizens. If the economy can be likened to a vast field of grain, then government spending is a high-pressure fire hose, riddled with thousands of leaks, pumping water purchased on credit from foreign suppliers, and held by a nearsighted madman. The free market is a vast raincloud that stretches for miles. The raincloud is vastly more effective for watering crops than the fire hose.

The destruction of value in this particular subsidy is even worse than usual, because it is a subsidy for the purchase of a product that depreciates with terrible speed—as the old saying goes, a car loses thousands of dollars in value the instant you drive it off the lot. Furthermore, since the C4C subsidy doesn't completely cover the cost of the new vehicle, the consumer must take out a loan for thousands of dollars to make up the difference—and the interest on this loan, extended over four or five years, will add thousands more to the effective cost of the vehicle. Of course, the socio-economic group most likely to trade in a clunker and make a new car purchase, specifically because of this subsidy, is the group most likely to default on their loans. This particular example of Obamanomics will end up using three billion dollars of deficit spending to cause consumers to take on ten billion dollars in debt—

and if the overall delinquency rate of 6% holds for these loans, one of the results will be $360 million in bad debt. The only way to make this money lose value faster would be to soak it in expensive champagne and set it on fire.

The media's urge to celebrate Cash for Clunkers as some kind of soaring success, because lots of people showed up to buy cars and grab their free money, is evidence to be collected at the latest of socialism's crime scenes. Socialism is always eager to shine a spotlight on its dubious "successes," while its victims are buried quietly in the dark. In an economy as large and complex as ours, letting government reduce the value of dollars, by reducing freedom of choice, has catastrophic effects. The difference between even the most intelligently managed command economy, and the immense value produced by the free markets, is the difference between subsistence and prosperity. The current bunch in Washington can't even manage to achieve subsistence.

The Fear Machine
August 9, 2009

Ken Gladney, the man beaten by union thugs at a town hall meeting, is the latest victim of the Fear Machine: an old horror from the early twentieth century, still in service after many upgrades. It is crucial piece of hardware for collectivists of all stripes, because the success of their grand designs requires a frightened populace—now more than ever. It isn't easy to persuade an Information Age society to forget all the lessons of the past century, and hand their money, freedom, and lives over to the same rancid ideology that bathed the world in blood and poverty. There aren't enough suckers willing to believe that this time, the collectivists will manage to construct utopia. There aren't enough people stupid enough to think the architects of the three trillion dollar deficit, stagnant economy, and runaway unemployment just need another fifteen or twenty percent of the economy under their control, and decades of miserable failure will suddenly turn into dazzling success. Ignorance is not a potent enough fuel to get socialism where it wants to go. It needs fear added to the mixture.

Brave and confident citizens are of little use to the socialist, because they have little appetite for government control of their daily lives. People who retain a measure of faith in their own abilities, and their ability to succeed in a free marketplace, are not looking for saviors. When a politician jumps in front of them and declares himself to be their messiah, they're likely to respond with laughter. People like Barack Obama, and the leadership of the Democrat Party, do not like being laughed at. They are even less willing to tolerate questions about their wisdom or good intentions. Their predecessors left them the keys to a well-tuned machine that suppresses laughter, and questions, with apprehension and dread.

The Fear Machine has claws and cudgels, but it's also wired into televisions and computers. It knows that chaos is more intimidating than raw violence. The purpose of dispatching the thugs who beat Mr. Gladney was not merely to silence him, or make other protestors feel physically threatened. The purpose is to make everyone who might attend a town hall feel as if they could be walking into a mob scene. Most Americans are decent people who don't want to become part of a riot. Notice how quickly the Left's media auxiliaries acted to muddy the waters, spinning tales of frightened Democrats hiding from imposing, probably racist mobs.

It's interesting how swiftly, and frequently, these weird allegations of racism were pumped into the media smog, even as Obama's minions left a black man bleeding on the pavement. Wild allegations of racism are the toxic exhaust of the Fear Machine. Upstanding citizens don't want to be accused of racism, or associated with groups that might have dark racial motivations. Few possibilities frighten them more. Notice how swiftly the President moved to inject racial themes into the arrest of his friend Henry Gates: another gallon of gas for the machinery Obama knew he would soon need to deploy, to suppress mounting opposition to his agenda.

Uncertainty nourishes fear. It's no accident that the biggest socialist power grab in American history is directed against the medical industry. Health care is complex and ever-changing. Most people don't understand the science of medicine, or the complex way their health care has been married to "insurance" programs that have little to do with insuring against catastrophic events. Because medical care is expensive, people incorrectly assume that poor folks must be dropping dead all over the place, for want of proper care. Because health insurance is tied to employment, people are as nervous about losing their health care as they are about losing their jobs. The vast majority of Americans tell pollsters they're happy with their own medical care… but they don't understand how it works, it could disappear tomorrow, and they're selfish for being happy with something denied to the least fortunate among us.

Economics is also an area where the public can be manipulated through terror. Few people understand how markets work. No one felt like they had time to master the intricacies of the subprime market when the financial collapse of 2008 hit. They had been conditioned to fear and hate the shadowy "fat cats" who run "the system" for their own personal gain, so they were ready to believe those same old hobgoblins were at fault once again. The Fear Machine is large and distracting, so it takes some effort to notice the people holding its remote control. The Republicans did little to shine the spotlight on them in the first, crucial days of the financial crisis. Unwilling to fight the nightmarish contraption towering over him on the evening news, McCain collapsed wearily on the side of the campaign trail, and crumbled into dust.

The Obama Administration expects Americans to live every day in fear. We're supposed to be afraid of the health insurance, energy, and banking industries. We're supposed to be so frightened of the damage our prosperity inflicts on the Earth that we'll pay literally *any* price to make it stop. We're told that everyone who speaks out against Obama's agenda is a well-dressed tool of sinister corporations, or the demonic servant of people who hate the President because of his skin color, or the storm troopers of a powerful new Nazi party coalescing from thin air. The Democrats believe they don't have to win debates, if they can make the public too afraid to listen to their opponents. They insist that their agenda must be implemented in haste, with no time for debate…and what makes people more nervous than being repeatedly told there is no time to lose?

Choice is frightening. The responsibilities of freedom are frightening. Freedom necessarily implies the possibility of failure, because not every action available to free men and women can be guaranteed to succeed. The Democrats present themselves as saviors who wish to liberate you from the burden of choice, and the duties that come with freedom. All they require is your blind faith, for just a little bit longer...until all the choices are made for you, forever, and you become the child of a maternal State that will protect you from harm, and punish you for disobedience.

There is a way to break the Fear Machine, and make it backfire on those who control it: **courage**. Brave men and women don't do *anything* blindly. Courage brings confidence, and confident people never stop asking questions. Confidence brings the wisdom to understand that a prosperous, happy future can be found through the creativity and spirit of millions of your fellow citizens, rather than the tortured and dishonest schemes of a few hundred politicians in Washington. Never forget that people who frantically point out "enemies" for you to fear and hate are usually the people you should be afraid of.

Above all, remember that *you are not alone.* The Democrats will desperately try to make you feel alone, in the coming weeks. It's a lie. You don't have to look over your shoulder to see the great body of Americans who share your values and beliefs, and your determination to remain in control of your health, wealth, and destiny. We're here. We always have been, and always will be. Be brave, and be of good cheer, because nothing frustrates those who demand fear more than laughter.

The Eff Word
September 7, 2009

Fascism.

It's the ultimate political epithet, the atomic blast that ends calm and measured debate. This makes those who seek to be reasonable and persuasive understandably reluctant to use the word...and those who aren't interested in either reason or persuasion eager to hurl it at their opponents. There is nothing surprising about the visceral emotions conjured by the mention of its name. The history of fascism is written in the blood of innocents, on a scale that challenges the limits of human imagination.

Our natural repulsion from the concept of fascism, coupled with the way it has been cheapened by decades of use as a casual insult by the Left, makes it difficult for us to study it dispassionately. It is important to make that study, because fascism was not a mystical phenomenon, a curse inflicted on the Axis nations through the supernatural charisma of Mussolini and Hitler. Too many people recall the garish and horrifying trappings of Nazi Germany, and think "it couldn't happen here." It *has* happened here. It's happening again now. We do ourselves no favors by refusing to see it, any more than we would be helping ourselves by throwing around baseless accusations of fascism where it does not exist.

Fascism, like communism and socialism, is a form of collectivist politics. As the great author H.P. Lovecraft put it, when describing the dark gods of his horror stories: "Many names, one nightmare." These philosophies share a belief in the supreme power and virtue of the central State. Under communism, government owns the means of production—there is no private industry. In a socialist system, the State is nominally separate from private industry, but it siphons large amounts of money from the private sector to fund the socialist agenda. Fascism maintains private industry, but places it under the direct control of the government. Private industry still exists, but the State sets production goals, directly controls economic activity, and dominates the management of corporations. Industry becomes enslaved to political goals.

Modern audiences, raised on a steady diet of movies about World War II, think of fascism as either inhumanly horrifying, or completely absurd, and wonder how anyone in their right minds could have fallen for the fascist sales pitch. In fact, fascism did not seem absurd at all to the intellectuals of the early twentieth century. They thought a wise and all-powerful State, run by the most brilliant minds, would be able to engineer a more advanced society, much as engineers were designing increasingly advanced scientific marvels. The pioneering

122

author of modern science fiction, H.G. Wells, was an outspoken advocate of authoritarian control by a benevolent government of geniuses and academics. His novel *The Shape of Things to Come* envisions such a government seizing control of the entire world to create a global utopia, called "The Dictatorship of the Air" because the government controls the technology of air travel—which it occasionally uses to drop bombs on those who resist. Here are some excerpts from a famous speech Wells gave to the British Young Liberals Society at Oxford in 1932, reprinted in Jonah Goldberg's indispensable *Liberal Fascism*—a phrase Wells actually coins in the speech:

> We have seen the Fascisti in Italy and a number of clumsy imitations elsewhere, and we have seen the Russian Communist Party coming into existence to reinforce this idea...I am asking for a Liberal Fascisti, for enlightened Nazis...And do not let me leave you in the slightest doubt as to the scope and ambition of what I am putting before you...These new organizations are not merely organizations for the spread of defined opinions...the days of that sort of amateurism are over-they are organizations to replace the dilatory indecisiveness of democracy. The world is sick of parliamentary politics...

The world is sick of parliamentary politics. This is an idea that occurs in every strand of collectivist thought. Collectivists only revere democracy until it has voted them sufficient power...then democracy becomes a cumbersome inconvenience that allows selfish, ignorant fools and corporate shills to interfere with the brilliant work of great men. The Democrats fleeing from town hall meetings are also sick of parliamentary politics, as is the President who defiles American government with dozens of unelected, unconfirmed, unaccountable "czars." Parliamentary politics proved very inconvenient for the President's healthcare takeover and cap-and-trade bills, and have been driving global-warming cultists mad with frustration for years.

Why is fascism bad? It seems like a ridiculously understated question, similar to asking why cancer is bad, but the answer is important. The grisly ornaments fascism has worn in the past should not distract from the deeper reality of what it is, and why it fails. The essential flaw of fascism is that it elevates the State to control of its citizens, because controlling the economy requires control of the people. A corporation is a voluntary association of people, not an inanimate machine that can be reprogrammed painlessly by wise government advisers. The people who comprise corporations must be kept alienated from the government's supporters—fascism requires enemies, and turns feral quickly. The government does not require a majority of the people to support it, in order to maintain power. It can make do with much less than fifty per cent, if they are sufficiently motivated and obedient. In fact, maintaining control through an energized minority is much easier than keeping the majority of the population on board, especially in a large country.

The proposition that enlightened government officials should control the economy sounds appealing to those who feel capitalism has not treated them well. No matter what name it operates under, fascism never works. It *can't* work. Fascist control might produce short-term gains for its favored constituencies, and the sense of organization it brings might benefit a highly disorganized or demoralized population, such as prewar Germany, for a while. In the long run, fascism falls apart because political control is always less flexible and innovative than free-market competition. The political masters of the economy have a list of alternatives they will not consider, mistakes they will not admit to making, and explanations that simply *cannot* be true. Since they see the free market as inferior to their intellect and moral judgment, they never study it carefully enough to understand how it really works. They become highly adept at killing the geese that lay golden eggs.

Government is a *terrible* senior partner for any industry, because it has only one thing to bring to the partnership, and that is compulsive force. Everything government does is an expression of force: it collects taxes under the threat of imprisonment or death, blocks access to markets through licensing, and changes the rules of market competition through regulation. A well-run government uses force to protect its citizens, from external threats and internal lawbreakers. As the size of government swells, so does the amount of force deployed to enforce its will. This is inevitable, because force is what a government *is*. The fascist views private industry as a work horse, yoked to the will of the State…and when the State has exhausted its minimal patience trying to talk the horse into moving faster, there remains only the lash. Political control of the economy never produces the results that would be needed to keep the vital constituencies of the politicians happy, and the only method they can imagine to make their industrial horses work harder is to swing the whip, with increasing anger.

The fascist impulse expresses itself differently in different societies. In America, it was first embraced by President Wilson and the Progressives, because it made sense to them, and everyone else in the industrialized world was already doing it—if you're unfamiliar with the intellectual literature of the Thirties, you would be surprised how often British and American academics fretted about "falling behind" marvelous, fascist Italy and Germany. Fascism's second life in America began because socialism failed. The system of providing social benefits to an increasingly large dependency class, by taxing a dwindling group of productive citizens, went utterly bankrupt. This is dramatically illustrated by the failure of Obama's health care plan, which even the most politically disinterested Americans can see we clearly don't have the money to pay for, with trillions of dollars in debt towering over us. Exit the tax collector…enter the "czar." When the American Left saw that it could no longer extract enough tax money from an increasingly grumpy, overtaxed electorate, it became logically necessary to compel industry to provide what the Left desires. Wrapping this strategy in high-minded language like "green jobs" does not change its essential nature.

The grim pathologies we associate with fascism come as consequences of its original sin, the assertion of direct State control over the economy. The cult of personality forms because the mighty politicians who command the economy *must* be brilliant supermen—how else could they handle the enormous task they have set for themselves? To support Obama's domestic policies, you must believe he understands medicine better than doctors and insurance companies, knows more about monetary policy than all the banks he has asserted control over, and has a greater mastery of energy production than the industries he plans to destroy with the cap-and-trade bill. He even knows more about making cars than General Motors... and *all* of the other auto-makers combined, since the automobile market wanted GM to die, and Obama commuted the death sentence to community service. No wonder the media loves to photograph the man with a halo, and Hollywood celebrities pledge their obedience to him on their knees!

Fascism acquires militaristic aspects because a society organized for war is easier to control, and opponents of the State are more easily dismissed as traitors. The American fascists, evolved from socialists and liberals, dislike aggressive wars of military conquest, so they co-opt the language of warfare for domestic policy issues, declaring their policy preferences to be the "moral equivalent of war." Fascism becomes violent because its supporters develop a tribal hostility to their domestic enemies, which eventually leads them to beat those enemies, and maybe bite off a finger or two. Fascism incubates racism because racial animosity is a powerful glue for holding constituent groups together, and milking them for political support.

Is America sliding into fascism? Not completely, or quickly...but it's a potent venom, deadly in small doses. We should not dismiss the menace of fascism by reasoning that it always comes dressed in black uniforms and jackboots, patrolling the perimeter of concentration camps—so we're in good shape as long as those horrors are not in evidence. We shouldn't be fooling around with such a toxic ideology *at all*. No matter how noble the stated goals at the beginning of the collectivist journey, it always ends at the same destination. Promoting his latest propaganda film, Michael Moore said that "capitalism is evil, and you cannot regulate evil. You have to replace it with something that is good for all people, and that something is democracy." This is more than just laughable hypocrisy from a millionaire leftist. Capitalism is the exchange of goods and services between free men and women. In the end, there is only one alternative to it, and it is not "democracy."

Many names, one nightmare.

The Spending Virus
September 12, 2009

Author's Note: This essay was written after the notorious address President Obama delivered to a joint session of Congress, in which the previously obscure Republican Congressman Joe Wilson of South Carolina cried "You lie!" after the President declared his health-care bill would never cover illegal aliens.

House Democrats are said to be mulling over a public reprimand of Joe Wilson, unless he formally apologizes from the House floor for calling President Obama a liar. Wilson and the Republicans should agree to this demand, provided every Democrat who called George Bush a liar follows Wilson in offering an apology to the former president. It would make for a very long session of the House. They could invite the Dixie Chicks to do the halftime show.

Wilson is a representative of South Carolina, but his outburst during Obama's address to Congress last week has also made him Speaker of the House for Inconvenient Truth. His ongoing passion play is the latest production from that Toho Studios of monstrous hypocrisies, the Democrat Party…because every politician attending Obama's address knows that he was indeed lying when he said his proposed government health-care plan would not cover illegal aliens. Of *course* it will. Anyone who tells you otherwise is insulting your intelligence.

It doesn't matter what the bill actually says, when the President signs it. It doesn't matter what steps House and Senate committees take to cover their legislative rear ends, after they choke on the sight of a couple million Tea Party protesters clogging the streets of Washington this weekend. They can add any amendment they like, and even build a statue of Joe Wilson triumphantly holding the amendment over his head, right in front of whatever brick-and-glass mausoleum they build to house the new Department of Health Care Hope and Change. It won't make any difference, because on the day Americans allow the President to sign a health-care takeover bill, the clock begins ticking on the extension of benefits to undocumented aliens. I wouldn't bet on it taking more than a year.

Every government program expands over time, because the spending virus is the most virulent contagion known to man. The primary purpose of any government agency is to demonstrate that its funding is insufficient, and needs to be increased. The best way to indulge this burning passion is to accumulate more dependents, and take on more functions. I can assure you that the very first meeting held in the Edward Kennedy Memorial Health Administration building will include discussions about how to get more people signed up for the "public option," or whatever they're calling it by then.

Remember those 17 million people who were suddenly subtracted from Obama's ever-changing estimate of the uninsured, during his speech last week? The Democrats don't want to deny those people coverage. They just know they can't get away with admitting it *now*. For the time being, their desire to sweep illegal aliens into their deficit-hardened arms must burn secretly in their hearts...but they'll be counting the days until they can announce their secret love to the tax-paying chumps that will be expected to pay for the nuptials.

This will not be a one-sided love affair. The illegal alien community will not wait quietly for their government health benefits. The first lawsuits will be filed within weeks of the health reform signing ceremony at Chappaquiddick. By the time Obama runs his first prime-time special, to explain why anyone who would deny government health benefits to illegal aliens is an astroturfing racist bigot on the payroll of big corporations, the first test case of an illegal demanding access to government health services will probably have reached the Supreme Court. How do you suppose Justice Sonia Sotomayor will rule?

Conservatives often speak of socialism's doomsday equation, when less than half the people pay all the taxes, and the remaining majority can vote themselves more taxes and greater benefits at will. In reality, it takes far less than 50% in the dependency class to begin the collapse of republican government into a socialist black hole. Thanks to progressive taxation, the costs of indulging dependent groups is spread among many taxpayers, and weighted against a very small group of top income earners. Thanks to payroll withholding, the cost of government spending programs is socialized into small increases in deductions that taxpayers barely see, with the really big payments coming from evil rich guys who can easily afford to part with their ill-gotten loot.

Each new spending program counts for pennies added to your taxes, or more likely passed along to you as hidden costs by the people paying the really serious taxes. Perhaps those pennies will be added to the whopping deficit that your children will be expected to cover. In each case, you barely notice another few drops of blood being squeezed out of you... but the beneficiaries of those spending programs will fight like demons to keep them growing, and the political class is anxious to harvest their votes.

We had a small taste of the spending virus in the Cash for Clunkers boondoggle, which Democrats are quick to assure us was a success, because lots of people lined up to get the free money that was being handed out. The budget for this program quickly tripled, to three billion dollars. About 690,000 vehicles were sold under the program, which paid up to $4500 per purchase. There are roughly 138 million taxpayers in the United States...so a little over 137 million of us, who didn't buy a car during the Cash for Clunkers program, paid three billion dollars to the 690,000 people who did. Every one of those people would be violently angry if you tried to take their four thousand dollar subsidy back, and would consider you a miserly penny-pincher if you complained about the handful of change you paid into the program—especially since progressive taxation ensures the middle class paid only a few cents apiece, while the "wealthiest Americans" ponied up rolls of quarters for their "fair share."

Government health care will work *exactly* this way, especially as it becomes a regressive tax against a group that generally doesn't use its political influence effectively—young people—to disproportionately benefit older people. Of course, when the rationing kicks in, the oldest cohort of Americans will find themselves on the wrong end of those Quality of Life spreadsheets, and their last few letters to the editor of their local papers will express astonishment over the dissipation of their once-formidable political influence. By then, it will be far too late for them to undo the awful mistake of allowing ObamaCare to pass.

Anyone who wastes your time arguing that government health care won't be extended to illegal aliens is guilty of producing unnecessary carbon emissions. There is absolutely zero chance that philosophically consistent Democrats will refuse health benefits to poverty-stricken immigrants, or that politically savvy Democrats will think twice about raising your taxes to purchase the votes of minority groups. The cure for the spending virus is difficult. It begins with bringing your tea bags into the voting booth in 2010, and burning out the infection that raised our national debt to astronomical heights. Once this is done, we can discuss a treatment plan for the much older New Deal pathogens that made us vulnerable to this deadly secondary infection.

A Memo To the Global Warming Cult
December 12, 2009

Author's Note: Both supporters and detractors made this one of the most widely referenced essays I've written. To this day, I occasionally get email about it, including some amusing hate mail from misguided souls who still think calling someone a "climate change denier" is somehow intimidating. I've reproduced it with an original typo and correction.

Dear global warming fanatics,

Please. Stop. You're embarrassing yourselves. Take a deep breath, and try to understand what has happened to you during the past month. You need to accept that your dreams of global domination are over. Increasingly shrill attempts to terrify the masses into ignoring Climagate are only making you look foolish. The con job you've been running for the last thirty years is busted forever.

I know this is difficult for you to accept. Things seemed to be going well. You've got the cap-and-trade bill lurking over the United States, ready to shatter an already weakened economy plagued with unemployment problems, and effectively end America's role as a dominant industrial power. Your beliefs have been instituted in public schools as the official state religion, whose rituals and incantations are forced upon millions of school children. The wealthy royalty of popular culture is pleased to produce an endless string of movies, music, and television programming to market your beliefs. Your critics were marginalized to the point where the presidential candidate from the 2000 Democrat ticket felt comfortable referring to them as Nazis.

I can see how losing all of this cultural and political power in a few short weeks would be stunning. I hope the shock has dissipated enough for you to understand where we are now, and where we are going from here.

You aren't going to frighten the world into reducing the human population. You're not going to succeed in terrorizing free people into embracing totalitarianism, to fend off a phantasmal catastrophe that no democratic nation has the discipline to combat. We're not going to politely ignore swarms of private jets and limos ferrying you to carbon-belching "climate summits," where you draw up plans for the Western proletariat to live as primitive hunter-gatherers. We're not going to let a pampered elitist, who once flew around the world to attend cricket practice, tell us that we need to make do without air travel and ice water.

We'll never be foolish enough to allow a band of fanatics to use "peer review" to rule all dissenting opinion out-of-bounds, then declare themselves the proud owners of a mighty consensus. You global-warming fanatics underestimate how much you *needed* those tactics to gain power. You'll never have that kind of unchallenged authority again, because we will never stop demanding the raw data, and we'll drown you in laughter when you mutter something about deleting it by accident. We will never forget that you began with a conclusion and sought to harvest data that supported it—the exact *opposite* of the scientific method.

Your arrogant condescension to your critics is horribly misplaced. You have completely lost the ability to call anyone "stupid." *Your* capacity for reason is the matter in question. Your status as "scientists" is on probation. It will take years of faithful adherence to the scientific method, and rigorous efforts to test and disprove your hypotheses, before you can regain the trust of thoughtful men and women. Until you have accomplished this, the attitude we expect from you is humility and contrition. You have much to answer for. The time for you to issue pompous lectures is over. The time for you to give sworn testimony may soon begin. We're a year away from the American voter's first opportunity to respond to the politicians who terrorized them by waving a loaded cap-and-trade bill in their faces.

We ask you to stop propagandizing our children, because it won't work any more. We will prepare them to deal with you. Informed parents across the industrialized world will explain what Climagate means to their children, and prepare them with questions your public-education minions cannot answer. The vindicated critics you've been working to silence will fill the post-Climagate void with publications, and some of them will become best-sellers. You'll always have your political allies and fellow travelers, but you'll never have a population ignorant of climate science to push around again.

You can stop trying to make Climagate go away by ignoring it, or lying about it. That won't work, either. Huge stories can no longer be suppressed by a handful of like-minded network executives and editors. Those glittering eyes you see in the darkness, beyond the comforting glow of the *New York Times* editorial board, are the massed ranks of the Internet's *Army of Davids*. They are a feral mixture of blogging curiosity and search-engine memory. If you think they're closing in around you…well, it's not just your imagination.

One of the worst sins you must answer for is the damage you have done to real science. We have much to learn about the Earth, its ecology, and its climate. We will not enhance our ability to learn those secrets by impoverishing ourselves in fit of primitive superstition and political opportunism. Desperate people don't do a good job of protecting the environment… it is a job suitable only to vibrant nations of industry and technology. Those of us who still cherish independent thought, and the spirit of scientific inquiry, would like to resume our studies of the universe. It's difficult to hear the truth whispered in the tides, the breeze, and the solar wind over the hysterical jabbering of fanatics, and the angry demands of greedy politicians.

Update: Thanks to reader "osogrande" for pointing out a typo where I referred to Al Gore as the 2000 vice-presidential candidate. I've corrected the mistake. I wanted to acknowledge the error, instead of claiming my original raw data was accidentally deleted.

The Chimera
December 15, 2009

In Greek mythology, the Chimera was a monster with a lion's head, a goat's body, and a serpent's tail. The term has come to be synonymous with nightmares and illusions. Modern America is infested with these monsters, and politicians are very dedicated to fighting them… with swords forged from billions of tax dollars, and shields woven from the dessicated remains of your shriveled liberties.

The proponents of Big Government programs frequently excuse their waste and inefficiency by hinting at the terrible things that *would* have happened, if they had not taken expensive action. The recent stimulus bill, a fountain of pork-barrel waste and theft, is defended in these terms. You should be thanking the Democrats for saving us from a 5000 Dow and other economic horrors, instead of asking tough questions about how that money was spent, and how minimal its benefits to anyone except targeted Democrat constituencies have been. If the Democrats decide they need another $300 billion in stimulus spending, you should be quick to hand over the cash. The Chimera is always lurking in the shadows, ready to strike, and no price is too high for keeping it at bay.

One of the most laughable attempts to excuse poor government performance with phantom terrors is the infamous "jobs saved or created" metric employed by the Obama Administration. It's the kind of reasoning employed by primitive witch doctors, demanding tribute and respect for keeping the demons of the night at bay, and taking credit for every morning where demon-related casualties are zero. It's not even political rhetoric…it's superstition.

The mythological Chimera was said to breath fire. The modern version breathes greenhouse gas. The global-warming scam is based on manipulating data to create the ominous shadow of a monster lurking in the indeterminate future—a shadow so terrible that questions dismissed as suicidal madness. Speaking in Copenhagen today, Tony Blair conceded the Climagate scandal renders global-warming science "not as certain as its proponents allege," but quickly added that it would be "irresponsible" not to take this fraudulent science seriously anyway. There is no escape from the Chimera.

If the global-warming cult is given the fantastic amount of money and power it demands, it will spend the rest of history assuring its victims that only swift and unquestioning compliance with its agenda prevented a global catastrophe…which could return at any moment. Make no mistake: giving in to the climate-change elite will bring about the creation of the most powerful, lavishly funded religion the Western world has ever seen, and it will *never* stop issuing dire threats to maintain its position. The Chimera can never be permanently slain, and you will never be allowed to stop fearing it, or paying for protection against it.

Even when statists are given the power and money they demand, they are quick to excuse their failures by claiming they weren't given *enough*. The absolute global failure of every form of collectivism—from fascism and communism to American-style liberalism—is always dismissed by saying enough money wasn't spent, the State was not given enough control, or the "right people" weren't put in charge. If 90% of a society comes under the domination of the State, every calamity will be blamed on the 10% who remain free. The American left demands more government spending, including a vast new government health-care system that will add trillions to a total government liability, including Social Security and Medicare, that already exceeds $106 trillion dollars. That's nearly double the GDP of the entire planet. There literally isn't enough money in the world to appease the Chimera.

It's instructive to note that no private industry would be allowed to use the kind of rationalizations and evasions Big Government routinely deploys. A business that justifies no return for vast payment, on the grounds that various hypothetical disasters were avoided, would be prosecuted for fraud. No corporation would be allowed to cherry-pick positive developments as evidence of its success, and write off the negative consequences of its actions as someone else's fault…or wave them around as further proof of its greatness, since things could have been so much *worse.* No business is large enough to make grandiose claims about controlling the entire economy, anyway. Politicians are small men who declare themselves titans, and expect us to pay for their battles against epic monsters. The idea that someone *could* control the commerce of a nation produces the imperative that someone had better try, or else.

The tendency to make grandiose promises, take credit for anything it finds worthwhile, and frighten the citizens with tales of hypothetical doomsdays that only Big Government can reschedule are hard-coded into its very nature. Few politicians can see a dead beast without feeling the urge to strike a pose of triumph over its remains. There will never come a day when government tells the voters they don't need its help any more. No government project is ever finished, and no liberty it takes from the citizens can ever be safely returned. We should bear this in mind when evaluating government's promises, or measuring its accomplishments… and most especially when we hear it describe the monsters it promises to protect us from.

The Illusion Of Design
December 20, 2009

The basic argument in favor of government-run health care, among people who sincerely believe it's the best way to reform the medical system, is that a program designed and administered by the State will provide health care to more people. As things stand, a certain number of people have no health insurance, and this is held to be unfair and dangerous…to the extent that the rest of us must endure a radical overhaul of the entire system, as the State takes control of the insurance industry first, and eventually all of medicine.

Why do these uninsured people lack coverage? The ostensible reason is that they cannot afford it, although in fact a sizable portion of the uninsured are young people who choose not to purchase expensive insurance, and many more are illegal aliens. Also, the nature of the laws surrounding health insurance make it very expensive to purchase privately, instead of receiving it as part of employment compensation, so rising unemployment (the signature feature of the Obama economy) means more uninsured. Still, the popular conception of the case for health care reform is based on the haunting image of millions of poverty-stricken sick people, wasting away from the lack of health insurance. As the slogan tossed around through Twitter earlier this year put it, "no one should have to die because they can't afford health insurance."

Why is health insurance so expensive that the poor cannot afford it? The Left believes this is a failure of the free market, with greedy health-insurance companies callously pricing their product out of reach, and slapping exorbitant premiums on anyone who isn't the picture of health. The true answer is that government is primarily responsible for distortions in the health insurance market, dating back to the wage controls that made it commonplace for employers to offer health benefits as a means of attracting skilled employees. The law preventing the sale of health insurance across state lines is an example of government-induced price distortions. For a contrasting example of medical services becoming more affordable in response to free-market competition, consider the constantly falling price of Lasik eye surgery. The Left refuses to think clearly on this subject, and maintains that health care is a "human right" that should be available "free" to everyone.

Liberals insist it is simply unthinkable to allow financial considerations to impact the distribution of this essential human right. As Kirsten Powers put it recently, "Americans will die if we don't provide universal health insurance." Because money is the instrument through which free people express their will and make choices, the argument for socialized medicine boils down to the superiority of design and control over competition and choice.

So, in summary, the case for nationalizing health insurance is that health care cannot be entrusted to the unpredictability and greed of the free market. The individual purchasing decisions of free men and women are too chaotic. The only way to ensure access to health care for everyone is for the State to install a massive, strictly enforced system, complete with huge fines and jail time for those who fail to comply. This system would be superior to the free market, because it would be carefully designed by brilliant minds…engineered to deliver an incredibly complex, ever-changing service to hundreds of millions of Americans.

Is anyone stupid enough to think a "carefully designed system" is what the Democrats are about to drop on us?

Senator Ben Nelson (D-Nebraska) held up the Senate reform bill over his heartfelt concerns over abortion funding…until he was bought off with hundreds of millions of dollars in enhanced funding for Medicaid in his state. In a similar vein, language worth over $100 million was added to the bill, targeting the state of Louisiana, to purchase the vote of "moderate" Democrat Mary Landrieu. In other words, this "carefully designed" health care bill has different rules for people who happen to live in Nebraska or Louisiana, because this was necessary to buy the votes of their senators.

The Congressional Budget Office scoring for the health care reform bill is based on tricks and gimmicks, including Medicare reductions and cuts of over 20% in physician payments, which no one seriously believes will actually happen. A great deal of this health care reform package is a delusional fantasy, if not an outright fraud.

Socialist senator Bernie Sanders of Vermont jammed a 767-page amendment into the bill, then violated Senate procedures to suddenly withdraw it when Republicans forced the entire amendment to be read on the Senate floor.

Far from being a brilliant plan constructed by top doctors and financial experts in a government brain trust, this health-care bill is a twisted, deformed political document, seen in its entirety by only a few high-ranking politicians belonging to a single political party. Its components have not been precisely crafted as part of a fantastic system calibrated to ensure the maximum access to quality health care for all Americans.

The bill is not being examined with transparency and careful deliberation by representatives who behave as humble servants of the people and their Constitution. Instead, it's being hastily rammed through in the dead of night, over the objection of powerful majorities of the American people, with desperate last-minute deals cut to acquire the necessary votes, financed by vast sums of taxpayer money. The primary consideration is not crafting the most sophisticated and intelligent health care reform…it's getting a bill pushed through before angry voters have a chance to blast the Democrats out of Congress. Look at it this way: if the average middle-class American paid about $5000 in federal income tax last year, then you might be one of the 20,000 people who paid for Mary Landrieu's vote, in the hope of giving Barack Obama a bill to sign as a Christmas present.

Aside from the nauseating payoffs, this kind of legislative taffy pull is to be expected in a representative republic. That's how it works. People elect Congressional representation to look out for their interests. Legislation is modified by demands that can range from mild objections to stubborn intransigence. Parliamentary procedures are invoked by experienced politicians to shape the debate. Regional interests and passionate beliefs are poured into a bubbling stew of sections and sub-paragraphs. All of this is inevitable, and therefore good reason to avoid the absolute madness of allowing the President and Congress to nationalize industries, or posture as wise stewards of a high-performance command economy.

The moral imperative for socialized medicine is the belief that government can design a system to distribute health care more efficiently than the free markets. I challenge anyone who sincerely believes this to review the recent events in the House and Senate, and realize that representative government is utterly incapable of designing any such system. The merciless and tyrannical enforcement techniques required to ensure hundreds of millions of people comply with health care reform are utterly indefensible in the service of a monstrosity stitched together from back-room deals and nine-figure bribes.

The only logical way to maintain the integrity of a vast, complex program designed to control a trillion-dollar industry is to dispense with the "representative" part of our government model. Those who seriously believe the State must control health care, which is tied into the bulk of our economy and technological development, should stop fooling around with half-measures of tyranny. If health care is truly a "human right" that must be provided "at any cost," then take a cold, hard look at the tortured gestation of the rough beast slouching from Harry Reid's office to be born…and understand that liberty, democracy, and representation must be sacrificed, as part of that cost.

Welcome To Subsidy Nation
January 15, 2010

As reported by the Associated Press, congressional Democrats appear to have reached an agreement with unions to get their awful health-care bill lurching forward again:

Rep. Joe Courtney, D-Conn., who led the opposition to the tax in the House, said the agreement involves several measures that would ease its impact. Among them: excluding the value of dental and vision benefits in applying the tax, as well as raising the $23,000 threshold at which it would take effect for families.

Union officials are also pushing to provide that anyone who makes $200,000 or less would be excluded from the health plan benefits tax, a concession that would benefit employees who are not unionized as well.

In a win specifically for union members, negotiators were working out a plan to delay the tax from being imposed on collectively bargained health plans for several years.

What a splendid "win" for union members! What percentage of our rapidly dwindling work force belongs to labor unions? Well, according to this article from Workforce Management, it was about 12.1 percent in 2007. This means the other 87.9% of you non-unionized working stiffs will be subsidizing the prize won by union negotiators today. As the Associated Press report explains, you won't be alone:

The agreement with labor came as the White House sought fresh concessions from drug makers and other health care providers as they looked for funds to sweeten subsidies the bill provides for lower-income families who cannot afford coverage.

Those "fresh concessions" from drug makers will rapidly become very stale price increases for consumers. I suppose it's entirely reasonable to expect non-union workers to subsidize these concessions, because our noble union comrades "sacrificed higher wages" to obtain their fabulous health benefits:

The proposed tax has been a major sticking point because early versions from the Senate would have hit union members, who have negotiated generous health benefits, sacrificing higher wages. House Democrats were strongly opposed, and did not include the tax in their bill. But Obama favored the tax, citing the consensus opinion of economists that it would help hold down costs by nudging workers into less pricey coverage.

As of 2007, the average union worker made about $629 per week, compared to $404 for non-union workers, putting union wages about $5 per hour higher on average. Of course, these figures vary widely in specific industries. In lower-level service industries, union workers earn roughly the same amount as their non-union counterparts. This means that, among the lowest-paid union members, the "sacrifice" they made for their sacred health care benefits amounted to accepting the same wage as non-union workers. That's without counting the panoply of fringe benefits available to union members, which can be extremely valuable.

Thus, our friends in the Democrat Party expect the rest of us to subsidize the expensive health-care benefits of their union allies, who are generally paid much more than we are. Union members won't be among the workers getting "nudged into less pricey coverage" to hold down costs, since they will be legislatively immunized against such nudging. When *you* get nudged into less pricey coverage, I hope you're comforted by the knowledge that your dental benefits and vision plan will be going to a deserving union member, who earned them by faithfully voting as instructed by his union leadership.

Welcome to Subsidy Nation, the midway point between a free-market democracy and a total command economy. The middle class has grown restless over endlessly rising tax rates, so the current statist strategy of choice involves using mandates on business, regulatory burdens, and special exemptions to pay off their favored constituencies. It's not a new idea, but it's *exploded* during the first year of this administration, and if the ObamaCare monstrosity is signed into law, it will become the fundamental organizing principle of our culture and economy.

We've already been treated to the spectacle of the other 48 states being told they had to subsidize lavish Medicaid funding for Louisiana and Nebraska, to purchase the votes of their senators. More taxpayer loot for special interests is stuffed into every corner of the bill. Earlier in the year, taxpayers and the used-car market were raided to finance the Cash for Clunkers program. The government has poured billions into General Motors, keeping it afloat for the benefit of the labor unions feeding from its carcass. The list goes on…and there were already plenty of subsidies and mandates in place, from both Democrat and Republican administrations, before President Obama took his oath of office.

The socialist vision of Big Government plays a game of diffuse costs and focused benefits. Subsidies and mandates give politicians an extra layer of protection from the voters. The politicians can even score points by demonizing the very businesses they are using to collect revenue for their agenda. The subprime mortgage crisis was a spectacular example of this: the entire financial sector was brought to the edge of the abyss because Clinton Democrats forced banks to make politically useful, but absurdly risky, loans to targeted constituencies. When the dust from the resulting implosion settled, the guilty political party was more powerful than ever.

The proper way to look at Subsidy Nation is to understand that *everyone* is part of the game. If you aren't receiving the subsidies, you're paying for them. *You* paid for the gas in the Fannie Mae ice cream truck Barney Frank and Chris Dodd have been driving around. If you didn't buy a car under Cash for Clunkers, you subsidized the rebates for those who did. If you don't live in Nebraska or Louisiana, you chipped in to buy the votes of Ben Nelson and Mary Landrieu. It's all very well hidden, even more than payroll check withholding hides your direct tax burden. You don't have to write a check to Nelson or Landrieu. You'll just notice that, over time, everything costs more and seems worth less. Your job might be pulverized in a collision of special interests. You'll be rationed out of health care services you could have purchased in 2009. Your life will be controlled with so many strings that you can't see the individual threads any more, just a grey tapestry that everyone complains about, but no one understands.

The long-term doom of Subsidy Nation is the entropy that comes with the evaporation of choice. Choice is the heartbeat of wealth. A $5000 health-care plan, forced on you by the government, is not worth as much as five thousand dollars in cash, any more than a ten-dollar gift certificate has the same value as a ten-dollar bill. We've already watched health "insurance" devolve into a clumsy voucher system for purchasing health care. By controlling the health-care portion of your compensation, the government reduces your overall wealth...and you'll never enjoy the level of quality you would get from health-care providers competing to earn money you can spend freely. Imagine the depressing quagmire of an economy where everyone is paid in coupons the government has already designated for food, housing, or health care—doled out according to the government's idea of your needs.

We've already got one foot in that quagmire. Subsidy Nation's elaborate schemes will always fail, because they are based on considerations of politics and ideology, not efficiency and growth. Vital constituencies will respond to those failures by howling for more subsidies. That is why the Cadillac health care plans of wealthy and powerful labor unions will be exempt from punishing taxation...while the rest of us are stuffed in the trunk of that Cadillac with a couple bags of lime, watching an irrational, emotionally unstable government fiddle with its knives and mutter something ominous about shoeshine boxes.

The Context Of Middle-Class Frustration
January 21, 2010

Last night, President Obama gave ABC's George Stephanopolous his first interview since the Massachusetts special election. Admitting that people were "frustrated" with the results of his administration's first year, Obama continued:

So the reason I say that we are not surprised by what happened in Massachusetts is because I'm frustrated, too.

I'm frustrated by the fact that **over the last decade**, we have not seen the kind of progress for middle class families that are needed. That's what I promised to deliver in the campaign.

It's not something that I believe we can get done in a year. But it is something that I think we are starting to make progress on.

The part of that statement I've highlighted should bring a groan from everyone who's tired of Obama endlessly blaming his failures on his predecessor. Later in the interview, the President spoke of the "broader context" in which he plans to "move the middle class forward." I don't think he sees the context broadly enough. The middle class can trace its frustration much further back than the election of George Bush, or Bill Clinton before him.

The middle class is the great enemy of collectivist politics, under any of its names: progressivism, communism, fascism, or "liberalism." As far back as Karl Marx, the apostles of collectivism have understood that they must subjugate the middle class before they can claim total victory.

The upper class isn't a big problem—they don't have the votes to block a collectivist agenda in a democracy, and they generally find ways to maintain, or increase, their power and wealth under a total State. The power of the State can be extremely valuable to them, for manipulating markets and thwarting upstart competitors. Many of them are willing to trade a little wealth for power, or find moral nourishment in supporting a collective agenda.

The members of the lower class are generally seen as the clients of a collectivist movement, the recipients of the social benefits it promises. Their desperation and anger become fuel for the movement, providing both righteousness and voting power. The collectivist only needs to conceal any hope of finding prosperity beyond the generosity of the State, and keep the lower class convinced that government is the only moral actor in the economy. Review the speeches of Barack Obama, and search for *anything* that suggests the poor should look *anywhere* beyond the government and its social programs for salvation.

It's clear that the middle class is the great enemy of collectivism. Only they have the combination of voting power, money, and economic self-interest to see the growth of government as undesirable, and provide effective resistance. They generally view their interactions with government in a negative light—they've all spent time in the Department of Motor Vehicles mausoleum, spent hours wrestling with tax forms, or been slapped with a traffic citation they don't think they deserved. They understand the inefficiency and emotional instability of government, and instinctively resent its intrusion into their lives. A health-care takeover is the best chance collectivists will ever have of persuading the middle class to vote itself into chains…but for the better part of a century, they've been able to hear the hammers of the State ringing on the metal of those chains, in the forges of taxation and regulation.

The middle class is a vast group in a capitalist society, which is one of the things collectivists really *hate* about capitalism. Its upper reaches include the entrepreneurs and small business owners that bring economic vitality. Virtually every aspect of Obama's agenda is designed to injure or burden small businessmen, and this is no accident. Despite their angry rhetoric about giant corporations, leftists have little trouble controlling them. They often do business directly with the government, as vendors…and, through lobbyists, as customers. They generally employ members of labor unions, which serve as a de facto arm of Big Government, injecting the agenda of the State directly into the corporate bloodstream. It's the small business owners and self-employed, along with those who aspire to join their ranks, who are the most difficult to control, and the most likely to muster effective electoral resistance to the statist agenda. The middle class is filled with people who pay attention to the second page of their paycheck stubs.

I realize all of the above sounds terribly sinister…and perhaps you find that appropriate, having reviewed the works of Saul Alinsky and the Cloward-Piven strategy of manufactured crisis. I believe it is crucial to understand that it doesn't *matter* if the people engineering a collectivist state have sinister motives or not. In fact, the belief that their intentions make a difference is *incredibly* dangerous. It's related to the catechism of the faculty-lounge Marxist, which holds that communism and fascism only failed because bad people were in charge of them. In his interview last night, the President gave this as his reason for pushing so forcefully for his health-care takeover plan:

The reason I tackled healthcare wasn't because this was my personal hobbyhorse. The reason I tackled it was during the course of the campaign, I traveled all across this country and I kept on hearing heart-breaking stories about families who were bankrupt because they got sick. If they had health insurance, suddenly insurance companies were doing things that were just plain wrong, and were leaving folks in an extremely vulnerable position.

It doesn't matter if this is his sincere belief, spoken straight from the heart. His health-care plan was still an awful idea that united the country in opposition against the increasingly thuggish and arrogant methods he used to advance it. Those methods are *integral* to the collectivist enterprise. It will always become thuggish and arrogant, because when all virtue resides in the State, those who oppose the growth of the State become villains by definition. Consider the President's assessment of his Republican opponents:

My hope was a year ago today when I was being sworn in that reversing that process was going to be easier partly because we were entering into a crisis situation and I thought that the urgency of the moment would allow us to join together and make common cause. That hasn't happened. Some of it, frankly, is I think a strategic decision that was made on the side of the opposition that…I think that some of it had to do with a sense that the best political strategy was to simply say no.

Here, in a nutshell, is the heads-we-win, tails-you-lose mentality that keeps the State plodding blindly forward, crushing a formerly vibrant economy beneath it. If you don't answer Obama's trillion-dollar health-care plan with your own trillion-dollar program, you're an obstructionist—not an opponent to be debated, but an obstacle to be swept aside. The middle class is frustrated because they understand the basic concept of fiscal responsibility, and they know they—and their children—will be expected to pay for these titanic solutions.

They also know they'll have very little to say about how the money is spent, because they don't have the lobbying power of the core Democrat constituencies. They certainly won't be "controlling" Big Government through their votes. It took a political apocalypse, triggered by an incredible Republican win in Massachusetts, to frighten the Democrats out of ramming their health care plan down America's throat. How many times can the middle class, composed of individuals trying to live their lives and take care of their families, expect to generate such a powerful shock wave? In the collectivist future, those individuals won't be waging epic battles to preserve their liberties. They'll be haggling over percentage increases in their benefits.

The frustration of the middle class is the angry confusion of people who can appreciate the opportunities Big Government denies them. It is the anxiety of those who hear the businesses who employ them relentlessly demonized, while the ruling class is *never* held responsible for its foolishness, waste, and theft. It is the resentment of people who suffer through disasters that President Obama and his allies regard as opportunities. It's the hearty distrust of a State, and its media apparatus, which declare every frigid blast of bad economic news to be "unexpected"—but expects us to believe it can predict market fluctuations, technological advances, and even the global climate.

The President says "I have every interest in seeing a unified country solving big problems." The rest of us have an interest in being allowed to pursue our *individual* solutions to those problems, according to the liberties our Constitution says belong to us as absolutely as our souls. We can see the wreckage of those "unified" solutions strewn through our past, and littering the rest of the world. Our frustration is born of intelligence and moral strength, not stubborn blindness.

The Blue Assumptions
January 26, 2010

*Author's Note: The following was written shortly before President Obama's first State of the Union address. I was not surprised to learn he failed to use this address the list the things "government will **not** do," as I suggested at the end of this essay. This was the first piece I discussed extensively on the air with Rusty Humphries, introducing me to the singular experience of discussing my work with someone who not only read it carefully, but clearly took notes.*

In "The Context of Middle-Class Frustration," I explained that I view collectivist politics, including what Americans call "liberalism," is at war with the middle class. Of course, lots of middle-class people vote for liberal politicians. Conservatives sometimes wonder why people would constantly extend their support to an ideology so hostile to their interests, and distinguished by such a long record of broken promises and failed programs. Some of it is tribal—not everyone backs up their voting with intense meditation on political philosophy. There are people on both the Left and Right who simply vote the way their parents do, or view politics as a team sport, and love rooting for one side or the other.

Among those blue-state voters who *do* put some effort into their politics, I find there are four mistaken assumptions about government that guide their thinking. Government is an exercise of authority, so it's wise to have a clear understanding of the nature of authority before voting to expand government.

The first, and perhaps most dangerous, assumption is that **authority confers virtue.** This seems to have become rooted in the American psyche after the exhilaration of victory in World War II, and the perceived success of the New Deal. Many people automatically assume liberal politicians are selfless servants of the people, who only want what is best for everyone. The media actively cultivates this mindset through its worship of bold Big Government initiatives, and the heroic statesmen who make them possible. If solving the problems of society is a noble endeavor, and the only solutions are titanic government programs, then the proponents of such programs *must* be noble!

Certain branches of the government, such as law enforcement and the military, tend to attract selfless and dedicated people. However, there is no reason entering government service, or winning elections, automatically makes someone virtuous. If this were not true, there would be no need for military police or internal-affairs divisions.

The federal government currently employs something like two million people. A system of this size *cannot* function if it must assume the majority of those employees will be tireless, self-sacrificing people of impeccable character and honesty. Government employees respond to incentives, just like private-sector workers. Politicians are no less avaricious than rich businessmen—especially since they can rely on their supporters, and the media, to conceal their greed beneath the pure white robes of the "public interest." Imagine the outcry if a captain of industry announced the kind of power and money grabs that litter the endless press conferences of President Obama.

The second assumption is that **authority bestows wisdom.** There is a powerful desire, among much of the American public, to believe the government employs the best and brightest experts in every field. This is one of the reasons the global-warming scam endured as long as it did. Top people from government agencies, such as James Hansen of NASA or former Vice President Al Gore, were credited with honesty and intelligence they simply do not possess. The underlying principle of government-controlled health care is the belief that brilliant people in the ruling class and bureaucracy can engineer a better medical system than doctors, hospitals, and free-market competitors. This belief finally cracked against the inescapably tawdry reality of the back-room deals and political favors in the House and Senate. One of the reasons polls have revealed Americans turning so decisively against ObamaCare is that they can no longer convince themselves the proponents of the plan have anything resembling a *plan.* In a free country, the authority of government does not long survive the public's loss of faith in its wisdom.

The third assumption is that **authority implies benevolence.** We elect our officials, and we like to think of them as "public servants" who work for us. The popular vote becomes a magic spell that transforms ambition into compassion. Liberals are comfortable with this Administration's mad scramble for power because they're serenely confident it will someday be used for the public good. They don't like to think about power being hoarded for its own sake, placing tenured lions of the Senate on the same moral plane as money-grubbing capitalists. Because they disdain materialism and sneer at the pursuit of the almighty dollar, they imagine some invisible, sacred currency allows the government to express the will of the people.

If there's one thing we've learned from the last few decades, it's that Big Government lives beneath a shroud of corruption that grows vaster, and darker, as the size of the State increases. The supposed benevolence behind a government program *cannot* be used to evaluate its performance. In a system woven from trillions of endlessly moving dollars, credit cannot be given for good intentions…any more than the honest good will of a Cessna pilot could suddenly give him the ability to fly an F-22 Raptor. It's no comfort to the people crushed beneath failed government programs that the authors meant well.

Finally, there is the persistent, but ridiculous, superstition that **authority creates wealth.** A shocking number of people believe, at some primal level, that government can produce goods and services out of thin air, or "create" jobs through brilliant spending initiatives. In reality, the sole resource of government is *coercion.* Its only "product" is compulsive force. This is a useful resource—you want plenty of compulsive force handy when criminals invade your home, or terrorists attack a city. However, it is *not* a substitute for wealth.

Government prints money, but it doesn't create value. It can use coercion to allocate resources, but this is a horribly inefficient and immoral system, compared to free enterprise. Like any other entity, the government "spends" more of its sole resource when it gets in trouble, imposing more compulsion through taxes and regulation.

Deployed wisely, coercive force enhances value. Your money is worth more because the government works to keep it (more or less) stable. Your buying power is enhanced when you can rely on the government to offer protection from fraud and theft. The authority of the government, when used sparingly, builds *trust,* and this makes its citizens wealthier.

When government power exceeds the limits necessary to build trust, and begins attempting to command the economy, value is *destroyed.* We're living through that right now. In an environment of nationalized companies, union payoffs, and reckless deficit spending threatening the stability of our currency, the trust and confidence which lead private citizens to invest, generate wealth, and create jobs is diminished. Government force is the destroyer of *possibilities*…and what is wealth, but the accumulated value of the possible? Our economy operates at such a high level that marginal reductions in our freedom generate awful shocks to our standard of living. As bad as the economy is now, it can get much, much worse…if the vital energy of freedom is not restored to it.

The first four steps on the path to a proper appreciation of liberty lie in the rejection of these four assumptions about authority. The free market has never accepted them, which is why an anemic economy is desperate to hear a State of the Union address in which this President lists the things he will *not* do.

The Great Crash
February 5, 2010

Author's Note: You might say this piece has been foreshadowed by those which come before it. I have linked back to it frequently from subsequent writings. My critique of American socialism is power- fully shaped by my conviction—backed up by any number of extremely disturbing actuarial tables— that it's doomed to crash completely, in a systemic breakdown unlike anything seen before...anywhere in the world. We are too big to disintegrate slowly, and with any degree of comfort for the common folk trapped in our collapse.

During my college days in the early Nineties, I read a study that projected tax rates into the future, assuming government spending remained fixed at early Clinton levels. Due to the explosion of entitlement spending brought about by the insolvency of Social Security and Medicare, even the lower income brackets would face something like a sixty percent federal tax burden by the 2020s. Reading this study was one of the most significant events of my intellectual life. I remember thinking, with terrible clarity: That's just not going to work.

I believe collectivist ideology is an offense against liberty, and also a tragically inef- ficient means of addressing the social problems it professes to care about. A study of history shows that every form of collectivist ideology has grown increasingly vicious, and eventually murderous, as its ruling elite struggle to retain power. There is one other reason I'm opposed to collectivism: it's doomed to fail. Even if I were willing to concede Big Government the intelligence and moral stature to control our culture and economy, I would be haunted by the knowledge of its inevitable failure...a destiny written into the DNA of American socialism since the birth of Social Security.

Socialism fails because it's a static solution imposed on a dynamic society. People re- spond to incentives, chasing carrots and avoiding sticks. The initial proposition of the New Deal was to provide for the needs of the desperate, by collecting taxes from the wealthy. Unsurprisingly, the system devolved into the vote-buying and corruption we live with today, becoming a heavy wagon hitched to a struggling middle class, which provides far more of the funding than those "fat cats" socialists love to use as whipping boys. Politicians respond to incentives too, and the machinery of the centralized state excels at sucking in tax dollars and spitting out votes. The ugly gears of that machinery are well-hidden behind an illusion of moral authority and seductive promises, alluring enough to compel the faithful support of nearly half the population, even as its unsustainable failures become painfully obvious.

The system was doomed to crash because its vast array of taxes, spending, and regulation destroy the very wealth that sustains it. It ran out of fat long ago, and began feeding on muscle…and now it has worked its way down to the bone. Wealth is a product of choice, and every action taken by a collectivist government destroys wealth by reducing the options available to its citizens. Liberal politicians assume the population will go on blindly producing the same extraordinary prosperity, no matter how much the government skims off the top. That's why every outbreak of bad economic news is "unexpected" to them, as well as the media who share their assumptions. Has a nation ever grown poorer after reducing the cost and power of its central government? Why would anyone assume a nation could grow richer by reducing the size and power of its private sector?

The towering heights reached by the American economy gives us a long way to fall. Of the dozen wealthiest nations in the world, only America has a nine-digit population. The next largest wealthy nation after us is Switzerland. The system imposed on a population our size is bound to fail with a mighty crash. We take the trappings of our prosperity for granted, and don't appreciate how complex, fast-moving, and fragile the upper reaches of our economy are. Politicians seeking to micro-manage the corporate world are tinkering with a high-performance engine while it's still running.

I don't know exactly what form the Great Crash will take. Social Security has been a ticking bomb for generations, and recently we learned its detonation is much closer than previously suspected. Instead of producing a surplus that helps fund the rest of the government, it has gone into the red…something that wasn't supposed to happen for over a decade. Social Security was never an "investment" safeguarded by the government. It's a pyramid scheme, with current payroll taxes funding the benefits of retirees. The original ratio of workers to recipients was over 40 to 1, but now it's down to three to one…in an economy with over 20% real unemployment, suffering under a government unwilling to do any of the things that would reduce its power, and promote long-term job growth.

Reckless deficit spending has weakened our currency, and hastened the day when Social Security and Medicare entitlements will grow to devour the entire federal budget. Massive tax increases are just over the horizon, awaiting the day when this President feels safe in assuring the voters that fiscal responsibility compels him to unleash them. The point of statist "health care reform" is to make the voters feel the only alternative to those tax hikes is death. The outer limit of New Deal socialism will be reached when overtaxed workers step back from the last few private-sector jobs, and refuse to support dependents who will fight to the death for their benefits.

I suspect the Great Crash would begin long before that ultimate moment of bankruptcy arrived. It could be triggered by an unforeseen catastrophe. By some estimates, the total cost of the 9/11 attacks exceeded *two trillion* dollars. Barack Obama's economy would not survive such a blow, especially since his immediate reaction to a systemic collapse would accelerate it, by nationalizing more of the private sector.

Even without a catastrophic trigger, the tragic end of our old system would begin when the job-creating upper class exercised its option to withdraw from the economy, taking money and capital with it. One of the most important attributes of wealth is the range of options it brings. The people targeted most aggressively by desperate socialists can simply leave the system. They can stop investing, hoard their wealth, or move overseas. They can do this very quickly, and they are, by definition, highly skilled at sensing the right moment for dramatic action.

The rich will play along for a good long while, and as you can see from the number of well-connected Democrats raking in fortunes during this recession, they can even profit handsomely by purchasing influence over a stagnant command economy…but when they feel the endgame approaching, they'll be gone before their old pals in Congress know what hit them. When you hear a leftist declare that all of our problems can be solved by soaking the rich, understand that will never happen, because the rich will jump out of the pool before they get soaked past the knee.

The time of the Great Crash has not arrived just yet. As bad as things may seem now, they can get an order of magnitude worse…and that means we still have time to change course. Your daily life depends on billions of transactions performed at the speed of light, millions of tons of goods shipped across vast distances, and oceans of gasoline flowing from convenient pumps. These complex systems cannot sustain much damage before your life changes in ways you might never have imagined. The people responsible will tell you it was inevitable, or it was all your fault for living so well in the first place. They'll try to divert your anger to their enemies, and expect you to trade your ambitions for the sustenance they will provide.

We don't have to let it come to that, if we remember that prosperity is inseparable from freedom, while command offers only obedience and survival. We don't have to lose much more freedom before we lose a great deal of our prosperity. Every dollar spent by the government is a dollar that won't be able to generate wealth through choice. We still have the imagination and energy to put the bankrupt ideology of liberalism behind us, before it bankrupts us. We can thank the deluded intensity of Barack Obama and the last true believers of the Left for making it clear how the story of the almighty State will end, in the absurdity of a $14 trillion debt that still isn't big enough for them. Our grandfathers broke the Axis and rebuilt the world. Our fathers made academics eat every word they wrote about the inevitable triumph of communism. We have one last pitiful offspring of the collectivist dream to bury. We can do it, but it will require vision and leadership.

Simply returning to the bloated budget of George Bush's final year would require a historically unprecedented cut of over 15% in total government spending. The budget President Obama just submitted would swell the federal workforce to over two million. Trimming it back to where Bush left it would put half a million people out of work. Correcting this ruinous course will be an achievement unlike any the world has ever seen. The world has also never seen anything like the crash that awaits us if we fail.

The Green Death
February 16, 2010

Author's Note: After a liberal reader challenged my contention that radical environmentalism has a cost measured in human lives, I decided to recount the story of Rachel Carson and Silent Spring. *I thought the broad outlines of the DDT hoax were well-known by now, and was surprised my contentious reader was unfamiliar with them. My response to this reader began in the comments to "Resolving the Global Warming Fraud," but grew long enough to merit their own post. It wound up generating the most single-day traffic my web site has ever seen. I firmly believe one of the reasons lunatic environmentalism retains so much cultural influence is because it's never held accountable for its crimes. Its founding myths are written into textbooks, and its victims are swiftly forgotten.*

Who is the worst killer in the long, ugly history of war and extermination? Hitler? Stalin? Pol Pot? Not even close. A single book called *Silent Spring* killed far more people than all those fiends put together.

Published in 1962, *Silent Spring* used manipulated data and wildly exaggerated claims (sound familiar?) to push for a worldwide ban on the pesticide known as DDT—which is, to this day, the most effective weapon against malarial mosquitoes. The Environmental Protection Agency held extensive hearings after the uproar produced by this book...and these hearings concluded that DDT should not be banned. A few months after the hearings ended, EPA administrator William Ruckleshaus over-ruled his own agency and banned DDT anyway, in what he later admitted was a "political" decision. Threats to withhold American foreign aid swiftly spread the ban across the world.

The resulting explosion of mosquito-borne malaria in Africa has claimed over sixty million lives. This was not a gradual process—a surge of infection and death happened almost immediately. The use of DDT reduces the spread of mosquito-borne malaria by fifty to eighty percent, so its discontinuation quickly produced an explosion of crippling and fatal illness. The same environmental movement which has been falsifying data, suppressing dissent, and reading tea leaves to support the global-warming fraud has studiously ignored this blood-drenched "hockey stick" for decades.

The motivation behind *Silent Spring*, the suppression of nuclear power, the global-warming scam, and other outbreaks of environmentalist lunacy is the worship of centralized power and authority. The author, Rachel Carson, didn't set out to kill sixty million people—she was a fanatical believer in the newly formed religion of radical environmentalism, whose body count comes from callousness, rather than blood thirst. The core belief of the environmental religion is the fundamental *uncleanness* of human beings. All forms of human activity are bad for the environment...most especially including the activity of large private corporations. Deaths in faraway Africa barely registered on the radar screen of the growing Green movement, especially when measured against the exhilarating triumph of getting a sinful pesticide banned, at substantial cost to an evil corporation.

Those who were initiated into the higher mysteries of environmentalism saw the reduction of the human population as a *benefit*, although they're generally more circumspect about saying so in public these days. As quoted by Walter Williams, the founder of the Malthusian Club of Rome, Alexander King, wrote in 1990: "My own doubts came when DDT was introduced. In Guayana, within two years, it had almost eliminated malaria. So my chief quarrel with DDT, in hindsight, is that it has greatly added to the population problem." Another charming quote comes from Dr. Charles Wurster, a leading opponent of DDT, who said of malaria deaths: "People are the cause of all the problems. We have too many of them. We need to get rid of some of them, and this is as good a way as any."

Like the high priests of global warming, Rachel Carson knew what she was doing. She claimed DDT would actually destroy *all life on earth*, if its use continued—the "silent spring" of the title is a literal description of the epocalypse she forecast. She misused a quote from Albert Schweitzer about atomic warfare, implying the late doctor agreed with her crusade against pesticide by dedicating her book to him...when, in fact, Schweitzer viewed DDT as a "ray of hope" against disease-carrying insects. Some of the scientists attempting to debunk her hysteria went so far as to *eat* chunks of DDT to prove it was harmless, but she and her allies simply ignored them, making these skeptics the forerunners of today's "global warming deniers"—absolutely correct and utterly vilified. William Ruckleshaus disregarded nine thousand pages of testimony when he imposed the DDT ban. Then as now, the science was settled...beneath a mass of politics and ideology.

Another way *Silent Spring* forecast the global-warming fraud was its insistence that readers ignore the simple evidence of reality around them. One of the founding myths of modern environmentalism was Carson's assertion that bird eggs developed abnormally thin shells due to DDT exposure, leading the chicks to be crushed before they could hatch. As detailed in an excellent *American Spectator* piece from 2005, no honest experimental attempt to produce this phenomenon has ever succeeded—even when using concentrations of DDT a hundred times greater than anything that could be encountered in nature. Carson claimed thin egg shells were bringing the robin and bald eagle to the edge of extinction...even as the bald eagle population doubled, and robins filled the trees. Today, those eagles and robins shiver in a blanket of snow caused by global warming.

The DDT ban isn't the only example of environmental extremism coming with a stack of body bags. Mandatory gas mileage standards cause about 2,000 deaths per year, by compelling automakers to produce lighter, more fragile cars. The biofuel mania has led resources to be shifted away from growing food crops, resulting in higher food prices and starvation. Worst of all, the economic damage inflicted by the environmentalist religion directly correlates to life-threatening reductions in the human standard of living. The recent earthquake in Haiti is only the latest reminder that **poverty kills**, and collectivist politics are the most formidable engine of poverty on Earth.

Environmental extremism is a breathless handmaiden for collectivism. It pours a layer of smooth, creamy science over a relentless hunger for power. Since the boogeymen of the Green movement threaten the very Earth itself with imminent destruction, the environmentalist feels morally justified in suspending democracy and seizing the liberty of others. *Of course* we can't put these matters to a vote! The dimwitted hicks in flyover country can't understand advanced biochemistry or climate science. They might vote the wrong way, and we can't risk the consequences! The phantom menaces of the Green movement can only be battled by a mighty central State. Talk of representation, property rights, and even free speech is madness when such a threat towers above the fragile ecosphere, wheezing pollutants and coughing out a stream of dead birds and drowned polar bears. You can see why the advocates of Big Government would eagerly race across a field of sustainable, organic grass to sweep environmentalists into their arms, and spin them around in the ozone-screened sunlight.

Green philosophy provides vital nourishment for the intellectual vanity of leftists, who get to pat themselves on the back for saving the world through the control-freak statism they longed to impose anyway. One of the reasons for the slow demise of the climate-change nonsense is that it takes a long time to let so much air out of so many egos. Calling "deniers" stupid and unpatriotic was very fulfilling. Likewise, you'll find modern college campuses teeming with students—and teachers—who will fiercely insist that DDT thins egg shells and causes cancer. Environmentalism is a primitive religion which thrives by telling its faithful they're too sophisticated for mere common sense.

The legacy of *Silent Spring* provides an object lesson in the importance of bringing the global-warming con artists to trial. No one was ever forced to answer for the misery inflicted by that book, or the damage it dealt to serious science. Today Rachel Carson is still celebrated as a hero, the secular saint who transformed superstition and hysteria into a Gospel for the modern god-state. The tactics she deployed against DDT resurfaced a decade later, in the Alar scare. It's a strategy that offers great reward, and very little risk. We need to increase the risk factor, and frighten the next generation of junk scientists into being more careful with their research. If we don't, the Church of Global Warming will just reappear in a few years, wearing new vestments and singing new hymms…but still offering the same communion of poverty, tyranny, and death.

The Terms Of The Deal
March 18, 2010

Author's Note: The fateful vote on ObamaCare did indeed occur the weekend after I posted this essay.

This weekend may see the fateful vote on ObamaCare, or it may be passed with twilight's last deeming. There is not much time left for Americans to consider what is about to be done to them, and raise their voices in a protest loud enough to frighten nervous Democrats out of their parliamentary maneuvers. The ruling class wants this bill badly enough to interpret anything less than fierce protest as implied consent.

Even discounting the sewer system of underhanded deals and bribes needed to push ObamaCare through Congress, distorting it beyond any semblance of a carefully-designed plan, it's foolish to accept it as a "solution" to health care "problems." **No government program is a solution to anything.** I'm not referring to their inefficiency or cost. I'm talking about their very *nature*.

A government program is not a carefully-designed system, or even an enduring commitment. It is a *promise*. Systems require discipline. For example, the operation of an aircraft carrier is a very complex system, which relies upon many individuals to perform carefully-defined duties. Failure to perform these duties results in punishment or dismissal. All of the crew members understand this, so the system is reliable. When the captain orders a fighter to launch, he knows the deck crew and pilot will quickly obey. The crew and pilot, in turn, know that the captain would not order a launch for no good reason. Everything happens with speed, efficiency, and precision, because the system is illuminated by trust.

Government social programs don't work that way. They *can't*. Today's Congress cannot bind future sessions with discipline. They can only saddle their successors with obligations. The national debt has grown to staggering proportions because debt is the only thing each new Administration and Congress inherit from those who went before.

When Barack Obama tries to convince you to accept a government takeover of the health-care industry, he is making a promise he won't be around to keep. ObamaCare's job-killing taxes are front-loaded, but in order to fool the Congressional Budget Office into giving it a respectable deficit score, its benefits are delayed for years. Even if Obama wins re-election, he would complete his second term long before the program was completely phased in…and

160

no external authority exists to compel either Obama, or his successors, to honor the promises he's been making.

Consider the question of public funding for abortion, which has led Democrat representative Bart Stupak and his little bloc of pro-life colleagues to withhold their support. They are ostensibly holding out for guarantees against government-funded abortions, but the odds that ObamaCare will never cover abortions are exactly **zero**. It's simply a question of *when,* not if. Once the government controls the health-care industry, there is nothing to prevent Democrats from paying for any service their constituents demand. A future law funding abortion can easily be passed, or maybe even "deemed" into existence. Abortion advocates can use lawsuits to squeeze funding out of the government. Control of the health-insurance industry will give the government massive leverage to erode determined public resistance against any steps it wishes to take.

Think about the evolution of ObamaCare health insurance into single-payer socialized medicine, something Obama and the Democrats quietly promise to left-wing audiences. The government will have every incentive to press for this transformation, and arrange it by pushing private competitors out of the market, then presenting single-payer government health care as tomorrow's "solution" to the problem they're working to create today. There is nothing to stop them from doing this.

The only guarantee you have that ObamaCare will provide the promised benefits, and remain within its boundaries, is the trust you place in the word of Barack Obama and his party…and your faith in future politicians who have yet to be elected.

It is madness to extend such trust to the party of Charlie Rangel, John Conyers, Nancy Pelosi, Christopher Dodd, Barney Frank, and Harry Reid. There is no reason to trust an administration that places billions of dollars into the hands of unaccountable "czars," including the odd Communist. Only a fool would believe the endless string of lies and deception from this President will magically transform into honesty and fidelity, after his angry demands for more power are fulfilled. A party that openly plans to subvert what little power remains in the tattered Constitution will not become *more* lawful after it seizes control of an entire industry. It would be idiotic to believe that a government whose economic projections have never come close to reality can suddenly predict the costs of the most enormous program it has ever produced. Remember, this Administration's idea of a "system working" consists of frantic airline passengers tackling a terrorist seconds before his underwear detonates.

It would also be foolish to place such faith in Republicans, or anyone else. Today's Democrats are not unique in their corruption, a cancer that can be driven into remission with electoral chemotherapy in 2010 and 2012. Massive government breeds massive corruption through its very nature—it is the predictable behavior of people who are no less greedy, ambitious, or deceitful that the most rapacious robber baron. They hide their avarice behind masks of finely chiseled sanctimony, but as the final maneuvers toward the passage of Obama-Care illustrate, they're just as quick to bend rules and perpetrate fraud as any white-collar criminal.

It would be a horrible mistake to accept a deal with the creators of history's most staggering national debt, based on assurances they will place your interests ahead of theirs, for *decades* to come. As Darth Vader memorably explained to Lando Calrissian, the State can always alter the terms of the deal, and your only recourse will be praying they don't alter it any further.

Part Three
Family

Ordinary people are tired of hearing every standard they hold is an insult to those who don't meet it, and every belief is an insult to those who don't share it.

The Tyranny of False Choices
May 8, 2009

Author's Note: This essay, along with "In Defense of Marriage" and its responses, form a trilogy about marriage and family, inspired by the infamous confrontation between gay activist Perez Hilton and Miss USA contestant Carrie Prejean. Fellow Green Room contributor Laura, who can be read at pursuingholiness.com, pointed out that Prejean's simple statement of support for traditional marriage caused her to be treated as more dangerous and undesirable than John Walker Lindh, the "American Taliban." This observation crystallized my own thoughts on the subject.

Carrie Prejean has been having a rough couple of weeks. She was denied the Miss USA crown because she gave an honest answer to an ambush question from an angry gay-rights activist. (Do you suppose they'll have an equally militant pro-life activist hosting the pageant next year, asking "gotcha" questions about partial-birth abortion?) The consequences of her honesty have included being dressed down with the kind of sexist language that had feminists screaming for the cops in the Nineties, before their movement burned itself to ashes in defense of America's most powerful sexual predator. Her views on gay marriage have been chalked up to childhood trauma, as if they were a subject for treatment, rather than debate.

The anger and vindictiveness of the gay-marriage movement is unsurprising. They are the aggressors in a cultural battle, which is entering a critical stage. Aggressive behavior is to be expected. Mainstream society has something they want, and they're going to have to take it, because it will not be surrendered voluntarily. They must take maximum advantage of every opportunity to put their cultural opposition on the defensive. What answer do you think Perez Hilton was *hoping* Carrie Prejean would give?

Whatever the merits of gay marriage, it must be understood that it's a tremendous change from the traditional understanding of marriage, which stretches back for centuries. This change is being pressed upon society with great speed and urgency. Two or three generations is a very short time to push an idea from unthinkable to inevitable. Many Americans don't like the way this particular change is being presented as mandatory, with all opposition dismissed as evil, insane, or ignorant. It's bad enough to be told you must put forth an opinion about something you'd rather not think about. It's even worse when you're told that only one opinion is acceptable. Perez Hilton wasn't asking Carrie Prejean a question—he was demanding submission. Thoughtless genuflection to "the right of gay persons in love to get married" is the *jizya* paid to the dominant culture, and you're not allowed to squeak out so much as a tepid salute to traditional marriage until you've paid it.

The question asked of Carrie Prejean was whether she thought every state should legalize same-sex marriage. The answer that got her in so much trouble was, "Well I think it's great that Americans are able to choose one way or the other. We live in a land where you can choose same-sex marriage or opposite marriage. You know what, in my country, in my family, I do believe that marriage should be between a man and a woman, no offense to anybody out there. But that's how I was raised and I believe that it should be between a man and a woman." She's not exactly getting in anyone's face there, is she? She even began with a polite disclaimer that made it clear she respected the "choice" of people that disagreed with the viewpoint she was about to declare. Are those who passionately believe in global warming expected to begin statements of their faith with cheerful salutes to the validity of their opponents' choices, and end with an apology to anyone who doesn't share their fanatical beliefs?

Carrie's declaration of respect for the advocates of gay marriage was, obviously, inadequate to a culture that needs the defenders of traditional marriage to "feel themselves subdued," as the Koran puts it. It was also unnecessary to begin with. Those who revere traditional marriage do not need to apologize for the defense they offer. For one thing, in a nation where everything has been politicized—down to the food you eat and the car you drive—I think we can take it as a given that any strong belief is going to offend somebody. Worse, offering pre-emptive apologies to the likes of Perez Hilton is a concession that the time-honored traditions of ordinary people are inherently vicious and offensive...and once you've conceded that, you've lost the argument over whether those traditions need to be junked. You're just negotiating over the timetable.

Ordinary people should strongly reject the idea that respecting the tradition of marriage is automatically an insult to those who do not share that respect. Elevating marriage does not require hatred of gay people. Celebrating marriage as among the highest achievements of the human race does not require us to dismiss those who will never be able to marry as less than human. You can say something is special without damning everything else as meaningless. I wish Carrie Prejean had explained that to Perez Hilton, instead of beginning her declaration of traditional beliefs with a weak apology for daring to hold them. I hope the treatment she has received will give other defenders of those beliefs the resolve to dispense with the apologies.

Everyone who believes in marriage as the union of a man and woman had better realize they are under attack, by an ideology that defines itself through attacking. The most zealous proponents of gay marriage will never be satisfied with legalistic civil unions, which I doubt straight America would have any sustained objection to—there's no reason any given group of people shouldn't be allowed to enter into contractual agreements to guarantee access to sick partners in a hospital, or the distribution of an estate, or similar practical considerations. Where middle America stands its ground is recognizing these arrangements as a "marriage"...and that very recognition is what the leading advocates of gay marriage demand. Its exclusivity is exactly what they desire. They cannot abide millions of tradition-minded men and women declaring that the bond they share is precious and unique, because they will not see that declaration as anything but an insult. To the leaders of the gay marriage movement—the people with microphones and cameras pointed at them—the battle to redefine marriage is not about *gaining* something, it's about taking something away from those who don't deserve it.

Initiative in defense is required, because in today's politically supercharged atmosphere, sitting quietly and waiting for your beliefs to be redefined as indefensible is suicide. All of the slanders directed at Carrie Prejean are variations on the tactics deployed against everyone who stands for traditional marriage. The attempt to treat opposition to gay marriage as a psychological disorder is an obvious bid to silence opponents with a Hannibal Lecter mask. The hypocrisy charge, currently being made by strangling Miss Prejean with her own swimsuit, boils down to an assertion that she opposes gay marriage out of pure, mindless hatred—if she's such a naughty little minx in every other respect, she can't have any logical reason for refusing to get on board with the gay agenda. The less subtle accusations that support for traditional marriage is motivated by "homophobia" imply there is no sincere respect or admiration for marriage itself—it's All About the Gays, as if your parents' next anniversary party will celebrate a thirty-year schoolyard taunt directed at oppressed homosexuals. The charge that marriage isn't worth defending, because so many marriages produce no children or end in divorce, misses the entire point of celebrating the ideal of raising a family through a loving union that lasts a lifetime: if it was easy, it wouldn't be worthy of celebration.

If the reader is strongly sympathetic to the cause of gay marriage, and finds any of the above to be harsh or confrontational, I can only say that traditionalists did not start the marriage wars. We reserve the right to offer a spirited defense of what we believe, and the hardball rules of engagement were set by the aggressors, as they are in every conflict. We will not allow the question to be framed as a choice between accepting gay marriage or endorsing hatred and bigotry, because that is the kind of false choice a tyrant offers his subjects. The real question is whether traditional marriage is worth defending…because if it is, then Carrie Prejean is being persecuted for taking a noble stand, and if it isn't, she foolishly threw away a glittering prize out of blind loyalty to a tired superstition.

In Defense of Marriage
May 11, 2009

Author's Note: This was the first time one of my essays was promoted to the Hot Air main page. If I remember correctly, it was the first time anything was promoted out of the Green Room to the main page. The technology for doing this was new, but once Ed and Allahpundit got the kinks hammered out, an epic discussion began in the comment forum. If you're interested in this topic, I highly recommend looking up the original post on HotAir.com, and reading those comments. Many good points were made on all sides of the issue, and considering the emotional temperature of the gay marriage issue, the discussion was extremely polite and substantial.

Recent events have made the legal recognition of gay marriage a hot topic. Social conservatives are fighting a battle to preserve the traditional definition of marriage, and this battle is entering a crucial stage. The other side of the argument has enormous influence in the popular culture, to the point where one of its most outspoken activists can be invited to judge the Miss USA contest, and use his position to score political points. Social conservatives are presumed guilty of bigotry for daring to speak in favor of traditional marriage—as the Carrie Prejean affair demonstrates, they are treated more like defendants at a trial, than participants in a debate.

Whatever the motivations of the outspoken leadership of the gay marriage movement, there's no question that many average gay Americans want the official sanction of marriage for the best of reasons: to honor passionate commitment and lifelong relationships. It's essential for those who defend the traditional definition of marriage to make the case that marriage is worth preserving, when the consequences of winning the debate include disappointment, humiliation, and anger among gay people who wish to be married.

Marriage between men and women is a tradition that stretches back for centuries, into the history of the European nations that colonized America, and the history of virtually every other civilization around the world. Marriage is vastly older than various other features of modern life that we asked to accept as eternal and unchangeable, such as progressive taxation, or federal control of public education. It was not invented in the Fifties by stodgy old television producers, and we are not designing our nation's law or culture from scratch, arbitrarily deciding to pencil in a mean-spirited homosexual exclusion to a newly minted "right." We should be clear that proponents of the traditional definition of marriage are being asked to redefine something that has been part of human law and custom for most of our recorded history. The longevity of marriage, and its presence in almost every human culture, speak in its favor. Modern Americans often embrace the delusion they are the first generation to be capable of changing their ways, but our forefathers down through the centuries were perfectly capable of redefining marriage, if they had wanted to. The definition of marriage as a bond between a man and a woman has endured through the development of Western culture, under the influence of various religions, because it's important.

Marriage is a basic building block for society. The marital bond creates families, and brings families together, creating an atmosphere of trust and loyalty that was crucial to the formation of ancient societies...but is also important to a technologically advanced democracy. The line of authority begins with man and wife, and builds into families, extended clans, communities, and nations. Men and women raised by parents who honor their lifelong pledge of devotion are better able to enter a democracy as strong, independent citizens who can fulfill their civic duties and use their voting power wisely. It's common sense to recognize the advantage of having an extended family you can fall back on for support in tough times, and which can build wealth that benefits all of the family members. Simply owning a family home, which has been largely paid for by the older generation, is an enormous asset. People who can turn to their families when they hit rock bottom are less likely to demand welfare from the government. The pathologies of crime and welfare dependency are strongly linked to the explosion of children raised by single parents, as the no-fault divorce culture has weakened marriage. Families also provide emotional support that no amount of sterile government spending can ever duplicate. We never should have accepted the Great Society notion that raising children was primarily an exercise in accounting, treating them as line items on Uncle Sam's budget sheet.

Solid marriages, and the families they produce, also contribute a powerful resource that has become scarce in modern America: **honor,** and by extension shame. Families help to build a sense of honor by holding children accountable for what they do to each other, and making them aware that they carry the family's honor with them when they move into the outside world. People who are mindful that their actions reflect upon the reputation of a mighty family tree are more likely to conduct themselves honorably, and more likely to feel the sting of shame if their actions don't measure up to the family's standards. It's sad that so many of us have to go through life without being able to look behind us and see the ghosts of our parents, and their parents before them, holding hands and standing united in their pride at our achievements...and their disappointment when we behave in a way that dishonors their memory. We live in a world that our great-grandparents could scarcely have imagined, and we should be grateful that they were able to build that world for us, and aware of our responsibility to build the world our great-grandchildren will inherit. A nation that runs up an incalculable national debt is not a nation that is paying enough attention to the needs of its great-grandchildren.

Those who were raised in a single-parent household, as I was, might object that it's possible to develop these virtues without both a mother and father to teach them. This is very true, but it's far easier to raise children and give them the strength of an extended family with an intact marriage. I doubt most single parents reading this would deny their jobs would be easier if the mother or father of the children was still around to help, and took their responsibilities to their spouse and children seriously. When you're talking about the evolution of a civilization—the interwoven life stories of three hundred million people—it pays for society to revere and encourage the traditions which are most likely to produce free-thinking, industrious, lawful citizens.

If raising children within an intact marriage makes it, say, 10% less likely those children will be criminals, you can keep thousands of criminals from haunting the streets by encouraging intact marriages…and that 10% hypothetical figure is probably a very low estimate of the beneficial effect of intact families, among the demographics most prone to violent crime, drug abuse, and long-term welfare dependency. Our cultural elite has constructed a society in which they can indulge their libertine instincts, and preen themselves over how marvelously open-minded they are, while passing the cost along to people whose lives became intolerable when they became a little bit harder. European states have collapsed into tired old socialist nursing homes by failing to produce enough children to keep their cultures and economies vibrant. In Europe, a half-dozen elderly grandparents have only one grandchild to share between them. In America, we have a vast population of children who never meet their grandparents.

There are those who say that assigning an exalted, officially sanctioned status to married couples implies that single people are somehow less valuable to society. Some argue that child-rearing isn't a sufficient argument in favor of marriage, because we don't frown on married couples who never get around to having children, or are incapable of having them. This misses the larger point that a healthy America has plenty of room for spinsters, playboys, and career-minded power couples who can't fit children into their lifestyle…but we can't *all* be like that. The next generation will come from families who make the incredible sacrifices necessary to have two, three, or even more children, when many of their friends look at the bill for a stay in the maternity ward, and think about what a cool plasma TV and home-theater system they could have bought with that money. Love and faith—in the future, and in each other—make it possible for a man and his wife to make those return trips to the maternity ward, without which the future would be empty and poor.

The advocate of redefining marriage will say that same-sex marriages can provide the kind of solid family environment that is so desirable, and modern technology can make it possible for them to have children. This ignores the value marriage has for the men and women who are joined by it, even if they never raise a family. Too much of our social evolution since the Sixties has been distorted by the ridiculous article of faith among the elites that men and women are interchangeable. Men and women are **different,** and they **need** each other. Marriage civilizes and focuses men, who have traded their clubs and spears for footballs and videogame controllers, but remain the same competitive and predatory creatures they have always been. It places their strength at the service of the women they love. For a man who doesn't choose to serve in the military, marriage is his greatest opportunity to swear absolute loyalty to someone in this world besides himself. When a man kneels before his love and asks for her hand, he is not kneeling because he's weak…he kneels because he's strong, and he's ready to share that strength with his wife. It's a promise that is not easy to make, or easy to keep. Four decades of increasing crime, declining ambition, and deepening poverty for the most unfortunate among us should have taught us beyond question how much husbands and wives, fathers and mothers, need each other. The freakish ideologues who sold American women idiocy like "a woman needs a man like a fish needs a bicycle" owe several generations of women, and their children, a groveling apology.

Some advocates of redefining marriage would laugh at this description of marriage, and call it an ideal too many couples fail to achieve. They might say the epidemic of divorce since the Seventies proves that traditional marriage has become a tattered and threadbare flag that is not worth defending. On the contrary, the divorce explosion proves the necessity of officially respecting and encouraging the difficult commitment of marriage. We weakened marriage by redefining it as a temporary business arrangement between men and women, to be dissolved without hesitation or remorse at any time. We would weaken it further by redefining it as a temporary business arrangement between anyone. We aren't doing ourselves any favors by abandoning ideals that are difficult to achieve. We haven't been helping our children by discouraging them from reaching for the future together…by telling them "forever" is a silly word, or "always" is merely the opening bid in an extended negotiation. We've done a poor job of setting a good example for the younger generation, and now we're trying to let ourselves off the hook by saying those marriage vows were unreasonably difficult to begin with. Marriage is valuable because it's difficult.

The libertarian objection to official recognition of marriage is that people should not look to their government to legitimize their moral preferences. This has always been a hollow argument, because the laws of a nation inevitably reflect the morality of its citizens. It becomes a ridiculous argument in the face of the gigantic, activist, sanctimonious government and ruling class of modern America. If the government is going to become agnostic on the question of sanctioning marriage, it will be the first time in decades it has decided to become agnostic on anything. Politicians who tell us we have a moral imperative to drive smaller cars should not be allowed to fall silent when asked if we have an even greater imperative to honor our marriage vows.

The idea that defenders of marriage are pleading for state and federal laws to "legitimize" their beliefs gets the situation exactly backward: the citizens of a nation have a right to expect the laws of their government to reflect their beliefs. The advocates of redefining marriage understand this instinctively. The point of their crusade is not to gain the "right" to declare themselves to be married…they can do that now, and many of them do. The point is to change the legal structure of the country, to express a revised, manufactured consensus that the sex of the people involved in a marriage doesn't matter, and eventually this would be further revised to say that the number of people involved doesn't matter either. The point of obtaining legal sanction for gay marriage is not to change how **gay people** feel about it.

Ordinary people, struggling to prosper and raise their children in a complex world, are tired of being told that everything they revere is subject to deconstruction and re-inter-pretation. They are tired of hearing that every standard they hold is an insult to those who don't meet it, and every belief is an insult to those who don't share it. They're weary of being used as test subjects in grand social experiments. To maintain a common culture, we must have ideals with intrinsic meaning, just as some of the words in any language must have a clear and unambiguous meaning. Government is not something imposed from above on its citizens, in a democracy—its authority flows upward from them. They have a right to expect that government to honor the vows and commitments they have made between themselves, dating back to centuries before the United States of America existed. They have a right to live in a society that doesn't expend its energies trying to condition them to forget something they have understood since the first time they saw their fathers and mothers standing together and smiling down at them in the cradle…and which they have respected since the first time they looked through a family photo album and dreamed about who would be standing beside them, when the picture of their own family was added. Redefining marriage doesn't make lasting unions between men and women less important. It just makes them harder to find.

In Defense of Marriage: Responses
May 14, 2009

Author's Note: There were so many strong critical responses to "In Defense of Marriage" that I decided to write a follow-up post addressing them, rather than tackling them individually in the comments section. It was a valuable lesson in refining my own thoughts on a subject, by considering the arguments against them. Leaving an essay open for comments creates a priceless resource for the author who relishes opportunities to strengthen his beliefs through challenge and evaluation.

In response to some of the points raised in the comments to the "In Defense of Marriage" essay I posted on Monday:

Aggression and Defense: It should be emphasized that the same-sex marriage movement is aggressively seeking to re-define an existing institution. The people who believe marriage is defined as "men marrying women" were there first. We are defending a centuries-old tradition. This doesn't automatically mean the tradition is worth defending, but it does mean those wishing to re-define marriage are the party which should demonstrate it is necessary and desirable, because they're the ones who want to change things. Many of the arguments against traditional marriage proceed as if we all just climbed from the wreckage of Oceanic Flight 815, and we're trying to write up the rules of our island civilization from scratch, before the Smoke Monster shows up.

It is often said that we are not discussing whether or not gay men and women can be married, because they can get married now, provided they marry someone of the opposite sex. A man and woman seeking a marriage license will not be asked if they're secretly gay, and sent packing if either of them answers "yes." This is not a trivial point. We are not talking about denying a civil right to a group of people, which is where glib analogies to the black civil-rights movement fall short. We are talking about changing the definition of marriage, as it is both customarily and legally understood. Changing the definition of an institution inevitably changes the institution. To use another institution as an example, the Boy Scouts stop being the Boy Scouts if you force them to admit girls. Again, this doesn't logically settle the argument about whether re-defining marriage is a good idea—sometimes institutions do need to be changed— but let's be honest about the magnitude of the change we're discussing.

Is traditional marriage good for society? Some advocates of same-sex marriage wonder if it's worth frustrating the desires of gay Americans to preserve a dusty old tradition. I believe both reasoning and evidence support the conclusion that traditional marriage has great value to society. Putting things in the most practical and unemotional terms, a nation must have an average birth rate of 2.1 or better to avoid population decline, and the only way to get past that 2.1 limit is to have a sizable number of families with three or more children. A male same-sex marriage cannot produce its own children at all, and while female same-sex marriages could bear children through artificial insemination, it seems very unlikely that they would produce enough of the large families we need.

Once the children are born, stable marriages provide the best environment for raising the children to be lawful and productive citizens. The evidence for this is overwhelming. Directorblue has an excellent post in the Green Room, entitled "The Racists," that lays out some of the sobering statistical evidence for the negative effects broken families have on children. You can be as dispassionate as a computer, and still see that society has a vested interest in promoting large, stable families. Raising such a family is extremely difficult and expensive, so it's in the best interests of society to encourage and honor those who make the necessary sacrifices. This is one reason I disagree with the notion that we could settle the marriage debate by abolishing marriage altogether. (Respect for the feelings of the large majority of people that take marriage seriously is another.)

Marriage is just a word: Many of those in favor of allowing same-sex marriage is to ask why permitting it would have any negative effect on traditional marriage. The answer is that words have meaning, and concepts have power. Some things are defined by their exclusivity. A Congressional Medal of Honor is just a hunk of metal hanging on the end of a ribbon, but not everybody can have one. Awarding such a medal does not transform the recipient into a hero—they receive the medal **because they are** heroes. Our nation needs a considerable number of people to make the difficult sacrifices necessary to serve in the military, and only the people who make those sacrifices are allowed to call themselves "soldiers." We reward those people with respect and deference—not as much as we should, in my opinion. Why do we show any special deference or appreciation to people who win Nobel Peace Prizes, or Academy Awards, if they're just pieces of paper or little golden statues?

Every society has methods of expressing special respect and gratitude for particular achievements. If we can agree that traditional marriage is valuable to society, and should be encouraged, why should we be eager to remove the special status afforded those marriages by re-defining them as one of many possible configurations for a humdrum legal partnership? Why should a huge majority—even in the generally liberal state of California—be forced to rewrite the meaning of words and ideas like "marriage," "husband," and "wife," which have been a basic part of their culture for generations, in order to accomodate a tiny minority? And why is that minority so desperately, even fanatically, dedicated to achieving that revision of meaning, to the point where they openly threaten to destroy the lives of people like the Prop 8 supporters or Carrie Prejean, if marriage is just a silly old word that nobody should be getting all worked up about?

People are not robots. They aren't emotionless social units that can be given a new set of behavioral directives on command. They respond to rituals, symbols, and traditions. They need these things to relate to one another. Those who criticize the defenders of traditional marriage often speak of them as if they were defective computers, in need of a reboot and the latest set of Progressive Attitude v5.0 patches.

Much of the power behind words and concepts comes from the authority of the common culture, and the government that (regrettably) exerts a powerful control over it. If you doubt this, consider a certain six letter word for African-Americans that begins with "N", and which is routinely used by black entertainers, but absolutely forbidden to whites. While you're at it, consider the history of the term "African-American." Words have power, and they shape culture. A hundred years ago, "African-American" meant someone who emigrated to America from Africa. A hundred years before that, it would have been a nonsensical phrase, which would have honestly confused anyone from either America or Africa.

Americans share a common culture, and it requires some core concepts to function. A culture with no shared values is like a language that consists of random sounds. One of the more absurd suggestions to appear in the comments to my original post was the childish taunt that people who don't like the idea of legalized gay marriage affecting school curricula should pull their kids out of class and home-school them. Sure, as long as we get to take all the tax money we fork over for those useless public schools with us. If the political class was ever foolish enough to seriously make that offer to Americans, the miserable, tottering public school system would collapse into rubble in the wake of the stampede fleeing from it. Of course, in order to complete that exodus, we would have to destroy the most powerful opponent of both school choice and gay marriage in the world, Barack Hussein Obama.

We don't really want to fragment the nation into little cultural enclaves, any more than it already is. It won't be permitted by the legal system anyway. Will the states that refuse to vote in favor of legalizing same-sex marriage be allowed to deny the validity of gay marriages performed in the other states? Will the answer to that question be different if the number of states that legalize gay marriage increases to 20, 25, or 30? The purpose of the gay marriage movement is not to win the "right" for people of the same sex to declare they are married, because they can do that now. The purpose is not to remove legal obstacles placed in the way of same-sex partnerships, because most of the legal benefits desired by same-sex couples are already available to them, or could be obtained with legal adjustments far less drastic than re-defining marriage. The purpose is to force people who believe in the traditional definition of marriage to submit to a different set of beliefs, imposed with the force of law. This is not being presented as a polite request, or a calm and deliberate attempt at reasoned persuasion.

Marriage and tax breaks: The legal benefits most uniquely associated with marriage are its tax advantages. I don't think the primary opposition to granting tax advantages to same-sex civil unions would come from conservatives—we think everyone's taxes are too high anyway. Taking away the benefits afforded to marriage, while leaving the rest of the bloated tax system in place, would make the desirable goals of stable marriages a little more difficult for struggling couples to achieve. If you want to eliminate the tax benefits of marriage by eliminating the income tax entirely, sign me up.

Marriage and religion: I didn't advance any form of religious argument in favor of marriage in my original post, but the comments were still peppered with people insisting the only reason to support traditional marriage is religious fanaticism. Of course, the people saying this are usually just trying to avoid all other arguments by pulling out a favorite straw man to beat. The idea that opposition to same-sex marriage is invalid, because many of the opponents are people of faith, is bigotry. It's a bigotry the proponents of same-sex marriage slip into frequently enough to wonder if it's one of their primary motivations. Did anyone in the gay-marriage movement offer Carrie Prejean the respect for her sincere beliefs that she favored *them* with?

Insisting that opposition to an idea can only be evidence of stupidity and hatred imposes the tyranny of false choices. Telling free people their only options are to support the re-definition of marriage, or be denounced as imbecilic close-minded hate-mongers, is not offering them a "choice"…and if they accept those terms, they aren't free people. Praising the marriage of men and women as an especially valuable and honored institution is not an insult to men and women who don't get married, for whatever reason…any more than honoring those who join the military denigrates civilians. The insults seem to be coming from the same-sex marriage advocates, anyway. If you sneeringly dismiss someone's revered traditions as no better than slavery, don't be surprised when they fight back.

Marriage isn't worth defending because it's imperfect: There's no doubt the institution of marriage has suffered over the last forty years. This is a worthy topic for an entirely different discussion. In the context of the same-sex marriage debate, I have to doubt the wisdom of further weakening such an important institution by radically rewriting its basic terms, when loosening the requirements for terminating marriage has already done so much damage to it. The shaky condition of marriage in 2009 is cause for improving it, not discarding it. As to the idea that stricter divorce laws would trap women in abusive relationships: I hope the reader can forgive me for being brutally honest and a bit emotional here, but I deeply believe in the value of marriage as a vow between a man and a woman, and someone who abuses his wife or children is no longer a man.

Same-sex marriage would serve the same social purpose as traditional marriage: I already mentioned that same-sex marriage is unlikely to fill the same reproductive needs as the traditional variety, and of course male same-sex marriages can't reproduce at all. Would relaxing the definition of marriage to include homosexual unions reduce the number of people who choose to enter traditional marriages? I don't think that concern can be as casually dismissed as some of the commenters in my original post did. Getting married is a tremendous commitment for everyone involved, and given the general slant toward women in divorce proceedings, it's currently an even greater risk for the man—who is most commonly the one who initiates the marriage through a proposal. Raising a family with lots of children is an immense sacrifice for both parents. If these unions have inherent value to society, as I argued above, doesn't society help to create them by granting special status and appreciation—not to mention financial benefits, under our complex socially-engineered tax code? Wouldn't taking those benefits away, or granting them to people who don't meet the traditional requirements for marriage, reduce the incentive for people to make that commitment? Same-sex marriage between homosexuals would only be one result of re-defining marriage—it would become equally legal, and sanctioned by society, for a couple of heterosexual best buddies to enter a non-sexual "marriage" as well. I don't think it's a stretch to suppose that would cut into the number of men who make the effort to grow out of their perpetual adolescence and marry a woman.

How significant would the reduction in traditional marriage be? I don't think we have enough data to compute this scientifically, based on the handful of states that have legalized same-sex marriage thus far, but when you're contemplating millions of couples across the country, a small percentage translates to a lot of people. Given the awful failure of most of the other social engineering experiments we've been subjected to in the past century, a lot of us would rather not be volunteered for this one. How many advocates of same-sex marriage are willing to wait a few years, to accumulate data from the states which have legalized it so far, before forging ahead?

Same-sex marriage would not lead to polygamy: Oh, yes it would. Inevitably. The other slippery-slope arguments are far-fetched, but not this one. The polygamists wouldn't even need to spend decades building pop-culture credibility. A few court cases, a lucky spin of the Supreme Court Wheel of Fortune, and they're all set. If the sex of the participants in a marriage can be ruled irrelevant, how could the number of participants be eternally fixed at precisely two? If everyone involved meets the criteria for informed consent, how can you rewrite part A of the marriage concept, but steadfastly maintain part B is forever off-limits to revision? There probably aren't that many people interested in entering polygamous marriages at the moment, even compared to the small portion of the population that wishes to enter same-sex marriages…but they are out there, they will sue, and they will win. Polygamy is a Very Bad Thing for any culture—it's the anti-matter version of marriage. Its most notable effect on society is to increase the number of sexually frustrated lower-class young men. That's something we most certainly do not need.

Where do the marriage wars go from here? My crystal ball is no better than anyone else's, but I strongly doubt the state-by-state approach will go much further for same-sex marriage advocates. The requirement for other states to honor those arrangements will breed resentment and energize those who are strongly opposed to them, and let's be honest: there are a lot of those people, and many of them are no more interested in being reasonable than the people who tried to stomp their jackboots on Carrie Prejean's neck. Eventually there will be no more talk of treating marriage as a "federalism" issue, any more than we are allowed to settle the abortion debate via federalism. In the end, my guess is that some form of civil union arrangement for same-sex partners, and probably multiple partners, will be arrived at. I can only guess at how rocky the road to that destination will be.

Government and the Marriage Business
May 28, 2009

Author's Note: I'm firmly convinced of the value of traditional marriage, but I also think our government is far too aggressive in pressing moral judgments on us. They're not usually judgments conservatives agree with. I would rather break the machinery of government down, than temporarily turn its controls over to people who share my views on social issues. Too many of our social debates turn ugly because the stakes are so high. As I remarked to a correspondent during a later discussion of gay conservatives, the American atmosphere is tense because it's filled with force, and resistance.

Pepperdine law professor Douglas Kmiec's suggestion that marriage should be replaced with neutral "civil licenses" has already drawn agreement from Ed Morrissey at Hot Air, along with a disagreeing post from Pundette, in which she quotes Robert George's defense of traditional marriage as an essential component of a healthy society. Having written extensively in defense of marriage myself, I wanted to add my own thoughts on the idea of "getting government out of the marriage business."

I wrote earlier that I believe society has a critical interest in promoting opposite-sex marriage. It provides the best environment for raising children, it celebrates the ideal relationship between women and men, and it creates nuclear families that supply the building blocks of authority for a democracy, in which authority is supposed to flow upward, from family to community to state to nation. There is also a strong economic argument for the traditional family, which accumulates lasting wealth in a unique fashion. Even a low-income family can provide significant economic benefits to its members: making sacrifices to put children through school, fostering an attitude of reliance on self and family instead of the state, building social networks that can benefit every member of the family, and gathering property and other assets that can be passed down between generations. Hillary Clinton's famous book on child-rearing had it exactly backwards—it doesn't take a village to raise a child in America, but it takes strong families to build a decent village. A backbone of solid marriages and families gives a society the strength to accommodate the people who never become married, or never have children. We're not going to get above the replacement birth rate of 2.1 without a significant number of families that have three or more children. You're just not going to get there with artificial insemination, and you sure don't want to get there with a horde of children raised outside of marriage. The first reel of *Logan's Run* was not a blueprint for a happy society.

The idea of getting government out of marriage has a certain libertarian appeal, but we're nowhere near the overall state of libertarian social and economic freedom that would make this a winning argument. Why should marriage be the only aspect of society the federal government isn't deeply involved in? Besides, the assertion that following Doug Kmiec's suggestion would "get government out of the marriage business" is mistaken. Erasing marriage as an official concept, and replacing them with legalistic "civil unions," would not reduce the involvement of our massive centralized government, any more than it has been able to keep its nose out of legalistic civil contracts between automobile companies, their bondholders, and their labor unions. Changing the language surrounding the relationship between men, women, and children will not make divorces any less messy or painful. No aspect of society has ever been improved by making it *less* exalted. You can devalue marriage by declaring it to be equivalent to same-sex relationships, polygamous associations, and lifelong buddies who decide to enter a "civil union" to enjoy its tax advantages…but none of these things will improve marriages.

Ed writes that "the advent of no-fault divorce, in which one party can abrogate the marriage contract without penalty or consideration of the other party, has completely destroyed the notion that the government plays a role in protecting the integrity and well-being of the family." I can't imagine how anyone sees that as a reason to make things *worse*. The no-fault divorce revolution Ed references occurred less than fifty years ago. Are we supposed to accept that a mistake made in the 60s and 70s has produced an immutable new social order that can never be changed or improved? Did the awful social devastation of the last fifty years really invalidate the accumulated wisdom and tradition of the previous two thousand years? Somehow "progressive" social theories always seem to mean "everything is doomed to get worse, and all we can do is try to manage the decline efficiently." If a review of social trends over the last half-century leads you to believe no-fault divorce was bad for women and children, just wait until you see what *non-existent* marriage does to them.

The argument in favor of separating government from marriage is made as if the central government was not already legislating morality in hundreds of different ways. Much of the titanic super-state is justified on moral grounds, or because its activities are supposed to be good for society. What's the point of pumping trillions of dollars into economic "stimulus" and rescuing companies that are 'too big to fail" if we simultaneously withdraw the respect and legal approval of the state for the *one thing* most likely to keep children from living in poverty? When we have seen Barack Obama out of office, and passed whatever laws are necessary to ensure the president of the United States is never again allowed to manage an auto company, force banks to accept government funds, appoint Supreme Court justices on the basis of their racial wisdom, or use "progressive" taxation to "spread the wealth around" in the name of social justice, then we might have a more reasonable discussion about whether government should be involved in marriage. For the time being, anyone who wants to beat the defenders of marriage with the libertarianism or federalism clubs is going to find themselves holding a wet noodle instead of a cudgel.

Coming to Terms With Abortion
May 31, 2009

Author's Note: I encountered some objections to the assertion that for many young mothers and would-be fathers, abortion is a procedure to "restore a life of casual sex and self-indulgence." I might have better phrased that as "too many." Since I wrote this piece, there have been encouraging signs that the younger generation is turning against abortions of convenience. Maybe in a future edition of this book, I'll be able to rewrite that sentence to say "for a few young mothers and would-be fathers."

With a Supreme Court vacancy, and a nomination battle under way, one of the most painful topics in American culture is once again in the spotlight: abortion. Looming at the intersection of individual liberty and the nation's moral conscience, turning upon questions that mark the boundary between science and faith, heated in the crucible of a tyrannical exercise of raw judicial power made in the name of freedom, the abortion debate is a bleeding wound the American political system will never allow to heal. I've mentioned it in passing, during my brief time writing for the Green Room…but, like everyone else who makes a serious attempt to study and comment upon American life, I realized I needed to address it directly, and fully.

I've never been personally involved in the decision to abort a child. Most people haven't, since there are roughly 1.2 million of the procedures performed each year, and over 300 million people live in the United States. Like many people of my generation, I also don't have any children—there are only about 4 million live births in the United States each year. Compare 1.2 million abortions to 4 million live births annually, and you can see the dimensions of the abortion question. Compare either of those totals to the overall population, and you can see that quite a few of the people passionately assuming the pro-life or pro-choice stances don't have any direct personal experience in the matter…a point I'll return to in a moment.

My first experience with public debate was a speech class I took in college, during which I was assigned the pro-choice side of the abortion debate. I gave a very good speech, and was almost unanimously held to have crushed my debating opponent. I thought it was entirely a question of "a woman's right to choose," a decision in which no one but the woman had any legitimate influence. I was eighteen years old at the time.

Over the years, I came to realize that on the subject of abortion, half of America is eighteen years old.

It takes a certain maturity to understand that, in the vast majority of those 1.2 million annual abortions, the woman was not forced to conceive the child she's choosing to eliminate. She had choices to make long before she headed for the abortion clinic. When the consequence of those choices became a viable human child, the issue became one of **responsibility,** more than choice. I understood that completely, on the day when I first held my infant niece. Maybe you have to hold a baby to understand it. Not enough of us get to hold babies, these days.

Recent polls show that a majority of Americans have come to consider themselves "pro-life," but this is a matter of degree. You can add the poll numbers up a different way, and conclude that over sixty percent of Americans favor keeping abortion legal in some form or another. I don't believe we would ever arrive at a national consensus that it should be eliminated completely. Speaking for myself, I always felt it should be available in the cases of rape, where the woman was made pregnant against her will; incest, where the woman was either forced to conceive, or is by definition mentally and emotionally incapable of being a mother, especially to a child all but guaranteed to have severe genetic defects; and the life of the mother. I would be awed and humbled to stand in the presence of a woman who insisted on carrying her child to term, even knowing it would probably cost her life, but I can't agree that she should be *compelled* to do so. The conflicting opinions of the American people on the topic of abortion come, in part, from the difference between medically necessary, extreme cases, and the far greater number of abortions performed for the convenience of the mother—or the father. You can't come up with a solid majority for outlawing abortion entirely, but a lot of people are growing uncomfortable with abortion on demand.

Much of the soft support for abortion comes from the essential immaturity of the electorate, who follow the path of least resistance when discussing an issue they'd rather not think about, and which probably doesn't affect them personally. Abortion is part of a culture that works to prolong the adolescence of men and women until well into their forties. Having a baby is such a *drag*. It forces people to grow up and take responsibility for their actions. It compels carefree and hedonistic couples to confront the massive reality of their obligations to each other, and the life they have created. For many young mothers and would-be fathers, abortion is not a procedure designed to remove an unwanted fetus—it's a procedure to restore a life of casual sex and self-indulgence, which went up in smoke when that home pregnancy test kit turned the wrong color. Young men who have never been involved in conception or abortion themselves find it easy to dismiss the entire issue by talking about "a woman's right to choose," which simultaneously allows them to sound enlightened, particularly in the campus environment many of them inhabit…and lets them off the hook for doing any serious thinking, or defending a morally serious but difficult position. When you force those young men to confront the question of whether elective abortions are wrong—rather than asking who should make the final decision about having one—the poll numbers shift. Saying you're "pro-choice" is the quick and easy way for teenagers, of all ages, to sound fashionably liberal and dodge the more telling question, which is: what would *you* choose?

Of course, the abortion debate is horrendously deformed by *Roe vs. Wade*, an exercise of raw judicial power that short-circuited the national discussion, and left the pro-life side feeling marginalized and helpless. The absolute supremacy of "the right to privacy" inescapably reduces the value of life, for no one would argue that someone's right to privacy allows them to murder a six-year old in the seclusion of their own home. Since no one would argue that privacy trumps life, the target of absolutely legalized abortion must not be alive. Further, *Roe* asserted that privacy trumps the *potential* of life, and since it does not exclusively address abortions directed at forced or life-threatening pregnancies, it ultimately asserts that *convenience* trumps the potential of life. The mother's right to be free of the consequences of her actions takes absolutely priority over whatever the child would have done with his or her life. The consequences that flow from this judicial assertion, and the cultural influence of the immensely wealthy nationwide abortion industry it enabled, are profound and deep. Life, sex, and death are the only social forces more powerful than money. We are quick to denounce the unquenchable thirst for money as "greed," but silent in the face of a reckless hunger for sex and death.

In the Sixties, it became fashionable for people to say it's wrong to bring children into the terrible, spoiled world we inhabit. Those who oppose abortion on demand often say that each terminated pregnancy might have resulted in the next Michaelangelo, George Washington, or Jesus. The difference between those viewpoints is defined by faith in the possibility of excellence, and redemption, in each human life. One of the reasons I was eventually ready to identify myself as "pro-life" is that I think the world is better with more people in it. It's not that any newborn child might be the savior of mankind…it's that *all* of them are. If you think the world stinks, do something to make it better, and bring children into the world to help you. The good guys need reinforcements. The paralyzing fear of a dark future is a despicable, cowardly reason to deny the next generation their shot at making it brighter.

If we had the maturity, as a nation, to accept the burden of weighing freedom of choice against the right to life, we would strike down *Roe vs. Wade* and return the decision to the states. I have no doubt that many—perhaps even most—states would vote to keep abortion legal, many more would take action to restrict the availability of elective abortions, and a few would vote to outlaw the procedure completely. The people who passionately believe that abortion is murder would be free to move to states that have declared it illegal, where they would not be forced to watch as their tax money is used to support something they consider obscene. The people who desperately desire an abortion, and believe they have the right to make that choice, would face nothing worse than the inconvenience of traveling to a state where they can have the procedure. We are better off having a robust argument about abortion, than being mired in a bitter, vindictive squabble about whether we're allowed to argue.

Once upon a time, when I was an eighteen-year-old student, I made a young lady cry because she thought her faith in the sanctity of life was no match for my debating skills. Now it's twenty-five years later, and I can only hope that somehow, she reads this and realizes she won that debate, after all. Too many people who call themselves "pro-choice" view their objective as scoring victories against sanctimonious pro-lifers, and savoring their tears. The true losers in this debate did their weeping in private, after they realized something can be perfectly legal but horribly wrong...and sought to reverse a "mistake" that might have grown into someone beautiful, only to discover their second judgment was final, and would never grow into anyone at all.

The Essential Fusion
November 15, 2009

Ed Morrissey relayed an interesting quote from Democrat representative Carol Shea-Porter of New Hampshire earlier today:

> "I think when you can pay for insurance, you must," said Shea-Porter. "For those who are blessed to have insurance through their companies, they should keep it."

Those who are *blessed* to have insurance through their companies? You might have thought your health insurance was part of your compensation, following a pattern set by decades-old wage controls which obliged companies to offer benefit packages to attract skilled workers. According to Congresswoman Shea-Porter, that health insurance is actually a divine blessing, like having a good singing voice. By extension, this would mean the people who don't have insurance through their companies are *cursed.*

This is more than just a linguistic quirk. Democrats speak often of those who "win life's lottery," insinuating their wealth is not their hard-earned property, to which they have an absolute right. Instead, it's pennies from heaven, and we should spare no pity for those who would catch an umbrella full of those pennies and scurry off to indulge their greed, while others are left to suffer. Those who believe government has a duty to "spread the wealth around" find it essential to compromise the idea that wealth belongs to those who earn it. Ownership is the truth that must be buried before theft can put on its Sunday best and introduce itself as "redistribution."

Congresswoman Shea-Porter's remarks are just the latest in a series of incidents that remind me why I become restless when social and fiscal conservatives argue. The philosophy of conservatism cannot be adequately expressed without the fusion of its moral and economic arguments. I've spoken with a number of liberals who became conservatives, and they rarely cite the fiscal arguments of conservatism as the reason they switched. I would imagine people who become more liberal over time say the same thing. Neither side seems to win many converts with its pie charts.

A strictly financial argument for conservatism never makes much progress with the electorate, because liberalism is presented as an explicitly moral enterprise. This is one of the big reasons it is never held to account for its practical failures. Every liberal talks up the latest huge expansion of the government as if the year is 1909, rather than 2009, and the ideas he advocates haven't been proven disasters around the globe. Collectivist agriculture yields starvation, the trillion-dollar War on Poverty produces more poverty, political control of industries crashes those industries...and yet, it's always Day One of the great socialist experiment, and no one has ever hit on the brilliant idea of making the "rich" pay their "fair share" to fund a government crusade against want.

This increasingly stale series of fresh starts is not merely a cynical attempt to keep the population from challenging liberal ideas, by exploiting the case of historical amnesia it gained by slamming its collective head into the public school system. Confronted with the grim history of their ideology, most liberals will say it doesn't matter if their ideas are efficient, because there is a moral imperative to follow them, and all opposition to them is fundamentally immoral. It doesn't matter that liberalism doesn't work, because it's the right thing to do...the *only* right thing to do.

Consider the liberal reaction to the concept of the Laffer curve. To put it simply, the Laffer curve explains that high taxes produce less revenue for the government than expected, because people change their behavior to avoid the taxes...and many of these behavioral changes result in an overall weakening of the economy, reducing the size of the economic pie government is trying to cut itself a slice of. This is why both Kennedy and Reagan *increased* revenue to the Treasury by cutting taxes. Young liberals try to deny the objective reality of the Kennedy and Reagan tax cuts, and become very confused and upset when shown the hard data. Old liberals are smart enough not to argue with the data. They just say it doesn't matter, because steep progressive taxation is morally correct, and "tax cuts for the rich" are absolutely immoral—regardless of their net effect on government revenue.

One of the reasons liberals always sound so foolish when they discuss economics is their belief that moral certainty trumps objective knowledge. In his infamous encounter with Joe the Plumber, Barack Obama expressed it like this:

> It's not that I want to punish your success. I just want to make sure that everybody who is behind you, that they've got a chance at success, too...My attitude is that if the economy's good for folks from the bottom up, it's gonna be good for everybody. If you've got a plumbing business, you're gonna be better off...if you've got a whole bunch of customers who can afford to hire you, and right now everybody's so pinched that business is bad for everybody and I think when you spread the wealth around, it's good for everybody.

In other words, the lot of underemployed plumbers will improve when the government seizes a huge amount of money from the wealthy, keeps a large portion for itself, and distributes the remainder to poor people, some of whom will doubtless use their welfare money to hire plumbers. Keep this logic in mind the next time some fossilized liberal makes a crack about "trickle-down economics."

The part of the conservative movement broadly defined as "social" is essential to defeating the moral argument of the Left. Electoral victory requires persuading moderate and independent voters, and even some liberals who are still open-minded enough to give the other side a hearing. Such persuasion is impossible without a compelling moral argument, because conservatism does not seem coherent without it. Say what you will about the fundamental argument of collectivism, but you can't deny it's simple and consistent: give us your vote and we will take care of you, at the expense of people whose greed is worthy of your hatred.

The difficulty faced by a strictly fiscal expression of conservatism can be seen in way Republican health care proposals have difficulty gaining traction. The recent House Republican proposal was given a $61 billion price tag by the Congressional Budget Office—something like 6% of the cost for the Democrats' delirious $3 trillion fantasy. It's a fine expression of fiscal conservatism…but without the accompanying moral argument against socialized medicine, it won't amount to much beyond a group of well-meaning Republicans clearing their throats, tapping stacks of paper on their desks, and wondering why no one is paying attention to them.

The ideas of the Left are both ineffective and immoral. They are not strictly economic proposals. Economics affect society, an idea the Left currently understands much better than the Right. When the State achieves the massive size of our federal government—and has cocooned itself in preparation for the metamorphosis into something incalculably larger—the difference between fiscal and social policy evaporates. What is the point of claiming to be "fiscally conservative and socially liberal" when the State controls so much of your life, and asserts first claim on so much of your income…which is another way of saying it has first claim on the majority of your time?

I have always thought the embrace of liberty is the key ingredient to achieving the essential fusion between social and fiscal conservatism. I sympathize with most of the goals expressed by social conservatives. I don't believe they can achieve those goals by imposing them through the power of a massive central State, the way liberalism has done for decades. They should see that State as an offense against the moral imperative of liberty, and relish the challenge of fighting their battles locally, after regaining the freedom we never should have been foolish enough to surrender. Collectivism is premised on the absence of respect for fellow citizens—they must be compelled to follow the collective agenda, or cared for by the State because they're too feeble to survive without it. Both social and fiscal conservatism can meet on the common ground of liberty, which demands respect for fellow citizens. This does not require social conservatives to abandon the notion of community standards. Instead, it means they must respect the decision of those who disagree with those standards to change them… or relocate to a different community.

From liberty flows competition, of both businesses and ideas. Success in a competition of ideas requires persuasion, not compulsion. No one who is confident in the power of their ideas should fear the challenge of persuasion, just as no one who believes in the quality of their business fears the competition of the marketplace. Liberty is both powerful and moral. The embrace of liberty is something both halves of the Right can agree they are right about. I think current events prove it's a mistake to think liberty can survive the attack of collectivism—a powerful illusion with the inherent aggression of a nightmare—without both halves of the Right defending it.

Joy To The World
December 24, 2009

Author's Note: With this post on Hot Air, I announced the creation of my own website…and abandoned my anonymity. I never had any particular reason to write under a pseudonym. As mentioned in the Introduction to this book, I just wanted a cool user name when I registered to comment at Hot Air. I was still nervous about "going public" when the time came. Clicking the "Publish" button on this post felt like taking a deep breath and jumping into ice-cold water, much as it felt when I published my very first essay. I'm happy to report that only good things have come from writing under my own name. I received my first invitation to appear on the Rusty Humphries radio show within a few weeks of going public, and began preparing the book you now hold in your hands. I haven't felt depressed in a long time, but if I ever grapple with depression again, I would treat it by reading the wonderful and moving responses to this essay. You can't imagine how incredible it feels to read people expressing their gratitude for the simple gift of your name.

I'm not a practicing member of any congregation, but I've never entertained a single atheist thought. No aspect of creation has led me to doubt the existence of the Creator. I have never doubted that life endures beyond the final beat of a mortal heart. Faith and feeling lead me to hold these beliefs, but I hold them in concert with reason, not in defiance of it. I don't believe any part of creation was put here for us to ignore, or deny.

I don't like the way religious people are treated by our popular culture. A search for virtue and enlightenment that has been in progress for centuries is too often judged by the sins of its past, or the oppression it is found pre-emptively guilty of wishing to enforce. A secular State that has no qualms about legislating morality responds aggressively to those who speak of transcendence. Churches are measured against a grim shade of Torquemada, entirely invisible to the happy congregations inside. Questioning the fitness of religious believers to serve in democracy is as absurd as constructing a theocracy. Ideas should be evaluated on their strengths. Far from the stereotype of thoughtless Bible-thumping drones, religious men and women—from the Founding Fathers to today—have been ready to show the philosophical homework that led them to their moral conclusions.

People of the Jewish and Christian faiths are not the proprietors of our civilization, but it's grossly unfair to deny their pivotal role in shaping it. It is equally unfair to plow over the true meaning of Chanukah and Christmas, and erect a thousand-watt generic monument to "happy holidays" and the Winter Solstice above them. I have *never* understood the increasingly common modern neurosis of taking offense at a hearty cry of "Merry Christmas!" Christians offer this wish as a *gift,* not a commandment. This is their season of joy, the celebration of what they believe is the most important moment in history. Joy is a flame that grows higher with kindling. It is music that bursts with the eagerness to leap from heart to heart. It is not a sacrament to be hoarded only by believers.

Who can embrace the full meaning of the birth we celebrate in this season, without loving the sound of laughing children playing with new toys, or young voices raised in carols of sleigh bells, snow, and mistletoe? Those who don't believe in the divinity of Christmas Day have no reason to injure the faith of those who do...and the faithful have no reason to suffocate anything that spreads joy through the world, on this day we take as proof that Heaven loves us, and wants us to be happy. Even the most confident atheist can appreciate the nobility of a "fairy tale" that says the Author of creation wrote his own son into the story, in a chapter that would end with unspeakable pain...but turn the first page of a new book, describing a world of redemption and forgiveness. If you believe Christmas is a superstition, you can at least wish that all of humanity's superstitions were as beautiful.

Some people doubt the sanctity of Christmas because the date was moved around in ancient times, to align with pagan festivals. With the modern understanding of reality, I wonder how the date would be measured on Mars, which takes just under six hundred and eighty seven days to orbit the Sun...or in the ribbon of light that stretches between the sisters of a binary star...or at the event horizon of a singularity. The theory of relativity tells us that it's always Christmas *somewhere*. December the 25th is as good a day as any.

Tonight, on Christmas Eve, some of us will long for husbands and wives, fathers and mothers, brothers and sisters who serve in distant lands, and sleep beneath different constellations...but we can all share the radiant memory of a single star, that burns forever above both the humble and the wise. Distance, and even death, are banished in the calm of a silent night, and a joyous morning. Not all of the guests at our tables will be visible to the eye, but all can be felt equally in the heart. No one *requires* you to believe in anything, to cherish Christmas as a special day...but we can all share the courtesy, and honesty, of remembering *why* this day is so special, to so many. This is not a season for demands. It is for gifts, and invitations.

I have two gifts for everyone, both simple, but heartfelt. The first is that I've finally found the time to put together my own website, where I've re-posted everything I've written for Hot Air, and set up a way for people to contact me. It's rather plain right now, but I'll keep working on making it better, and maybe do some more interesting things with it in the future. The address is **http://www.doczero.org/**

My other gift is even more humble, but people have frequently asked for it. My name is John Hayward, and it has been...and will continue to be...my delight and honor to write for you.

Merry Christmas, everyone!

Victory Against Despair
January 23, 2010

Friday brought the annual March for Life to Washington, D.C. Held on the anniversary of *Roe vs. Wade*, it brings us the bittersweet comedy of watching the media studiously ignore a massive, peaceful protest in the nation's capitol, even on a slow news day. Imagine the coverage that would be afforded a fashionable leftist cause that brought a couple hundred thousand people together for 37 years, often on a workday. If you could find that many people still deluded enough to protest on behalf of the climate-change fraud, the weekend news programs would discuss little else.

When the media does pay attention to the March for Life, it typically describes the event as a dreary vigil held by a graying herd of humorless, elderly scolds. Look at any photo gallery of the 2010 event and decide for yourself if this is an accurate description. Consider also the remarkable Marist survey that shows six in ten young people believe abortion is morally wrong. Pro-lifers are not a dwindling band of tired foot soldiers decomposing at their posts. They're also not the doctrinaire zealots dismissed by Democrat Party propaganda and popular culture. They were both wise and gracious in their support of Scott Brown during his run for the Massachusetts Senate seat, even though he doesn't share all of their views. The pro-life movement understood that no face-saving deals with nervous House Democrats would prevent abortion funding from creeping into socialized medicine, sooner or later.

It's tempting to look upon the pro-life struggle as deadlocked trench warfare against a culture that values self-actualization above duty to the family, especially a family that doesn't exist yet. Strung above the trenches are the barbed wire of the abortion industry's financial interests, and the rusted political power of the radical feminist movement. The latter is much diminished from its peak in the pre-Clinton years, but still has disproportionate influence over media coverage, as can be seen from Newsweek's hit piece on the March for Life rally.

Perhaps it was inevitable that progress would come slowly for the pro-life movement, as every great moral struggle is waged on the battlefield of individual minds and hearts. I've always thought *Roe vs. Wade* was a terrible law, a poorly-reasoned attempt to end an important debate through raw judicial power. Americans could render this law irrelevant, without ever setting foot in a courtroom…by refusing to set foot in abortion clinics. *Roe vs. Wade* did not accurately express the moral sense of the nation, either in 1973 or today. No law can prevent us from asserting that moral sense through our free choices. I doubt America will ever make abortion completely illegal, particularly in terrible situations, such as pregnancies which threaten the life of the mother. We *can* understand that extending abortion to the horizons imposed by *Roe* didn't make it any less terrible.

The odds against convincing an increasingly self-absorbed culture to make sacrifices on behalf of unplanned children are formidable. It's interesting that our political class is comfortable demanding all sorts of *other* sacrifices from us, laid on the altar of our collective good under the guns of our huge, complex government. We are forever told that we must pay our "fair share" and accept the control of the State to achieve social justice...while absolute sexual liberty, including the inconsequential relationships promised through abortion on demand, are offered as a relief valve for the pressure of the State's demands. We're told to accept a sexual freedom that bypasses reason, in exchange for Constitutional freedoms which transcend the designs of government.

Those who gather in the March for Life each year are not daunted by the odds they face. Why should they be? Life *exists* in defiance of probability. Love is an act of faith, a leap from the lion's head over a chasm of past disappointments and future peril. If your faith does not come from religion, you might find it in statistics. The universe is filled with poison and vacuum. Everything that lives had to win a million coin tosses in a row. Measured against the vast and frigid sweep of existence, the odds that you would be sitting here, reading *this,* are absurdly small...and yet, here you are. We owe our children the same fighting chance to be miraculous.

Our busy, distracted, abundant lives give us many reasons not to make the incredible sacrifices necessary to bring an unplanned baby into the world. Every year, on January 22nd, thousands of voices fill the calculating air of Washington with *one* beautiful reason for young mothers-in-waiting to rise above their understandable loneliness and fear, and become incredible. Our bitter politics may never give us a chance to overturn *Roe vs. Wade,* but we can make it crumble to dust through faith in ourselves, and the future we can share with our children.

I have never wasted a single moment in anger at those who see their lives as a dark labyrinth that ends at the doors of an abortion clinic. I also won't count a single moment spent in reverence of those who climbed *over* the walls of that maze as wasted. I don't torment myself with the celestial question of exactly when life begins, because that's not the point. The alternative to the awful extremity of abortion is the indispensable joy of introducing this flawed world to someone who might make it better. The timetable of the procedure doesn't change the nature of the alternatives.

The birth of every child is a victory against despair. Over ten thousand children were born in the United States yesterday. We are winning.

The Power Of Women And Life
January 29, 2010

The National Organization for Women has protested the decision of CBS to allow a pro-life ad from Focus on the Family to air during the Super Bowl game. The ad features Heisman trophy winner Tim Tebow and his mother, Pam. Pam returned the kickoff of a life-threatening pregnancy to put Tim in the red zone for claiming that Heisman trophy. NOW has called on CBS to dump the ad, prompting Sarah Palin—currently the starting quarterback of the pro-life team, and a player with serious skin in the game—to respond with a characteristically bold forward pass from her Facebook pocket:

> What a ridiculous situation they're getting themselves into now with their protest of CBS airing a pro-life ad during the upcoming Super Bowl game. The ad will feature Heisman trophy winner Tim Tebow and his mom, and they'll speak to the sanctity of life and the beautiful potential within every innocent child as Mrs. Tebow acknowledges her choice to give Tim life, despite less than ideal circumstances. Messages like this empower women! This speaks to the strength and commitment and nurturing spirit within women. The message says everything positive and nothing negative about the power of women—and life. Evidently, some women's rights groups like NOW do not like that message.

NOW president Terry O'Neill says Palin is missing the point:

> The goal of the Focus on the Family ad is not to empower women. It's to create a climate in which Roe v. Wade can be overturned. There are always going to be women who need abortions. In this country, one in three women will have an abortion.

So, the point is that people who think Roe vs. Wade should be overturned lose their right to free speech? Does this principle apply to all Supreme Court decisions? If so, I guess we'd better get started on the Obama impeachment hearings, after the embarrassing disrespect he showed the Supreme Court during the State of the Union address.

It's nostalgic to read a press release from NOW again. The organization was last seen sinking into the bubbling tar of the Clinton impeachment saga, babbling incomprehensibly about how sexual harassment really isn't such a big deal when pro-abortion Democrat presidents do it. Like every appendage of the socialist state, NOW has no principle beyond fealty to the political party that grants it power, and the Democrats used to grant them a remarkable amount of power—enough to end the careers of Navy officers and combat pilots, after "investigations" that stopped just short of waterboarding. When NOW talks about "empowering" women, it speaks in the collective sense. Empowerment comes from obedience to feminist organizations, which use that power to drag an oversized chair up to the grim carving table where the Democrat Party wields its redistibutionist cleavers.

Some critics cite unquestioning support for unrestricted abortion rights as the primary demonstration of loyalty power feminists seek from their supporters, but the NOW offensive against the Tebow ad, and their response to Sarah Palin, suggest the true sacrament of radical feminism is not abortion…it's **opposition to the pro-life movement.** Power in a collectivist system comes from tribal loyalty, and hatred is a powerful glue for holding collectives together. As with leftist racial groups, NOW has very little positive to offer its supporters these days, so it thrives by pointing fingers at its enemies. Religious people in general, and outspoken pro-life advocates in particular, look very good on the business end of a trembling finger.

The Tebow ad will not call for the overturn of Roe vs. Wade. It's meant to be a heartfelt endorsement of life, from a mother who chose it against the recommendation of doctors, in the face of her own suffering and possible death. As Palin says:

NOW is looking at the pro-life issue backwards. Women should be reminded that they are strong enough and smart enough to make decisions that allow for career and educational opportunities while still giving their babies a chance at life. In my own home, my daughter Bristol has also been challenged by pro-abortion "women's rights" groups who don't agree with her decision to have her baby, nor do they like the abstinence message which she articulated as her personal commitment.

My own opposition to abortion-on-demand is not religious in nature. I believe there aren't enough people in the world. The decision to deny a human being his, or her, opportunity to enter the living world and make the *choices* that compose a lifetime should never be made lightly. For people of religious faith, the exercise of free will was a parting gift to creation from its Author. For the atheist, the expanding nova of human choice brings light and meaning into a universe of cold dust and searing plasma. Either way, life is precious, and it follows that those who follow Pam Tebow's path are worthy of respect. How can we render that respect, if we insist her choice was *absolutely* equivalent to terminating little Tim, right up to the moment when his head emerged from the birth canal?

We're nowhere near the repeal of *Roe vs. Wade*, a naked exercise of raw judicial power… which is apparently so fragile that a son thanking his mother for the gift of life could tear it to shreds. I wonder how many of the other iron laws supporting statism are actually written on tissue paper. If *Roe* were repealed, the question of abortion restrictions would return to the states, and people contemplating the examples of Sarah Palin, Bristol Palin, and Pam Tebow would gain the dangerous freedom to express their beliefs through smaller, more responsive governments. I can understand why NOW and its fellow travelers would be terrified of that possibility. It has nothing to do with "keeping abortion legal," for there is no chance Americans would ever vote to outlaw it completely, in every state. It has everything to do with siphoning power from the useful fantasy of a world that will never exist, and the ugly caricatures who tower above it with scourges and holy books.

A society reveals much of its character in the way it treats its women and children. Palin finds common cause with NOW in calling out "advertisers and networks for airing sexist and demeaning portrayals of women that lead to young women's diminished self-esteem and acceptance of roles as mere sexed-up objects." Abortion on demand has been very useful for preserving the self-esteem of men who desire casual sex without consequence. Perhaps those men would be less likely to view the women in their lives as *problems*, if they didn't know there was an easy *solution* right around the corner.

The Tebows are not planning to use their Super Bowl minutes for a sermon, or to impose their views on anyone. They only want their chance to testify that life, liberty, and the pursuit of happiness are not an equation that balances out to zero. The idea that such a statement is unacceptably political is further evidence that our lives have become too politicized, because too many decisions have been bumped to an upstairs office that doesn't even have a suggestion box.

NOW is mistaking a compelling narrative for compulsion. No organization that demands suppression of the other side's free speech is "pro-choice" in any sense of the words. Feminists are certainly free to produce their own Super Bowl ad, trumpeting the virtues of partial-birth abortion, or any other practice they don't think Pam and Tim Tebow support with suitable enthusiasm. Something tells me most people would *choose* to change the channel during that ad.

Challenge and Respect
February 3, 2010

A recent study, published in the *Archives of Pediatric & Adolescent Medicine*, found that a group of sixth- and seventh-graders exposed to abstinence-based sex education was significantly less likely to participate in sexual activity over the following two years, compared to a control group that did not receive such education. This is an intriguing development in the long, bitter war over sex education. It also has implications for the wider debate about the importance of *culture,* and whether it can be shaped to the benefit, or detriment, of both children and adults.

Conservatives take a lot of heat for expressing concerns about cultural matters. Some prefer to identify themselves clearly as "fiscal conservatives," advertising their unwillingness to engage on cultural matters. Much of the prejudice against religious conservatives stems from the generally accurate perception that they consider cultural issues important, and address them from the disciplined standpoint of religious faith.

There is a sense that cultural issues are a quagmire for conservatives, a pool of radioactive quicksand that resists all efforts at positive change, and repels vitally-needed independent allies. The Left's control of popular culture is presumed to be absolute—they spent forty years marching through film, literature, and academia, salting the earth behind them. There's no way to re-fight the old battles of past decades. Culture only moves forward and down, with today's *Jersey Shore* becoming tomorrow's *Brady Bunch.* Our grandchildren will laugh about the bygone days of the squaresville Two Thousands, when the worst thing that happened to women on reality shows was a sock in the jaw.

Those who accept this analysis should observe how much *effort* the Left puts into maintaining its cultural dominance, and controlling the education of children. Why do they pummel kids with so much "green" propaganda, if the tide has forever turned in their direction? The people who assure us we can't possibly teach kids the logical, sensible virtues of abstinence spend a *lot* of time programming them to believe in "climate change" without question. They're also rather desperate to keep our kids penned up in public schools, so they can be thoroughly seasoned by the gestalt and pepper shakers of the teachers' unions. From the panic over Tim Tebow's pro-life Super Bowl ad, to the relentless hatred of prominent figures like Sarah Palin, no organ of the Left behaves as if *they* believe their cultural victories to be eternal.

Culture is a fine clay, to be worked with sensitivity for the weaknesses of human nature...but also appreciation for our soaring aspirations, and our beautiful appetite for nobility and heroism. Even our most pampered and indulged children have an instinctive urge to excel. They find an environment in which nothing is *demanded* of them to be so enervating that it drives them mad. No young athlete dreams of playing for an outcome-based NFL or Major League Baseball where scores are not kept, and everyone is declared a winner, to avoid damage to their self-esteem. Kids become cynical in response to an adult world that worships their youth, but doesn't respect them enough to be honest with them.

Small bits of pop culture are harmless amusements, but large doses of it pack an emotional wallop. Pick up a CD from a hard-core rap or death metal group, check out the cover art, and give the disk a spin. No big deal, right? Now imagine yourself listening to nothing but that type of music, day after day, and remodeling your room to resemble the album cover. It would *change* you. I'm personally fond of horror stories and films, but if I read and watched nothing else, and invited Pinhead over to give my house an Extreme *Hellraiser* Makeover, it would certainly produce a noticeable drop in my normal levels of sunny optimism. We live in an atmosphere charged with terabytes of sound and graphics...a level of radiation that inevitably produces mutations.

We should also understand how much power the government has to change us. As Mark Steyn puts it, "a determined state can change the character of a people in the space of a generation or two." One of the unfortunate conceits of the modern age is the belief that we can unleash gigantic social programs on people without reprogramming them. The architects of the modern progressive state, feverishly scribbling cookbooks for the preparation of a new mankind in the early twentieth century, certainly believed a powerful government could re-shape its people. The salesmen of the New Deal and Great Society understandably chose not to make that a bullet point in their advertising to the common man.

Conservatives *must* involve themselves in popular culture, particularly with respect to young people...because otherwise, we're trying to win a debate with the Left on points, before an audience that is rapidly forgetting how to keep score. It's tough to persuade a nation when you no longer speak its cultural language. The challenge is not merely to criticize, but to offer something *better.*

The success of the abstinence program reported in *The Archives of Pediatric & Adolescent Medicine* is an encouraging example. I wonder how many of the kids in that program responded to it because they appreciated being given something to *aspire* to, instead of one more weary load of training to manage the damage from surrendering to their worst instincts. Our young people have shown a remarkable tenacity in the face of a sedative culture. You can find plenty of evidence—from the graduating classes of universities to the battlefield valor on display in Afghanistan and Iraq—that the transformation of American society is far from complete, or irreversible.

There is a growing appetite for the wisdom and traditions we conservatives are working to conserve. Our children should expect more than a life of standing in line for their ration of a rapidly dwindling economic pie, or tending the dying embers of a civilization that made itself forget how to **burn**. We can begin by teaching them how love is an act of faith, loyalty is an act of courage, and passion mixes with fidelity to become immortality. We honor ourselves by showing respect to others. The boys and girls in those abstinence classes aren't being given easy answers to the problems of adolescence, but they're receiving the respect of honorable men and women. It's said that asking kids to embrace abstinence is "unrealistic." The future needs people who view unrealistic expectations as a challenge, rather than a eulogy.

A Prayer From the Living World
February 26, 2010

*Author's Note: Arthur Conan Doyle once said that if he was only remembered for writing about Sherlock Holmes, he would consider his career a failure. If I am only remembered for writing **this**, I will consider my career a success. I've received a number of requests from church groups for permission to reprint it, which I have happily granted. I'm not so arrogant as to think I can talk people out of committing suicide…but maybe I can slow them down a little, and that might be enough. Death is always in such a damnable hurry.*

The body of actor Andrew Koenig was found in Vancouver's Stanley Park yesterday. His father, Walter Koenig, said that his son "took his own life, and was in a lot of pain." Like most of my generation, I grew up with Walter Koenig as Chekhov on *Star Trek,* and he played a superb villain much later, on *Babylon 5.* Until his press conference yesterday, I didn't realize he was a man of such incredible strength and dignity. He asked for his family to be left in peace to mourn their loss. I hope he won't mind if I take this sad occasion to address others who might be following the road that ended in Stanley Park for Andrew. No matter how far you have gone down that road, there is *always* a path that leads away. I could offer no greater tribute to Andrew and his family than trying to help you take it, or at least see it.

You won't find the beginning of that path in your house, or your room, or any other private place where you torment yourself, and wonder why a world you're hiding from can no longer see *you*. You'll have to step outside, and take a walk through your town. You'll pass hospitals where the gift of life is unwrapped and presented to the universe. In another wing, life is held as precious treasure by families gathered around quiet beds, surrounded by tireless machines and their tired, but determined, keepers. Perhaps you'll find a hospice, where the dying embrace their last opportunity to share their lives with all who receive the blessing of a seat beside them. You'll pass churches and temples, filled with the sworn enemies of despair.

You may find yourself wishing you could give the unwanted years of your future to the clients of those hospitals and hospices. I did, years ago, when I stood where you are standing now. I was on my knees at the time, offering that trade with all my heart. It doesn't work that way. Those who tend the hospices can tell you why, and the people in the churches and temples can explain why it shouldn't.

Stroll past your local police station, where the noble calling to risk your life in the service of others is answered…and the worship of death as a solution to problems meets its humiliating end. Maybe you'll spot a recruiting station, where men and women who love their friends and families accept a duty that could take them away forever…because they know others love their families too, and there is no *safe* way to build and protect the future for them.

If your walk takes you past sunset, watch the cars rolling into the driveways of apartments and houses. If you walk from night into morning, watch the people reluctantly leaving their homes, to provide for their families. Those people are not wasting their lives, but fulfilling them. They return home to enjoy their reward, and renew their inspiration. Every day, they write new pages in the human story. None of us will see the end of that tale…but I know you share my appetite to read another chapter, and then one more after that. You may have convinced yourself to ignore it, but it's still there.

Step into a convenience store for a cup of coffee or chocolate, and take a look at the newspapers. They are filled with pleas for help that *you* could answer. From the inner cities of America, to the broken streets of Haiti, and around the world, there are places where the clocks are filled with nothing but desperate hours. Another pair of hands, or another few dollars of support, are always needed. The years ahead, which you regard as a painful burden, *can* be given to them. It will take effort, and courage…but along the way, I can promise that your life would stop feeling like a burden.

You may view suicide as your last chance to shake the pillars of a world that has turned its back on you. The world doesn't need any more shaking. If you've been telling yourself that no one will miss you when you're gone, you are wrong. Your suicide would tear a hole through the future, and *nothing* could ever fill the space where you used to be. You might think you're alone, but you don't have to walk more than a couple of miles from your house to see a building full of people who would be delighted to meet you. There are places like Suicide Hotlines, staffed by men and women who have spent their entire lives preparing to hear the sound of your voice, and greet every day hoping to learn your name.

You may be afraid to face the years ahead. You're not the only one, and if you extinguish the light of your faith and wisdom, you consign others to darkness. You might see death by your own hand as the end of unbearable pain…but I ask you to think about Walter Koenig, facing a wall of cameras with quiet grace in the hours after finding his son's body, and understand that it's only the **beginning** of agony.

You might have decided your fellow men are rotten to the core, and you're weary of their company. Listen to the music of Mozart, or look upon the work of Michelangelo, and consider the argument of those who profoundly disagree. Maybe part of your problem is that you've been listening to the wrong music, or looking at the wrong pictures. Dark waters are easy to drown in. The judgment of the human race will not lack witnesses for the defense, and they will make their case to *you*, if you give them a chance.

Now, take the last few steps back to your home, and set aside one sorrow or terror with every footfall, until your mind is clear. If you're thinking of incinerating the remaining years of your life, surely you can spare a few minutes for quiet reflection, and hear this prayer from the living world:

Please don't leave us. We need you.

It is a quiet prayer, spoken in a soft voice, but it's *never* too late to listen.

Part Four
Freedom

We are lions, and the free people of the world are our pride.

The Fragile Flame of Freedom
June 4, 2009

That does not lessen my commitment, however, to governments that reflect the will of the people. Each nation gives life to this principle in its own way, grounded in the traditions of its own people. America does not presume to know what is best for everyone, just as we would not presume to pick the outcome of a peaceful election. But I do have an unyielding belief that all people yearn for certain things: the ability to speak your mind and have a say in how you are governed; confidence in the rule of law and the equal administration of justice; government that is transparent and doesn't steal from the people; the freedom to live as you choose. Those are not just American ideas, they are human rights, and that is why we will support them everywhere.—From Barack Obama's Cairo speech, June 04, 2009

President Obama's speech had some good moments, but the tone of the above paragraph reflects some dangerous delusions about the nature of freedom, and America's role in promoting freedom around the world. He spent far too much time equivocating and apologizing, in an address to people who should be sitting at our feet as students, not addressed as fellow professors in the faculty lounge. The proper tone doesn't have to be rude, but it does have to be confident. If Obama was this timid about his beliefs when he was a teacher, then he was a rotten teacher. No one learns a lesson presented as an interesting suggestion.

The President labors under a delusion common to latter-day American politicians: that freedom is an irresistible, unbreakable tide flowing forward through human history. His predecessor suffered from this illusion as well, as George W. Bush once declared, "Freedom is the direction of history, because freedom is the permanent hope of humanity."

No, it isn't.

Freedom is all the more precious and valuable because it is a fragile flame. We like to tell ourselves that everyone around the world is yearning for American levels of political, economic, and cultural freedom, and only brutal dictators with thugs and secret police prevent them from realizing this dream. We often meditate on Ben Franklin's famous assertion that "those who can give up essential liberty to obtain a little temporary safety deserve neither liberty nor safety," in the belief that no one who considers Franklin's wisdom could possibly conclude that trading liberty for safety is a good idea.

I can show you a lot of recent public opinion polls that would demonstrate most *Americans* don't reject the idea of making that trade out of hand, never mind the rest of the world. People long ago lost their reverence for the ideal of freedom, and became increasingly willing to trade liberties they regard as abstract notions, for concrete benefits. If you ask modern-day Americans whether they would trade the freedom to choose between different styles of automobile for a miserable, Soviet-style government-designed car with hardware that limits how far it can be driven each week, provided "free" by leveling confiscatory taxes against the evil rich and their foreign car purchases, don't be surprised if you get a frightening number of takers. The guiding purpose of the Obama Administration is the belief that dusty old liberties can be pawned for material benefits.

The sad truth is that most people around the world wear chains, and they are not entirely forged from bullets and barbed wire. The history of successful revolts against tyranny is not brimming with success stories. If the people of Cuba "yearn for government that is transparent and doesn't steal from the people," they have spent the last fifty years doing this yearning in stony silence, except for the brave souls who speak out and end up in Castro's dungeons. They've sat quietly by as the reins of their kleptocratic dictatorship are handed off to Casto's brother, who displays no signs of being a democratic reformer. Of course the Cubans are afraid of the heavily armed thugs Castro calls "soldiers," but they were afraid of the Batista thugs, too. If they all rose up and spoke with one voice, the regime could not silence or kill them all. The same is true of the Middle East, where the precarious freedom of Iraq and Afghanistan was won through the matchless skill and courage of American fighting men and women, after decades of brutal tyranny. Neither Saddam Hussein, nor the Taliban, were going anywhere until the United States military sent them howling down to hell, and the job will not be finished with the Taliban unless America finishes it.

Most of the people on Earth live under the dominion of small, savage ruling cliques, who are vastly outnumbered by their oppressed subjects. It will remain so until America fully remembers, and accepts, its position as the champion of freedom…not just religious freedom, which Obama returned to half a dozen times in his speech in Cairo, and seemed to be the only brand of liberty he was interested in talking about. Religious freedom does not long survive in the absence of other liberties. Show me a dictatorship, and I'll show you an underground church movement that lives in fear of raids by the secret police. Freedom is a comprehensive ideal, whose power is easily diluted by fear, greed, or the desire to satisfy smoldering hatreds. Once a people begin listing the freedoms they're willing to trade away for security or ideological purity, the list inevitably begins growing longer. After you've been shamed or frightened into trading away your property or speech rights, it won't be long before the total state decides it doesn't have much respect for your right to worship, either—especially when your religious beliefs keep coming into conflict with the government's objectives.

We do the Muslim world no favors by qualifying our support for liberty and equality. When Obama says that "America does not presume to know what is best for everyone," he pretends to a false humility that clouds the severity of radical Islam's deficiencies. We *do* know some things that are best for everyone. Here's one: **stop murdering people because you**

think your religion demands it. Here's another: no leader is legitimate, except one chosen by all of his people, and bound by laws that require him to respect their rights to life, liberty, and the pursuit of happiness. We've known these things for two hundred and thirty years. We aren't performing any service for the rest of humanity by pretending they're just interesting theories we're still experimenting with, or that we're interested in hearing a totalitarian culture's alternatives to them.

If you're planning on attending a Fourth of July Tea Party, you might contemplate the circumstances of the original Boston Tea Party, in which the principles of freedom led our forefathers to embark on a path that led to a desperate struggle against the most powerful nation in the world...because of a tax that quite a few Americans did not find unbearable. *That* is how you defend freedom: entirely and unapologetically, because tyranny is intolerable long before it becomes unbearable. Ronald Reagan, a far better and wiser president than Barack Obama, knew that "freedom is never more than one generation away from extinction." Freedom is fragile, so its champions must be strong. Americans are not a helpless endangered species, apologizing for any inconvenience we might cause the world's dictators before we die off. **We are lions**, and the free people of the world are our pride. The one thing President Obama unquestionably has in common with the leaders of the "Muslim world" is that his long-term goals depend on preventing the American people from remembering that.

What the President Should Have Said In Cairo
June 7, 2009

*Author's Note: This is a companion piece to the preceding essay, written after President Obama gave a tepid speech about Islamic terrorism in Cairo. I knew perfectly well that he wouldn't have said any of the things which follow. This is how I think the speech in Cairo **should** have gone. I liked the first sentence of the President's actual address, so I kept that.*

I am honored to be in the timeless city of Cairo, and grateful for your hospitality. I will honor you in return by addressing you directly. I came here to speak to *you*, not to European leaders or American media commentators. I hope you will forgive my frankness, but we have much to talk about, and some of what I came here to say will not be easy for you to hear.

I will not waste your time by carefully selecting quotes from the Koran, in a misguided attempt to tell you what your religion means. I am here to tell you what membership in the community of civilized nations means. Your faith is your own affair, but it ends where the rest of our lives begin. It is fashionable among the Western elites to say that we have much to learn about the Muslim world, but the truth is precisely the reverse. One of the bedrock principles of Western democracy is that we don't need to understand, or even like, a particular religion in order to respect its faithful and their rights. There are some things the West is long overdue in teaching its Muslim neighbors, however. Let us begin with dismissing the notion of a "Muslim world." There is no such thing. There is *one* world, made increasingly intimate by the easy movement of people, resources, and ideas. We are all in the process of learning how to live with our fellow men, and while the West is far from perfect, we are much further ahead in our studies than the nations of the Middle East. Our security, and yours, will be greatly enhanced if we can lend you some of the wisdom we have accumulated.

We did not come by this wisdom easily. We learned by taking incredible risks…and making terrible mistakes…magnified by the power of Western military tradition and technology. The people of the Middle East have never known anything to compare with the industrialized slaughter of the two World Wars, in which millions of lives were lost to decisively settle the question of what makes a government just and legitimate. You have never watched five thousand of your sons die on a single day, to secure a beachhead against the forces of genocidal fascism—a battle we commemorate on the sixth of June every year. Your fighting men have not faced anything like the battle for Okinawa, where American Marines faced an eighty percent chance of death—and did not waver. You have not sacrificed half a million soldiers to destroy the evil of slavery, as America did during its Civil War. You have

214

not spent blood and treasure around the world to save other nations from the savage darkness of communism. You have no leaders to equal the Founding Fathers who pledged their lives, and sacred honor, to win America's independence from imperial domination.

You have not burned and bled for freedom, as we have. We would spare you that pain, if we could. We are willing to burn and bleed for *you*—and we have been doing so, for eight long years. Instead of indulging in foolish paranoid fantasies about crusaders and oppression from America, open your eyes and look to the mountains of Afghanistan, where over a thousand Coalition troops have died to overthrow the Taliban, after their despicable complicity in the murders of September 11, 2001. We did not have to send those troops into harm's way, to avenge the slaughter at the World Trade Center. We could have eliminated all life in that region, in a matter of hours. If we followed the standards of our enemies, we would have. We sent our best and bravest into battle because of who we wished to spare, not who we wanted to kill.

Open your eyes and look to Iraq, where we allowed thousands of Iraqi troops to lay down their arms and go home, instead of killing them where they stood. We paid an awful price for this act of mercy, as many of those men went on to join the brutal terrorists who dreamed of keeping the Iraqi people enslaved. Some in America and Europe find it politically expedient to draw moral equivalency between American soldiers and the terrorists they fight. I ask you to show me the al-Qaeda "equivalent" of Private First Class Ross McGinnis, who climbed down *into* an armored vehicle and smothered a grenade to protect his crew, when he could easily have leaped from his gunnery hatch to safety. Show me an "insurgent" who can match the valor of Sergeant First Class Paul Ray Smith, who flung himself into an impossible battle against odds of a hundred to one...to save the lives of a hundred wounded men. These two soldiers are among those who have won the Congressional Medal of Honor for their sacrifices in Operation Iraqi Freedom. *No one* on the other side is worthy of such an honor. I say this to you because keeping silent—whether from misguided modesty, self-loathing, or the desire to avoid offending your vanity—is an insult to *your* honor, and an injury to your future.

We have made a fetish of "tolerance" in America, and it has curdled into poison. I am here to tell you what the civilized world is no longer prepared to tolerate. We will not stand silently by while women are enslaved, brutalized, or murdered. We will no longer hypnotize ourselves with self-criticism over gay rights, while you bury gay men and women under piles of jagged stone. We will not swallow our tongues for fear of offending Islam, when Islam oppresses all other religious beliefs within its borders. We know you can do better. We also know that nothing will improve unless we *demand* you do better...and we **do** demand it. The world has turned, and the old days of totalitarianism and pillage are done. There is no more place in it for barbarians. Believe what you will, follow your customs, honor the holy writings of your Prophet, and strive to understand God's will through prayer, music, and scholarship. You will find nothing but honest respect and admiration from the West. But when you stand among civilized people, you will *be* civilized people. When you are shown respect, you will answer with respect. As the West reveres and protects the life of your innocents, so you will revere ours.

I speak to you as the democratically-elected leader of a great republic, which has earned the right to walk tall and proud through the halls of history. It is a right earned on battle-fields...but also at humanitarian relief camps, pharmaceutical laboratories, civil-rights march-es, and field hospitals. It is a right earned by rebuilding shattered enemies after terrible wars, by tearing down the statues of tyrants and building schools for the children of their liberated victims. Ours is a hard-won glory that can be seen in six men raising a flag on Mount Surib-achi, or one man planting that flag in the dust of the moon...or millions of men and women stepping into voting booths. Look at the free people of Iraq, with their fingers proudly cov-ered in purple ink after they vote, and know that America is eternally eager to share her glory. Indeed, we believe we can only render it proper honors by sharing it with all of our brothers and sisters around the world. But also remember this: the Middle East stands at a crossroads, and the heavy responsibility of reconciling faith, tradition, and the demands of the modern world rests with you. You must choose between old hatreds and new possibilities. You must choose between murder and prosperity. I have come here today to tell you clearly, and without reservation, that you cannot have both. May the next leader chosen by the American people stand in my place someday, to congratulate you on a wise choice.

The Vulnerability Of Black Men In America
July 24, 2009

Author's Note: Henry Louis Gates is the Harvard professor who made national news after he was arrested trying to break into his own home. Cambridge police officer James Crowley charged Gates with disorderly conduct. Gates had connections with the President, who declared the police had acted "stupidly." Professor Gates is black, while Sergeant Crowley is white, so the incident became part of the national passion play over "racial profiling." It could more accurately be used as a teachable moment about the perils of acting like a pompous jerk to the police, and it led me to a conclusion about the role of capitalism in defeating racism, discussed at greater length in essays you will find later in this volume.

On the subject of his now-infamous arrest, Henry Gates said, "This isn't about me; this is about the vulnerability of black men in America." We are saddled with entirely too many arrogant people who think of themselves as icons, their lives needing only a sprinkle of controversy and media attention to blossom into historical moments. If this incident turns out to be "about" anything more than a rude man being treated rudely by a cop, it would be about the lack of responsibility and humility in our floundering President. Maybe the President's unseemly haste to turn a legal matter he admitted to knowing nothing about into a major racial incident, along with an offhanded insult to the intelligence of police officers, will turn into a "teachable moment" for black voters, and make them less vulnerable to voting for shadowy con artists because of their skin color.

One thing black men are definitely vulnerable to is violent crime. Blacks represent about 14% of the general population, but they make up nearly half of murder victims. For decades, they have been thirty to forty percent more likely to suffer from violent crime than the general population. You will notice that white liberals are much more enthusiastic about springing black criminals from their "disproportionate levels of incarceration" than the law-abiding black citizens who must deal with them, once they've ditched their orange jump-suits. The best things society could do to help innocent black men avoid being robbed and murdered are providing enhanced access to lawful, registered firearms for self-defense, more aggressive prosecution of the criminal element, and more police protection. Professor Gates is not doing black men any favors on the latter count, and I doubt they can expect much help from President Obama on the first two, even if he can get through the rest of his term without calling the police "stupid" on national television.

Another thing black men are vulnerable to is unemployment. The black male unemployment rate runs about 5% higher than the national average. According to this report, it stood at 15.4% as of June. Some of this high unemployment rate seems likely to come from the high concentration of black workers in urban areas, which tend to be hit hard by recessions. Another factor could be the relatively low median age of black males, which is about six years younger than the national average—putting a high number of black workers in the sort of entry-level jobs that evaporate most quickly in a recessionary climate. The political party that enjoys over 90% support from black voters is currently pushing a cap-and-trade energy bill that would cause a recession lasting decades. I would suggest that black men who wish to improve their economic fortunes consider a change of voting habits.

A major factor in high black unemployment rates is their high vulnerability to receiving horrible educations from the public school system. The greatest obstacle faced by black parents who want to secure a better education for their children is Barack Hussein Obama, who wasted no time killing a successful school voucher program in Washington D.C. The Democrat Party stands ready to fight school choice to the death, thanks to the dominant influence of the teachers' unions. Perhaps some concerned black voters will catch a Democrat some day, while he's picking up his children from their expensive private school, and ask him what it would take to get him to stop blocking school choice for his loyal constituents.

One other thing black men are vulnerable to is racism. White racism, the obsession with white racism, and black racism are all toxins that can damage their chances for success. Blacks are not well-served by the sort of racial paranoia stoked by the Gates incident, or Obama's high-profile reaction to it. They are also injured by serious white racism, of course. There is only one tonic that can reliably dispel every form of racial hatred, without injuring the liberty of any citizen, of any race: *commerce*. The first steps in achieving black equality may have been necessarily political, but the last dregs of racism can only be drained away by men and women united in common effort for mutual gain. Irrational hatred can never survive familiarity…. it lives only in the abstract, in the darker halls of the mind, where it can feed on illusions and memories. Every day in America, someone begins working side-by-side with a partner of the "wrong" color, and forgets how to hate him.

Commerce cannot completely purify the human heart…but it doesn't have to. The heart only needs to be softened a bit, just enough to let people offer each other a chance for success, or have the wisdom to accept the offer. In the unity of our quest for prosperity, we learn how wasteful violence and ignorance are. No government program or draconian law can ever duplicate the cleansing power of the bond that forms between two people, when one of them needs something built, and the other one has a hammer. No decent person of *any* color would sacrifice the welfare of his family to indulge foolish hatreds.

Black men are vulnerable to a politics of government control and withered liberty, whose final insult is that it destroys the economic vigor that has the power to make racism irrelevant. Based on what we have learned about the background of Police Sergeant James

Crowley, who has taught classes in how to avoid racial profiling, and fought to save dying black basketball star Reggie Lewis from his fatal heart attack in 1993, it seems he could teach this lesson to Professor Henry Gates...if the professor had the wisdom and humility to listen.

Clarity In The Defense Of Freedom
June 21, 2009

Author's Note: This was written after the murder of Neda Soltan, the young woman gunned down in the streets while attending a protest against the rigged election that kept Mahmoud Amadinejad in power. The line about "hundred and forty word Tweets" is a reference to Twitter, the social network that restricts users to short messages, which became an important means for the Iranian democracy movement to stay in communication with the outside world.

Once again, people are dying for freedom. Some have pointed out it's a somewhat threadbare freedom, a revolution that began because one mullah-approved, America-hating politician with a shady past was robbed by the other mullah-approved, America-hating politician with a shady past. Foreign-policy realists remind us the Iranian people have, as a group, been violently anti-American for decades, and they wouldn't have transformed into allies just because Mousavi managed to win a recount over Amadinejad.

The stakes are higher than that, now. The entire oppressive theocratic regime is tottering, and it will only be able to shore up its foundations with a mountain of bones. People have rarely been able to achieve freedom without bloodshed, because tyranny is death—its willingness to kill is the only way it can keep its captive populations in line. We in the West are not always honest with ourselves about how well that usually works for the tyrants. The cudgel for those speak out of turn, the lash for those who try to escape, a bullet for those who resist…it's a brutal formula practiced for ages, around the world, because it's effective. Modern technology gave oppressed peoples more ways to organize, and plead their case to the outside world—but it also gave the tyrants more efficient ways to murder them, when they have satisfied themselves the outside world will do nothing. Hundred and forty word Tweets turn cold and silent when a fifty-ton main battle tank rolls into view. The Tweets are only powerful when someone listens, and answers. Otherwise, the tank will always have the last word.

We don't have to like the Iranian people as a whole, or the government they might erect to replace the mullahs, to respect and support their struggle for freedom. America's sacred duty is the defense and promotion of liberty, and we do this because it's right and just, not because it will create useful allies. Let this bloody day stand as an enduring lesson that free men must **never** stand silent in the face of oppression, no matter what geopolitical tacticians might say about carefully calibrated messages and surgically precise displays of indifference. It didn't take long for the Iranian regime to blame the strangely subdued Obama Administration for manufacturing the uprising, as part of their justification for suppressing it. This should surprise no one. Why are we always crediting totalitarian dictators with some modicum of honesty and fair play, when they never display any of those traits? Why do we elect people who stand there with expressions of dumb shock on their ice-cream stained faces, when their carefully crafted non-statements of non-interference and "deep concern" dissolve in a hail of bullets, acid, and fire…followed by dictators pointing accusing fingers at their exquisitely disengaged and non-committal selves? The thugs who rule Iran were going to blame the Great Satan for this crisis anyway, as anyone with an ounce of common sense knew all along. The president should have raised his voice and earned the blame. As it stands, an army of anonymous posters on Twitter have done more to befriend and support the Iranian people than the American government.

Biting our tongues and looking the other way while captive populations are brutalized never gets us any of the benefits our highly nuanced foreign policy elite promise. It only earns us the scorn of struggling peoples, and makes us vulnerable to the charge of hypocrisy. Obama's pathetic attempts at self-justification to the contrary, no one in the Revolutionary Guard is going to take their fingers off a trigger because they suddenly remember Obama's milquetoast Cairo speech, and decide they can't be killers in a world where the American president vowed to defend the rights of Muslim women to wear the hijab.

The president's statement today said that "we are bearing witness" to the Iranian people's belief in justice, "and we will continue to bear witness." **No.** The task history has given to the American president is not "bearing witness" to the brutalization of innocent people, the way her neighbors "bore witness" to the murder of Kitty Genovese. Our task is to speak out, call evil by its true name, and let all the world know exactly where we stand. Our government should have done that days ago, weeks ago. Whether they win or lose, the survivors of the Iranian uprising will remember that dozens of their friends and family were dead by the time Obama got around to clucking his tongue at the regime that murdered them.

Thomas Jefferson warned early Americans against "entangling alliances." Now we have a president who tries to preserve his entangling alliances by hoping the rest of the world will forget he's an American. We have a United Nations Security Council to handle sending out weak and ineffective letters of "grave concern" for us. **Our** duty is to speak with passion and clarity in the defense of freedom. We may be forced to deal diplomatically with torturers hiding behind chests full of "decorations" they awarded themselves, or gutter trash thugs robed as divine lawgivers, but they should never look into an American leader's eyes and see anything except barely controlled distaste. No one on Earth should have cause to spend one instant wondering where America comes down in a battle between brutal dictators and those who courageously resist them. No American should have cause to spend one instant wondering where their President comes down, either.

The Ethics of Ferocity
August 25, 2009

The Obama Administration has decided to drag CIA interrogators and Bush Administration officials into court, where they will be persecuted for their role in defending America from terrorist attacks. Apparently Obama and his accomplices decided to distract their liberal base from the fiery *Hindenburg* crash of socialized medicine, by offering them a relaxing cruise on the *Titanic* of leftist foreign policy. As with everything else the current Administration does, it's a remarkably foolish move: dangerous for America, and self-destructive as a strategy.

I don't have much patience or understanding for people who play games with national security for political benefit, so let me dismiss the political strategy of this outrage by saying it once again demonstrates the danger of believing your own political spin, and taking the lovestruck panting of a sycophantic media seriously. Real Americans are not anxious to punish the people who shut down al-Qaeda's domestic operations. While liberals wave the Justice Department's report on CIA interrogation techniques at the rest of the world and tearfully beg them for forgiveness, the rest of us are wondering why we don't reduce the deficit by selling the rights to these interrogations on pay-per-view. The contestants on your average Japanese game show go through more intense ordeals.

Obama should understand that he was elected *in spite of* his childish posturing as a messiah and redeemer, not because of them. A weary public allowed itself to be badgered into electing the first black president, after they ran out of patience waiting for John McCain to explain why they shouldn't. Normal people don't define their relationship with the government by taking pleasure in the humiliation of political figures they dislike. We're six months past the point where American voters can be kept quiet by suffocating them with the pillow of Bush hatred. We're about a month past the point where anyone capable of independent thought believes Obama is a better president than Bush was.

Political strategy aside, America needs to resolve its argument about the morality of self-defense, and quickly. It's my contention that a peaceful democracy has a moral imperative to demonstrate ferocity in defense.

Because we are not an aggressive, conquering nation, we don't seek to subjugate the world and eliminate opposition. This means we will always be playing defense. One of the most dangerous delusions of the Left is the idea that we might be able to create a civilization that has no enemies. Civilization *always* has its enemies. Liberals should understand that, since they draw their own political strength from the unhappy remnant that always feels cheated by free-market capitalism, no matter how prosperous it might become. Even the most peaceful and compassionate nation will always be at risk from savages who wish to drown it in blood.

Anyone who has studied any form of self-defense knows the danger of hesitation. Effective defense requires swift and decisive action. When a fist is flying at your face, you don't have time to flip through your mental catalog of Jet Li movies and pick a cool counter-move. Hesitation can defeat even superior strength and technical skill. The most powerful weapon in the world is useless as long as it remains in its holster...and it provides no deterrence value if your assailant *knows* it will remain there.

To suggest that enduring six months of Obama has made the CIA more hesitant to conduct effective intelligence operations is an understatement. Democrat political double-dealing is a crime that strikes at the heart of our venerated belief in civilian command of the military. We respect this arrangement, in part, because we believe it is proper for the civilian government to exhaust all peaceful, diplomatic avenues before we commit to war. You don't send Marine recon units to conduct subtle diplomacy. The Bush Administration did its duty in this regard—for all the liberal caterwauling about "Bush's rush to war," it took a hell of a lot longer than Barack Obama's rush to nationalize the health insurance industry and triple the deficit.

The other side of this arrangement must also be honored: we must allow the military to act with decisive speed, working within clearly defined rules of engagement. The military requires, and deserves, the assurance that they will not be used as political pawns by the civilian authorities. This is the duty a peaceful nation owes to the men and women who risk their lives, and make countless personal sacrifices, to ensure our safety. It is also logical, because the safety of American civilians, along with the hope for minimal collateral damage to foreign populations, depends on giving our defenders the confidence to take swift and decisive action. We know from experience that modern America does not have the political and cultural endurance to fight protracted wars—and, frankly, protracted wars stink. If war is forced upon us, it's better for everyone involved if we make quick work of the enemy.

The Left has demonstrated a willing eagerness to sap American endurance in times of war, again and again. The antiwar movement is a fusion of many agendas, including domestic political hatred of the sitting President, and outright sympathy with the enemy. There is little that can be said to these elements of the Left...but to those who sincerely oppose extended military action on humanitarian grounds, I would say it is deeply immoral to apply political sanctions and legal penalties to the very people who have the best chance of ending a war quickly, or preventing enemy attacks from claiming innocent lives. Nothing will prompt a determined enemy to attack faster than the belief his target is paralyzed with uncertainty. Nothing will break the will of a terrorist organization faster than capturing or killing its command structure, and that requires timely intelligence. There is exactly one way to obtain that intelligence, and you can read all about it, in the Justice Department report on CIA interrogations. The options to wish determined enemies away, hug them into submission, or instantly penetrate their command structure with double-oh super-spies are not on the table. The option of surrender is *underneath* the table, and a few hundred million patriotic Americans will stomp on your damned fingers, if you try reaching for it.

If a group of people took your family hostage, and one of their associates fell into your hands, you would do *anything* to extract the location of your family from him. **So would Barack Obama**, and Eric Holder, and every Democrat who ever sullied the halls of Congress by referring to American soldiers as Nazis. President Obama would not dither about the finer points of a criminal's hypothetical "rights" while the man's accomplices were taking power tools to Michelle and the kids. Anyone who would is a lunatic…and I don't want to leave the security of our country in the hands of lunatics. The moral justification for relying on professional military and law-enforcement personnel is the understanding that their training will allow them to do all the terrible things we would do to protect our family, more dispassionately, carefully, and efficiently than we could. Double-crossing them for political gain is using the families of other people as poker chips, in the smug certainty your own loved ones are in no immediate danger. If we don't let the professionals do their jobs against a relentless enemy now, then one day, we will *all* be soldiers.

A few weeks ago, Eric Holder saw nothing wrong with Black Panthers using billy clubs to intimidate voters. Today, he thinks intimidating terrorists with cigars is a crime. Holder is the one who should be answering tough questions under oath.

Falling Through Fire

September 11, 2009

Author's Note: Sometimes I put a good deal of planning into an essay: writing notes, gathering web links for reference, and editing several times before I post. Other times, the writing comes quickly and instinctively. This was one of those times. I wanted to write something special to commemorate 9/11, but I found myself parked on the wrong side of a writer's block all through the evening of September 10. Just after midnight, my hands started moving across the keyboard on their own, and didn't stop until this was done. I was overwhelmed to learn it had such a profound effect on people. I'm proud to think I did well on behalf of all the people who died on that terrible day.

When someone told me a plane had just hit the World Trade Center, I thought they meant a Cessna. I would imagine a lot of people had that reaction on 9/11. The truth was difficult to comprehend. The fear we inflict upon ourselves is electric with anticipation. Real horror, dropped before our eyes without warning, is dry and hollow. It can be difficult to focus your eyes on something you never saw coming.

In the afternoon hours of 9/11, *everything* became possible, except what actually happened. No one could have guessed that al-Qaeda's attack on America would be defeated aboard United 93, only minutes after it began. I hope, with all the ferocity of a broken heart that will never mend, their defeat came as a stunning surprise to those animals. I hope every one of them died with a passenger's hands around his throat.

United 93 may have crashed in the fields of Shanksville, but it came to rest in the sands of Omaha Beach, after gliding over the snow of Valley Forge, and it sleeps beneath the quiet midnight stars of Ia Drang. The American Revolution has raged for over two centuries, and one mighty company of heroes has fought through every battle. The proposition that free men cannot be broken by the will of tyrants is a challenge. No one can look at the rowdy, mismatched, vital, beautiful sea of Americans, and doubt that challenge will forever roar beyond our borders. We will liberate the world, eventually, if the tyrants don't stop us. The enemy keeps returning to that conclusion…usually a few bloody days before we do.

It's really not surprising that the united American spirit of the days after 9/11 proved to be short-lived. Beneath the political disputes of today turn vast gears of philosophy and doctrine, forged generations ago, by people who looked beyond their own lifetimes. We like to trivialize political disputes, perhaps because most of us understand the love of a single friend is more valuable than a million pages of ideology…and how many people lack at least one friend who disagrees with them? Maybe we also look down at politics because we retain a little of the Spirit of 1776, and dislike the notion that our lives should be shaped by the agenda of others. No matter what we think of them, those vast gears are still there, and nothing could have stopped them from grinding for long.

The idea that we should have given Saddam Hussein the benefit of the doubt on his weapons of mass destruction, and cease-fire violations, always seemed strange to me. In the hours after the World Trade Center fell, a great many Americans wanted to do a lot more than invade Afghanistan or Iraq. We certainly have the power to do a lot more. It is to our eternal credit that we did not use it. In the aftermath of an unspeakably brutal attack, we could have done our worst, but we did our **best** instead. The flag-draped coffin of an American soldier blazes with the glory of a man or woman who sacrificed everything to defend American lives, while also cherishing the value of innocent foreign lives.

If we are to defeat the evil that brought down the World Trade Center, we must do more than dig a handful of vermin from the mountains of Afghanistan. Brave men and women have made a breathtaking start in Iraq. Celebrating the honor of their achievement does not require us to forget the mistakes our leaders made along the way. Failure to learn from the mistakes made in war is a sin against the fallen. As we measure those mistakes, we should consider that changing a people without destroying them first is the undiscovered country of warfare, and Americans are its lonely pioneers.

Eight years later, it's a lot to ask people to think about 9/11 every single day. On this one day, at least, we can remember three thousand people who began an ordinary morning, and ended it by falling through fire. It was not a natural disaster, or a "tragedy," and by God I am weary in my soul of people who amuse themselves by pretending it was a government conspiracy. It was an attack. It was murder. Across the Middle East tomorrow, there will be people who celebrate the murderers. Don't turn away from the sight. We cannot afford to allow this enemy to become invisible. We can't afford to let our heroes become invisible, either. The savages with box cutters were real. So were the men who ran **into** those collapsing towers. In their name, with love for their memory, and luminous with their spirit, we will prevail.

The Leader of the Free World
September 24, 2009

The leader of the free world spoke before an international assembly yesterday, and said:

> We believe in the rights and the responsibilities and the inherent dignity of the individual…. We don't believe that human nature is perfectible; we're suspicious of government efforts to fix problems because often what it's trying to fix is human nature, and that is impossible. It is what it is. But that doesn't mean that we're resigned to, well, any negative destiny. Not at all. I believe in striving for the ideal, but in realistic confines of human nature…

> [We're] not going to impose our values on other countries. We don't seek to do that. But the ideas of freedom and liberty and respect for human rights, it's not just a U.S. idea. They're very much more than that. They're enshrined in the Universal Declaration of Human Rights and many other international covenants and treaties.

These remarks were made in Hong Kong, not the United Nations building. The speaker was not the current President of the United States, who is sadly irrelevant to the cause of freedom. It was Sarah Palin—who is, for the moment, the *de facto* leader of the free world. It's very unusual to see the position occupied by a private citizen, with no official power to back up her words. I doubt Mrs. Palin likes the situation any more than I do. It's a position with absolutely no tenure, outside of high office—a new standard bearer could speak with greater clarity and passion tomorrow. Someone with power *must* soon fill the role…but for now, a voice pouring the right words into hungry ears will have to suffice. The free world holds ideals above power anyway. It cannot be led through force. It uses power to *defend* its ideals, not to impose them.

In the best of times, the President is also the leader of the free world, putting American economic and military power behind the cause of freedom. Instead, Barack Obama is the leader of the **indentured** world. Every action he has taken in office has been designed to reduce the freedom of Americans, in exchange for what he believes are noble goals. It's not necessary to question his sincerity to understand that his vision of the future is less *free* than the nation we live in today. No one can carry the banner of freedom in one hand, and a 1200-page cap-and-trade bill in the other. The language of freedom cannot be spoken convincingly while the President's minions are using intimidation, wild charges of racism, and physical violence to suppress dissent. Talk of democracy and the rule of law is hollow when it comes from a man laboring to install a deranged Marxist as the dictator of Honduras, over-riding that nation's constitutional law. Every fraudulent vote produced by Obama's close allies at ACORN was an offense against the freedom of the legitimate voter it nullified. A vigorous defense of liberty cannot be mounted from the sick bed of a welfare state.

While Palin expounded on political and economic liberty in simple, but forceful, terms, Obama was offering disposable nonsense like this to the petty thugs and tyrants at the United Nations:

> I took office at a time when many around the world had come to view America with skepticism and distrust. Part of this was due to misperceptions and misinformation about my country. Part of this was due to opposition to specific policies, and a belief that on certain critical issues, America has acted unilaterally, without regard for the interests of others. This has fed an almost reflexive anti-Americanism, which too often has served as an excuse for our collective inaction...

> We have also re-engaged the United Nations. We have paid our bills. We have joined the Human Rights Council. We have signed the Convention on the Rights of Persons with Disabilities. We have fully embraced the Millennium Development Goals. And we address our priorities here, in this institution—for instance, through the Security Council meeting that I will chair tomorrow on nuclear non-proliferation and disarmament, and through the issues that I will discuss today...

> We have sought—in word and deed—a new era of engagement with the world. Now is the time for all of us to take our share of responsibility for a global response to global challenges...If we are honest with ourselves, we need to admit that we are not living up to that responsibility. Consider the course that we are on if we fail to confront the status quo. Extremists sowing terror in pockets of the world. Protracted conflicts that grind on and on. Genocide and mass atrocities. More and more nations with nuclear weapons. Melting ice caps and ravaged populations. Persistent poverty and pandemic disease. I say this not to sow fear, but to state a fact: the magnitude of our challenges has yet to be met by the measure of our action.

Brutal terrorist attacks, blowing off a young woman's head because she dared to protest a stolen election, insufficiently draconian global warming legislation.. it's all the same, really. We've all made mistakes. Who are we to judge? The next time terrorists are preparing to saw off the head of a blindfolded captive, I hope they'll remember Obama outlawed "torture" at Guantanamo Bay, and appointed a special envoy for Middle East peace. Why *wouldn't* they be eager to set aside their ancient hatreds, and join America in squandering their prosperity over "climate change?"

Later in his speech, the man who incessantly blames George W. Bush for all of his failures managed to say this with a straight face: "Nothing is easier than blaming others for our troubles, and absolving ourselves of responsibility for our choices and our actions." Evidently, the international quid pro quo for Obama's endless concessions is that they didn't laugh at him. At least, not out loud.

When Ronald Reagan spoke the words that shattered the Berlin Wall, he drew strength from the confidence of his nation's commitment to freedom. That commitment cannot be conditional. Obama can't be the czar of czars, supreme executive of nationalized industries, and distributor of trillion-dollar "stimulus" checks, while also serving as a plausible champion of liberty. The wealth of free men cannot be "spread around" to suit a politician's ideas of fairness, without compromising the freedom of both the providers *and* the recipients. Embracing freedom means allowing others to choose their own course in life, earn and spend their own money…and take responsibility for their occasional failures. Freedom is meaningless in the absence of responsibility. Children are not free.

The increasingly bitter and frustrated man who addressed the United Nations yesterday was not the leader of the free world, challenging the forces of tyranny and offering hope to the oppressed. He went there to offer pleasing words and concessions to the tyrants, so they would leave him alone, while he draws a burial shroud over the American century. No dictator will ever be moved to free his captive people by an appeal to prevent the polar ice caps from shrinking.

When he finished his remarks, the President politely turned the stage over to creatures like the Holocaust-denying president of Iran, and the lunatic dictator of Libya. By tomorrow, not even the sycophants at MSNBC or the New York Times will remember a single thing Obama said, although they will continue to insist it was magnificent.

Meanwhile, the unlikely champion of liberty and capitalism scooted back to her hotel room in Hong Kong, to update her Facebook page. It takes nothing away from Mrs. Palin's accomplishments to say that we need more than words in support of liberty—it's *our* responsibility to take it further, in the voting booth. If you don't think Sarah Palin should be the leader of the free world, vote for someone who can do the job. If you *do* think it should be her, convince her to stand for office. We could use more people saying the things she told her audience in China, but for this lonely and perilous moment, she's the only one who has both the ideas, and the audience. The free world has plenty of demand for more leaders…but it has no room for either masters or servants.

The Peace Of The Grave
October 9, 2009

I'm not really surprised by the Nobel committee's decision to grant the Peace Price to Barack Obama. I assumed they would give it to him at the earliest opportunity. I forgot the award had not been given for this year. It would have been slightly better for their credibility if the Nobel committee had waited until next year, but perhaps they didn't want to take the chance that current events would make that impossible by the end of 2010. The kind of "peacemaking" favored by the Nobel committee is the kind that usually gets innocent people killed, and frequently ends in the kind of war that comes as an even bigger surprise than Obama's award.

Obama had been in office for less than two weeks before the Nobel nominations were finalized, so his nomination was not based on anything he had done as President. The Nobel Price long ago became a joke, and an insult to the people who suffer under terror and tyranny around the world, but I don't think the committee just threw Obama the award because he's so wonderfully special, and not even because he won the election to succeed the only man who has truly deserved the award since 2001. Maybe Obama won the Nobel because of his courageous youthful defiance of murderous evil, when he was brutally tortured for months but refused to submit to totalitarian brutes? Oh, no, wait, that was the guy he defeated in the election.

The Associated Press says the Nobel committee "praised Obama's creation of a new climate in international politics, and said he had returned multilateral diplomacy and institutions like the U.N. to the center of the world stage." Of course, he hasn't actually changed any of the hated Bush's foreign policies, until this week, when he began talking about embracing the Taliban savages as partners in peace, who might just deserve to control a big chunk of Afghanistan after all. A while ago, I suggested you could ask the women of Afghanistan for a testimonial to Bush's achievements in the realm of women's rights, now that the upholstery has been removed from their faces. You'd better ask quickly. The new Nobel Peace Prize winner doesn't seem all that disturbed by the thought of seeing them muffled again.

Obama was given the Nobel Prize, not because of anything he has done as President, but because of what the committee thinks he will do. His achievements are as non-existent now as they were on the day he was nominated. His agenda, however, is clear. He spelled it out in that insipid speech he gave to the United Nations a few weeks ago. Speaking as the leader of the indentured world, he made it clear that he plans to dim the lights on an America in decline, and humbly step aside as the post-American century begins. That's why he won the Peace Prize. The

Nobel committee has long seen the United States as the greatest threat to world peace, and the man who plans to bankrupt and disarm it has earned their admiration.

There are only two responses to tyranny: submission and resistance. Submission is easy. It can be negotiated. It is filled with nuance, and requires a large staff of diplomats and state functionaries to administer in style. Organizations like the United Nations make the first concessions to dictatorship by their very nature, as they allow thug states like Iran and Libya to take seats next to peaceful democracies. Obama's dismal eulogy for America at the U.N. was followed by lunatic rants from the blood-splattered clowns who will be the new masters of the global future. Entertaining such creatures is easy, if you can just ignore the piles of faceless victims buried behind them. You may rest assured that the name Neda Agha-Soltan was not spoken during Obama's Peace Prize deliberations, and it will not be spoken when the prize is placed into his hands.

Resistance is **hard.** It requires the courage to call evil by its name, and sacrifice universal adoration in the process. The Left likes to rail against intolerance. The defense of peace and freedom requires the absolute intolerance of evil. It requires leaders who don't need a few days to decide whether to cancel the Fourth of July picnic invitations of a dictatorship that guns down peacefully protesting citizens. It relies upon a nation with the strength and resolve to project both humanitarian assistance and military power around the world.

Barack Obama's America, mortgaged to the hilt and several trillion dollars beyond broke, with a stagnant economy trapped in government amber, will no longer be such a nation. The Nobel committee is pleased to reward him for that, because a muscular United States rocks a lot of boats. The "international community" has never forgiven George W. Bush for backing it into a corner over Iraq, and forcing the United Nations to enforce its own resolutions. "Resolution" is harmless and exciting when it's a word spoken by important diplomats, and scribbled into strongly-worded letters. It's scary when backed up by forceful leaders who take it seriously.

The cultural and political elite of Europe is delighted to give Obama an award for his bold work in turning America into the same kind of dilettante basket case they are. The people who sat helplessly and watched the slaughter in Bosnia may come to regret sacrificing their last shred of credibility to shore up a weak President, so he can finish the task of hobbling the only nation on Earth that can do a damned thing to prevent a slaughter. Europe thinks it can do business with the Islamic fascism creeping through its streets, but it will find any deals it makes with them have expiration dates, as surely as all of Barack Obama's promises do. When they once again turn to America to save them, they had better hope we've had the wisdom to replace the confused and helpless man clutching his shiny Nobel Peace Prize with someone who can saddle up and ride to the rescue. Negotiation without principle is submission, and the only peace brought by submission is the peace of the grave.

The Consent of the Governed
November 29, 2009

Jonah Goldberg of *National Review* recently wrote about the high-stakes political battle over health care reform:

> Some moderate Democrats are making a side bet that they can vote for it out of solidarity and then run back to the center come the 2010 elections.

> Well, I say let it ride. And just to make it more interesting, Republicans should promise to repeal "ObamaCare" if they get a congressional majority in 2010. As *National Review's* Ramesh Ponnuru argues, that way moderate Democrats won't be able to run away from their votes come 2010. They'll be on notice that this will be the campaign issue of the election. And moderate Republicans will be on notice to resist the temptation to tinker with ObamaCare rather than defenestrate it once it's passed.

> Sure, I'd rather see this health-care proposal die stillborn (and that's still quite possible). But if it passes, the upside is that Americans will finally be given a stark philosophical choice on a fundamental issue. That's much rarer than you might think (recall that the Iraq War and the bailouts were bipartisan affairs).

Earlier in the article, Goldberg complains that "the quest for the middle ground usually rewards the worst kinds of politicians—those devoid of any core convictions and only concerned with feathering their own nests—and yields the worst kinds of policies." The health-care debate presents the kind of sharp ideological contrast that makes it hard for unprincipled politicians to seek shelter in the mushy bog of the middle ground. Over the weekend, the libertarian Cato Institute calculated that the true cost of ObamaCare would exceed $6 trillion, after the various deceits used to make it seem close to revenue-neutral are stripped away. How much does real estate in the "middle ground" of such outrageous spending cost? Three trillion? When a radical program of such massive size is proposed, anything less than determined opposition is equivalent to submission.

I appreciate Goldberg's point about the kind of muddled, confusing, and ultimately ineffective legislation produced by the quest for the middle ground. However, I wonder how truly desirable these uncompromising contests between capitalism and socialism are. Aren't elected officials, especially Congress and the President, supposed to represent *all* of their constituents? Wouldn't that mean listening to the concerns of both liberals and conservatives, and trying to craft legislation that satisfies both sides to some degree? Are the members of a winning political coalition supposed to have absolute power to do whatever they want, even if

236

they won with only about half the popular vote, while the other side sits in obedient silence until their next chance at the ballot box?

In the course of endorsing a Dick Cheney run for the Presidency in 2012, Jon Meacham of Newsweek writes:

One of the problems with governance since the election of Bill Clinton has been the resolute refusal of the opposition party (the GOP from 1993 to 2001, the Democrats from 2001 to 2009, and now the GOP again in the Obama years) to concede that the president, by virtue of his victory, has a mandate to take the country in a given direction.

I don't think most Americans are under the impression they're voting for a dictator every four years. Bill Clinton won the Presidency with a mere 43% of the popular vote. What sort of "mandate" did that give him to "take the country in a given direction?"

Of course, we cannot parcel out presidential powers based on the scale of the candidate's electoral victory. The proper functioning of our government, and the harmony of our democracy, demand that we acknowledge the full legitimacy of the man or woman who sits in the Oval Office. The Left did their country no favors by bitterly dragging the 2000 elections out until 2008. The complementary aspect of this principle is that strong electoral victories cannot logically yield enhanced "mandates" to take the country in various radical directions. If close elections don't produce miniature Presidents who just keep the seat warm until the next election, then landslide victories don't produce super-Presidents with turbocharged authority. A President who carries 49 states, and wins 70% of the popular vote, is not entitled to stuff the opposing 30% of the electorate in the trunk and take America out for a joy ride.

The Declaration of Independence states that governments derive "their just powers from the consent of the governed." The American understanding of democracy does not envision voters as slaves who enjoy the privilege of voting for a new master every few years. When the Declaration speaks of the right—and, later the duty—of the people to abolish tyrannical governments, it renders the notion of "mandates" to impose radical change on unwilling citizens absurd.

The vital role of consent in the structure of a just government is one of the most powerful ideas ever advanced by the human race. On the other hand, the belief that consent can be manufactured by democratic majorities is one of the most cherished illusions of activist government. The dissent of a minority is not rendered irrelevant by victory in a popular vote...but the health-care debate in the Senate proceeds on the assumption that victory in a parliamentary struggle between a hundred elected officials will compel the consent of the millions of citizens—now a sizable majority of the population, based on the latest polls—who strenuously object to ObamaCare. If Senate Democrats win this debate, huge amounts of your liberty will be destroyed, and vast sums of money will be seized from taxpayers…and you will not be allowed to object. Any attempt to withhold your consent from this economy-shattering, life-changing radical legislation will end with you sitting in a prison cell.

The consent of the governed cannot be expressed solely through a semi-annual vote for elected representatives. It can only be respected by placing strict limits on what those representatives can vote for. Some would argue that requiring the consent of the entire population to authorize massive government programs would effectively render those programs impossible, because 100% agreement is virtually impossible to achieve. **Exactly.** The entire apparatus of socialist government is a Constitutional violation that would never receive the total support of those who are controlled by its regulations, or compelled to pay for its agenda. For this reason, its agenda should never even reach the serious discussion stage, never mind legislative implementation.

Americans concerned about the size of their government should not be forced into a permanent defensive posture against an endless series of aggressive initiatives. If the needs and desires of some can transcend the liberty of others, then liberty itself is a meaningless concept. Freedom is not what you have left after everyone else is finished making demands of you. The need for your consent is not respected when your only hope of withholding it lies in historic midterm electoral victories and the rapid construction of huge Congressional majorities. The patriots who declared their independence from England perceived an essential truth about the nature of just government, which we have become almost afraid to contemplate.

Love The Warriors

January 2, 2010

Author's Note: The original posting of this essay included pictures of the men who died in the Karbala attack. I thought it was important to see them. I couldn't stop staring at the photographs I found while I was researching them. I dearly hope that if any of their families reads this, they judge I have done proper honor to the memory of these brave soldiers.

"You don't have to love the war, but you have to love the warrior."—**Private Johna-thon Millican**

The author of those words was twenty years old when he died. He used a web camera to talk with his wife from Iraq on the morning of his final day. He had been in Iraq for about three months. The quote above comes from his MySpace page.

1st Lt. Jacob Fritz was a graduate of the United States Military Academy. His younger brother Daniel graduated from West Point a year after his death. He looks like a man who knew how to laugh. "Sometimes, when there's a whisper in the wind, I feel he's walking with me," says his mother Noala. His parents bought 70 acres of farmland across the highway from their place for Jacob to settle on, when his military career was over.

Private First Class Shawn Falter had twelve brothers and sisters. Three of his older brothers preceded him in military service. At his funereal, his older brother Andrew, an Air Force master sergeant, said, "Rest, Shawn. You've done your part. Your brothers will take it from here." Pfc. Falter once gave up his own leave time, so a fellow soldier could return home to be with his wife and children.

Specialist Johnathan Bryan Chism was a month away from coming home for two weeks of rest and recuperation when he died. A few years ago, he was a Boy Scout.

On January 20th, 2007, these four men were abducted from the Provincial Joint Coordination Center in Karbala, Iraq, during a sophisticated insurgent attack. The operation was believed to have been coordinated by the Qods Force of the Iranian Revolutionary Guard. Within a few hours, they were executed by their captors. Their bodies were left with some abandoned vehicles. Two of them were tossed on the ground, while two were still handcuffed together inside one of the vehicles.

A fifth soldier, Captain Brian S. Freeman, was killed in the initial attack. He was a world-class athlete who won a bronze medal as part of a bobsled team in the 2002 America's Cup race. Some of the bobsled drivers he trained with went on to compete in the last Olympics. One of them, Steven Holcomb, called Captain Freeman "one of the greatest men I have ever known."

The architects of the attack that killed Captain Freeman, and the subsequent murders of the other four brave soldiers, are brothers named Qais and Laith Khazali. They were captured in a March 2007 raid in Basra. On New Year's Eve, we learned that Qais Khazali has been released, apparently as part of a prisoner exchange for British hostage Peter Moore. Laith Khazali *was already released six months ago.* Peter Moore was kidnapped in May 2007, explicitly to be used as a bargaining chip for the freedom of the Khazali brothers.

The circumstances around Qais Khazali's release are murky, with the usual denials and clarifications swirling around like a cloud of confetti over Times Square on New Years' Eve. Multi National Force spokesmen claim this was not a hostage trade, but rather an attempt to comply with "the implementation of the U.S.—Iraq Security Agreement" and support a "reconciliation process." Some suggest this is all part of an elaborate intelligence operation.

Republican Senators Jeff Sessions and Jon Kyl have already sent a letter to the Obama Administration, citing an executive order signed by President Reagan in 1986 that prohibits concessions to terrorist hostage takers. With the New Year holiday behind us, more Republican congressmen will doubtless be right behind Sessions and Kyl with their own hard questions. It's even possible some Democrats will join them, now that they're finished with midnight votes to take over the health-care system, and desperately need to fool their constituents into thinking they're "moderates" who care about national security.

Was that harsh? *Prove me wrong,* Democrats. Make me eat those words. I'll gladly slather them in barbecue sauce, and savor ever last consonant.

International conflicts are a messy business. We know that Iran has been supporting the Iraqi insurgency with money, equipment, and personnel. We don't have the manpower to completely lock down the thousand-mile border between Iran and Iraq. Attacks on Qods Force bases in Iran would swiftly escalate into all-out war. Intelligence is the key weapon in defeating a terrorist insurgency, and it must often be obtained through sins committed in deep shadow. We must also make efforts to respect the sovereign dignity of the Iraqi government we have been nurturing for the past six years. Even with all of these uneasy truths in mind, it's difficult to see how the release of the men behind the Karbala attack can be justified.

It seems unlikely that the Khazali outrage could have happened without President Obama's authorization. I'm ready to hear him explain this...and then, considering his reputation as a liar, every thinking American should be ready to fact-check **every word he says**. I don't mind admitting I'm a hostile audience. You should be, too. Nothing this President has done since taking office has earned him a shred of trust or faith, especially in the area of national security.

We just watched his utterly incompetent Secretary of Homeland Security, Janet Napolitano, stammer her way through a terrorist attack. Her only useful purpose was preparing the infamous Defense Intelligence Estimate that indicted "radicalized right-wing extremists" as potential terrorists, thus transforming an important security document into a piece of scornography to titillate the far Left. No one who takes the defense of America seriously would put an unqualified piece of bureaucratic furniture like Napolitano in charge of Homeland Security...and, a week after a defective set of exploding underwear was the only thing keeping her from standing trial for three hundred counts of negligent homicide, *she's still there*. There is still no evidence Barack Obama takes defense issues seriously, or even understands them. His Administration stands by while Navy SEALs are persecuted for allegedly punching a terrorist in the mouth...while the enemy murders handcuffed hostages with head shots.

I can think of a hundred bad reasons Obama would let the murderers of Karbala go. He needs to help us imagine a good one. America's military men and women pledge their last full measure of their devotion to our defense. We owe it to them to return that devotion.

I humbly devote this space to remembering Private Johnathon Millican, First Lieutenant Jacob Fritz, Private First Class Shawn Falter, Specialist Johnathan Bryan Chism, and Captain Brian S. Freeman, and I encourage you to join me in demanding the full story behind why the filth who orchestrated their murders are walking around free. We won't get those answers unless we push for them, with the same courage and dedication our fallen heroes gave to their duty. This story *will* go away, unless *you* keep it alive. Love the warriors, by making it clear to Washington that their lives are worth more than *any* politician's career.

If I may borrow a few words from Private Falter's brother: Rest, my friends. You've done your part. Your countrymen will take it from here.

The Joyous Daybreak
January 18, 2010

When the Founding Fathers penned the Declaration of Independence, they wrote the first chapter in a mighty saga that continues through the present day, and whose final pages will not be written until the world is bereft of a single man or woman who calls themselves an American. We have been blessed across the centuries with hands bold and steady enough to write new pages in the gospel of liberty. Martin Luther King, Jr. was one of those authors.

When he spoke from the steps of the Lincoln Memorial on August 28, 1963, Dr. King used a voice that rang from the Liberty Bell in the east, and rolled across the mountains of the west, to echo through every corner of the Earth. All of the great American speeches are like that. They do not rest comfortably within our borders. Like Washington at the First Inaugural, Lincoln at Gettysburg, or Reagan at the Berlin Wall, King's words were spoken from the American heart, charged with universal truth that made them the property of all mankind. He was a pioneer, the first to describe one of the most challenging aspects of liberty: *no one* in a nation is truly free, until no one is oppressed.

Why are we still cursed with racism, when its greatest enemy spoke with an eloquence its vicious little servants can never hope to match? We commemorate King's life every year on this day. We share his speeches with our children. How can so many people accept such a glorious cup, and pass it along without drinking their fill?

Racial hatred endures because it is useful, and we are practical creatures who don't set aside useful tools easily. Racism enforces a *conformity of thought* that is precious to every brand of despotism. Tyrants love to burden their subjects with an enemy they only need to point at. The cellar of every squalid little dictatorship includes bottles full of machetes and bullets, labeled with the names of racial enemies, to be uncorked whenever the populace dwells too long on the misery of their lives. The American brand of useful racism is considerably watered down, but people do occasionally die from overdoses.

Racism endures because it provides a dark mirror, in whose depths can be seen a cheap illusion of righteousness. Nothing brings the rush of moral superiority more quickly than a casual accusation of racism. The notion that particular racial groups, including whites, are especially liable to indulge in ethnic hatred is, itself, a deeply racist notion. We *all* carry that taint in our blood. No race of man can claim it has never looked upon others with prejudice. Lazy accusations of racism are really a different flavor of the same poison as vile assertions of racial superiority. Both are an easy way to declare other people beneath contempt, so their ideas can be discarded as rubbish without a second thought. Like any narcotic, racism is seductive to lazy minds...and powerfully addictive, with violent withdrawal symptoms.

Ugly prejudice lurks in the deep shadows around the understandable human tendency to seek the comfort in the familiar. Our Constitution enshrines the right of free people to choose who they will associate with. People of every color have used that choice to build "communities" that might better be described as enclaves. No just law can ever bring the walls of those enclaves down. They must be dismantled brick by brick, one friendship at a time. It won't be quick, or easy. We shouldn't hate ourselves for that. The Bible carried by Martin Luther King taught him that "love is patient, and love is kind. It does not envy, it does not boast, it is not proud. It is not rude, it is not self-seeking, it is not easily angered, it keeps no record of wrongs." Does that sound like a fair description of racial relations in America, three decades after King fell to a murderer's bullet? Perhaps not...but we are closer than we were, on the day that shot rang out, tiny against the mighty echoes of the voice it silenced.

Racism endures because we've thrown away the most effective weapons against it. We built a system of government that strangles the free enterprise which brings people together, united by their ambitions. We scowl at the healthy laughter that builds fellowship, timid at the thought of giving offense. We haven't put enough effort into maintaining our common language, the mortar of a peaceful and open society. The most impoverished among us indulge a subculture that violently dismisses the pursuit of excellence as racial treason. Meanwhile, the ruling elite have constructed a system that stands Dr. King's dream on its head: we bring our children into a world where the color of their skin unlocks a million pages of legislation, while attempts to judge the content of their character are a felony offense.

From his vantage point on the steps of the Lincoln Memorial, Martin Luther King Jr. beheld a "joyous daybreak" in the sky above his country, and the free world it leads. He saw clearly. The clouds have parted slowly, but inexorably, every day since then. No man or woman of character can listen to the "I Have a Dream" speech without feeling a part of their soul rise to meet the challenge that waits on the other side of those clouds.

To Keep And Bear Arms
March 3, 2010

Author's Note: The anecdote that begins this essay used to be very painful for me to recount. Over the years, it has lost its terrible hold on my imagination. I offer it here in the hope that it might prove educational, for anyone seriously contemplating the right—and responsibility—of self-defense.

Twenty-five years ago, a little after sunrise on a Monday morning, the front door of my house was kicked in by a man who had blown his mind with crack cocaine. He marched my family upstairs at gunpoint. When I reached the top of the stairs and turned around, he put the gun in my forehead and pulled the trigger.

I've always heard it was good to begin a composition with an arresting opening paragraph. That's the catchiest one I can offer from an otherwise modest biography. I hope the rest of this essay lives up to the opening. I'll do my best.

I don't mind admitting this incident gave me a lifelong aversion to guns. I don't have any objection to *other* law-abiding citizens bearing arms—in fact, I'm strongly in favor of it. It's just not a right I have chosen to exercise, although I'm working on getting over it. I'm fascinated by the beauty and science of firearms. I rarely pass a gun magazine on the stands without flipping it open, and I love attending gun shows. My first close encounter with a gun was rather…*intense,* so I'm understandably nervous around them. I recently discovered I'm a remarkably good shot with a target rifle, after some friends invited me to shoot with them. I've decided twenty-five years is long enough to be uncomfortable around the reality of something I've always supported in theory.

The Second Amendment is once again in the news, as the Supreme Court considers a case that would invoke the Fourteenth Amendment to apply it to the states, striking down restrictive state and local gun-control laws…oh, wait. You're probably wondering why I'm still here, having been shot in the head and all. Well, I got lucky. I was able to knock the gun out of the way just in time, and the bullet wound up in the wall, instead of my brain. I had managed to make a hasty call to the police as the door was being kicked in, and they arrived to find the perp and I wrestling for control of the weapon at the bottom of the stairs. No one died in my house that day.

I wish the Supreme Court would do more than rule the Second Amendment applies to the states. It's long past time the last, ridiculous cobwebs of ambiguity were cleared away from the right to keep and bear arms. Gun control has been simmering on low heat for a while, after boiling over in the Nineties. We should clear it off the Constitutional stove al-together. We have better things to do than slip into another bitter, tedious argument about whether the government can interfere with our right, and duty, to defend ourselves.

The notion that citizens have no good reason to be armed, because the State can protect them from violent crime, is one of the most dangerous lies Big Government has fed its subjects. The government reduces crime through the police and court systems, but no matter how tirelessly the police work, there is very little chance they can actively defend you from assault. There aren't enough of them, and there never could be. The very areas of privacy that allow us to relax with our friends and families will always be soft targets for criminals... unless we fortify them ourselves. The police arrived at my house several minutes too late to play a role in my attempted execution. They made excellent time—there happened to be a unit in the area. If things had gone a little different, they might have arrived just in time to avenge me.

Citizen access to firearms has reduced crime rates time and again, but this is more than a matter of practicality. It's a question of principle. The people of an orderly nation surrender the business of vengeance to the government, replacing it with the rule of law. They cannot be expected to surrender the right of *defense*. The right to protect yourself, and your family, from injury and death is an essential part of your dignity as a free man or woman. Without the First Amendment, you are a slave. Without the Second, you are a child.

The Western nations which have abandoned this essential understanding of an individual's right to self-defense have become rotting orphanages filled with dependent children. They're not dealing very well with the invasion of a determined ideology that has complete confidence in its own righteousness, and few reservations about using violence to assert itself. Losing the dignity of self-defense is part of the degeneration from master of the State to its client. As this dignity fades, the people and their government speak less of *responsibilities,* and more of *entitlements.*

The Second Amendment is a concrete expression of the American birthright of independence. With the right of self-defense bargained away, our rights to speak and vote give us modest influence in a collective. The Founders wanted more, and better, for us.

Sometimes liberals sneer at the idea we might keep arms against government tyranny, because a bunch of pistol-packing Tea Party types have no chance of repeating the success of the Revolution against a modern military force. This completely misses the point. A disarmed populace has little choice but to obey orders. If the population is armed, a tyrant's forces have to do more than just brandish their weapons...they'd have to start pulling triggers. Victory for a righteous populace would come in the military's refusal to pull those triggers. Tyranny should never be *easy*. Of course, it should never come to that again, in the United States. As long as the population is armed, this is an understanding, and a duty...not an assumption.

The right to keep and bear arms is a crucial intersection of liberty and obligation. A gun owner is entrusted with the solemn duty to tend his weapons carefully and securely. In accepting this duty, we remove the destiny of our loved ones from the hands of madmen, and it is no longer measured by the distance of a friendly police car from our homes. It would be a mark of our maturity as a nation if we stopped telling ourselves that freedom can exist in the absence of responsibility...or danger. The shards of those illusions carry sharp edges, when they shatter.

The *New York Times* article about the case before the Supreme Court ends this way:

The Supreme Court's conservative majority has made clear that it is very concerned about the right to bear arms. There is another right, however, that should not get lost: the right of people, through their elected representatives, to adopt carefully drawn laws that **protect them against other people's guns.**

Carefully drawn laws will not protect you from other people's guns. Believe me. None of the people carefully drawing those laws will rely upon them for *their* protection.

What Freedom Demands
March 21, 2010

Author's Note: I was away from the Internet, on a camping trip, during the weekend of ObamaC-are's passage. I was tired when I got home, and wanted nothing more than a long nap. Instead, I opened up a word-processing document, stared at the screen for a while, and suddenly began writing this. I don't think I've ever done less advance preparation for an essay—it came straight from the heart, in one sitting, just as fast as I could hit the keys. I think it got such a huge response because of its sincerity. Blog writing is usually like preparing a piano concerto…but there are hours that demand the unrestrained blast of trumpets.

Tonight, self-appointed wise men in Washington are steamrolling the objections of sixty to seventy percent of the population, and forcing a massive health-care bill down our throats "for our own good." Presumably the backroom deals, corrupt payoffs, Congressional Budget Office accounting tricks, threats of unconstitutional parliamentary maneuvers, and betrayals of principle are *also* for our own good. What do you know? Banana republics turn out to be the highest evolution of government—the only form of the State equipped to take proper care of its citizens, by lying to them and trapping them in legislative cages, over their howling protests.

Tonight is not the end of the ObamaCare saga, but it does mark the beginning of a slow turn by the American ship of state. It doesn't have to be a turn to the left. On the contrary, it could be the first overture in a rebirth of our commitment to freedom, and the last gasp of an exhausted statist ideology, long overdue for its disposal in the waste bin of history.

The decision is up to us. Our representatives will fight various legislative battles in the months to come…and then we will speak in November. As the voters of the United States ponder what to say, it would profit us to think long and hard about the freedom Democrats are trying to take from us tonight, and *what freedom demands.*

Yes, it makes demands. Freedom is not a gift. It is not given to you by the government, in a precise dosage that can be adjusted to match a politician's diagnosis of what ails the body politic. Your forefathers won an impossible Revolution against an invincible foe to declare the self-evident truth that your rights descend from your Creator. Whether that Creator is a transcendent God, or a random combination of genetic material in the primordial soup, it is a power that existed before the first king assumed his throne, or the first president was elected. Liberty burns in your imagination, flows through your veins, and rings through your words.

This radiant idea has burned through all the bloody clouds of the last three centuries: *you are not clay to be sculpted by the will of another.* You are not a racially inferior inconvenience, to be marched into a concentration camp. You aren't a class enemy to be exiled by dictators. You are not a disposable cog in the machinery of collectivist economics, or a mouth to be starved by the failure of collective agriculture. **You are an American,** and through a dereliction of their duty as elected representatives, the Democrats have forced you to choose whether you will retain the full measure of the honor and dignity your Constitution asserts for you.

If you choose to obey their demands, it will be the last such choice you make. Your opinion was disregarded on this travesty of a health-care bill. It will not be solicited in the future. Fifteen thousand new IRS agents will ensure that you comply with endless future "adjustments" to socialized insurance, until it mutates into socialist medicine, and bankrupts us along with the crushing weight of other unsustainable entitlements. On that dark day, you will be fighting battles, not making choices.

Like your muscles, heart, and lungs, freedom is a part of you, and it makes demands. You cannot exercise freedom in the absence of responsibility. That means you must accept the challenges of a complex, fast-moving world. You must exercise your influence in that world, and money is the medium of exchange that transforms your labor into your will. You have to demand the best return on your investments, and the best quality for your purchases. This requires education, to gather the information necessary for making wise decisions.

We are currently paying the price for decades of turning away from those demands, and trusting government to insure our quality of life. It's understandable. The free market is huge and powerful, and it does not pause to adore the millions of individuals passing through it…and occasionally stumbling. We feel overwhelmed by the waves of information crashing around us. In the case of an arcane discipline like medicine, we don't feel as if we understand it well enough to make informed decisions, and our will is expressed through an insurance system that has already been turned into an incomprehensible mess by government regulation. It would be so easy to let righteous politicians with limitless power and money take care of us, tapping into the vast fortunes of the super-rich for the benefit of all, and transforming health care into a "human right"—which means the little people won't have to think about it any more.

If you are in thrall to this temptation, consider what you are being asked to surrender. Hidden in ObamaCare's thousands of pages are countless legislative snares, and subsidies designed to convert your freedom into benefits for favored constituencies. The money drained from our economy into this health-care sinkhole will reduce *your* freedom—even when it's money from the wallets of other people. That's because a collapsing free market will eliminate choices and options you currently take for granted. Mandates that wipe out part-time employment will destroy services your family needs. Jobs shipped overseas to avoid crushing penalties are employment opportunities forever denied to you. Higher taxes on corporations slither down to you as elevated prices on goods you may no longer be able to afford.

A swelling government reduces the size of the private sector…the galaxy in which free Americans burn as stars. Common sense tells you that a nation with a gigantic government is less free. What is the proper name for a system in which the State controls everything, and the private sector is completely gone? Why should free men applaud heavy steps taken in that direction? What about the freedom of Bart Stupak's constituents, who foolishly trusted him to resist the tyranny of forcing pro-life taxpayers to fund abortions? Today they watched Stupak's honor shrivel into a meaningless piece of paper, offered by a compulsive liar, whose every commitment comes with an expiration date.

The call of freedom requires you to turn away easy solutions offered by corrupt politicians. It's not a "solution" anyway—just the gateway to another, heavier imposition on your liberty down the line. If its authors believed otherwise, why would they use tricks and lies to chisel out a "deficit-neutral" ten-year forecast from the Congressional Budget Office? A free man dismisses such deception with *contempt,* and demands to know what happens in Year Eleven. A free woman looks at a "crisis" in a heavily regulated market and commands government to *remove itself* to undo the damage it has already caused. What is the final form of a State that is rewarded for its failures with more power? We already know that name, don't we?

Tonight, the Democrat Party declares war on the American middle class. They are gambling on the forced creation of an entitlement we'll be too exhausted and weary to reject—no matter how poor its quality, corrupt its inception, or unbearable its cost. We *do* have one last chance to strike this down. There is no reason **any Democrat** up for re-election in 2010 or 2012 needs to retain their seats. They don't own those seats, any more than the Kennedys owned Massachusetts. There's no reason the Democrats need to exist as a viable political party after 2012. Obama can be their last President.

It would be incredible if the American people could bring about such a transformation of their decadent political class, in these coming elections.

Sometimes freedom demands that you do the incredible to preserve it.

A Word To The Weary
March 27, 2010

I get a lot of email from people who ask if the final degeneration from capitalism to collectivism is now inevitable. Entitlements are never repealed, after all, and we just got saddled with a *back-breaking* entitlement, piled atop a national debt that was already crushing us. It seems like it would take a miracle just to undo the damage Barack Obama has done in a single year…and that would just get us back to where George Bush left us. Dependency, unemployment, economic contraction, and socialist politics are a perpetual-motion engine of national decline.

I also hear from people who wonder just how bad things really are. If they're so awful, we should be thinking about unthinkable alternatives. If not, maybe we should follow David Frum's advice, and work out reasonable terms of surrender with our new socialist overlords. After all, Obama's not the first guy to wipe his feet with the tattered "Don't Tread on Me" flag. Perhaps none of the wounds from 2009 and 2010 are all that deep, and we're just a few elections away from Bush-era prosperity again.

Thoughts about the future shape our actions in the present. If you believe the events of the past week have permanently and irrevocably deformed the American economy and culture, your feelings are likely to consist of anger, or despair.

I can understand why some are tired of fighting the good fight. Robin Koerner at The Moderate Voice reacts to the Obama Administration's plan to offer incentives if mortgage holders will forgive part of the principle on overvalued homes:

> A few months ago, the principal on my mortgage was comfortably more than the place was worth, and my low income was in decline. So I did the responsible thing, cut my expenses back to the bone, and raised and moved whatever money I could to cover it, and to try to pay it down. I wanted to deal with the fact that I was upside down on the mortgage and dangerously exposed to future rate increases; most of all, I wanted simply to reduce my monthly payments.
>
> Why did I bother?
>
> If I had not been so responsible, Obama's plan (I still cannot quite believe it) would have given me (via my bank) YOUR money, humble tax-payer, as a gift to reduce my mortgage, and I would have gained to the tune of many thousands of dollars.

Those who play by the rules find themselves dealing with a lot of these sucker punches lately. It's the nature of a politicized economy. Health care will work the same way. If you're not part of a favored constituency, the government will milk you for the money it needs to buy the votes it requires.

When you object that such behavior is wildly inconsistent with the Constitution, you're quickly assured that, on the contrary, these outrages are legally unassailable. Decades of court precedents, often laid down by activist judges, have become a weird quantum formula that somehow proves the Constitution was actually designed to guarantee a titanic redistributionist State with virtually unlimited powers. The ruling class can even spend weeks openly discussing the idea of passing laws without voting on them, when it's not sure it has the votes to do what it wants.

My own vision of the future includes peril, but not doom. We're in a bad place right now, but we can turn things around. We can do better than pacing slowly backward through the wreckage of Obama's term, until our feet begin crunching on the empty pill bottles of George Bush's unsustainable prescription-drug entitlement.

When I look to the past, I see a central government that has *never* been able to keep the promises of its welfare programs, or respect the limits of its budget projections. Even among those who accept the premise that health care is some kind of "human right," I find it astonishing that anyone could ignore history to the degree necessary to believe politicians can provide it. It's even more amazing that anyone could watch those politicians blindly stumble across various legislative land mines—*less than a week* after passing the bill—and convince themselves these people have *any idea* what they just signed. Only someone with religious faith in the State could look upon the rotting heap of fraudulent budgeting, deception, and last-minute deals that spawned this monstrosity, and believe it will have a happy ending in which its promises are kept.

The future holds the final, systemic crash of the New Deal and Great Society. How far away is it? It's hard to recalibrate the doomsday clocks fast enough to keep up with our current tidal wave of deficit spending. I think we have about fifteen years, after factoring in the poisonous effects of desperate measures taken to hold off disaster, like the Value Added Tax. I can imagine many world events that would accelerate that timetable considerably.

Social Security is running deficits *now.* Its collapse is a matter of actuarial fact, not opinion. The Congressional Budget Office just released a report that says the national debt will reach 90% of our gross domestic product by 2020…and the CBO usually under-estimates the effects of economic slowdown on federal tax revenue. Two years ago, the CBO thought Social Security would not be in the red until 2019. Five years ago, Barack Obama's party confidently assured us the program would remain solvent for decades. These people have **always been wrong.** They just compounded their errors with trillions of deficit spending from a bill none of them read.

So, yes, the situation is serious. You can't wait fourteen years to deal with a meltdown that's fifteen years away. Even if the system was not due to implode into a black hole of unfunded liability, the offenses against freedom required to create and sustain it would still be wrong. Those offenses did not begin with the current President. They began long before I was born. That doesn't make them any more excusable. We should not accept decades of error as an insurmountable obstacle to doing better.

The task awaiting us at the ballot box is difficult, but not impossible. Laws have no magical, talismanic power—if they did, we wouldn't need law enforcement. We can change laws. We can dissolve any body that tells us otherwise. No one can hold us down in our national deathbed. We are instructed to worship the political traditions of the 1940s, 60s, and 70s, when vast and eternal departments of limitless appetite and wretched inefficiency were constructed. Our birthright as Americans includes a far older, stronger tradition from 1776, which teaches us that *only our liberty* is eternal.

There's no reason a country with vast natural resources, tended by a bold and innovative people, should suffer double-digit unemployment and capital flight. A compassionate nation, whose daily industry has done more for the downtrodden than every utopian scheme combined, has no reason to lower its head in shame, and tolerate the extraction of "charity" at gunpoint. The veterans of bloody wars against lawless tyranny should not accept a system that makes fools of the industrious. A great people, who live in reverence of equality, require no lists of class and racial enemies from opportunistic politicians.

This is the hour for passion and reason, not anger and disgust. The strength to restore our prosperity lies in the muscle and imagination of citizens who have been programmed to think of themselves as sheep, by those who seek power as their shepherds. The time for averting a painful disaster is short...but the most amazing chapters of American history were written in the last seconds before midnight.

It's time for us to be amazing again. I hope you find that as invigorating as I do.

Part Five
Culture

Not all of the guests at our tables will be visible to the eye, but all can be felt equally in the heart.

Walter Cronkite And The National Will
July 18, 2009

Walter Cronkite's death on Friday evening will doubtless fill the weekend news programs with career retrospectives and fond tributes. He was an extraordinarily accomplished newsman, and a transitional figure for the rise of television news. It is the nature of celebrities that their lives are celebrated when they pass on, so there's nothing surprising about Cronkite receiving far more public honors than the world's greatest baker, or neurosurgeon, could expect. There are also strong words of criticism to be spoken at Cronkite's national funereal. He achieved much during his career, and many other print, broadcast, and Web outlets will spend the weekend recounting these achievements. His most unhealthy achievement was finding the limits of American will, ending an era of confidence that began with victory over the Axis in World War II. Some would say that confidence *needed* to be shattered. If you have a Ouija board, I can put you in touch with a couple of million dead Cambodians who might beg to differ.

For the conservative student of recent history, and of course for the surviving veterans of Vietnam, the nadir of Cronkite's career was his reporting in the wake of the Tet Offensive. For the younger reader who might not be familiar with this event, the Tet Offensive was a massive, coordinated attack on all the major cities of South Vietnam, during the normally quiet Vietnamese New Year celebrations, in January and February of 1968. The U.S. Military had been making public statements of Communist weakness, so the large-scale attacks seriously undermined the military's credibility with the American public. From a military standpoint, Tet was a disaster for the Communists, who were estimated to have suffered over 8000 casualties, severely damaging the Vietcong insurgency in South Vietnam. The operation produced no strategic gains for the North Vietnamese, who had to compensate for the decimation of the Vietcong by committing more regular army troops to subsequent combat operations. It was a huge propaganda victory, however, as Cronkite—a newsman with respect and influence far beyond any single figure in journalism today—declared the Vietnam War to be unwinnable. "We are mired in a stalemate that could only be ended by negotiation, not victory," America's Anchorman declared.

Cronkite's editorial about the war represented a considerable departure from the previous journalistic ethic of reporting objective facts, and allowing the audience to make up their own minds about their meaning. It certainly wasn't an ethic observed with unshakeable fidelity before him, but Cronkite's stature made his reporting on Vietnam a significant moment in journalistic history. President Johnson famously declared, "if I've lost Cronkite, I've lost Middle America." The military found itself unable to sell its strategically correct assessment of Tet as a defeat for North Vietnam to the public. Consequently, their request for a troop surge, to finish the job in Vietnam, was denied by the President, who became despondent and largely stopped communicating with the media. In the wake of Cronkite's declaration of inevitable defeat in Vietnam, public support for the war dropped fifteen to twenty points in public opinion polls…in a matter of months.

If any of this sounds familiar to you, it should. The congressional Democrats of 2006 remembered the Tet Offensive very well. You might have thought Harry Reid looked like an imbecile, desperately searching for a live al-Qaeda commander he could surrender to, and you might have considered the "General Betray Us" Moveon.org swill on the eve of the Iraq troop surge to be mindlessly stupid…but they were just trying to reproduce what Cronkite did for the North Vietnamese, the way a cargo cult hopes to bring gifts from the sky gods by building crude replicas of airports.

Cronkite's reporting on the Tet Offensive was a signature moment in the evolution of asymmetrical warfare. The Vietcong resembled modern terrorists in many ways—they even had suicide bombers. North Vietnam realized, by the spring of 1968, that they could never defeat the American military in battle. The NVA field commander, General Giap, was said to be despondent over the failure of the Tet offensive, and felt his situation was likely to deteriorate even further. Then, as now, American soldiers were proving highly adaptable, and were developing increasing skill at countering enemy tactics, along with a naturally improved knowledge of Vietnamese terrain. The gallantry and skill of Vietnam's soldiers paved the way for America's astonishing battlefield victories in Operations Desert Storm and Iraqi Freedom, much as tomorrow's soldiers will study the long and painful story of the Iraqi occupation, to perfect their counterinsurgency tactics. The soldiers and commanders of 1968 were learning, too.

I will leave it to military historians to debate whether a full-scale surge of troops in the wake of Tet would have secured the defeat of North Vietnam. For myself, I think it highly likely. We'll never know, because the age of modern terrorism—tactics designed to sap civilian will and destroy political support for a powerful military—began when Walter Cronkite took to the air on February 27, 1968, and informed the American public it should not "have faith any longer in the silver linings they find in the darkest clouds."

Walter Cronkite was not an active agent of the North Vietnamese, in the sense Jane Fonda was. He spent the rest of his life steadfastly insisting his editorial judgment on Vietnam represented his honest and heartfelt opinion. When measuring an event of such enormous importance, it hardly matters what his deeply felt personal reasons were. What he did **not** do was simply and clearly report on the outcome of the Tet offensive, and allow his viewers to decide what they made of it. The Communists came to understand the value of their propaganda victory, with General Giap later saying "The most important result of the Tet offensive was it made you de-escalate the bombing, and it brought you to the negotiation table. It was, therefore, a victory…The war was fought on many fronts. At that time the most important one was American public opinion." (Contrary to Internet rumors that will probably start floating around again this weekend, Giap did not specifically credit Walter Cronkite with making this "victory" possible.)

Cronkite's career saw the rise of advocacy journalism in the modern sense, along with the birth of terror warfare. The two developments are not unrelated. Terrorism benefits from access to a media that sees itself as international and "open-minded," rather than aligned with the patriotic interests of its mother country. Journalists of Edward R. Murrow's day would have named al-Qaeda killers as vermin, without hesitation, and applauded American soldiers for exterminating them. Cronkite decided the vermin were invincible. His descendants give interviews where they proudly state they would not warn American troops of an impending terror attack. They pass along terrorist propaganda and doctored photographs as news, and dispatch reporters to search for signs of defeat when victory is imminent…provided a President of the wrong party sits in the White House, of course. Say this much for Cronkite: he didn't care that Johnson had a (D) after his name. To Keith Olbermann, nothing else would matter.

After Cronkite came the deluge. Consider the trajectory of his successor, Dan Rather, who began his career lying about schoolchildren applauding the assassination of JFK, and ended it by trying to pass off falsified documents in a partisan hit job on President Bush during the 2004 elections. Cronkite was a powerful and accomplished newsman who made a fateful decision to become the news, instead of reporting it. His replacement was a ridiculous hack. Whatever you think of Walter Cronkite, it seems clear that his profession became smaller, and less trustworthy, after he passed through it. We would be wise to remember the lesson he taught us about the limits of American will in the Age of Terror. It's better for us to win our battles fast and hard, and let the media weep for the enemy, than give the media time to dictate our strategy, and declare victory impossible.

An Excerpt From Meghan McCain's Totally Awesome Six-Figure Book
August 12, 2009

Author's Note: Meghan McCain, daughter of 2008 presidential candidate John McCain, has been heavily touted as fresh young face for a new, more liberal conservatism. She's supposed to have a six-figure book deal with Hyperion, although I don't believe her work has been published as of this writing. Ms. McCain spends most of her time slamming everyone to her right, usually in a more entertaining manner than her father. Hot Air links to a sizable number of her essays in its Headlines section. Some Hot Air readers felt she received a disproportionate amount of attention for writing that often seems rather lightweight, but I always thought the considerable effort invested in pushing her to prominence warranted keeping tabs on her—and her sillier pronouncements are usually hilarious. One such pronouncement came in August 2009, when she declared herself more influential and important than Michelle Malkin...on the grounds that McCain has more Twitter followers. As soon as I stopped laughing, I grabbed my keyboard and produced the following satire of what McCain's book might be like. A surprising number of Hot Air readers thought this was legitimate, which I took as high praise.

From Chapter 16, "Staying Extremely Cool In The Face Of Extremism":

...having a hard time understanding why people were so slow to follow my warnings, and steer clear of extremely extremist ppl like that extreme Michelle Malkin. I mean, like, we're right in the middle of this historic debate about giving people health care so they won't die any more, and she's pushing some stupid book that says our historic black president is actually some kind of crook. Talk about ankle-biting! I mean, President Obama is not only historic and totally cool, but he probably has even more Twitter followers than me, and here's this nasty little book by a woman that has less than half as many Twitter followers as I do, trying to cut him down! How stupid is that? Hello, Michelle? This President is a giant walking through history, and you're like a little blob of pink bubble gum on the pavement, and I would totally be honored to be the curb he uses to scrape you off his shoe after he steps on you.

Uncool people like Michelle Malkin just want to block health care so everyone will get sick and die, I guess. That's the kind of cruelty I'm doing battle with, in my righteous quest to reform the party of hateful, retarded, gay-bashing rednecks that I love so much. I sincerely believe there is a place in my party for evil far-right homophobes like Michelle...but it's *way* behind the hot, fresh young vanguard of the new conservative generation. One of the basic principles of conservatism is that young people know more than old people, and make better leaders. You know who all the top news anchors say is the leader of those cutting-edge young Republicans? I'll give you a hint: her initials are "MM", but it isn't Michelle Malkin.

Maybe the old fossil conservatives could do our laundry and make sure we have a steady supply of Funions and frappucinos, while we fight the battle for a brighter Republican future. Only hip young tattooed New Republicans have a chance of winning major conservative victories, like chopping a few thousand dollars off the national debt, and forcing fundamentalist extremists to attend gay weddings if they want to keep the tax deductions for their hateful little churches.

My party will need leadership in the years to come. We need someone who can win the approval of the same media that worships me, then go on to run a principled, respectable campaign to lose gracefully to President Obama in 2012. We need to show America that we Republicans are totally inclusive and moderate, like the Democrats. That way, everyone will love us, and we'll enjoy friendly and respectful media coverage in 2016. If we run some kind of fundamentalist extremist gay-bashing animal-hating extremist from some weird state nobody ever heard of, like Alaska, we're just going to nuke the fridge for a whole generation of young Republicans.

I mean, if we want to win like the Democrats, we have to *be* like the Democrats, right? It's just common sense, like everything that guy Kewie Dee says. Democrats are *soooo* cool and inclusive, they make me want to giggle like a giddy schoolgirl. Like, one time I'm walking from the limo to a trendy restaurant in D.C., and I bump into Sheila Jackson Lee, and she's all like "Meghan, I'm buying," and I'm like OMG, this place is really expensive, but she says no problem, she can write it off as a travel expense—she had to cross the street to get there, and that's travel, right? So she has her bodyguards clear all the riff-raff out of our way, and this one guy—he looked like one of those nasty old extremists that shows up at town-hall meetings— he starts shouting questions about health care legislation at Sheila, quoting entire paragraphs from the freaking bill. Sheila was just totally cool about it. She had the guy tasered without breaking a sweat. I mean, how awesome is that? No one who needs Regnery Publishing to handle their dead-tree stuff can approach that kind of refined, elegant style..

You know who would be a completely fantastic leader for a hip, young, reinvented Republican party? My dad, that's who. He sure knows better than to get snarky with people who have more Twitter followers than he does. He is also the undisputed black-belt grand master at losing gracefully to President Obama, which, as I mentioned, will be a key component of Republican strategy in 2012. Here's a little juicy inside dish for you: my dad wanted to cancel his campaign and concede the race in, like, September of 2008…but that witch from Wasilla wouldn't let him. It would have been a totally brilliant move, because it would have built up so much love and respect from reporters, and it would have showed moderates just how inclusive our new Republican Party can be. But You-Know-Who was too extreme and homophobic to listen to reason.

My party should learn from my dad's example, and quit trying to sell hate and fear. We should be more like the Democrats, who just want to stop greedy doctors from stealing children's tonsils, give people free money for cars, and pass environmental legislation before greedy businessmen destroy the Earth. We should stop trying to scare everyone by talking about runaway spending, Constitutional principles, political corruption, and similar extreme topics. In my next chapter, I'll explain how support for gay marriage will lead my party back into control of the White House and Congress, after President Obama is finished using them...

Glenn Beck and the Unforgivable Curse
August 19, 2009

Author's Note: The boycott against Beck described in this essay wound up accomplishing nothing. Defending Beck against the boycott, on the other hand, was tremendously entertaining. Liberal hate sites were filled with inarticulate mobs grunting in fury over this essay. There's something in the liberal psychology that reacts blindly, and viscerally, to any suggestion that they are not the sole arbiters of what constitutes "racism," or that any leftist in good standing (let alone The First Black President!) could be guilty of harboring racist thoughts. For the uninitiated, "Avada Kedavra" and the Unforgivable Curse are references to the Harry Potter books.

Radio and television host Glenn Beck finds himself confronting an advertiser boycott, organized by people who don't watch his show anyway. The primary effect of the boycott will be denying advertisers like Best Buy, CVS, and Travelocity access to Beck's immense and rapidly growing audience. (By the way, one of the participating advertisers is GMAC. Don't we taxpayers own five or six billion dollars worth of GMAC? Something tells me the boycott supporters include a far larger percentage of people who don't pay any federal income tax than Beck's audience does. GMAC should require permission from actual taxpayers before it's allowed to engage in a silly boycott that could damage its profitability, and devalue our five billion dollar investment.)

The comment that got Beck in hot water involved calling President Obama a racist, who has "deep-seated hatred for white people of the white culture." Calling any liberal a "racist" is the *Avada Kedavra* of political discourse, the Unforgivable Curse. Admittedly, it seems like an unprovoked act of rhetorical aggression. It's not like Obama and his party have been running around calling everyone who disagrees with them racists, mindless drones, un-American traitors, Nazis, assassins, or Astroturf lawn gnomes who get their opinions from their corporate paymasters. Oh, wait, it's *exactly* like that.

Perhaps we could defuse the tension by asking the boycott organizers if they think someone who sat quietly at Klan rallies for twenty years could credibly be accused of racism. I'm sure they would say "no"…and since that's an accurate analogy for Obama's decades at Jeremiah Wright's Church of Racial Hatred, Beck would doubtless be moved to offer a polite apology, and we could call the boycott off. Maybe Beck could give President Obama an autographed copy of his book, with a "Sorry, dude!" inscription. Beck's thoughtful gift would doubtless secure a place of honor in the White House library, alongside *Rules for Radicals* by Saul Alinsky, *Open Veins of Latin America: Five Centuries of the Pillage of a Continent* by Eduardo Galeano, and *Fugitive Days: A Memoir* by Bill Ayers.

The rest of Beck's comment, asserting that Obama has "deep-seated hatred for white people of the white culture," should be easy for the President's defenders to disprove. All they have to do is cite one positive thing Obama has said or written about white culture. Anywhere. Ever. Hopefully they can get back to us before GMAC needs another taxpayer bailout, to address the self-inflicted financial damage from its participation in the boycott. I wouldn't recommend wasting any time going through Obama's university compositions, assuming you can find where they're buried, and get past the three-headed guard dog. He graduated from Columbia and Harvard, where "deep-seated hatred for white people of the white culture" is written in green on your thesis when the professor hands it back to you, along with "excellent sentence composition!" and "good use of original sources!"

There's no question that Beck's comment was provocative and rude. If you happen to be in a room with Glenn Beck at the moment, and you're reading this to him out loud, he probably just shouted "Exactly!" Political and cultural debates always feature provocation and rude behavior. The American media occasionally becomes very prim about this. Strangely enough, these occasions always coincide with the election of a Democrat President. The same people puckering their lips over the heated tone of Beck's assertions, Sarah Palin's "death panel" commentary, or the behavior of town-hall protesters, thought the temperature was just *peachy* when liberals were openly fantasizing about assassinating President Bush. The average liberal couldn't order a burger and fries at McDonald's without informing the cashier that Bush was a subhuman cowboy moron.

Our political discourse is heated because the stakes are so high. Obama has wasted trillions of dollars in taxpayer money, threatened the economy with permanent recession through his cap-and-trade bill, and tried to ram through a federal takeover of health insurance without debate. The Administration openly asserts that certain Americans "shouldn't do a whole lot of talking," and labels dissent from its agenda un-patriotic. Today we hear rumors that Democrats plan to shove their health-care debacle down the throats of a public that has become increasingly united in opposition to it, using parliamentary "nuclear options" to muscle it through Congress. The public is right to feel a bit testy when Congress talks about using "nuclear options" against it.

We have arrived at a moment when politics determines the survival of entire industries. Broken companies are dug up from shallow graves at the edges of the free market, and reanimated with massive infusions of tax dollars, for the benefit of the politically-connected union infestations that killed them. People who end up on the wrong side of health-care rationing could pay for their unwise 2008 presidential votes with their lives. There is no place where a taxpayer can go to secure a refund for his share of the squandered $787 billion "stimulus" bill…just as there will be no place to go when they discover socialized medicine is a disaster. There will only be a comment box at the local Post Office / Government Surgical Clinic, where you can scribble your complaint on the back of your organ donor card.

It wasn't supposed to *be* like this. Average people should not require advanced degrees in medicine and economics to make informed decisions in the voting booth. They don't have time to study the effects of deficit spending on the bond market, or the sad history of attempts to repeal the laws of supply and demand through subsidies and price controls. They have lives to lead, children to raise, and jobs that give them plenty to worry about. They respond to loud, rude, spectacular things, because they desperately want to believe the situation is *simple* enough for them to comprehend it, and cast informed, meaningful votes. The Left understands this very well, and grits its teeth when the Right starts playing the game. The people who blew billions of tax dollars fooling voters into thinking they could get "free money" to buy a new car, have no right to complain when a smart lady with a Facebook page coins a phrase that galvanizes opposition to their agenda...or when a guy with 2.5 million viewers uses harsh language to bellow a challenge the media should have issued much more politely, during the presidential campaign, for the benefit of their 50 million viewers.

Americans are becoming increasingly uneasy with the degree of politics that has been infused into every aspect of their lives. They're only just beginning to realize how much worse this President has made the situation, in the seventy years since his election. (That's what it *feels* like, anyway.) People trapped on a runaway train can be forgiven for screaming, especially when the conductor has made it plain that he cannot be talked into easing back on the throttle, and thinks anyone who tries it should be thrown off the train. It's too bad the media gave Obama so many free passes during the campaign. I can forgive the angry look on Glenn Beck's face as he tears them up.

Crimes Against the Party
September 29, 2009

The Left is mobilizing to protect Roman Polanski from being extradited to the United States, after his arrest by Swiss authorities for the crime of raping and sodomizing a 13-year-old girl in 1977, then fleeing from justice. Polanski spent his thirty years in exile from the United States on a rocky island off the coast of Madagascar, where he subsisted on a diet of roots and grubs. His only companion was a mangled Barbie doll with a cracked face, which he named "Natasha." No, not really. He's actually lived a life of opulence in Europe, hailed as a great artist, toasted in the salons of Paris. The only thing he's been deprived of is the thrill of threatening to leave America when a Republican wins the presidency.

Polanski's defenders cite his brilliance as an Important Director of Important Films as a reason it's not only wrong, but outrageous, to punish him for his past crimes. This is similar to the arguments made in favor of releasing convicted cop-killer Mumia abu Jamal from prison, a point of view enthusiastically held by at least one high-ranking member of the Obama Administration: that fabled Rohrschach inkblot of liberal stupidity, Van Jones. Mumia's delicate writing hand is much more important than the one he used to shoot Officer Daniel Faulkner in the back.

The Left also issues Get Out of Jail Free cards to people other than artists. The Polanski defense is a nostalgic karaoke rendition of the 1998 anthem "Perjury About Sex Is Not A Crime," sung on Bill Clinton's behalf. Perjury, infidelity, and what the antique feminist movement used to call "sexual harassment" were small prices to pay for Clinton's inspirational leadership.

You can't say the Left is entirely soft on crime, however. There are some scofflaws they'll never stop trying to put behind bars. CIA agents who kept America safe from terrorists, for example. None of the terrorists held at Guantanamo Bay was innocent, or thirteen years old, and none of them were drugged, raped, and sodomized, but the Obama Administration is keen on prosecuting the people who interrogated them. If Roman Polanski had covered his victim's face with a wet towel, maybe his defense would be a bit less energetic.

Another individual the Left wants brought to justice is Karl Rove, for the crime of being Karl Rove. The other charges against him range from being nebulous to absurd, but rest assured, it would be a great day for America if we could frog-march that villain into the vacant cell left behind by a liberated Mumia abu Jamal. Best of all would be the trial and imprisonment of George W. Bush, a fantasy the Left holds with the intensity of a small child shivering through a sleepless Christmas Eve. Bush actually did the stuff Clinton just talked about, such as liberating the people of Iraq from monstrous tyranny, or fighting AIDS in Africa, but it earns him no slack from liberal vigilantes. He did more for womens' rights than anyone alive today—you can ask the women of Afghanistan about it, now that their faces aren't wrapped in upholstery—but he didn't do anything really important, like make a movie about the sexual oppression of suburban America.

The Left is primarily interested in prosecuting people guilty of crimes against the State. Not the American government *per se*—Polanski's flight from the American justice system doesn't count, because like all great and fashionable artists, he is a Citizen Of The World. The State stretches beyond the American government—in fact, it was born and nourished overseas, in the writings of European progressives and fascists at the dawn of the twentieth century, and it still draws much of its intellectual nourishment from European sources today.

The State has only one Party, with franchises and local sub-divisions around the world. The Party may have factions that quibble over relatively minor issues of policy, but America is one of the few developed nations where the Party has any serious opposition…and even here, it's remarkable how deeply the Party's ideology has penetrated its nominal opponents, and how many of its foundational assumptions and myths they accept. Still, most American Democrats feel greater kinship with European socialists than with the greedy, racist teabaggers staging massive protests outside their windows. The previous Democrat candidate for President, John Kerry, was remarkably honest about this.

The Party makes a very clear distinction between its political masters, the elevated elite class surrounding them, and the little people who provide its electoral muscle. The elite are permitted indulgences that could not be made available to the unwashed masses. No matter how faithfully you might have voted Democrat for your entire life, the Clinton defenses against perjury and adultery would not be accepted from you. Likewise, your odds of successfully fleeing the rape of an underage girl, to become the toast of Paris, are extremely slim. The elite will not join you on the farm, in the socialist agrarian paradise they've been designing for the industrialized West. They will still be ferried around in limousines and private jets, long after you're expected to surrender your automobile. You would serve time in prison, or be bankrupted by enormous fines, for behavior that Obama cabinet officials are allowed to discreetly forget about. Some of this immunity comes from sheer political power, but any Republican who thinks he will be allowed to join Tim Geithner on the tax-evasion ice skating rink is a fool with a big surprise in his future.

The Party is primarily concerned with prosecuting crimes against itself, particularly against its elite members. It has little passion for crime among the little people, which it believes its advanced social-engineering theories can resolve, if it gains enough power to fully implement them. Justice is synonymous with the power of the Party—who's got time to fret over ancient sexual assaults and silly presidential perjuries when there is income inequality in the world? The elite cannot be expected to rattle around in the labyrinth of regulations they impose on the proletariat. They've got important work to do, including the kind of consciousness-raising that requires big name stars and directors.

George Bush's first offense was denying America the brilliant, socially aware, technocratic leadership of Al Gore. The statue of limitations will *never* run out on something like that. Meanwhile, forcing a beloved Hollywood director to end his life in the slammer for a little error in judgment, like rape, would be unthinkably crass...as long as his Party credentials are in order. That is why the same people who turned their backs on Elia Kazan weep for Roman Polanski today, and will weep again at his career retrospective, on some future Oscar night. The Party may have changed its name, and adjusted its methods, but it still remembers what Kazan did to it, and his sentence extends far beyond the end of his life.

Socialism: a Hate Story
October 6, 2009

Ann Althouse was one of the few people who bothered to drag herself to see Michael Moore's latest exercise in agitprop, *Capitalism: A Love Story.* Her reaction to the film is interesting. Describing a sign she saw in the lobby, she says:

> "Dump ¢apitali$m/Join the Socialists." And, indeed, the movie was a big promotion of socialism. Capitalism is "evil"—Capitalism is a "sin"—we were told over and over. And if only all the downtrodden masses would see this truth and join together we could have socialism.

Here is how she describes two of Moore's typically dishonest examples of sinful capitalism:

> There were some teenagers in Wilkes Barre, PA who had suffered a terrible abuse of their due process rights, and the fact that a for-profit detention institution was involved didn't transform what was a criminal scheme into a broader indictment of our economic system.

> And there were the life insurance policies that companies take out on their [low level] employees. Maybe these shouldn't be permitted—and calling them "Dead Peasant" policies was kind of outrageous—but if they are wrong, we can make legislation banning them. We have plenty of regulation in this country that keeps us away from a completely free market, and we can procure that legislation if that's what we want. I was disgusted by the camera trained on the face of a boy who cried over the death of his young mother. The real villain there was asthma. It said nothing significant about capitalism, which made it grotesque exploitation to use that boy in the movie.

Moore's method involves finding people who are unhappy with their circumstances, lying about the particulars of the cases to make them illustrate his points better, and converting them into wholesale indictments of the free market, and America in general. Althouse captures the overall flavor of Moore's work with this observation:

> Moore shamelessly and repeatedly advocated the violent overthrow of the economic system. It was somewhat humorously or moderately presented—such as through the mouth of a cranky old man who was being evicted from his home—but it came across that Moore wants a revolution. He kept advising the workers—and the evictees—of the world to unite and shake off their chains.

Socialist and fascist agitators have always relied upon the support of the disaffected. No system of government, from the most rigid collective state to the most energetic free-market democracy, can ever achieve a completely satisfied population. There are people who don't do well in a capitalist system. Some of these people suffer from bad choices—freedom cannot exist without the possibility for error. Some suffer reversals of fortune through no fault of their own. Prosperity requires risk, which carries the possibility of loss. Some people will be wronged by criminal enterprises, large or small. No system of laws is invulnerable, and even the most dedicated law enforcement personnel are not infallible.

The irony is that no system of government is **more** brutally unfair to the disaffected than the kind of total State that Michael Moore lusts after. A central State has more power to rob its citizens, waste their resources, cause devastating economic fluctuations, and cause physical injury than any private corporation. The State is far more difficult to change, and more likely to persist in its mistakes. It is utterly inescapable, to a degree that Microsoft and Wal-Mart can only envy.

One of the most persistent and dangerous illusions of socialism is the belief that money becomes magically virtuous when government handles it. Politicians are at least as greedy as any captain of industry. The installation of a politburo does not eliminate ambition from a society—it changes the means used to fulfill those ambitions. The political class achieves its desires through force, by definition. Unlike commerce, force produces no side benefits for the larger population—the politician and his constituents get what they want, at the expense of everyone else.

The people Moore caricatures as cold-hearted fat cats don't go away under a socialist government—what a silly, childish notion! The million-dollar marketplace of high-level transactions still exists, but now the most important commodity is political power. You can already see this happening all around us, as the transition to a command economy has radically accelerated under Obama, after puttering along in a lower gear for decades. What high-rolling mega-corporate CEO doesn't love the idea that his company is "too big to fail," and thus insulated from market forces by a shield of taxpayer money?

Political influence is one of the smartest investments those "fat cats" can make, which is why the immense Obama government became so fabulously corrupt so quickly. When you slide billions of dollars across the landscape, you can't be surprised to see a crowd of ruthless people chasing it. Those people won't go away when you complete the transition to complete socialism—they'll just become Party elders and commissars. They're not terribly inconvenienced by having to wear Party jewelry, and learn a few new songs. Their children might have already been taught the lyrics in school.

What about the little guy? Doesn't he benefit under benign socialist control? *Of course not.* He never has, anywhere on Earth, during the many times collective governments have gained power. The common man might realize some short-term gains when the socialist government marches into power—wow, free health care! It never lasts. It *can't.* Socialist control destroys the very mechanisms of prosperity it needs to pay off on its promises. The capitalist incentives for hard work and risk-taking are replaced by the collectivist impulse to do the least that is required of you, and accept whatever benefits you are given. People are, in the main, rational actors. They respond to incentives. There are always exceptions—people who answer a religious calling, or give 100% effort under any circumstances, due to their inner drive. Those people are never numerous enough to produce prosperity for a nation of millions.

Socialists despise competition—they find virtue in the idea that everyone deserves everything, and benevolent leaders have a responsibility to provide it. Competition doesn't disappear under socialist control—that's another childish fantasy. Instead, socialism replaces competition between individuals with competition between **groups.** The former is energetic and constructive, while the latter is bitter, and almost inevitably violent. In a total State, the individual has no way to improve his situation, no way to build a better life on his own. Instead, he must join a collective—a group large and powerful enough to influence the government, which dispenses all benefits. You can see this sort of thing all around you today, since our government is already titanic, and has confiscated much wealth to spread. It will get much, much worse if we're ever foolish enough to slip all the way into Michael Moore's idea of a total State.

The architects of the State can have all the good intentions in the world—they can be paragons of selfless virtue—and it doesn't change a thing. The nature of the system they create will inevitably corrupt it, because the nature of the people trapped in the system doesn't change. They want more for themselves and their families, and if they can't earn it, they will band together to demand it. There is only one reliable way to hold those bands together over the long term, only one predictable response to the diminishing returns gained by each sacrifice of liberty…and only one emotion the leaders of each collective entity can easily encourage, to maintain their own power: hatred.

When everything you have is provided by the State, you will easily come to hate anyone whose demands take priority over yours. They are not your competitors. They are your enemies. Even now, in what may prove to be the last days we can regard ourselves as a free nation with a bloated government, we can see how much *anger* simmers among those who believe the urgency of their demands outweighs any consideration of the cost to others. You may recall an attempt by ObamaCare supporters to launch a viral meme last month, with a Facebook and Twitter message that said something like "No one should have to die because they can't afford health insurance." A slogan like that does not allow for argument, or even picky questions. You either support socialized medicine, or you want people who can't afford health insurance to die. What attitude is appropriate, when confronting people who want those who can't afford health insurance to die?

Capitalism is indeed a love story, born from the enduring respect of free men for the maturity and liberty of their fellow citizens. It is better to be poor in a capitalist society, than middle-class in any of the miserable "worker's paradises" that litter the world. Free people working together, and in competition, generate the prosperity that stands as the only medicine against poverty. Children and pets might be loved without respect, but not adults. The alternative to respect and love is clearly visible in the ugly hypocrisy of a bitter millionaire, who charges the dwindling number of suckers foolish enough to take him seriously for the privilege of being told a dark fairy tale, which requires them to become slaves before they can live happily ever after. Listen to the desperation and anger growing in the air around you, and ask yourself if Michael Moore's hate story is likely to end well for anyone who isn't already rich, powerful, and ruthless.

The Blatant Beast
October 16, 2009

In the 16th-century epic poem *The Faerie Queene*, Edmund Spenser writes of a monster called the Blatant Beast. which had "a thousand tongues of every kind and quality", which "poured forth abuse, not caring where or when…speaking hateful things of good and bad alike, of high and low, not even sparing kings or kaisers, but either blotting them with infamy or biting them with baneful teeth." In one of my favorite books, *The Compleat Enchanter* by Fletcher Pratt and L. Sprague deCamp, a pair of modern-day psychologists discover a method for traveling to the worlds of fantasy and literature. When they visit the world of the *Faerie Queene,* they encounter the Blatant Beast, who demands they tell him a story he hasn't heard before, in exchange for their lives. The hero of the story responds by reciting an extremely bawdy limerick, the "Ballad of Eskimo Nell," embarrassing the Beast so much that it slinks off in defeat with its ears burning.

The mainstream media is the modern incarnation of the Blatant Beast, and its defeat calls for the same strategy by conservatives: tell it a story it can't ignore, then hit it with a punchline it can't help repeating. Like the Blatant Beast, the media does have a certain capacity for shame…because nothing bothers professional "journalists" more than amateurs besting them at the sacred ritual of reporting news.

The media beast is wounded, but still powerful. It's hard to measure the full extent of its influence, although it seems to have diminished somewhat with the rise of alternative media, including talk radio and the Internet. The modern style of agenda journalism dates at least as far back as Walter Cronkite and the Tet Offensive, but I've always thought it mutated into the form we recognize today during the 1992 elections. The media may have climbed into the tank for Obama to an unprecedented degree, but in '92 it was driving an armored fighting vehicle for Clinton. *60 Minutes* openly provided cover for his infidelity, helping to bury the Gennifer Flowers story. The press was happy to provide all sorts of assistance to the Clinton campaign, including assistance for the ridiculous "worst economy in the last 50 years" campaign slogan, and warping Bush's polite question about a grocery store bar code scanner into a heavy-handed theme about how "out of touch" he was.

These tactics were effective, in large measure, because Bush allowed them to be. He never got the hang of working around the media. Like Bob Dole and John McCain after him, he seemed trapped in a perpetual state of surprise about how unfairly he was being treated, and spent his re-election campaign waiting for a sympathetic wave of public outrage that never came.

Of course, Bush was working against the real pressure of economic turbulence, and the general public perception that incumbent Presidents—unlike incumbent members of Congress—are responsible for everything bad that happens during their term. If this tempts you to discount the influence of partisan journalists, try to imagine Barack Obama being held to the same standard during his re-election campaign in 2012. It's likely that he'll be running under the cloud of an economy at least as bad as the elder Bush's was, and possibly much worse…but the media will never hang it around his neck, as they did with Bush. The economy of a huge industrialized nation is a complex affair, and you can be sure every possible benefit of the doubt will be given to Obama.

The media's power to influence the public is not limitless, as we saw during the 2004 election. The wounds of Rathergate run deeper than many journalists like to admit. The 2004 media strove mightily to drag John Kerry across the finish line, but they couldn't quite pull it off. Kerry's thudding lack of charisma, and the transparent cynicism of his war-hero routine, were part of the reason, but it was fascinating to watch the media try to work around them. They seemed perplexed over their inability to discredit the Swift Boat Veterans for Truth by repeatedly calling them "the discredited Swift Boat Veterans for Truth." Dan Rather *still* doesn't understand what happened to him.

The media's credibility has continued to bleed steadily away. It would be a mistake to believe them powerless, or on the verge of re-discovering the honor of honest, unbiased journalism. No matter how popular a blog like Hot Air becomes, it will never be broadcast in hundreds of airport terminals to a captive audience of weary travelers, like CNN. The newsstands will always contain a sea of conventionally liberal publications, with a few National Reviews and Weekly Standards peeking out.

The media effort to secure the re-election of the Nobel Prize-winning First Black President will be ferocious. The MSM's control over the popular culture is still formidable—just look at what happened to Rush Limbaugh this week, as media outlets ran with ridiculous fake quotes posted by a few leftist bloggers, and hammered the man's reputation hard enough to eliminate his position in the group seeking to buy the St. Louis Rams. Rush has a vast audience, and simple common sense would tell anyone who isn't part of that audience that he could never have gotten away with making the statements attributed to him. The actual rape hoax perpetrated by a vile creature like Al Sharpton is held against him far less than non-existent "racist" comments were held against Limbaugh.

Still, the media will pay a price for the "successful" campaign against Limbaugh. It will never take the form of huge masses of people swearing off the *New York Times* and CNN all at once. It happens a little bit at a time. The Blatant Beast dies from many small wounds that bleed slowly. This week, all across the country, a number of people watched the Limbaugh debacle and decided they just don't trust the mainstream media any more, joining the people who reached that conclusion during the savaging of Sarah Palin, the unraveling of the global-warming hoax, and many other incidents, large and small.

The successful conservative candidates of 2010 and 2012 will learn how to speak to these people. More importantly, they will learn how to use their time in the spotlight to speak past the media gatekeepers, with memorable words and powerful ideas that haunt the imaginations of voters. We won't find these candidates by looking for people the media supposedly likes, or approves of. The press liked John McCain more than any other Republican candidate of the modern era, and he'd barely clinched the nomination before the first trumped-up story of a supposed affair with a staffer began floating through mediaspace. The search for a Galahad candidate, of such noble purity that the mainstream media is awed and humbled into giving him a fair shake, is futile. If the press can't find something real to work with, they'll cruise the lefty web sites until they find a juicy lie they can use. If there aren't already blogs full of imaginary "racist" comments from Mike Huckabee, Mitt Romney, Sarah Palin, and every other potential Republican candidate, there will be.

Conservative candidates can't keep the Blatant Beast from blotting them with infamy, or biting them with baneful teeth. They can make sure the voters see them battling with with skill and grace, and leave the Beast's ears burning with a few white-hot words it can't help repeating to everyone it meets.

Defending The Invincible
October 18, 2009

Author's Note: In October 2009, conservative superstar Rush Limbaugh attempted to join a consortium that wished to purchase the St. Louis Rams. His membership in this group was blocked, after an incredibly vicious and dishonest campaign to smear him as a racist. I've rarely been as angry as I was during this sorry exercise in liberal character assassination. I realized there was more at stake than the slander of someone I've long admired, so I followed Rush's example and set anger aside to make the larger point.

Almost every column written in defense of Rush Limbaugh over the last few days, following the vicious campaign to slander him as a racist, has included a statement along the lines of "Rush is rich, powerful, intelligent, and articulate, so he can take care of himself, and he'll be just fine." I don't mean to disparage the authors of these sentiments, but I must disagree. I know the most popular conservative broadcaster in America doesn't *need* some anonymous guest-author on a blog to defend him, but I'm going to do it anyway, without the slightest reservation due to his wealth and power.

Much strife and misery has been visited on this country by the idea that the rights and prerogatives of the rich and successful are diminished by their fortunes…that we should feel no remorse about seizing their property, or insulting their honor, because they'll still be comfortably rich at the end of the day. We have become much too relaxed about laughing off vile slander, because the target can nurse his wounded soul from the plush accommodations of a West Palm Beach mansion. Honor is as valuable to the millionaire as to the pauper.

I'll probably never be part of a consortium that purchases a football team, but I understand what it means to watch a dream bleed to death. My hopes and ambitions may be smaller than Rush Limbaugh's, but they have *exactly* the same value to me. Whether those dreams are carved from pixels, paper, or platinum, they are equally priceless. It requires only a drop of the moral imagination **utterly lacking** in the people who slandered Limbaugh to guess what it feels like, when a man whose life revolves around words and ideas sees his dreams boiled away by words he didn't speak, and ideas he has never held.

The events of the past week were about more than simply thwarting Limbaugh's desire to buy into a football team. There was the naked greed of parasites like Al Sharpton, desperate to maintain his relevance in a world that has wisely stripped him of the power to destroy a man's life with a phony rape allegation, or launch murderous riots. There was the blind personal hatred of Limbaugh, by people who long ago tired of watching him rewrite their plans for the part of America that refuses to submit to them. And, of course, this was the latest offensive in a bitter war against the ideas that Limbaugh has long served, as their most cheerful and effective defender. Limbaugh's enemies in that war are angry because they're frightened. They're frightened because all of their estimates and projections said they should have been able to claim victory by now.

Backed up against the wall, and forced to admit the most damaging quotes used against Limbaugh were forgeries, his accusers are left stammering that he's simply too "divisive" to be involved with ownership of an NFL team. What a bleak example of the totalitarian mindset! If you disagree with the approved ideas distributed by the collective, you're "divisive" and unfit for membership in polite society. I suppose Limbaugh is *saturated* with divisiveness particles, whose half-life will extend for decades, but the warning to others is clear: rid yourselves of those "divisive" ideas and get with the program.

Perhaps the President could direct one of his many czars to prepare a list of certified "divisive" positions, and which aspects of society are closed to offenders. It would save people like David Checketts, the investor seeking to purchase the Rams, the time he wasted inviting Limbaugh to join his consortium. Imagine how much more convenient it would have been for Checketts, if he could have pulled up a handy whitehouse.gov web page and learned Rush was too divisive to be minority owner of a football team! The Homeland Security spectrum of terrorist alert levels could be used to measure divisiveness ratings. I'd be willing to give them an email address, so the system could send me a warning message when I approach Level Orange. What do you suppose the divisiveness rating for someone like Jeremiah Wright would be? He built a tidy personal fortune from his Ministry of Hate—would he be allowed to buy a stake in an NFL team?

Only the most gullible dupes, and people who rely on CNN for "news", seriously think Rush Limbaugh is a racist. The dishonesty and cynicism behind dimwitted assertions that he wanted to buy an NFL team to role-play the life of a plantation owner is breathtaking. His accusers don't *really* think he harbors some elusive racist demon, which he suppresses just long enough to become friends with Walter Williams, Clarence Thomas, Thomas Sowell, and Tony Dungy. The people who read this crap should be at least as angry over the insult to their intelligence as Limbaugh is about the insult to his honor. This kind of weapons-grade stupidity is one of the things America can no longer afford.

Limbaugh's accusers want him burned at the stake for the crime of effective conservatism, not the racism they were so eager to lie about last week. The American public should think long and hard about which side of this ideological struggle should be on trial. Rush Limbaugh's ideas did not produce a titanic deficit, double-digit unemployment, and global adversaries who can barely stop laughing at our President long enough to pretend they respect him. His ideas did not put disciples of Saul Alinsky, Chairman Mao, and Alex Jones in positions of power. His words are not deployed to conceal hundreds of billions in stolen "stimulus" money, thousand-page Mad Lib bills riddled with blank paragraphs, and massive offenses against individual liberty. His EIB Network endorses $1500 Sleep Number beds, not "saved or created" jobs costing half a million bucks apiece. Unlike the "Hope and Change" Administration, he doesn't spend his three hours on the radio each weekday listing all the things you will no longer be allowed to do. He is the champion of ideas so powerful that his enemies fear the merest *taste* of them.

Rush Limbaugh has raised his voice in defense of freedom countless times over the years. I'm happy to exercise my freedom to raise my voice in defense of him. I invite you to do the same. It doesn't matter if he doesn't "need" it. He *deserves* it. All of us do. There is little we can do to reverse the injustice of the St. Louis Rams affair, but we can make it up to Rush by giving him the chance to deliver a *hell* of a show on the day after Election Day, next year. If CNN is foolish enough to continue employing cretins like Rick Sanchez by then, all of *them* should be turning in a very enjoyable performance on that day, as well.

Tapping The Golden Vein
November 20, 2009

Centuries ago, at the beginning of the Obama Administration, we were told that the "obscene" bonuses of AIG executives should be taxed away, with special taxes that amounted to bills of attainder. This is not the first time we've seen specific industries targeted with massive taxes because they were deemed immoral. The outstanding example is the tobacco industry, which the government uses as a trained vampire, sending it forth to suck tax revenue from the lungs of smokers. Big Oil gets soaked with a lot of taxes, too, justified in part by the merciless profiteering and environmental disdain of its chief executives. Of course, Big Tobacco and Big Oil still make money, but the government makes more from their products than they do.

One industry has thus far been able to escape punitive taxation, despite routinely employing shadowy accounting practices, spending fantastic amounts of money, and reaping obscene profits. It produces a product that often causes significant damage to the social environment. It raises its price to the consumer relentlessly, with no measurable increase in quality. Top employees can rake in $20 million or more in a single year, while frequently maintaining foreign residences to escape high tax rates. They often extract fat paychecks from their companies, even when their failures cost the company staggering amounts of money. While it generates much of its income in the United States, it's one of the worst industries for outsourcing jobs overseas.

It's time to tap the last untouched golden vein in the American economic bloodstream. Let's tax the crap out of Hollywood.

Hollywood actors are generally outspoken in support of "social justice," so they shouldn't mind picking up the tab. Will Ferrell, recently named Hollywood's most overpaid actor by Forbes, is an aggressive advocate of socialized medicine—but strangely enough, he hasn't used any of his millions to buy insurance for the poor. We can change that with some carefully targeted taxes. After pulling in $20 million a pop for a string of lousy movies, Ferrell is Salvation Army kettle full of undeserved loot just waiting to be rolled into the soup kitchens.

Canadian actor Jim Carrey railed against "personal greed" after collecting millions to record the voice of Scrooge in this year's computer-animated *A Christmas Carol*. Carrey's not dumb enough to submit himself to the wonders of Canadian health care or economic policy, but he thinks *you* should. We could help him overcome his bad feelings about personal greed by grabbing seventy or eighty percent of his huge fortune, and using that money to fund emergency medical services for the poor.

Let's just ponder Michael Moore for a moment, and move on.

Big-name actors aren't the only sources of golden fleece in Hollywood. Studio executives could teach the Enron crowd a few things about creative accounting. They spend gigantic amounts of money on awful big-budget "tentpole" films, while some of the biggest hits in recent years were modestly-budgeted movies like *The Hangover, District 9, Paranormal Activity*, and the *Twilight* films. Those huge budgets obviously aren't buying proportional amounts of quality.

Hollywood is a source of both social and political corruption. Its movies are often toxic waste thrown in the faces of parents trying to raise their children with decent values. Its stars and directors gain disproportionate influence within the Democrat party, and relentlessly shove their politics into the faces of their audience. They're certainly entitled to their opinions, but perhaps a little fiscal restraint would focus them more on the business of entertaining, and give them less money and idle time for proselytizing.

Why should actors and directors be the super-wealthy patrician class of America, gazing down upon toiling masses they claim to speak for, but scarcely understand? Why should the guy who brought you *Land of the Lost* be hauling in twenty times the loot of a top surgeon, brilliant inventor, or hard-working businessman?

You might wonder if our entertainer-monarchs would give us the same level of performance, after we began confiscating their huge salaries. The price controls and fee limits on medicine in the Democrats' health-care proposals assume doctors will provide the same care and effort if their incomes are controlled, so why wouldn't actors? They constantly claim to have a high degree of devotion to their art, so wouldn't they give their best even if we limited them to a handsome upper-middle-class lifestyle? And would the cinematic arts really suffer if some of the dreary, overpaid Hollywood elite stopped appearing in all our movies, making way for more young talent that would be overjoyed to receive a mere five or six-figure paycheck?

I can see nothing but upsides to dropping massive new taxes and regulation on Hollywood. To those who object that I'm supposed to be a champion of free markets…well, I am. But why should Hollywood be the last one?

The Suicide Fantasy
December 21, 2009

Author's Note: The movie Avatar *became an enormous hit, and its plot became the subject of much debate. I wrote this essay within a few hours of seeing it. I was trying to find a way to express why the finale, in particular, left me feeling profoundly uneasy. As I said to fellow Green Room contributor, and* Avatar *defender, C.K. MacLeod during a lively exchange some days later, I found myself actively rooting for the evil Colonel Quaritch during his thrilling escape from a crippled command vehicle. I think he became the true protagonist of the story during that sequence, bravely fighting a losing battle against an entire universe rigged against him by its author. I got an enormous response to this essay, so I gather a lot of other people were harboring similar thoughts. I'm an old-school sci-fi geek who would love to see some classics of the genre brought to the screen with a measure of* Avatar's *craftsmanship and budget, so I really hated to slam a high-profile, popular science fiction movie. If you want a less pedantic, more intelligent treatment of environmental and military themes in a fantastic setting, I highly recommend* The Legacy of Heorot *by Larry Niven and Jerry Pournelle. It's the story* Avatar *wants to be when it grows up.*

I went to see *Avatar* on Sunday evening, and found myself generally in agreement with Ed Morrissey's review—the visual effects are stunning, and James Cameron remains one of the great action choreographers of cinema. Although many reviewers have complained the film takes too long to reach its climax, I thought the early and middle sections were the most enjoyable parts. The visual achievement is dazzling, in both design and execution, making the exploration of both the human and alien portions of *Avatar's* beautiful world very entertaining.

Right after our hero consummates his relationship with his alien love, the whole thing goes very sour. I couldn't quite put a name to its disagreeable flavor at first—it's preachy and predictable, to be sure, but that isn't what makes its gorgeous rainbow soup curdle during the grand finale. I figured it out later that night, while reading a seemingly unrelated post from Mark Steyn on National Review Online, discussing angry global warming fanatics reacting to their disappointment over the pointless "global warming summit" at Copenhagen.

As quoted by Steyn, George Monbiot snarls, "Goodbye Africa, goodbye south Asia; goodbye glaciers and sea ice, coral reefs and rainforest. It was nice knowing you. Not that we really cared." Meanwhile, Polly Toynbee shrieks, "What would it take? A tidal wave destroying New York maybe—New Orleans was the wrong people—with London, St. Petersburg, and Shanghai wiped out all at once."

Avatar is the CGI-enhanced, $400 million version of the dark dreams peddled by Monbiot and Toynbee. It's a suicide fantasy, the Hollywood blockbuster equivalent of a troubled teenager's notebook sketches, scribbled by someone who hates himself only marginally less than he hates the rest of the world. To elaborate further, I must include some mild spoilers from the movie's plot—although, really, if you're more than twelve years old, you already know *exactly* what happens in this film. The only element of mystery awaiting you is finding out who kills the bad guy. I promise not to ruin that.

Science fiction and fantasy provide a storyteller with the fantastic power of an infinite blank canvas, upon which any setting can be created, to sustain any sort of plot. In *Avatar,* James Cameron has created a world that justifies the smug arrogance and bitter alienation of the radical environmentalist. The alien world of Pandora really *is* a maternal Gaia spirit, with every bit of the flora and fauna connected in a mystical web, which capitalists and soldiers are too blind and stupid to see. The alien Na'vi really *are* what infantile liberal mythology has made of the American Indian: innocent, peace-loving, simple, and so harmonious with nature that they can literally plug it into their pony tails. Lacking the conflict and flaws that make the Indians so fascinating and tragic, the Na'vi are utterly boring—aside from the heroine, brought vividly to life by a remarkable performance from Zoe Saldana. The childlike environmentalist daydream of a "perfect" society, sustainably at peace with Mother Nature, is captured in the image of the Na'vi tribe snuggled in hammock-like leaves, embraced by the vast branches of their goddess tree. No ambitions, no failures, no questions, no achievement, no future. These giant blue aliens leave absolutely no carbon footprint.

What happens to this wish-fulfillment watercolor of eco-paradise? Why, greedy idiots with guns and bulldozers show up to mow it down, of course. Humans *suck,* man. They deserve to die…and die they do, in a hail of arrows, fangs, teeth, and lots of screaming plummets from great heights. All those military toys beloved by the right-wing warmongers of the military-industrial complex prove to be useless against the righteous fury of an aroused Gaia and her chosen champion, a redeemed soldier who has seen the error of his ways. Take *that,* Marine killbot slaves of Big Business.

During the big battle scene, as dinosaurs were chowing down on soldiers, the middle-aged couple seated next to me were grinning happily…delighted by the defeat and destruction of their own miserable species. The dialogue in *Avatar* makes it clear that humanity's future depended on the success of the Pandora mission. "We sent the aliens back to their dying world," intones the hero, narrating scenes of the defeated humans as they're perp-walked off the planet, just the way environmentalist radicals have dreamed of handling the executives of Exxon-Mobil. Earlier, the hero tells Pandora's nature spirit about the evil of his fellow man: "They killed their mother, and they'll kill you." Good thing for the universe we're doomed!

Just as Cameron brings the primitive superstitions of radical environmentalism to life on Pandora, his portrayal of the human invaders matches the stereotypes of Big Business, and its blood-for-oil military stooges, held by campus crusaders. The corporate and Marine villains of *Avatar* are incredibly stupid. For one thing, if the fate of humanity rests on the Pandora mission, you'd think the governments of Earth could find someone other than a backstabbing middle-management weasel and a blatantly psychotic colonel to run the show. Even if you can accept their moral bankruptcy, their incompetence is shocking. It never occurs to them to solve their Na'vi problem with a missile from orbit—and they're explicitly shown watching orbital surveillance of the gathering alien armies. For that matter, they could have nuked the troublesome Na'vi goddess tree from orbit, then arrived at the blast site with medical supplies and tearful condolences for the horrible cosmic tragedy of a "meteor" they just couldn't stop.

The villains are also as willfully blind as the Left imagines its capitalist boogeymen to be. They laugh down the report of a scientist who obviously knows what she's talking about, and has hard evidence to back up her position. They also clearly never bothered to read the best-selling book on Na'vi culture written by said scientist, because if they had, they could have used their miraculous cloning technology to whip up a swarm of sacred milkweed pods and a big red dragon, and flown into their negotiations with the aliens as epic heroes of legend. They also could have made those negotiations, and violent conflict, completely unnecessary by simply tunneling horizontally into the huge deposit of vital minerals beneath the Na'vi tree city. But, you know, capitalists prefer genocide to creative thinking. Bullets are so much *cheaper* than drilling equipment.

The key to understanding the intentions behind *Avatar,* and the response of its audience, is to remember that the tale is set in the far future, and we are never shown the suffering billions dying on a ruined Earth. This is a suicide fantasy, exactly like those many of us indulge as teenagers: we're so much wiser, smarter, and empathic than the bummer adults running the world around us. They don't understand the mystic truth burning in our young hearts. They'll be sad when we're gone, and they'll finally realize how *righteous* we were. They'll finally understand their grim obsession with money and material goods is soul-crushing, because they'll be standing over the pulverized dust of our radiant souls. Death and tragedy will tear the scales from their eyes.

The can of holistic whup-ass opened by the magical world of Pandora at the end of *Avatar* comes from the same grocery of doom that supplies George Monbiot and Polly Toynbee with their nightmares. Read their words again, and understand they don't really *believe* those things will happen—no one is stupid enough to believe the twaddle about submerged cities dispensed by the global-warming cult. They **want** those things to happen. They daydream about glaciers melting and creating tidal waves that deposit soggy clumps of coral reef and rainforest in the middle of London. They shudder with orgasmic delight as they imagine drowning capitalists and politicians coughing out a spray of ice water, dodging the enraged polar bears swept into Fleet Street by the morning tide, and crying "George! Polly! You were *right!* You were right all along, and we were so *blind*...Save us!" But it will be too late, and George and Polly will only be able to fold their arms and blaze with smug satisfaction, glowing bright enough to remain clearly visible as they sink into the frigid depths.

Avatar was written by a man who thinks those who disagree with his environmentalist obsessions are so blind that, in the future they will create, the last decent man in the universe will lead a far more noble alien race to victory over us, and literally renounce his humanity as part of his reward. James Cameron invites you to join him in the most beautifully rendered adolescent daydream of suicide ever created, and share his sense of righteous superiority over those who refuse to applaud at the end. I'm a sucker for good-looking dragons, so I gave him a golf clap for those.

The Shroud Of Contempt
February 20, 2010

Author's Note: On February 18, 2010, a deranged man named Joseph Stack flew his small airplane into an office complex in Austin, Texas, killing an IRS manager and injuring thirteen other people. Stack left a rambling suicide note expressing anger at the government. The so-called mainstream media immediately tried to link him to the Tea Party movement. This attempt failed rather spectacularly—I think it led more people to distrust the media and declare their sympathy to the Tea Party.

Washington Post contributor Jonathan Capehart provoked outrage when he became one of the first mainstream media figures to try linking the deranged killer Joseph Stack with the Tea Party movement:

> Joseph Stack was angry at the Internal Revenue Service, and he took his rage out on it by slamming his single-engine plane into the Echelon Building in Austin, Texas. We now know this thanks to the rather clear (as rants go) suicide note Stack left behind. There's no information yet on whether he was involved in any anti-government groups, or whether he was a lone wolf. But after reading his 34-paragraph screed, I am struck by how his alienation is similar to that we're hearing from the extreme elements of the Tea Party movement.

Stack's suicide note contains nothing to substantiate this smear. In fact, Capehart had to deliberately edit the last lines of the note from his piece, because they repeated the Communist Manifesto and adapted it into an insult to capitalism—"The capitalist creed: From each according to his gullibility, to each according to his greed." This was obviously unhelpful to the nasty little action line Capehart wanted to manufacture, so it had to go.

Strangely enough, the *Washington Post* continues to employ Capehart, when his manipulation of the Stack suicide note, and apparent ignorance of the decidedly un-Tea Party sentiments that filled the bulk of the madman's screed, would have been taken as cause for dismissal by a paper with serious editorial standards. The following day, he posted on the subject again, making some amazingly disingenuous attempts to defend himself. "When I wrote my last post on Joseph Stack, I was very careful not to get ahead of what was already known," he begins. No, but he was *also* careful not to mention the information that didn't fit into his narrative, wasn't he? I guess I can see why the *Post* didn't sack him. He's got the methodology of the dying legacy media down pat.

Retreating into the herd-think that characterizes the establishment media, Capehart argues "I'm not the only one to make the connection between Stack's alienation from government and the anti-government extremists who have latched on to the broader Tea Party movement." Well, that makes it all right, then. I guess if we can get a quorum of reporters to agree, we can declare any inconvenient group beyond the pale, and set about demonizing them.

Would it be equally fair to make the connection between the ugly power politics of Al Sharpton and the NAACP, and the anti-democracy extremists who have latched onto the broader civil-rights movement? When those extreme elements were prowling around voting booths with nightsticks, the Attorney General was remarkably uninterested in connecting them with anyone. Might we speculate that an activist super-State, determined to choose winners and losers on considerations of "social justice," could inspire extremists to violently prevent members of the oppressor class from casting unhelpful votes?

Instead of fretting about "alienation from government" as a psychosis, shouldn't we be looking at the connection between slavish devotion to Big Government and outbreaks of violence? Soon after top Democrats fled from health-care town hall meetings, shrieking that constituents with tough questions were Nazis wearing swastikas, we had union thugs beating people up, and feral astroturf goons biting off their fingers.

The attempts to paint Joseph Stack's face onto a tea bag are part of a larger effort to cultivate contempt for the growing backlash against Big Government. Much of the bile directed at Sarah Palin, including the painfully unfunny "Family Guy" episode, is meant to serve the same purpose, finger-painting an image of her as an eccentric figure who can be dismissed with casual malice. Another example is the bizarre attack on Jason Mattera's appearance at CPAC by the *New York Times,* insinuating racism based on the sound of his voice. The media has been circling CPAC, looking for an opening, and Mattera was caught in a hail of ink from a drive-by slandering.

A distinctly unamused Andrew Breitbart called the *Times* reporter "despicable," and Palin spoke out against the "Family Guy" insult…eight months after dragging a root-canal apology out of David Letterman for spitting rape jokes about her daughter. They were right to raise their voices. The purpose of cultivated contempt is to alienate the sort of independent voter who can be strongly influenced by media atmospherics. The greatest political weapon remaining to our increasingly unpopular legacy media is their ability to cast a shadow of doom over selected targets, building a sense of unease that drives away those who pay only cursory attention to politics. When support for a person or group becomes unthinkable, their words become unintelligible.

Not all of the drive to excommunicate Republicans or the Tea Party comes from pure partisanship. Establishment media figures, including some nominally on the Right, are made confused and uneasy by the notion of "alienation from government." They understand that the *system itself,* not merely individual politicians, is coming under sustained and **principled** assault. Far from a witless mob chanting slogans of mindless anger, the increasingly libertarian Right is drafting manifestoes and designing action plans for the post-Big Government era. They are asking moral and practical questions for which command-economy socialism has no answer. The plan to intimidate them into silence didn't work, so the new plan is to intimidate moderate voters out of listening to them. Meanwhile, the witless mobs with mindless slogans and pitchforks are filled with union members demanding a government takeover of health insurance.

The Left still has a powerful media loom upon which to weave the ugly shroud of contempt, but it's a weapon that only works against inarticulate victims. Cutting through it quickly and forcefully is the best defense. No Republican, Tea Partier, or concerned citizen should quietly suffer insults that would *never* be tolerated against the consecrated constituencies of the Left. Linking Joseph Stack to the Tea Party movement is no more reasonable than linking homicidal maniac Amy Bishop to the National Education Association, because they share her fawning obsession with Barack Obama. The implication that mistrust of our bloated, blind government is a gateway drug to terrorism reduces the American tradition of independence to a psychosis.

Instead of making ridiculous stretches to sell Stack as a Tea Party Minuteman to their dwindling audience, journalists should be probing the connection between Big Government corruption and Amy Bishop's long career of unpunished violent lunacy. That's the kind of investigation that might just save lives…and end the degenerate politics defended by its media janissaries, with a chorus of sneers aimed at the people who pay for it.

Part Six
Politics

A moderate Republican is someone who lives in a state of perpetual surprise as he ponders the monthly bills for nanny-state government.

Krauthammer And Palin
July 3, 2009

Author's Note: This was the first of two occasions upon which I found myself disagreeing with the great Dr. Krauthammer over Sarah Palin. The disagreement was considerably more strenuous the second time, as you will see from "Why Sarah Palin Should Not Leave The Room." After posting this essay, I found myself away from the computer and radio during a long dinner engagement. Logging into Hot Air later that night, I began reviewing the comments thread…and discovered radio host Mark Levin, author of the magnificent "Liberty and Tyranny," had read the entire post on the air. After a lifetime of drinking modestly and staying away from drugs, I finally knew what it felt like to have my mind blown.

I admire Charles Krauthammer and usually agree with his take on the issues of the day, but I disagree with his recent dismissal of Sarah Palin as a serious candidate for 2012. It's far too early in the game to declare anyone either out of the running or inevitable…well, except for Mark Sanford. Krauthammer's statement that "You cannot sustain a campaign of platitudes and clichés over a year and a half if you're running for the presidency" is so powerfully contradicted by recent history as to be surreal. It would be a more defensible statement if he'd clarified it by adding "…without the enthusiastic support of the entire mainstream media apparatus, which Palin is definitely not going to have." I don't think that's what he meant to say, however…and there lies the key to understanding his views on Palin.

Charles Krauthammer is a brilliant writer, and a very perceptive analyst. He's also a denizen of the Beltway, which inevitably alters his perceptions. He lives and works at the very heart of the machinery of the superstate. If you've never been to Washington D.C., I highly recommend making the trip someday. Besides the wonderful sightseeing opportunities and museums, you'll also gain a sense of how much pure power hums in the air, radiating from the massive government buildings, and refined by the monuments to great moments in our nation's history. Washington has a sense of both age and modernity. You can see both the past and the future from the Mall.

Some would say that living inside the Beltway tends to make one turn into a liberal, but it's more accurate to say that the Beltway lifestyle brings a greater appreciation of the power of government. Every Beltway pundit, including Krauthammer, sees the ideal political candidate as a brilliant technocrat, combining charisma with a vast knowledge of history, economics, and the minute workings of Washington. The ideal leader has the intelligence and vision to steer the nation into the best of all possible futures, and Washington is the helm of the American ship, with the ship's wheel planted firmly in the Oval Office. The primary point of disagreement among Beltway pundits is the precise course we should be setting for the mighty central government. Few of them agree with the conservatives out in flyover country, who think we should be heading for the lifeboats.

If the ideal candidate for mastering the *U.S.S. Federal Leviathan* is not available, the Washington and New York elite will happily manufacture him, provided they can find someone who gives them suitable raw material...and flatters their intellectual vanity. The liberal dominance of the Beltway media grants liberal candidates the proper credentials, merely by virtue of their being liberal. All that is necessary is for the candidate to have attended a few of the right schools, to allow the pundits to proclaim him a gifted intellectual. Thus, an undistinguished junior senator from Chicago, with a wafer-thin resume, mediocre academic career, spotty attendance in the Senate, and shadowy past associations was magically transformed into a "brilliant community organizer" and awarded presidential stature. In fact, the award was most loudly bestowed by his putative opponent, John McCain. Meanwhile, the equally young and charismatic governor of Alaska is dismissed with a snort and wave of the hand, because she didn't go the right schools, and doesn't have a stack of detailed five-year plans for the U.S. Economy.

Krauthammer is no liberal, but he shares the common Beltway vision of the President as a super-genius micro-manager, the CEO of America, Inc. He doesn't see Sarah Palin as a serious candidate, because if she does decide to run, she won't be applying for the position he has in mind for her. He parts company with red-state conservatives, because we don't think our President should be expected to be a human super-computer, with every aspect of a three trillion dollar economy routed through her sleepless intellect. Searching for such candidates is a fool's game, and building a gigantic centralized government that can only function with such a person at the helm is a recipe for unending disaster. The desperate longing for such a Technocrat-In-Chief makes the media elite highly vulnerable to being conned by anyone who can brandish the right diploma and make it clear he has big plans for the office. He doesn't even need to present any detailed plans—Obama certainly did not. He only has to convince the elite that he has those plans rattling around in his gigantic, policy-wonk brain. Add a dash of heroic narrative, and you're all set: Obama is the First! Black! President! John Kerry was a super soldier in Vietnam! Bill Clinton was The Man From Hope! Even the most ridiculous fraud of a candidate can be taken seriously, if he pretends to be what the Beltway elite are looking for.

I think the unfolding events of the Obama presidency will continue to validate the views of we who write from flyover country. The Beltway romance with the Wilsonian ideal of the professor President, acting as an elected philosopher-king to solve all of the nation's problems from his Washington palace, is increasingly divorced from reality. Like all romances, this one tends to blind the smitten party from seeing the unpleasant truth. America does not need kings, and they are no more acceptable because their palace is granted with the consent of the voters, with a maximum lease of eight years. The colossal failure of a titan with Big Ideas may be a thrilling narrative for Beltway pundits to chronicle, but those of us who have to live through the fiery carnage are tired of clutching our wallets and waiting for the next titan to take center stage.

Krauthammer's practical advice to Sarah Palin is quite reasonable: study up on the issues she felt uncomfortable with last year. He's not entirely correct when he says "she has to stop speaking in cliches and platitudes…it won't work." It would work, if her desire was to seize that huge ship's wheel in the Oval Office, and tack just a few points to the right. I can only hope that if she does run, she has the kind of bold conservative vision that will make her campaign an epic battle, against the people who think the Presidency is the kind of job Barack Obama is qualified for.

There's No One Else Like Sarah Palin
July 6, 2009

Three days have passed since Sarah Palin allegedly committed political suicide by announcing she would resign from the governorship of Alaska. She looks pretty spry, for a dead person.

The commentary on her resignation was interesting, in that a lot of people worked very hard to make it seem more complicated than it was. Palin has a well-earned reputation for plain speaking, and she obviously didn't run her announcement past a team of script doctors, or read it off a teleprompter. Nevertheless, the media treated her like the freaky oracle from "300", portentously informing the rest of us What She Really Meant. These are the same people who insist that the confused, indecisive, deceitful current occupant of the Oval Office is a man of soaring principle. When Barack Obama attempts to obscure his sudden reversals by describing them as "what he's always said," news analysts nod their heads in agreement, and quietly delete his previous positions from their laptops. When Sarah Palin clearly lays out her reasons for resigning her governorship, the same people crank out a flood of "Ten Real Reasons Why Palin Might Be Quitting," with her actual stated reasons somewhere in the bottom half of the list.

Palin's decision to resign her post was surprising, but not irrational, or cowardly. She could be forgiven for wanting out of politics, after the savaging she and her family have taken. I've often wondered what she said to her daughters after David Letterman used them as props in his disgraceful "comedy" routine. How do you console your thirteen-year-old daughter after a late-night comedian makes a rape joke about her, in front of a national audience, to thunderous applause? What do you say to the kids when the comedian "clarifies" his remarks by saying he was really talking about the 18-year-old, rather than the 13-year-old? I cannot imagine what those conversations were like, and I can't criticize a mother who decides she's not going to endure any more of them.

I don't blame her for refusing to take any more personal or financial pounding from political operatives using Alaska's odd government ethics system as a weapon. Some have said she was foolish to cite the cost to Alaskan taxpayers as a reason for her resignation, since it was a paltry two million dollars. To me, that doesn't sound like a criticism—it's a campaign slogan. **Sarah Palin: She Still Thinks A Million Bucks Is A Lot of Money.** If she runs for president in 2012, it will be against an incumbent who thinks a billion dollars of graft or waste is a rounding error in one of his big-government schemes. A lot of people will like the idea of voting for someone who doesn't use rolls of taxpayer dollars to wipe the ink off their hands after signing legislation.

I also think Palin has the foresight to understand that Democrat efforts to bankrupt Alaskan taxpayers were going to intensify dramatically as 2012 drew closer. Groups like ACORN have pockets full of taxpayer subsidies, and legions of hungry lawyers on speed-dial. The abuse she's faced already was a warm-up act. The half-million dollars sucked out of her personal funds in legal fees was nothing but the price of admission to the coming horror show.

Palin would have needed to resign anyway, if she wanted to run for President in 2012. Doing it now leaves the governorship in the hands of her loyal lieutenant, and gives him time to build his own support for re-election. The first serious political damage to Palin will occur if polls show Alaskans are unhappy with this arrangement. I'm certain attempts are being made to generate such a poll at this very moment.

I don't think Palin's resignation represents the fiery end of her career in politics, if she wants one. A cursory review of the blog-melting traffic she generated over the weekend reveals the depth of interest and affection people retain for her. I doubt many of the people who support her are any less inclined to vote for her in 2012 today, any more than her most vocal detractors would have been any more likely to vote *for* her if she campaigned from behind a desk in Juneau—her eyes propped open by matchsticks as she tirelessly filled out gubernatorial paperwork, pausing only to record interviews and campaign commercials.

It would, however, be foolish to suppose her resignation will not pose a problem for her in the future. We can predict with absolute certainty that every single news article about her will mention it, and she will be asked about it during every interview she grants, if she runs for president. The media will pound her with the "quitter" charge, in a way they would never think to question any Democrat candidate, including the current President—who would have been summarily dismissed from any private-sector job he ignored as completely as his Senate seat, while he was campaigning. Dwelling on the unfairness of this will be much less useful than preparing to deal with it. Ronald Reagan proposed an Eleventh Commandment, "Thou shalt not speak ill of a fellow Republican." I would suggest a Twelfth: "The rules are different for Republicans." I don't blame Republican voters for being angry about this, but we've had enough of Republican politicians acting surprised by it.

I suspect many of the obituaries written for Palin by well-meaning conservatives are based on the fear that swing voters will be driven away when the media throws the "quitter" charge at her. This is a valid concern. "Swing" voters often base their decisions on such things, which is why the media has so much influence on them. The answer is to give the press something else to talk about. Controlling the direction of campaign coverage was never something

John McCain had any skill at. He labored under the misconception that reporters were still his pals from the Straight Talk Express days, but he could scarcely distract them from their rapt adoration of his opponent. If there's one thing Palin proved over the holiday weekend, it's that she has no problem drawing the attention of the media.

One of the crucial factors in McCain's defeat was voter apathy. A huge number of Bush voters couldn't be bothered to slog to the polls for him. If Sarah Palin climbs into the ring against Barack Obama in 2012, there won't be many empty seats in the stadium. If she hits hard enough, I don't think very many people will care that she has "Ex-Governor of Alaska" embroidered on her boxing trunks. Politics is all about possibilities, not certainties. Even those who feel skeptical about Palin's chances after Friday afternoon must conclude, from the passionate reaction of the public, that an awful lot of people are very interested in voting for someone like Sarah Palin…and there **is** no one else like Sarah Palin.

A Seemingly Very Nice Middle-Class Girl
July 11, 2009

Author's Note: Throughout 2009, and well into 2010, nothing drove blog traffic to greater heights than writing about Sarah Palin. She drives liberals, and a certain breed of left-leaning Republican, absolutely bonkers, prompting them to write wonderfully stupid things when they attack her. One morning, I found myself reading an incredibly dimwitted piece from Republican-turned-Obama-worshipper Peggy Noonan, while I waited for my coffee to brew. I wrote the response before having my first cup, so I was cranky and mean-spirited. That's what made it work. Few of my posts at Hot Air have generated a livelier response. I've edited this reprint to account for the absence of a joke that can only work on the Internet: in the original online publication, I linked to a Rick Astley video instead of Noonan's piece—a practical joke known as "Rickrolling."

Peggy Noonan used her Friday column in the *Wall Street Journal* to throw some dirt on Sarah Palin's grave. It's vintage Noonan: airheaded, dripping with condescension, and completely missing the point. No serious conservative needs to hear anything from Noonan except her groveling apology for being so horribly wrong about Barack Obama, who she energetically supported for president. However, it's worth picking through the flotsam and jetsam of this embarrassing column, to appreciate the kind of intellectual fat that conservatives need to trim from the Republican Party.

Let's begin by setting the stage: Sarah Palin resigned her governorship last week, and has no stated plans to run for elective office as of this writing. She has made it clear that she intends to remain on the public stage, and has a bright and useful future of public speaking, writing, and helping her party raise funds for 2010 and beyond. I personally disagree with the assessment that her resignation killed her political future, if she wants one. It will be an obstacle for her to work around, but I think she could overcome it—especially if Alaskans are clearly pleased with her successor, and think well of her as the 2012 elections get under way.

After referencing the way "The left and the media immediately overplayed their hand, with attacks on her children," Noonan says of Palin:

> She went on the trail a sensation but demonstrated in the ensuing months that she was not ready to go national and in fact never would be. She was hungry, loved politics, had charm and energy, loved walking onto the stage, waving and doing the stump speech. All good. But she was not thoughtful. She was a gifted retail politician who displayed the disadvantages of being born into a point of view (in her case a form of conservatism;

elsewhere and in other circumstances, it could have been a form of liberalism) and swallowing it whole: She never learned how the other sides think, or why.

I always thought the Wall Street Journal had editors that would review columns to make sure they don't have annoying run-on sentences that don't use commas but maybe they don't and never will. Poor sentence construction aside, Noonan couldn't be more wrong to say Palin's point of view "could have been a form of liberalism." No, Peggy. A charismatic woman espousing a form of liberalism would *never* have to suffer attacks on her children in the media. People who swallow forms of liberalism are never required to understand the first thing about conservative points of view. They aren't really expected to know anything about the intellectual history of liberalism, either. Barack Obama couldn't articulate the principles of conservatism if Thomas Sowell hacked into his teleprompter and fed him the words.

Later, Noonan zeroes in on the moment Palin decisively lost the "moderate Republican" snob vote:

> She couldn't say what she read because she didn't read anything. She was utterly unconcerned by all this and seemed in fact rather proud of it: It was evidence of her authenticity. She experienced criticism as both partisan and cruel because she could see no truth in any of it. She wasn't thoughtful enough to know she wasn't thoughtful enough. Her presentation up to the end has been scattered, illogical, manipulative and self-referential to the point of self-reverence. "I'm not wired that way," "I'm not a quitter," "I'm standing up for our values." I'm, I'm, I'm.

Palin doesn't "read anything," you see. She's probably not even literate. The moment Noonan is fretting over came when Katie Couric asked Palin which newspapers and magazines she reads regularly, and she couldn't name one. Given the cratering circulation of print media, Palin is clearly in good company. I suspect the sin that truly damns her in Noonan's eyes is her failure to read Peggy Noonan columns. At least America was spared the horror of a Vice President who doesn't spend much time reading newspapers. Instead, we got a Vice President who should have left his debate with Palin in a straitjacket, and shows no sign of coherent thought at all.

Of course, it's risible for a breathless supporter of the Lightworker, Barack Obama, to criticize anyone else for self-referential speech. Obama couldn't deliver a movie review of "Transformers 2" without referring to himself thirty-five times. Maybe Peggy could publish some guidelines on how often female Republican candidates are allowed to refer to themselves, per minute of speech, without being guilty of arrogance. Would she feel better if Palin talked about herself in the third person, like Bob Dole?

Dismissing the affection conservatives supposedly feel for Palin because of her "working-class roots," Noonan sneers:

She is not working class, never was, and even she, avid claimer of advantage that she is, never claimed to be and just lets others say it. Her father was a teacher and school track coach, her mother the school secretary. They were middle-class figures of respect, stability and local status. I think intellectuals call her working-class because they see the makeup, the hair, the heels and the sleds and think they're working class "tropes." Because, you know, that's what they teach in "Ways of the Working Class" at Yale and Dartmouth.

...and you've got that "Ways of the Working Class" textbook on your desk, don't you, Peggy? I'll bet it's heavily indexed with Post-Its, sticking out from the thick pages in a pastel rainbow. Does anyone else find it surreal that she tries to dismiss Palin's alleged pretensions to middle-class origins by explaining that her father was a school track coach, and her mother was the school secretary? Whoa, you got her there, Peg. She might pose as a moose-hunting soccer mom, but she was *to the manor born*. What fools we middle-class conservatives were, to accept this scion of soccer-coaching royalty as one of us, just because she hid her imperial velvet beneath a plaid shirt.

Of the idea that Palin made the Republican Party look inclusive, Noonan snarls, "She makes the party look stupid, a party of the easy manipulated." Well, that's what they say at the high-toned Washington cocktail parties, where the elite liberals keep Peggy Noonan as a pet, so it must be true. The vast number of Palin admirers will be thrilled to know that Peggy Noonan thinks they're stupid. I'm sure that will make them rush right into the waiting arms of Noonan and her weak-tea wing of the GOP.

Speaking of phony appeals to middle-class roots, here's what Noonan had to say about her Prince Charming, Barack Obama, back in 2008:

He climbed steep stairs, born off the continent with no father to guide, a dreamy, abandoning mother, mixed race, no connections. He rose with guts and gifts. He is steady, calm, and, in terms of the execution of his political ascent, still the primary and almost only area in which his executive abilities can be discerned, he shows good judgment in terms of whom to hire and consult, what steps to take and moves to make.

No attempts to manipulate voters with sob stories about humble upbringings in Barack Obama's biography, no sir!

Noonan responds to the charge that "the media did her in" by saying "her lack of any appropriate modesty did her in." Remember, **an Obama supporter** wrote this. For Peggy's dreamboat, a replicated Greek temple shows appropriate modesty when giving a convention speech. She probably swooned when Obama modestly spent fifty million bucks on his inauguration, prompting outgoing President Bush to declare a state of emergency, to release federal funds for the event.

310

Granted that the older column I quoted above was written a couple trillion wasted tax dollars ago, before the advent of Turbo Tax Tim and the rest of Obama's Epic Fail Cabinet, but you still have to love the way Noonan celebrated Obama's "good judgment in terms of who to hire and consult." He sure knew how to pick a spiritual advisor, that's for sure! If only Sarah Palin could have the good judgment to consult with aging hippie radical terrorists, Peggy might finally admire her for something more than being "a very nice middle-class girl with ambition, appetite and no sense of personal limits." By the way, Noonan delivers this backhanded compliment *immediately after* the paragraph where she declares Palin's middle-classness to be a fraud.

Noonan could have used this column to praise Obama's good judgement in hiring a deranged eugenicist who favors forced abortions and mass sterilization as his "science czar." Why did she waste it pouring salt into Zombie Sarah Palin's mouth and sewing her lips closed, so she could never rise from her political grave to threaten Republican voters again? Here's why Peggy made the effort to snap you out of your stupid, illiterate, soccer-coach-daughter-loving trance:

Here's why all this matters. The world is a dangerous place. It has never been more so, or more complicated, more straining of the reasoning powers of those with actual genius and true judgment. This is a time for conservative leaders who know how to think.

Here are a few examples of what we may face in the next 10 years: a profound and pro-longed American crash, with the admission of bankruptcy and the spread of deep social unrest; one or more American cities getting hit with weapons of mass destruction from an unknown source; faint glimmers of actual secessionist movements as Americans for various reasons and in various areas decide the burdens and assumptions of the federal government are no longer attractive or legitimate.

It never occurs to Noonan that those "glimmers of actual secessionist movements" might be caused by freedom-loving people fleeing the "actual genius and true judgment" of the shady, unqualified junior senator she couldn't wait to sweep into the White House. Hey, Peg, that "admission of bankruptcy" you're quivering about? That's coming because your boy Obama crashed the economy, looted the treasury of the future to serve the ultimate pork dinner to his faithful allies, and appointed fools and frauds to supervise his programs. He's trying to pass a ludicrous energy plan that will cost each American family thousands of dollars, and guarantee a recession for decades to come. If America doesn't rally to stop him in 2010, he'll bury what's left of the moribund economy under the bloodless husk of a nationalized health-care industry. If McCain had won in 2008, then immediately resigned for health reasons and left Palin in the White House, would she have cost us less than a trillion dollars? If so, she'd be a bargain compared to the nightmare Peggy Noonan helped to unleash.

Noonan is symptomatic of a defeated, collaborative wing of the GOP that wants nothing more than to be thought well of by the Left, which they believe has decisively won the political and cultural battles of the twentieth century. Their idea of a "conservative" is someone who can eke out a small discount on the price tag of mammoth liberal programs. Their goal in 2012 is to find a bland, pleasant, "moderate" Republican, who can win the approval of the media mullahs as a "serious candidate," then lose gracefully and give America's First Black President his second term.

The idea of serious conservative reform terrifies them: radical overhaul of the tax system, dramatic reduction in the size of government, a system that compels Congress to live like humble servants of the people instead of Renaissance royalty...Who will throw those wonderful cocktail parties in Washington, if the conservatives burn half the city down? Who will tell Peggy bedtime stories of dashing social engineers with titanic government schemes? Where will she find hip, exciting statists she can celebrate with schoolgirl treacle, like this nonsense from her 2008 endorsement of Obama: "Something new is happening in America. It is the imminent arrival of a new liberal moment. History happens, it makes its turns, you hold on for dear life. Life *moves*." She was on to something with that last bit. Obama has made a lot of American businesses think about moving.

In her conclusion, Noonan writes, "And so the Republican Party should get serious, as serious as the age, because that is what a grown-up, responsible party—a party that deserves to lead—would do." This is frothy, delusional milk, sprayed on top of a long, boring latte of condescension. Nothing could be less serious than fawning over a hollow President, who wastes his citizens' time with absurd fantasies about multi-trillion-dollar health care takeovers, piled on top of an already astronomical national debt. The latest polls suggest the public is becoming impatient with the infantile antics of the party Noonan thought should control both houses of Congress, and the presidency. If Peggy wants to see what an unserious, immature party looks like, she should watch video of Nancy Pelosi stammering about how the CIA lied to her, or leaf through the avalanche of scandals engulfing nearly every major Democrat. She could complete her education by dropping by to watch Al Franken squatting in his brand-new Senate seat.

I have a suggestion for the *Wall Street Journal*: make this Peggy Noonan's farewell column, and hire Sarah Palin to take her place. Peggy could head over to the Huffington Post, where she'd be received as a martyred hero. The Journal's circulation would skyrocket. This economy needs a success story.

Is America A Conservative Nation?
July 31, 2009

A recent Gallup poll shows a majority of Americans reporting their political views are becoming more conservative. Conservatives naturally welcome such reports of movement in public opinion, but the question of whether America is a fundamentally conservative nation is not easily answered. Polls proclaiming us to be a "center-right" country have appeared for decades, even as the nation's practical politics have moved inexorably leftward. There has never been a time, since the heyday of the New Deal, when liberal philosophy has received enthusiastic support from the public...and there has never been a time when liberalism has not grown in power and influence, except perhaps at the height of Reagan's strength. American politics orbit on the right side of a center that has been creeping leftward for the better part of a hundred years.

The Gallup article includes a good deal of head-scratching about the obvious contradiction of an electorate that describes itself as generally "conservative," but elected a leftist radical to the Presidency in 2008, along with solid majorities for the Democrats in both houses of Congress. A look at the disastrous politics of Obama's most extreme initiatives, such as health care or cap-and-trade, suggests the public that voted him into office was fooled into thinking he wasn't as far Left as he turned out to be. This is probably true for a certain segment of the population, which had essentially non-ideological reasons for supporting Obama: they enjoyed his speeches, they voted for him because he was black, they hated Bush or disliked McCain, or they followed the advice of media celebrities. Such voters were looking for ways to be comfortable with voting for Obama, and probably didn't dig into his past, or the actual content of his speeches, as much as they should have. I think there is more to the story than mere deception or self-delusion, however.

How do we reconcile a public that claims to be increasingly conservative, with a government that has become increasingly liberal throughout our lifetimes? I think the key lies in understanding the increasing obsession Americans have with "crises," and their belief that government should stand ready to take quick action in resolving them. Most voters are not ideologues. They haven't invested much effort in putting together coherent philosophies of government. They generally think of both "liberal" and "conservative" as bad words, describing extremes they would prefer to avoid. They are eager to identify themselves as "moderates" or "independents," and pride themselves on being thoughtful and flexible. A sizable portion of voters who do describe themselves as liberal or conservative hasten to add that they aren't rigid extremists, and will consider good ideas from both sides.

In their personal lives, most of these people—including a great many of those who consider themselves proudly liberal—follow principles we have come to associate with modern conservatism. In fact, the idea of applying liberal principles to their daily lives seems absurd. Most of the conservative positions that saw the strongest gains in the Gallup poll can be viewed in the context of people thinking about their own lives, and answering in a manner consistent with their behavior, or at least their ideals. Of course most people would not sacrifice their economic success to protect the environment, or casually surrender their right to defend themselves from criminal assault, and they're squeamish about relinquishing control of their health care.

In matters of public policy, however, Americans have generally accepted the idea that only government action can resolve the most serious problems we face...and a sensationalist media assures them we face many serious problems. The size, scope, and number of these problems seem overwhelming to the average citizen. He has no idea how to deal with the meltdown of gigantic financial institutions, heal the country's racial divisions, or "save" the environment. He desperately wants to believe there are smart people in Washington who know how to handle these issues. A century of astonishing technological development has convinced us that every problem has a large-scale, scientific solution. There is no aspect of the future we don't believe we can design and build, if we place our trust in the right group of social engineers.

The leftward movement of American politics has tracked almost exactly with the development of mass media, from radio to TV to the Internet. Overt political bias from the media is not as damaging as the general environment of permanent crisis they foster, accompanied by heroic narratives of brave and compassionate politicians with Big Ideas about how to rescue us from this week's nightmare. This attitude is essentially inevitable from the media, because fearful crises and bold actions are the product they sell to their consumers. You'll never see a news anchor kick off his nightly report by admitting nothing much happened today. Not even Fox News, routinely described as the "conservative" news network, is immune to sensationalism—far from it. Like all the other networks, Fox has a prestigious Washington bureau, staffed with people who are breathlessly eager to report on the latest adventures of our executive and legislative action heroes.

The idea that government is morally or legally prevented from addressing a major issue—the very heart and soul of the Constitution—is dismissed out of hand. James Madison's assertion that "I cannot undertake to lay my finger on that article of the Constitution which granted a right to Congress of expending, on the objects of benevolence, the money of their constituents" would be a complete non-starter in today's political climate. Rewrite that statement to make it sound like it came from a modern leader, and it would be swiftly denounced as uncaring and out-of-touch, the mutterings of a callous tool of the rich who foolishly thinks government should let poor people suffer, to finance tax breaks for his wealthy friends.

The GOP has not been vigorous in fighting the rising tide of dependence on government, or the disintegrating faith in private institutions. Republicans are largely willing to go along with the relentless accumulation of central power—they just have different ideas about how to use it. George Bush's "compassionate conservatism" was an expression of this attitude. Even Bush's tax cuts, like those Bob Dole half-heartedly campaigned on with his little "15%" signs, were presented without any connection to a larger conservative philosophy about the size and role of government…making them amount to nothing but a discount on the purchase of a deeply defective product.

As long as the basic principle of ever-growing, activist central government is accepted, the nation's politics will continue to slide leftward, no matter how conservative the population thinks it is. Belief in the State necessarily requires diminished confidence in free enterprise. The most encouraging development for conservatives is the mounting sense of frustration with Obama's clumsy policies, and their absurd price tags. The surest sign we are a conservative nation is that every Democrat since Walter Mondale has felt compelled to lie to the American people about the cost of liberalism, as well as over-selling its supposed benefits.

The challenge for conservative politicians is to express matters of national policy to the voters in the same terms which guide their daily lives. As the Gallup poll shows, most people find liberal ideas ridiculous or immoral when applied to the behavior of individuals and families. We should help them understand that liberalism does not become more efficient, or righteous, when it governs millions of lives and spends trillions of dollars. President Obama has done a great deal to help us make that case. The Republicans should build on the framework of Obama's failures in 2010, and begin moving America's center of gravity back to the right, where it belongs.

Who We Are
August 5, 2009

Author's Note: I think this remains the most widely quoted and distributed essay I have written. I wrote it in response to Democrat efforts to slander the people speaking up at their health care town hall meetings, by dismissing them as racists and cranks, or paid operatives of insurance companies. My own website tag line is drawn from this text: "Our freedom is not for sale, and we reserve the right to defend it from theft." The line about "wise Latinas" is a reference to Supreme Court Justice Sonia Sotomayor, who infamously cited her status as a wise Latina when discussing her qualifications for the Supreme Court. I've been told it's a popular read at Tea Party meetings. It is my delight and honor to serve as a voice for the people described in this piece.

There seems to be a bit of confusion among Democrats about the nature of the opposition to their plans. Maybe I can help clear things up, by telling them a few things about us.

We're not paid minions of any corporate interest or lobby. Most bloggers working to stop the Obama health-care disaster are like me, writing when they can find the time, because we care about the future of our country. The same is true of the people showing up at town hall meetings, and organizing rallies. Some of us are well-dressed in tailored suits. Others wear jeans and T-shirts. Most of us are dressed in what we wore to work.

Our support for a massive government program does not increase when you tell us we're not allowed to ask questions about it.

We're not racists. We're also not racialists. We don't think a wise Latina is inherently more qualified to do *anything* than a wise Asian woman, a wise white woman, or a wise white man. We're tired of being fed excuses for high government offices staffed by anything but the best people for the job. There are too many high government offices, so we'd like some of Obama's absurdly incompetent appointees to take their titles with them when they leave. We remember what it was like when we got rid of the Clinton mob, so we'll be conducting inventories on the contents of those vacated offices, before we turn out the lights and pour cement in the locks.

We don't like having to fight desperate battles to save our freedom and future from socialist politicians every ten or twenty years. We don't like having our time wasted with trillion-dollar statist fantasies, when our government is already trillions of dollars in the red. We're tired of checking the papers each day, to see which group of us has been targeted as enemies of the State. We're growing impatient waiting for the Democrats to come up with ideas that don't require their supporters to hate someone. We've had our fill of "progressives" who act as if we're living in 1909, and none of their diseased policies have ever been tried before.

We believe government should be punished for failing to live up to the expectations of its citizens, not the other way around. We don't think people who destroy thousands of jobs and billions of dollars in market value should get a pass because they meant well. We've had enough of dodging a massive State that wants to organize, subsidize, penalize, and divide us. We refuse to pay tithe to a religion we don't support, including the official State religion of global warming. We demand honesty, humility, and transparency from our public servants, no matter how many elections they've won. We won't settle for making the only important decisions about our futures in the voting booth, once every couple of years.

We don't blame people for showing up to grab their share of a government handout. We blame the people who stole the money from the rest of us, and put it on the table for them. We don't think respect for private property ends at a certain income level, or that only some people should be applauded for doing their best to get ahead in life. We believe in the power and righteousness of capitalism, the exchange of goods and services between free people acting in their own best interests. There is no moral substitute for it. Every other scheme for governing human affairs amounts to a few dominating some, to the applause of others. Our freedom is not for sale, and we reserve the right to defend it from theft.

We don't invest our hopes in the government. It is beneath the dignity of free men and women to spend their days hoping a politician decides to provide for our needs. We face the future, not with passive and helpless "hope", but with active and dynamic **faith** in ourselves, and our fellow Americans. We are opposed to a political class that tries to cultivate our hopes by showering us with fear. We don't trust politicians with our fortunes, much less with our lives. In fact, we don't trust politicians much at all...but we absolutely require *them* to trust *us*.

We do not regard America as the sole country on Earth that should be forbidden from taking pride in its history, traditions, and achievements. We reject the notion that celebrating our traditions is an automatic insult to anyone else. We owe absolutely no apologies to murderous dictators or unelected tyrants, and we care little for their feelings. We believe there are many lessons to be learned from our history, by all the people of the world, and we cannot teach those lessons if we allow ourselves to be shamed into silence. We will never hesitate to call evil by its proper name, or give evil men good reasons to fear us.

Now, if you'll excuse us, we have a lot of work to do. There's an election coming up next year.

Deconstructing Obama
August 17, 2009

Author's Note: This was written in response to an editorial penned by President Obama, who was coping with rapidly deteriorating public support for his health-care proposals. The Velociraptors of Supply and Demand made their first appearance in this text, and went on to appear in several photoshops and YouTube videos created by clever readers.

The president's weekend editorial in the *New York Times,* written to shore up support for his collapsing health-care takeover plan, offers an opportunity to begin the vital task of taking back control of our language from the Left. Too much of our public debate is held in the Red Queen's court, where words mean exactly what the Left wants them to mean.

The president opens his editorial with this piece of boilerplate rhetoric:

> Our nation is now engaged in a great debate about the future of health care in America. And over the past few weeks, much of the media attention has been focused on the loudest voices. What we haven't heard are the voices of the millions upon millions of Americans who quietly struggle every day with a system that often works better for the health-insurance companies than it does for them.

No one from the Left has any standing to complain about the media focusing on the "loudest voices," Mr. President. More importantly, no one from the government has any right to whine about "the system." Well-meaning liberals did not recently stumble upon a terrible, unjust health-care system, created by evil insurance companies during the eight years of the Bush Terror. Nothing has shaped American health care more than the statist wage and price controls of the World War II era, which created the system of medical services paid through "insurance" provided as a benefit of employment. Health care is not a free-market maiden, trembling as it awaits the first caress of benevolent socialist government. They have been married for a long time, and their relationship will not be improved by an expensive second honeymoon.

The President follows his opening paragraph with yet another attempt to justify radical change by relaying a couple of heart-tugging anecdotes. After repeating the tired lie about 46 million Americans lacking health insurance, he claims his reforms will provide "more stability and security to every American." (Apparently the system is improving dramatically on its own, because the bogus number tossed around by Democrats used to be 47 million) Government involvement in private industry *never* brings more stability. Big Government is inherently unstable, prone to wild mood swings based on elections, and the actions of influential power brokers and pressure groups. Stability requires predictability, and nothing is less predictable than an activist government with deep pockets, run by a party that seeks to divide Americans into warring factions for its political advantage. The idea that anecdotal evidence from a handful of people should justify seizing huge chunks of the American economy, re-defining entire industries with minimal debate allowed on the fast-track legislation, is the very opposite of "stability."

It's also important to understand that nothing the government does, other than securing the borders against foreign enemies and prosecuting domestic criminals, benefits "every American." Obama's agenda is explicitly designed to penalize groups of Americans, whose assets will be seized through taxation, to pay for the benefits Obama plans to shower on his favored constituencies. As the President memorably explained to Joe the Plumber, Big Government's agenda is redistribution, which benefits some at the expense of others.

Obama claims his plan would bring four main improvements to American health care:

> First, if you don't have health insurance, you will have a choice of high-quality, affordable coverage for yourself and your family—coverage that will stay with you whether you move, change your job or lose your job.

Big Government does not bring more "choice" to **anything.** Government involvement inevitably *reduces* choices, as bureaucrats design the limited menu of options they think should be available, and foreclose attempts to act outside their system. The "public option" in the Obama plan uses titanic amounts of government money—extracted from taxpayers on a progressive scale, which forces the people least likely to be interested in the public option to pay most of its cost—to create a heavily subsidized federal insurance "company." The government will offer plans that would be impossible for legitimate private insurance companies to compete with, since they don't have bottomless pits of taxpayer cash to cover their losses.

Obama's proposed legislation includes clauses specifically designed to force private insurance companies out of business, and funnel more of the population into the public plan. Anyone who tries to offer "choices" outside of Obama's blueprint will be prosecuted with the full intensity of the law. You'll have "choice," all right—*one* choice, and you're making it right now, if you don't do everything in your power to oppose Obama's agenda.

Obama claims the second virtue of his plan is cost control. See if you can get through this paragraph without laughing out loud:

> Second, reform will finally bring skyrocketing health care costs under control, which will mean real savings for families, businesses and our government. We'll cut hundreds of billions of dollars in waste and inefficiency in federal health programs like Medicare

and Medicaid and in unwarranted subsidies to insurance companies that do nothing to improve care and everything to improve their profits.

Yes, nothing cuts waste and inefficiency like handing control over to a bloated federal government that thinks it has access to unlimited taxpayer funding and deficit spending. I suppose it's more "efficient" to pour all those unwarranted subsidies into one huge "public plan," instead of spreading them out among dozens of evil insurance companies. Everything this President says is tailored for an audience of people who were born yesterday, and never had contact with a single government agency. He also seems to think no one reading the *New York Times* has any experience with Medicare, an underfunded program heading for total collapse, which many doctors already refuse to participate in:

> Third, by making Medicare more efficient, we'll be able to ensure that more tax dollars go directly to caring for seniors instead of enriching insurance companies. This will not only help provide today's seniors with the benefits they've been promised; it will also ensure the long-term health of Medicare for tomorrow's seniors. And our reforms will also reduce the amount our seniors pay for their prescription drugs.

Government cannot make *anything* "more affordable." This idea comes from the delusion that prices are arbitrarily assigned by greedy fat-cat executives, who ignore the laws of economics to charge the highest price they think they can squeeze from their victims. It doesn't work that way, and it also doesn't work when government tries to ignore the laws of economics, to set prices according to a political agenda. The history of price controls and government subsidies is an unbroken tale of misery and failure. Applying price controls to a complex product, such as medicine, is like trying to clutch a fist full of water. The only predictable result will be the dumb amazement of the politicians, when they find themselves trapped in the Jurassic Park of inevitable statist failure, with the laws of supply and demand coming at them like hungry velociraptors.

We might have avoided this whole costly debate if the President understood the meaning of the word "insurance." He clearly doesn't, as demonstrated by the last virtue he claims for his proposals:

> Lastly, reform will provide every American with some basic consumer protections that will finally hold insurance companies accountable. A 2007 national survey actually shows that insurance companies discriminated against more than 12 million Americans in the previous three years because they had a pre-existing illness or condition. The companies either refused to cover the person, refused to cover a specific illness or condition or charged a higher premium.

> We will put an end to these practices. Our reform will prohibit insurance companies from denying coverage because of your medical history. Nor will they be allowed to drop your coverage if you get sick. They will not be able to water down your coverage

when you need it most. They will no longer be able to place some arbitrary cap on the amount of coverage you can receive in a given year or in a lifetime. And we will place a limit on how much you can be charged for out-of-pocket expenses. No one in America should go broke because they get sick.

"Insurance" is sold according to actuarial tables. The insurance company sells inexpensive policies to a large number of customers, most of whom will never file a major claim. The customers voluntarily participate in this transaction, paying a small premium to gain protection against the possibility of catastrophic future expenses. The company makes money, because the amount paid out in claims is less than the income from premiums. A customer who anticipates no catastrophic expenses might choose to buy minimal coverage, or decline to purchase insurance at all. Using the force of law to compel universal coverage for the same price, regardless of existing conditions and risk factors, is not "insurance," and the captive providers are not "insurance companies." Orwellian distortions of terms like "insurance" and "premiums" cloud the health-care debate, and make meaningful discussion difficult.

This seems to be a feature of Obama's agenda, rather than a bug, based on the panicked, authoritarian way he pushes it. For example, later in his editorial, he says "Despite what we've seen on television, I believe that serious debate is taking place at kitchen tables all across America.." What have we been seeing on television that suggests serious debate has not been taking place at kitchen tables? This is just another backhanded slap at the grass-roots inferno of resistance that has erupted against the Obama agenda, implying those angry town-hall protesters are actors in some sort of scripted television production, designed to intimidate your family into nursing its corn flakes and pre-existing illnesses around the kitchen table in bitter silence.

The President writes in praise of "vigorous debate," which is the same phrase he used to describe the Iranian government dispatching thugs to murder demonstrators. The rest of his editorial is a stern warning to keep that debate from getting *too* vigorous, coupled with an alphabet soup of professional associations and lobbies that feel the debate is already over. Obama could have expressed his love of vigorous debate by allowing ample time for it to occur, instead of trying to ram his bill through Congress in July. He's still trying to sow panic at the end of his supposedly calm and reasoned editorial:

> In the coming weeks, the cynics and the naysayers will continue to exploit fear and concerns for political gain. But for all the scare tactics out there, what's truly scary—truly risky—is the prospect of doing nothing. If we maintain the status quo, we will continue to see 14,000 Americans lose their health insurance every day. Premiums will continue to skyrocket. Our deficit will continue to grow. And insurance companies will continue to profit by discriminating against sick people.

Americans should vigorously resist the Left's attempt to equate resistance to government spending with "doing nothing." They should *never* be allowed to get away with pulling that card out of their boots. Wow, the only choices are total government control of the medical industry, or "doing nothing?" Is that the kind of "choice" he boasts about giving Americans with his health-care plan—the false choice between blind obedience and paralyzed decay? I love the way he tosses in the line about the deficit continuing to grow. Another couple trillion dollars in spending, on a half-written socialized medicine bill, should be just the thing to rein in those rascally deficits!

Allowing the Left to control the language of public debate gives their harebrained schemes a dangerous head start. Examples about beyond Obama's editorial in the New York Times. Government does not "invest" in anything—investment is a conscious decision to risk your own money, in pursuit of reward. Government is not a "partner" in anything—partnership involves equals working together for a common goal. No one willingly chooses a gigantic, emotionally unstable "partner" who puts chains on your wrists, and a gun in your back. Government cannot "guarantee" anything, because the political winds of the future can blow today's promises down the memory hole. The benefits a group secures through government pressure will only last until a larger, louder, hungrier group comes along.

My advice to conservatives, and the politicians who would represent them, is to deconstruct the language of the Left at every opportunity. Take back the language...then take back Congress, the White House, and the country.

Why Sarah Palin Should Not Leave The Room
August 23, 2009

Author's Note: The comments forum for this essay grew to over a thousand entries, which holds the record as the most intense discussion to follow one of my posts. Half a year later, I still don't understand why Charles Krauthammer wrote the words which prompted this response.

When I began writing for Hot Air, I never imagined I would find myself critical of Charles Krauthammer twice, after only blogging for four months. I've followed his work for years, and still eagerly read everything he publishes. He writes brilliantly on many topics, but he just doesn't get Sarah Palin, or by extension her supporters...which by further extension means he misunderstands the precarious moment America finds itself in, and the opportunities that lie ahead for conservatives.

Let me dispense with the most controversial part of Krauthammer's recent Town Hall column first: this condescending nonsense about asking Palin to "leave the room" while "we have a reasoned discussion about end-of-life counseling." There's only one group of people who needs to leave the room during that discussion, and it's the socialist zealot in the White House, along with the craven cowards in his party. They've already demonstrated a remarkable gift for swiftly leaving the room when people start asking tough questions, so we'll hardly notice when they slink out. Maybe while they're gone, they could find the billions in Cash for Clunkers money that vanished into thin air.

Those Facebook pages she's tossing around like ninja throwing stars are eloquent proof that *no one* has the right to pat Sarah Palin on the head and send her out of the room, while the grown-ups settle down to serious talk. She isn't just writing snarky rants. She's providing both devastatingly effective criticism, and substantial policy alternatives. It's fairly obvious the White House paid a great deal of attention to her infamous "death panel" column. I haven't seen that many people turned into nervous wrecks by Facebook since the last time the "Mafia Wars" servers went down.

As many others have noted, Krauthammer begins his latest essay with his bizarrely offensive demand that Palin "leave the room," then spends the rest of the essay essentially agreeing with her. It seems fair to say that his problem is more with her style than her substance. He misconstrues the "death panel" comment in a manner that suggests he might not have read her original Facebook posting. The "death panel" solar flare occurs in this paragraph:

The Democrats promise that a government health care system will reduce the cost of health care, but as the economist Thomas Sowell has pointed out, government health care will not reduce the cost; it will simply refuse to pay the cost. And who will suffer the most when they ration care? The sick, the elderly, and the disabled, of course. The America I know and love is not one in which my parents or my baby with Down Syndrome will have to stand in front of Obama's "death panel" so his bureaucrats can decide, based on a subjective judgment of their "level of productivity in society," whether they are worthy of health care. Such a system is downright evil.

There is no doubt Obama and his allies want to drive the United States toward a single-payer health system. Some of his more colorful co-conspirators, like Barney Frank, aren't particularly cagey about it when they speak in front of friendly audiences, and Obama himself has expressed that desire in the past. A health-insurance industry dominated by a tax-subsidized public option, whose vampiric "providers" can re-write the laws of the industry to destroy their nominal competitors, will inevitably collapse…leaving only the government. Tossing a shark into your aquarium is not a good way to enhance "competition" among the fish. When America inevitably loses enough blood to lapse into a single-payer coma, there will be rationing, and that means government functionaries will decide how the limited pool of medical resources is allocated. I don't think "death panel" is an unfair metaphor for the resulting system, and the sense of dread it provokes in the listener is *entirely* appropriate.

The death panel doesn't have to take the form of nine robed Sith Lords, stamping your grandmothers' termination orders with a giant red skull, then handing them to a ghoul in surgical scrubs. It will be no less deadly if it consists of thousands of faceless government drones in cubicles, processing Quality of Life spreadsheets and crossing out the unlucky Social Security numbers with pink highlighter pens. In fact, my only quibble with Palin's prediction is that, given the style of the current Administration, it is much more likely that we'll have a Death Czar. Using the same Noonan-swooning judgment that gave us a tax cheat for Treasury Secretary, Obama will appoint a serial killer to the position. The Death Czar's first official act will be spending $2 billion in taxpayer dollars to hire a Brazilian company, which will extract organs from Americans after they receive their end-of-life counseling, then ship them overseas for use in foreign patients.

What Palin brings to the health-care debate is the energy, wisdom, and wit to make complex ideas understandable to ordinary people. Let me once again restate my admiration for Charles Krauthammer before saying, with regrettably brutal candor, that Sarah Palin had more impact on the health-care debate with one Facebook note than everything Krauthammer has written in the past year. That's not because people are shallow, and didn't pay attention until Palin kicked off a media firestorm. It's because they understandably seek out leadership on complex issues, and leaders have a knack for rendering fearfully complicated issues down to their essential truths. Ordinary Americans are more eager to entertain appealing speech from an engaging personality, than sign up for a long series of dry lectures, no matter how brilliant the lecturer might be...and they don't view their ballots as comment cards, to be completed on their way out of the lecture hall.

Every political movement needs both academic intelligence, and vital charisma. The Left has always viewed the relationship between its intellectuals and politicians as something like the production and marketing departments in a business—and when it comes to accumulating power, socialists are *all* business. People like Saul Alinsky and Bill Ayers spent decades weaving the strings that control the Obama marionette. They openly wrote of their understanding that savvy merchandising would be needed to make the public accept their agenda, at least until the public no longer has a meaningful choice about accepting it. When was the last time you heard a leftist intellectual belittle a popular liberal politician, the way Charles Krauthammer treated Sarah Palin?

The challenge for conservatism is to educate the voters in its basic principles, since they received no such education in the public schools. Conservatism always triumphs on the elementary questions of freedom and capitalism. The ideas of the Left are diseased in root and branch—history has shown there is no need to allow them to blossom, in order to see they are poisonous. Conservatives who allow themselves to be dragged into bickering about page 945 of a 1200-page bill have already conceded far too much of the debate. Americans deserve better than being told to sit down and shut up, while Washington plays Jenga with Obama's obscene health-care proposals. They should be angry and insulted their time and money were ever wasted with this madness.

If Obama were the CEO of a private company, he would have already been "asked to leave the room" by the shareholders, and he'd be driving home in tears, listening to voice mail messages from the company lawyers. Unfortunately, it's not so easy to dispose of corrupt and incompetent elected officials...which is why they should be provided with the smallest possible operating budget, watched like hawks, and kept out of everything that isn't their explicit Constitutional duty. We can begin the process in 2010, and finish it in 2012. I'd like to have both Charles Krauthammer and Sarah Palin in the room while we prepare for battle. I know *she* won't ask *him* to leave.

A Tribute to Ted Kennedy
August 26, 2009

Author's Note: The following was written on the occasion of Senator Ted Kennedy's death.

First things first: my condolences to the family and friends of the late Senator Ted Kennedy on their loss. The hours after a loved one passes from this world are a quiet cave of ice, where all of us must journey from time to time, and the memory of that place is the fellowship shared by all mortal men and women. I am here to speak ill of the dead today, and will make no pretense otherwise, but I also wish to respect the feelings of the living. I have been to that cave of ice. I wish Senator Kennedy's survivors as swift a return as their hearts will allow.

It's unfortunate that the personal sorrow of a man's death must become a topic of political discussion, but it's only fitting, because Ted Kennedy helped write the field manual to the politics of personal destruction. Politicians have been spreading scurrilous lies about their opponents since the early days of the republic, but Kennedy used scurrilous lies to destroy a man who wasn't a politician: Judge Robert Bork. Kennedy kicked Bork's Supreme Court seat out from under him, by questioning his very humanity. Let me repeat a Kennedy quote you have probably heard a few times today:

> Robert Bork's America is a land in which women would be forced into back alley abortions, blacks would sit in segregated lunch counters, rogue police could break down citizens' doors in midnight raids, schoolchildren could not be taught about evolution, writers and artists could be censored at the whim of government, and the doors of the federal courts would be shut on the fingers of million of citizens.

Thus began the modern era of below-the-belt, win-at-any-cost politics, played for the highest of stakes. Kennedy's Democrats have never been shy about throwing elbows while the media referees are taking one of their frequent naps. Kennedy was the chief programmer for the endless loop of Great Society liberal arrogance, in which the Left used various social problems as the pretext for power grabs, which invariably made the problems worse…justifying further power grabs. This is the virus Democrats wish to introduce into the health-care system. The initial injection of a government-funded "public option" would lead to the total collapse of the health insurance industry, which would require even more sweeping government control of medicine, leading to a grim future in which titanic amounts of taxpayer loot would be shoveled into a system that produced sub-standard care and wealthy politicians.

Kennedy was a prince in the Aristocracy of Intent, absolved of every crime by the soaring nobility of his intentions. His constituents were delighted to watch him emerge from a warm bath of incredible wealth, to rail against men who were crass and selfish enough to accumulate their fortunes by creating jobs and meeting consumer needs. A straight line can be drawn from his limousine liberalism to Al Gore's Learjet environmentalism. To be a Kennedy supporter is to endorse the notion that only the wise elite of the ruling class are morally entitled to the trappings of wealth. In the workers' paradise, the masses will be uniformly poor, controlled, and maintained...while the commissars live in mansions, the Castros are billionaires, and the Kennedys hold court at Martha's Vineyard. The desperate slobbering of people like Chris Matthews is an embarrassing illustration of the liberal's enduring need to believe his leaders are giants in the earth, the elite of the elite. Of *course* the Left is feverishly working to deify Kennedy. Liberals see themselves as moral and intellectual heroes, and heroes kneel only before gods.

Kennedy is praised for his "passion" by the same people who recoil in horror from the passion of town-hall protesters and pro-life advocates. Awarding political power, and respect, on the basis of "passion" is another road to totalitarianism. The passion of the State's acolytes will always eclipse that of hard-working taxpayers, who scurry home with one hand on their wallets, hoping to avoid the notice of a hungry government. There will never be a shortage of passionate advocates for billion-dollar spending programs.

Lust and sanctimony are a dangerous combination. We've had enough of politicians who believe their duty to their party, and its vision of the future, transcends their loyalty to the real America that lives beyond their ideology. Ted Kennedy unquestionably believed this, when he offered to help the Soviet Union defeat Ronald Reagan...or when he found it expedient to portray George Bush and the American military as the new management of Saddam Hussein's torture chambers, even as American troops were locked in mortal combat with al-Qaeda terrorists. We've had enough of Senators-for-life, and royal families who use safe districts as dynastic thrones. We don't need any more "visionaries" who think the purpose of the private sector is helping government to realize its true potential.

There's no doubt that Kennedy was a towering figure with a legendary career full of important legislative achievements. The most important legislative achievement of a reborn America will be strangling all the other legendary careers in their cribs with term limits. Congressmen and Presidents were meant to bow before their constituents, not tower over them. I'm all in favor of naming the term limits bill after Edward Kennedy. It would be a fitting tribute.

Avenger of the Bones
August 27, 2009

Author's Note: This was written in response to fellow Green Room contributor Robert Stacy Mc-Cain, also known as "The Other McCain."

I noticed The Other McCain took exception with a comment in my "Ethics of Ferocity" post from Tuesday:

We're six months past the point where American voters can be kept quiet by suffocating them with the pillow of Bush hatred. We're about a month past the point where anyone capable of independent thought believes Obama is a better president than Bush was.

In response, The Other McCain commented on the American Spectator blog:

This is a bad argument, setting up an unnecessary comparison which does nothing to bolster the opposition to Obama. Furthermore, one can easily argue that George W. Bush was a very bad president and that one of the worst aspects of his presidency was that Bush confused people about the meaning of "conservatism" in a way that damaged the Republican Party and made possible Obama's election.

I'm surprised Other McCain read my original comment as an attempt to elevate Bush. Can't I just as easily argue that Bush was a bad president, and Obama is worse? I didn't think the overall tone of my essay conjured an image of Bush atop the Philadelphia Museum of Art steps, arms raised in victory, while an exhausted Obama catches his breath a few steps of greatness beneath him.

It's fair enough to ask me to clarify my opinion of George W. Bush. I've only been a blogger for a few months, and the Bush Administration was thousands of years ago, in the Second Age of Middle-Earth, when hobbit unemployment was less than half what it is today, and mortal men were not running a seven-ring deficit. I also think my assessment of Obama's inferior presidency is objectively true, and demonstrable, without waxing nostalgic about the troubled tenure of his predecessor.

Bush's greatest flaw was his failure to appreciate, and employ, the persuasive powers of the presidency. His second term was particularly appalling in this regard—he essentially disappeared after his re-election, and was rarely seen again. His problem was not entirely one of delivery. His successor is widely praised as a marvelous speaker, but he's no better at persuading the electorate than Bush was. Obama's problem is arrogance, and the urgent need to leverage his brief window of total Democrat power into a permanent victory in the Left's long war against the middle class. Bush's problem was a lack of vision.

He could have overcome his clumsy speaking style. A few malapropisms won't destroy a generally memorable speech. People have been fondly quoting Yogi Berra for decades, after all. The problem is that Bush rarely had anything memorable to say, outside of a few tragic, heroic months in 2001…and in those moments, he spoke to the ages. Nothing Bush or his enemies did, in the uncomfortable latter years of his presidency, diminished the magnificence of his "We Will Prevail" speech. We *will* prevail, thanks in no small part to the efforts of a generally mediocre president who had a moment of true greatness, in the hour his country needed him most.

For the rest of his tenure, Bush puttered quietly in the political greenhouse, trying to breed the same weird hybrid of conservative ideas and liberal ideals as his father. Both Bushes discovered, too late, that it's a man-eating plant. George W. Bush's major conservative domestic achievements were his tax cuts and Supreme Court picks. These were important and desirable, but not enough to slow down the awful leftward pendulum swing that's killing us.

Tax cuts are not a philosophy, and without a strong conservative philosophy built around them, they are too ephemeral to effect permanent change, especially in a country where only half the citizens pay any income tax at all. Their economic benefits are too easy for the Left to dismiss, particularly with the assistance of a media that reported five percent unemployment as a crisis for the poor damned souls in the job-placement industry. The economy is too complex to be guided by one input factor, while the maze of regulations, subsidies, and other government distortions are left in place. The American culture is too complex to be guided solely by adjustments to the economy. Outside of his tax cuts, Bush either agreed with, or submitted to, far too much of the Left's agenda, paving the way for the current tragedy.

A great President must be a teacher, with a deathless enthusiasm for teaching the basics, over and over again. This was part of Reagan's brilliance. Listening to any of his speeches is like replaying a recording of a jovial professor, holding forth in the only class you never wanted to skip. A president must also serve as the leader of his party, without being in complete *control* of it. This is not easy to do, but Bush didn't even seem interested in trying. The degenerate state of his party in 2006 is not entirely his fault, but it *is* his responsibility.

That's an awful lot of bad stuff to lay on the ex-president. Let me speak in his defense by relaying a personal anecdote. My mother passed away, very suddenly and unexpectedly, on November 11, 2001—an awful day that fell exactly two months after another awful day. Watching the news one evening, during those two months, she told me how grateful she was for George Bush's courage and determination in the face of unspeakable evil, and how much safer he made her feel. After she was gone, I wrote a letter to the President, to pass along her thanks and add my own. I never got a reply, and never expected one. I could recite that letter from memory...and if I ever have a chance to meet George W. Bush, I will.

President Bush didn't do enough to cut the size of government, and rein in runaway spending. His deficits were too high...and his successor tripled them in six months. Bush never sent thugs to beat the protesters who were camped down the street from his house. He didn't try to prosecute people from Bill Clinton's administration for political advantage. I don't recall him blaming any of his problems on Clinton, ever. He didn't set up Orwellian email accounts to collect information on his critics. He sacrificed his political capital for the benefit of America's defense, not the other way around. His strategy in Iraq was executed poorly in many respects, but I believe it is a strategy that will prove to have saved countless American and Iraqi lives, in the long run. An Iraqi dubbed him "Avenger of the Bones," and that name always seemed right to me. Because Americans are not aggressors, conquerors, or helpless victims, we will sometimes need to be avengers.

On balance, I agree with The Other McCain: Bush was a bad president. He was *vastly* superior to the current occupant of the White House. I see nothing to be gained by keeping quiet about that observation. We owe President Bush that much, because in the horrified silence that followed a cowardly act of mass murder, he raised *his* voice for us.

My Disagreement With the Kennedy Narrative
August 30, 2009

Author's Note: After a week of soaking up the media reaction to Senator Kennedy's passing, I felt a second post on the topic was in order. This one struck a nerve with conservative readers, who were largely trying to forget about Kennedy…and found themselves frustrated in this endeavor by the endless media hagiography.

After five days of flood-the-zone news coverage, eulogies, and encomiums, filled with hundreds of op-ed pieces and blog posts, the Democrats have made their vision of Senator Edward Kennedy's life and career crystal clear. I've had some fun at their expense, but the late Senator has now been returned to the earth at Arlington, and fun time is over. I have some serious disagreements with the things I've heard from the Left over the last few days.

I do not believe a political career is worth a young woman's life. **Period.** I don't think Mary Jo Kopechne was proud to die for Ted Kennedy. I don't think her horrifying death was a necessary human sacrifice to enable his "fortunate fall." Ted Kennedy was not the victim of Chappaquiddick. Anyone who believes those things is a degenerate who should be shunned by civilized people.

I disagree with the notion that any aspect of Kennedy's life "redeemed" him for the death of Mary Jo Kopechne. Redemption requires contrition, an admission of guilt. Kennedy never admitted responsibility or guilt for what happened at Chappaquiddick. I wish he had, because the idea of so many people rushing to grant him undeserved absolution is nauseating.

I disagree that the world will "sorely miss" the "moral clarity" of someone who enjoyed jokes about the woman who died because of his cowardice and lust for power. The human race will be greatly improved when it is infested by fewer such creatures.

I disagree that we should be *more eager* to pass an increasingly unpopular, blatantly unconstitutional, ridiculously expensive bill that would destroy the health-care industry, just because a dead politician from a wealthy and powerful family would have wanted it.

I don't believe that destroying the reputation of a judge, through insane and reckless allegations that challenge his very humanity, represents great statesmanship. He tried the same slimy tactics he used on Robert Bork against Clarence Thomas. I don't think the legacy of personal destruction Ted Kennedy inaugurated during the Bork confirmation hearings has been a plus for America.

I don't believe that a man who worked with the Soviet Union to undermine American policy, slandered American troops while they were fighting battles in the streets of Iraq, and helped abandon the Cambodians to genocide was either a patriot, or a noble citizen of the world. His loyalty was to his own ambitions, to his Party, and to the country he thought America *might* become, if it would submit to his ideas. The loyalty of an arrogant man is always diluted by a measure of treachery.

I don't believe a man fighting for his life against a brain tumor should be denied care under a quality of life formula, in a rationed government health-care system. I also don't think those quality of life spreadsheets should add a million extra points for being a powerful politician. The idea that Senator Kennedy would have been denied the care he needed, to gain his extra year of life, under socialized medicine is ridiculous—the government will *never* apply rationing to its ruling elite, or make them wait in line. The idea that everyone *else* should be expected to surrender in their struggle for life is monstrous.

I disagree that the architect of the "Big Dig" debacle, who saddled the country with trillions of dollars in debt, and tried to change the rules of Massachusetts senatorial succession in an embarrassingly transparent bid to keep those seats permanently in his party's hands, is "the greatest legislator of our time," as President Obama called him. If he is, then his career is proof that we need fewer "great legislators." We can't afford them any more. Did he support some important legislation? Certainly. The most indisputably noble bill he was associated with was the Voting Rights Act of 1965. Mary Jo Kopechne died in 1969. That should have been the end of him.

I don't think a man who lied to the police, and dispatched henchmen to destroy the reputation of the victim, to help his nephew beat sexual assault charges is any sort of feminist hero. Let me know when the feminists think it's okay for a Republican to be one of the slices of bread in a waitress sandwich. The idea that political positions convey a supreme virtue, trumping abhorrent personal behavior, should be buried with Kennedy.

I disagree that someone's party affiliation, position in the government, or last name should put them above the law. I disagree that four decades of squatting in a safe Senate seat is admirable, for anyone of any political party. I don't see anything to applaud about a notorious womanizer with a spotless record of abortion extremism. I don't find anything noble about a man born to wealth and privilege seeking moral authority by socking struggling middle-class businessmen with the bill for his high-minded social programs…especially when he took every opportunity to shelter his own income from taxes.

Many reasons have been offered for Ted Kennedy's long, expensive, debased career: He was trading on his family name. The voters of Massachusetts thrust him on the country by perpetually re-electing him. It was America's collective fault for letting him get away with Chappaquiddick. The media loved him because they love epic tales of heroic liberal politicians. We can learn not to repeat all of those mistakes.

When you go into the voting booths next year, remember what the past week has taught you about the Democrats. It would have been one thing to offer a salute to the parts of his political agenda they agreed with, while acknowledging the dark side. The full-on hagiography, coupled with the disgusting attempts to dismiss Mary Jo Kopechne's life as a small price to pay for political power, reveal that this party knows *nothing* about the meaning of redemption, responsibility, and the value of individual human lives. The rest of us can neither afford nor tolerate anyone like Ted Kennedy, ever again.

The Death of the Individual
August 31, 2009

Liberalism has given itself many different names over the years. The American Left and its political vehicle, the Democrat Party, are most accurately described as collectivists. The belief that unites the various factions within the party is their determination to accumulate power in the central government, which they believe is morally and intellectually superior to individual citizens and free enterprise. To accommodate this philosophy, they must break faith with the Founders' devout belief in individual rights, which are not merely granted by the State, but which transcend it…rights every citizen is born with, which the State must respect.

Collectivism requires the denial that absolute individual rights exist—there can be no such rights, for the existence of one would imply the possibility of others. To quote a popular expression of collectivist philosophy, consider Mr. Spock's famous line from *Star Trek II:* "The needs of the many outweigh the needs of the few, or the one." This is close, but incorrect in one crucial detail: the collectivist believes that the needs of the many outweigh the **rights** of the few, or the one.

This is why the death of Mary Jo Kopechne doesn't trouble liberal intellectuals all that much. In fact, they think you're a bit childish and primitive for being obsessed with it.

The meme floated by the Left over the past few days, that Kopechne's death was a reasonable price to pay for Ted Kennedy's wonderful political career, is a brutally candid expression of the principle that even an individual's right to live is negotiable—a commodity to be measured against the "needs of the many," which the Left believes were far better served by Kennedy's politics than Kopechne's insignificant little life. The striking thing about the two most infamous expressions of this opinion, by Melissa Lafsky and Joyce Carol Oates, is how *breezy* they are. They don't caution the reader to brace himself for an outrageous, controversial assertion, which the author plans to defend. Both Lafsky and Oates are rather wistful in tone. They don't understand why anyone *wouldn't* think Kopechne's life for Kennedy's legislative agenda was a sweet trade, the deal of the century for America. As Mark Steyn puts it, the Left doesn't see why we should dwell on the bit players in the epic saga of Ted Kennedy's life.

The attempt to dismiss Kopechne's death as a down payment on Kennedy's mountain of legislation is not merely an act of political convenience, a smokescreen blown by Democrats eager to paint Kennedy into the "Last Supper" of liberal apostles, with oils of their choosing. The Left is speaking from the dark heart of collectivism, a belief system that will collapse if it acknowledges any area in which the rights of an individual absolutely trump the needs of the State. The modern super-state depended heavily on Ted Kennedy for its existence, as dozens of news anchors have been eager to explain over the last few days. The idea that the epic narrative of the State should be compromised in the name of justice for a random citizen is ludicrous to the Left.

Collectivism is inherently dehumanizing, no matter how benevolent the intentions of the collectivist, because it's completely incompatible with the notion of unalienable rights. The belief that Kopechne's life was more valuable than any legislation Ted Kennedy could ever pass, which leads conservatives to denounce the Lasky and Oates pieces as disgusting, is a belief the collectivist can never accept. For one thing, it would do an awful lot of damage to the pro-choice movement. For another, it would lead to uncomfortable questions about other inalienable rights, such as the right to own property. Progressive taxation, the beating heart of modern liberalism, is based on the notion that a millionaire does not have the same property rights as a pauper. You can't "spread the wealth around" without accepting that the "needs" of those who serve as the bread trump the rights of those who provide the peanut butter.

The Left makes its peace with the opulent, hedonistic lifestyle of people like Ted Kennedy, Michael Moore, and other trust-fund or Hollywood liberals by reasoning that if all virtue resides in the State, then its princes and priests are supremely virtuous by definition, at least in the political, collective sense. Rich rewards are their due. For everyone else, the Constitution and Bill of Rights are infinitely adjustable, as required by the complex needs of a gigantic government that wants to micro-manage the destiny of an even larger nation. When the executive, legislative, and judicial branches of the federal government become Clotho, Atropos, and Lachesis, spinning the loom of fate for millions of citizens, you can expect some threads to be cut rather clumsily.

Collectivism always becomes ugly and brutal. Frankly, every collectivist society before ours became openly murderous. There is no gentle way to deal with the human remainder from every equation the State designs. Liberals criticize capitalism by saying it doesn't make adequate provisions for taking care of everyone. Neither does liberalism—it only pretends otherwise. Collective politics requires compulsion, which in turn requires the death of compassion for the inconvenient individual.

A noble society owed Mary Jo Kopechne a measure of undying anger over her death, and should have denied any position of high honor to the man who never repented for his part in it. A truly wise society should work forward, from the inherent rights of the individual, to fair and just laws that respect those rights. Collectivism works backward, from a desired outcome to the elaborate political theories necessary to justify it...and like any other massive vehicle being driven in reverse, it sometimes runs people down.

The New Contract With America

September 1, 2009

Observers of the political scene are increasingly willing to entertain the possibility that the Republicans could retake the House in 2010. They have an opportunity even greater than 1994, but thus far they haven't demonstrated anything like the organization Newt Gingrich and his team brought to the party. The last thing I heard from a prominent Republican politician in either house of Congress was Orrin Hatch suggesting we present Ted Kennedy's Senate seat to his widow as a gift.

The time is unquestionably ripe for a new Contract With America. It only makes sense to nationalize the election, in response to the growing discontent voters feel with the President's agenda. It's also wise for the Republican Party to come together around a clear statement of policy and principle, as a way of re-introducing themselves to an electorate that couldn't find many reasons to love them in 2006 and 2008.

The new Contract With America should set out a bold vision for undoing the damage Obama has done to the country. This will be a more delicate project than it might seem at first glance. Obama was a radical who ran as a moderate, and a certain degree of radical change will be necessary to undo the damage. It will take some heavy lifting to get America back to where it was just one year ago, a journey that will double back across a barren wasteland of wasted tax dollars, past bottomless deficit pits and pools of poisonous regulation, where a murder of czars picks at the bones of long-dead liberty. The media will assure the public this journey is a suicide mission, and their only choice is to plod along the irreversible course the Democrats have plotted, no matter how dreary it might be.

The task for the Republicans is to both excite and reassure the public. Average folks always say they want "change," but they're understandably nervous about massive upheavals. They won't be eager to hop off the Democrat log flume and jump right onto a Republican roller coaster. A well-reasoned agenda, backed up with resolute common sense, will go a long way toward convincing them that the fate Obama had in mind for them is neither desirable, nor inevitable.

I hope the new Contract With America features massive **reductions in government spending** as a centerpiece. The government must release its death grip on the private sector. Private industries grow, produce new products, generate wealth, and create jobs. Government-controlled industries are corpses that decompose at varying speeds. Why would the economy grow, and spur new job creation, if the private sector keeps contracting? Let the new Contract

With America explain the staggering size of Obama's deficits, and the radical explosions in government spending…then show how the two are related, and why they can only be reduced in tandem. Pledge that no new agencies will be created, and the process of trimming the fat from the bloated federal government will begin in earnest under Republican leadership.

The new Contract should **shatter the ridiculous myths** Democrats have been concocting about their failed policies. Purge America of the economic ignorance necessary to believe something like Cash for Clunkers was a success. Promise a full accounting for the billions that disappeared from Cash for Clunkers and the "stimulus" bill. Pledge the full and timely release of vital economic data, which Obama has gone to great lengths to conceal. Explain why the Post Office is not a model which the health-care industry should emulate.

Republicans should vow to bring **transparency and accountability** to the shady maze of back alleys and smoke-filled rooms Obama spilled on the already mean streets of Washington. Michelle Malkin's new book is a detailed indictment of the new Culture of Corruption. She already did the heavy lifting for you, Republicans. Present her table of contents to the American people as a target list, and promise none of those targets will be left standing by the end of 2010. An awful lot of Americans already own that book. Maybe they can use red pens to draw little bulls-eyes next to the names, as they are taken down. Election day should see a massive run on red pens. Don't make Michelle publish a second edition of the book in 2011.

The new Contract With America must, inevitably, **address health care.** The Republicans should take this opportunity to explain how government intervention has caused many of the problems that exist in the health care system. More intervention is not the solution. The answer lies with treating health care like other commodities, and allowing competition, and the creative energy of the free market, to make it less expensive, and therefore more available. Socialism can only increase supply at the expense of quality, and it can never increase supply enough to meet skyrocketing demand. Prices are not reduced by grinding them into dust and hiding them in everyone's tax bills.

Competition requires more companies to enter the insurance industry, while a government-funded insurance option will inevitably have the opposite effect. Competition also requires greater consumer participation, which means more awareness of exactly what they're buying, and how much they are paying for it. Too much of health care is hidden behind the bureaucratic complexity of health insurance, which isn't really "insurance" at all, but rather the medium of exchange for the purchase of medicine—a baffling foreign currency minted from a blend of payroll deductions, employer contributions, and government subsidies. Let people have "insurance" for catastrophes, and purchase rational health plans for routine care with their own money, bringing patients and doctors together. Reduce the legal costs to the medical profession, through tort reform…and explain, in clear and fearless language, why that will *never* happen under Democrats. Free markets can only exist in bright daylight—choice requires knowledge.

The new Contract With America should include a firm **commitment to America's defense**. Pledge to end all political prosecution of American intelligence agents and military personnel, and make a strong declaration that our soldiers are not chips to be tossed on the political poker table. Make a promise to America's defenders that they will always go into battle with clear rules of engagement, and never need to worry about being second-guessed by politicians after the shooting stops. Include a heartfelt, long overdue thanks to *all* of the men and women who have kept America safe since September 11, 2001.

The Republicans should pledge to hold regular, well-attended **meetings with their constituents**, and promise that both supporters and dissenters will be kept safe, and respected. This is a long, slow pitch over home plate, and it would be foolish not to knock it out of the park.

These ideas, and many other worthwhile proposals, must be expressed in both **practical and moral language**. When the Left is confronted by the failure of its ideas, it always tries to foreclose alternatives by declaring them unthinkable. No liberal has ever been more likely to mount this defense than Barack Obama, who has nothing except the assumed mantle of moral superiority to offer in defense of his party. Few have looked more ridiculous trying to don that mantle. There has been too much corruption in this Administration, too many Obama cronies getting rich while unemployment and the deficit explode, too many knives in America's back with Nancy Pelosi's fingerprints all over them. The case for freedom and capitalism should begin with the simple understanding they are inseparable.

I'm sure I left some things out. There is no shortage of things the Republicans can do for their country. If they can't rise to the occasion, in this of all election seasons, it will be time for them to step aside—or more to the point, it will be time for us to push them aside. They need to do more than convince us they're a bit less awful than the Democrats. They need to make us *believe* in them again. It's a tall order. That's why I want some time to study the menu.

Judgment Day
September 4, 2009

Barack Obama is trying to install a self-described communist and "black nationalist" as an unelected, unconfirmed "czar" with indefinite powers to force private companies to engage in economic activity that meets the President's political agenda. The would-be czar, Van Jones, turns out to be a paranoid lunatic who believes in a disgusting conspiracy theory, which stands as an insult to the people murdered on 9/11, the heroes who died trying to save them, and the heroes who died avenging them. The truth of Jones' revolting beliefs, including his signature on a manifesto, was easily discovered through simple Internet searches. This means either Obama knew about it and hoped to hide it from the public, he knew about it and thought it was not a big deal, or he was ignorant of vital information about someone he planned to appoint in defiance of Congress and the Constitution.

What was Barack Obama's major qualification for the presidency, the one thing we were repeatedly told to consider above his paper-thin resume, shadowy associations with racists and terrorists, and troubling ethical background? Ah, yes: his **judgment**. Do you remember these chart-topping hits from the 2008 presidential campaign?

> He has within him the possibility to change the direction and tone of American foreign policy, which need changing; his rise will serve as a practical rebuke to the past five years, which need rebuking; his victory would provide a fresh start in a nation in which a fresh start would come as a national relief. He climbed steep stairs, born off the continent with no father to guide, a dreamy, abandoning mother, mixed race, no connections. He rose with guts and gifts. He is steady, calm, and, in terms of the execution of his political ascent, still the primary and almost only area in which his executive abilities can be discerned, he shows good judgment in terms of whom to hire and consult, what steps to take and moves to make. We witnessed from him this year something unique in American politics: He took down a political machine without raising his voice.—*Peggy Noonan, October 31, 2008*

> President Obama will (I pray, secularly) surely understand that traditional left-politics aren't going to get us out of this pit we've dug for ourselves. If he raises taxes and throws up tariff walls and opens the coffers of the DNC to bribe-money from the special interest groups against whom he has (somewhat disingenuously) railed during the campaign trail, then he will almost certainly reap a whirlwind that will make Katrina look like a balmy summer zephyr. Obama has in him—I think, despite his sometimes airy-fairy "We are the people we have been waiting for" silly rhetoric—the potential to be a good,

perhaps even great leader. He is, it seems clear enough, what the historical moment seems to be calling for.—*Christopher Buckley, October 10, 2008*

Many more examples would be easy to find. I highlight Buckley and Noonan because they were nominally people of the Right, working to make other conservatives comfortable with the man who had dazzled them. Of course, most liberals are inclined to believe any liberal candidate has good judgment. Buckley and Noonan viewed themselves as ambassadors of Hope and Change to the hopeless and unchanging Right, asserting that Obama was qualified for the presidency because his judgment and temperament were objectively excellent *despite* his political philosophy.

It's not unreasonable to promote judgment as an important qualification for the presidency. It's a rather broad concept, since virtually everything a person does reflects on their ability to make reasoned decisions. Anyone who supports a leadership candidate, for any reason except blind faith or a romantic response to their charisma, is endorsing their judgment. Voters are attracted to candidates with military backgrounds, in part, because an honorable military career demonstrates courage, self-sacrifice, and the ability to remain focused under intense pressure.

In Obama's case, the independent voter was presented with only two reasons to vote for him: his vaguely defined policy agenda, and his supposedly marvelous judgment. (I know many will suggest an obvious, but uncomfortable, third reason was the color of his skin, but that was always more about the voters wishing to purchase virtue at a discount price, rather than a reason to vote for this specific candidate.) The vaguely defined policy agenda turned out to be even more ephemeral than any independent voter might have thought, since few of Obama's actions in office bear any resemblance to the policies he campaigned on, even judged on the usual dismal curve for politicians of either party. This leaves only the matter of Obama's decision-making skills, and the Van Jones debacle is only the latest, and most outrageous, evidence that his media cheerleaders were wrong about that, too.

The position Jones was appointed to fill is as much of an outrage as the man himself. Here is a working definition of fascism, from *The Concise Encyclopedia of Economics:*

> Where socialism sought totalitarian control of a society's economic processes through direct state operation of the means of production, fascism sought that control indirectly, through domination of nominally private owners. Where socialism nationalized property explicitly, fascism did so implicitly, by requiring owners to use their property in the "national interest"—that is, as the autocratic authority conceived it. (Nevertheless, a few industries were operated by the state.) Where socialism abolished all market relations outright, fascism left the appearance of market relations while planning all economic activities. Where socialism abolished money and prices, fascism controlled the monetary system and set all prices and wages politically.

Does all of that sound familiar? How else do you describe an unelected political operative, appointed without the advice or consent of Congress, and gifted with a thirty billion dollar budget for the purpose of shaping private industry to fit the President's political agenda? I've always been wary of using the Eff Word to describe domestic political figures…but after seven months of corporate takeovers, stolen "stimulus" money, political destruction of inconvenient citizens, pointed insinuations that the public's right of free speech is a secondary concern against the urgency of the Obama agenda, and the deployment of organized squads of thugs to use violence against dissenters…capped off by the green banner raised above a phalanx of czars, and the man chosen to hold it…

If this isn't fascism, the word has no meaning at all, aside from being a historically inaccurate synonym for German National Socialism. At this point, the burden of proof is upon Obama, to explain how his actions are *not* fascist. If he does that during his upcoming address to schoolchildren, first period homeroom class would finally become interesting. I would tune in. I'd buy it on DVD. I'd even pay extra for Blu-Ray, if there were some decent extras, like maybe an interactive game where you match up Obama's cabinet appointees and czars with the crimes they have committed.

Fascism is a particularly ugly form of collectivist economics because it retains the illusion of private industry, which is dominated by the state. Private industry does not like to be dominated; it resists. This gives the fascist an early, and urgent, need for domestic enemies he can rally the public against. Van Jones signed a document alleging that Obama's predecessors, in collusion with a huge number of military and civilian government personnel, conspired to murder thousands of American citizens for financial gain. Obama wanted to put him in charge of an agency that would use its lavish funding to assert that uncooperative businesses are conspiring to destroy the planet for financial gain. It would disburse taxpayer subsidies to politically connected businesses that support the President's environmental agenda, which is marketed as a mystical religious faith, with dissension treated as heresy. Does any of that sound designed to bring Americans closer together?

The media is trying to ignore the Van Jones outrage. Don't let them. This is not a "mistake." A mistake is a matter of chance, a momentary failure of reason and wisdom. This is part of a pattern. Are we supposed to believe Obama knew nothing about *any* of his appointees? Are we expected to believe his White House staff is utterly incapable of matching the research a bunch of bloggers managed in less than twenty-four hours? Would President John McCain have been indulged if he'd appointed a "white nationalist" who signed a petition calling for the investigation of Bill Clinton in the murder of Vince Foster? The paper Van Jones signed says that every soldier who fell in Iraq died to cover up an act of mass murder, joining thousands of willing accomplices. That's not an "indiscretion." It's an insult to everyone who died on September 11, everyone who mourns them, everyone who comforted the mourners, and everyone who fought to bring justice to the murderers.

I suspect Obama will realize his deadly mistake, possibly by the time you read this, and Jones will be urged to make a quiet withdrawal into obscurity. Perhaps he could apply for a future position as ambassador to Honduras, after Obama installs Manuel Zelaya as dictator. He should not be allowed to do get away with this. Obama should be compelled to withdraw his name from consideration, along with a detailed accounting of Jones' objectionable beliefs, and a full explanation for why such a person would be appointed to a position of power and authority under his Administration. Voters can keep this explanation in mind when they have a chance to vote the President's party out of Congress next year. Democrat leaders can keep the voters in mind while they contemplate the ghostly footsteps that lead from Congress to the Nixon White House, and ask themselves how much is enough.

As for those of us who had enough of Barack Obama long before Election Night 2008, our judgment has been utterly and indisputably vindicated.

Defending the Honor of President McCain
September 22, 2009

TV and radio host Glenn Beck recently sat for an interview with Katie Couric, in which he asserted that John McCain would have been "worse for the country than Barack Obama." Beck's remarks were deliberately provocative—he was laughing in a "try this one on for size" spirit when he repeated them. He might have been looking to stake out some unique, independent ground, in the manner of his Fox associate Bill O'Reilly, who awakens every morning to discover the center of the political universe is planted squarely between his toes. I'll take Beck at his word, however, and strenuously disagree with him.

John McCain was not my choice for the GOP nomination. He ran a perfectly appalling campaign, all the more heartbreaking because he squandered the only exciting opportunity he managed to create: the selection of Sarah Palin. McCain's greatest mistake, which America has not finished paying dearly for, was allowing the Democrat crooks behind the subprime crisis to skate away without penalty. The miscarriage of justice involved in leaving Barney Frank to happily count the money he looted from American taxpayers *pales* beside the damage he continues to inflict on the economy. In fact, the Washington Examiner just ran a story about the return of the very same policies that produced the subprime crash. McCain is accountable for every bit of the damage people like Barney Frank and Chris Dodd cause in the future, an accessory through his silence. He spent far too much of his campaign dreaming of a big, old-fashioned wedding with The Media, flanked by honored Senate colleagues in tuxedos and bridesmaid gowns…while the object of his affections staggered out of a tattoo parlor with Obama's name written all over her, fell into the back seat of the Lightworker's muscle car, and roared off in a shower of empty beer cans.

He was an awful candidate…but McCain would not have bitten his tongue while Iran murdered its citizens, leaving their Fourth of July picnic invitation on the table. He would not be working to install a Chavez puppet as dictator of Honduras. He wouldn't have tried to sacrifice American intelligence agents in a show trial for political gain. He wouldn't shower America's adversaries with concessions while gaining nothing in return. McCain would have plenty of opponents, but he wouldn't spend an unseemly amount of time designating groups of his constituents as enemies. He would know better than to casually accuse a cop of racism on national television.

I don't see McCain setting up an Orwellian email address to rat out political enemies to the White House, or dispatching a horde of thugs to beat up demonstrators at town hall meetings. I doubt he would greet the disappearance of billions in "stimulus" money by shrugging and demanding another trillion. He wasn't lying when he said he wanted victory in Afghanistan. He would have fewer unelected, unconfirmed "czars," and none of them would be a Truther, a supporter of cop killer Mumia Abu Jamal, or a communist...let alone all three. His Supreme Court nominations would not have to defend their racial theories of judicial supremacy at their confirmation hearings. Enemies of America wouldn't have to test John McCain to find out what he was made of—they could just ask the North Vietnamese. I always thought "The Straight Talk Express" was a silly name for his campaign bus, but at least it wasn't splattered with the political blood of people thrown beneath it.

This is not to say that President McCain's domestic policies would have been superb. It's impossible to predict exactly what anyone *would have done* in the Oval Office. The butterfly effect from swapping out presidents is so huge that it comes with pair of tiny Japanese girls, who speak in unison when they warn of its approach. However, nothing McCain said during the campaign made me anticipate a presidency of bold conservative reform. I suspect we would have gotten something like the lazy Bush slide to the left in most areas, sprinkled with the occasional conservative policy, and the unmitigated disaster of amnesty for illegal aliens.

During the campaign, disgruntled Republicans often said it would be better to have Obama in office, showing everyone just how horrible Democrat policies are, than tolerate a RINO like McCain pushing the same policies in low gear, with bipartisan fingerprints. Glenn Beck's slap at McCain is a retroactive expression of the idea that conservatism is just one crushing defeat away from total victory. Anyone who thought it was worth putting Obama in office, as some kind of object lesson for the American voter, gravely underestimated the amount of damage he could do. Look at how far we've sailed past the edge of fiscal sanity, in only nine months. It would take decades of careful, moderate reform just to get us back to where George Bush left us...and that wasn't exactly an enviable position. Freedom is an endless voyage, while tyranny has far too many points of no return. The course we steered away from President McCain has taken us perilously close to those terminal waters.

The Obama presidency has been a flash forward to where the post-Reagan glide path might have taken us, in ten or twenty years. It is *not* the same thing to arrive at this moment in 2009 instead of 2029, any more than spending the night drinking a bottle of whiskey is the same thing as draining it all in one gulp. Toxicity increases with dosage. Many things might have occurred over the next few decades, to help us cope with the coming crash. Instead, the time bomb of Social Security begins detonating *next year.* Even if Obama left office tomorrow, it would take dramatic reforms to pull us out of our nose dive...and the American voter *hates* dramatic reforms.

I've got a lot of bones to pick with George Bush's domestic policies, and I doubt President McCain's would have been much better, but if either of them replaced Obama tomorrow, the economy would begin improving immediately...not because they would do anything particularly brilliant, but because they wouldn't pummel us with the insane crap Obama serves up as daily fare. At least the markets would have less reason to be terrified of the White House. Simply refraining from the dramatic transformation of our economy and culture would be a huge improvement at this point.

McCain wouldn't be a worse president than Obama. He *would* be more politically inconvenient for the conservative movement. Speaking for myself, I'd pay that price in a heartbeat…to spare my country what it has already endured, and what is yet to come.

The Omnipresent Leader
September 27, 2009

Much outrage has accompanied the release of a video showing little kids at the Bernice Young Elementary School in New Jersey, being led in a creepy North Korean-style song of praise to Barack Obama. I like to call this clip "The Best Home School Endorsement Video Ever." Ed Morrissey posted another example of musical indoctrination on Hot Air today, which he felt was a bit more harmless, although it includes lyrics like this:

Obama is the President!

First African American in history

44th president of the United States

The ground has shifted

The world has changed!

I don't recall many schoolteachers leading hymms to George Bush when he shifted the ground under Saddam Hussein and changed *his* world. Something tells me no one in the educational establishment would be leading musical worship sessions for the equally historic President Sarah Palin or President Condoleeza Rice, either.

The great HBO miniseries *Band of Brothers* includes a scene where a World War II Army officer is reluctant to salute a superior officer he dislikes. The superior officer gently reminds him, "We salute the uniform, not the man." Even the less infuriating kiddie sing-along referenced above is offensive to this ideal, because it drills campaign rhetoric about the Historic First Black President into the children. Inducting these kids into the Mickey Mouse Club division of the Obama personality cult will not help them make a reasoned, independent evaluation of his presidency as they grow older. During the later Clinton years, when it became difficult to actually *look* at the man, the Left lectured us that respect was due to the office he held. Now, we're told to ignore a tsunami of policy failures, and revere the historic skin color of the man in the Oval Office.

Besides the understandable anger parents feel when their children are used as political props, the Bernice Young sing-along is grating because it's another aspect of the Obama omnipresence. The guy is **everywhere**, all the time. He's been stalking the American voter all summer, muttering the ever-changing details and phony rationale for his health-care takeover plan. Mercifully, he stopped just short of filling our inboxes with spam emails, or dropping pop-up spyware onto our computers. I have a recurring nightmare that the Microsoft Office Assistant will rap on my monitor to get my attention, and start talking about the urgent need for health-care reform.

The omnipresence of our political leadership will only grow worse over time, if we don't begin scaling back the super-State. Everything in life has become politicized, and politics have become highly centralized. The President, and the majority leadership in Congress, have an increasing amount of influence over every aspect of your daily life—not in a remote theoretical sense, but literally. If the government takes over health care, your body will become property of the State, which will have a vested interest in controlling your diet, exercise, and everything else that might affect your consumption of tightly-rationed medical resources. The cap-and-trade bill puts the federal government in charge of your kitchen appliances and light bulbs. These latest extensions of federal power come after decades of more gradual increases.

Since command economics never work, and statists believe the solution to all problems is more government power, your life will become increasingly dominated by political leaders. Liberals, including most media figures, find this a desirable state of affairs, so they are naturally inclined to revere and worship fashionably liberal politicians. The liberal very much wants the country to be led by a genius who can control the economy, reshape entire industries, and wisely redistribute wealth to achieve social justice. Any Democrat who achieves high office automatically becomes such a genius to them. Of *course* Barack Obama is a moral, intellectual, and physical superman! He *has* to be. It's only natural to feel awed and humbled in the presence of such a being.

The logic of statism assumes that politicians are a superior breed, better suited to run industries than any corporate CEO, and qualified to spend the stupendous amount of money extracted from taxpayers more intelligently than they could. Once the functions of government move beyond essential expenses, such as national defense and border security, the rationale behind every additional tax dollar is based on the greater wisdom of the political class. You cannot be trusted to support the arts, care for the indigent, respect the environment, or do any of the other things Washington spends your tax money on. Soon, you will not be trusted to manage your own health care—in fact, under the Max Baucus health-care plan, you would be *jailed* for failing to purchase government-approved health insurance. If all of this money is taken from you because you can't be trusted to spend it wisely, it follows that the people spending it *must* possess supreme wisdom. Likewise, the displaced private owners of a nationalized industry must be inferior to the politicians who now control it. No rationale for Big Government can escape these conclusions.

The bigger the government, the greater its leaders. The unfortunate citizens of the biggest governments in the last century were told their maximum leaders were demigods. After all, nobody fills their cities with statues and ten-story portraits of ordinary men. Similar cults of personality are forming in modern America...because the democratic election of a government, or the declared benevolence of its nature, do not change the logic of political superiority. People who are intelligent enough to spend half the income of a vast country better than its citizens will naturally seem like fitting subjects for songs of praise, to their most dedicated admirers. Why *shouldn't* your children be made to learn those songs?

Rogue Warriors
October 4, 2009

Author's Note: This was written after the massive pre-order sales for Sarah Palin's then-upcoming book, Going Rogue, *were made public. Of course, the book wound up breaking records and becoming a huge hit, without the benefit of recipes or sudoku puzzles.*

The unprecedented pre-order sales of Sarah Palin's memoir, *Going Rogue*, have prompted numerous attempts to either explain, or dismiss, her popularity. Steve Schmidt, the chief strategist for the McCain campaign, pins his hopes for the future on Mrs. Palin…squarely between her shoulder blades, with a knife. Says Schmidt:

> I think that she has talents, but my honest view is that she would not be a winning candidate for the Republican candidate in 2012, and in fact, were she to be the nominee, we would have a catastrophic election result.

> In the year since the election has ended, she has done nothing to expand her appeal beyond the base….Th[e] independent vote is going to be up for grabs in 2012. That middle of the electorate is going to be determinative of the outcome of the elections. I just don't see that if you look at the things she has done over the year…that she is going to expand that base in the middle.

Schmidt adds, "The leadership of the party cannot be outsourced to the conservative-entertainment complex." Oh, so *that's* why zillions of people are pre-ordering her book—they're hungry for entertainment. With any luck, Palin will throw in some recipes, and maybe a few sudoku puzzles. The sour grapes about Palin's supposed inability to "expand her appeal beyond the base" are ludicrous. If the hardcore Republican base has become large enough to push an unwritten book to the top of the best-seller lists, 2010 is going to be even more unpleasant for the Democrats than I suspected. The last remaining Democrat senators will be able to carpool in the last remaining Saturn.

Schmidt's position is unpleasant, but understandable. As the architect of a disastrous campaign, he needs someone to blame for his failures, or else his career is over. A much less hostile analysis from Raphael Alexander of the *National Post* offers this explanation for the Palin phenomenon:

> Sarah Palin is a classic populist politician. What makes her so popular is her very nature. She is the definition of "grassroots", a working mother who successfully entered politics at the municipal level and worked her way up to the governorship. She didn't

manage this by impressing people with her five different institutions of education, or how many books she had written on Russian foreign policy. No, she managed it because she inspired Americans who felt that Sarah was "one of them."

For every housewife who dreamed of being more, but had to contend with the responsibilities of raising a family, Palin inspires a strange kind of anti-feminism. There is a perceptible sense of pride that one can be "just average", with all of the same human failings and shortcomings as everybody else.

So people are scrambling to order Palin's book because she's "one of them?" She's the new Erma Bombeck? Certainly her approachability and friendly, common touch are part of her appeal, but they're not the most important part. She's not sitting on top of the Amazon and Barnes & Noble best-seller lists because she's *average*.

What fascinates people about Sarah Palin is that she's **provocative.**

Every movement needs its scholars, the engineers of its philosophy. It also requires representatives, people who can get elected to office and implement its ideas. To get those representatives elected, there must be people who can master the scholarship, make it understandable to people who aren't political junkies...and add a little extra zing, a jolt of electricity to capture the imagination of those non-political people.

There are many ways to be provocative. Some of those methods are rude, or confrontational. The only memorable moment in President Obama's address to Congress on health care reform came when a previously obscure Republican representative couldn't stomach any more mendacity, and called him a liar. It was an ill-mannered outburst, for which the Congressman apologized...but it was also devastatingly effective. It got people buzzing, and because the Congressman was correct, his outburst prompted furious last-minute adjustments to the President's legislative proposals, along with weakening the already soft public opinion of those proposals.

The most aggressive provocateurs walk a tightrope across a canyon of bad taste and controversy. Glenn Beck says some wild, hilarious, and outrageous things, in his desperate struggle to awaken rubber-frog voters before the waters of mega-state socialism boil them alive. He's also been spectacularly right about some very important things, like the Van Jones scandal. Even as Beck reaches new heights of popularity, and drags sleazy characters like Jones out of an administration that major media outlets worship as flawless, a couple of soft-spoken young people with a video camera shock America into action against ACORN, an organization they should have become enraged about long ago. Sometimes you don't have to say anything to be provocative—you just have to show Americans something their media gatekeepers didn't want them to see.

Sarah Palin is provocative by her very existence, having followed none of the scripts prepared by the media, or the bitter vampires of McCain's campaign staff. She electrifies people by speaking with confidence and cheer, to convey ideas that strike the average listener as simple common sense…and which make them realize how radical and deranged the world outside their window has become. Palin's recent speech in Hong Kong was upbeat and plain-spoken, describing an America of liberty and opportunity, and frankly addressing the murderous evil of our terrorist enemies. The speech becomes electrifying when you realize these ideas would be as incomprehensible to the current Administration as Quaddafi's lunatic rant before the United Nations.

Palin's famous "death panel" commentary was powerful because it brought the midnight whispers of an unpleasant truth into the public consciousness. The provocations of someone who used to carry the ancient banner of a great political party must be delivered with elegance and wit…especially if they contemplate taking up that banner again.

The conservative movement requires champions who can make both moral and practical arguments, and show how they are woven together. America has swung so far to the left that simply standing athwart history and yelling "Stop!", as William F. Buckley put it, makes one into something of a radical. I don't think we conservatives appreciate our provocateurs enough. The editorial power of the mainstream media has been greatly diminished by the rise of alternative news and commentary sources, but the media still has the power to keep *silent*, and bury important stories. More importantly, they control the culture, which administers endless injections of their ideology to the apolitical "swing" voters who are so critical to elections. The parade of businessmen and religious zealots who serve as Hollywood's corps of villains, plot lines designed to make liberalism seem irresistible, a thousand little jokes and asides that paint the Right as psychotic…It takes a lot of wattage to blast a conservative idea through all that white noise.

Look at the way our major media culture has treated Obama's radical ideas to take control of the medical insurance industry: a blatantly unconstitutional scheme that becomes sheer insanity in the face of towering government debt, and self-destructing Medicare and Social Security entitlements. The media regards this as a perfectly reasonable, almost uncontroversial idea. What would be an equally dramatic conservative idea? Instead of nationalizing a massive industry, what if a conservative politician proposed privatizing one, like the embarrassing public school system? The proposal would be immediately treated as unthinkably radical, an unacceptable heresy, and the media would portray its advocates as borderline lunatics.

You can't fight your way across a slanted battlefield like that with quietly respectable speeches and erudite policy papers, submitted as genteel points of order. You can't have leaders whose monocles drop from their widened eyes, as they reel in astonishment from savage and unfair attacks. You get around the media by saying things they have to repeat, expressed in language the public will find unforgettable. You provoke so much interest that people shove biased journalists aside, as they rush to pick up a copy of your book.

The Obama presidency has given many people who dislike politics no choice but to become political. Political control has infiltrated every aspect of their lives. As they awaken to this reality, they're looking around for someone besides Obama, someone who can show them an alternative to the total State, which they can no longer pretend not to see. They will not turn to someone quietly waiting to be noticed. The announcement of Going Rogue marks the moment when Palin's future became more important than her past. What she "used to be" is no longer as important as what she is, and may become.

Rogue Stars Rising
October 23, 2009

Author's Note: This is part two of a series that began with "Rogue Warriors," covering the epic New York District 23 special election. It continues through the next three essays. I think the conservative movement and the GOP got a lot of arm wrestling done during this strange drama, and the conservatives were the ultimate winners. Certainly no one who backed Dede Scozzafava could consider themselves winners.

Two stories are unfolding out in the 23rd Congressional District of New York. In the foreground, we have the three-way contest between hapless Republican Dede Scozzafava, upstart Conservative Party candidate Doug Hoffman, and some generic Democrat whose name no one can remember. This race is a microcosm of our strange politics, which have become like a speeding car with jammed door locks, cut brake lines, a dead steering wheel, and air vents that pump nitrous oxide. Everyone is dimly aware the country is heading for the edge of a cliff, but no one can muster the energy to search for alternatives.

The President took time away from his losing wars against Fox News, the Taliban, and economic reality to endorse the Democrat, who would doubtless prove a useful ally in the only war Obama is winning: the war on the American middle class. He probably should have endorsed Scozzafava instead. She'd only be marginally less useful to him—does anyone see her leaping to the well of Congress and declaring her iron-willed opposition to ObamaCare in all its forms? Does anyone have difficulty imagining her sudden decision to support a bill that will address her "concerns" while guaranteeing "affordable access to insurance" for the twenty, thirty, or forty-seven million Americans, legal and otherwise, who will surely die without a government health plan?

At least Obama would have been doing something interesting and unpredictable by endorsing Scozzafava. She clearly shares his views on the use of state power to suppress annoying journalists. Instead, he flew into the district to cough up some more empty rhetoric nobody will remember tomorrow, on behalf of a candidate no one cares about, but who stands a good chance of winning by default.

The other story, playing out in the background, is the second act of one political saga beginning, even as another draws to a close. The rising star of Sarah Palin passes over the melancholy ruins of Newt Gingrich, who spent the last of his credibility endorsing Scozzafava. The Republican Party of Gingrich dies, unloved and irrelevant. Something else is replacing it. The new opposition party is not guaranteed of victory—such guarantees are issued to no one. Palin may never choose to campaign for an office beneath its banner, but she's an integral part of its identity. She'll certainly never be a governor, or anyone's vice presidential candidate, again. For the Republicans, it will never be 1996 or 2006 again. There's no more room for school-lunch debacles, government shutdown miscalculations, Trent Lott, George Allen, Mark Foley…or Newt Gingrich.

It pains me to say this about Gingrich. He accomplished some amazing things, in the mid-90s. He's a smart man who has offered some interesting ideas, in his second life as a conservative intellectual. The problem is that Newt is a political tactician, and in the final stages of a losing war against collectivist ruin, the time has come to focus on grand strategy, rather than tactics. The second decade of this century will be an existential war for the American soul, not a police action.

Gingrich is always thinking about the tactics of the moment, trying to win on points that will *never* be awarded fairly. He spent far too much of his time as Speaker of the House shouting in vain for media referees to throw penalty flags that remained stuffed in their pockets. Meanwhile, the political battlefront has shifted into the fatal terrain of essential liberties and economic freedom. This is the time for courage, conviction, and bold action…not whining about "big tents," while pushing a product of the Pataki machine with a Margaret Sanger award dangling around her neck. A Republican party that embraces Scozzafava over Hoffman isn't a "tent." It's not even a lean-to.

The most urgent task for conservatives is building a logical, consistent *vision* to place before the voters. They're looking for a comprehensive explanation of why Democrat policies are wrong. They can see Obama's failures all around them, but in the absence of a compelling narrative from the opposition party, they're likely to conclude those failures were inevitable, and learn to accept them. If no one presents a coherent alternative to socialism, it wins by default, because too much of the political and media culture desires it. We've already tumbled far past the point where anyone views the Constitution as even a speed bump, let alone a barrier to socialist ambition. The principles embodied in that incredible document *will* perish, if they are not respected, explained, and defended.

A party that supports Scozzafava over Hoffman *cannot* mount that defense. They can't run candidates to the left of the Democrats, then expect a spellbound audience when they explain why the Democrats are wrong. This is not a question of rigid idealism, or remaining a "perfect minority." The voters, including the fabled "moderates," need to be persuaded, not pandered to. Running a liberal squish in a largely conservative district will not cause moderate voters to squeal with excitement over the billowing expanse of the GOP's enormous tent, and rush to see what other wonders might be hidden inside.

In her endorsement of Doug Hoffman, Sarah Palin said:

Our nation is at a crossroads, and this is once again a "time for choosing."

The federal government borrows, spends, and prints too much money, while our national debt hits a record high. Government is growing while the private sector is shrinking, and unemployment is on the rise. Doug Hoffman is committed to ending the reckless spending in Washington, D.C. and the massive increase in the size and scope of the federal government. He is also fully committed to supporting our men and women in uniform as they seek to honorably complete their missions overseas.

And best of all, Doug Hoffman has not been anointed by any political machine.

Doug Hoffman stands for the principles that all Republicans should share: smaller government, lower taxes, strong national defense, and a commitment to individual liberty.

She's clever to throw in that jab at political machines. Dede Scozzafava rolled off the conveyor belt of such a machine, to stand blinking in confusion outside Hoffman's headquarters, drowning in a sea of his campaign posters as she babbled about how she finally wanted to debate him. Voters impressed by political machines will be unable to tear their eyes from the stupendous contraption of media wiring and corrupt money that grows from Barack Obama. Those who are still capable of independent thought need to hear Palin battle cries, not Gingrich apologies.

The GOP is doomed if it holds the course Newt Gingrich set for it, in the waning days of his troubled tenure as Speaker of the House. It should set a new course, following the rogue stars rising to starboard. Palin and Hoffman are among the first of those stars. She's taking a risk by endorsing him, since her detractors would savor his defeat. That's good. America needs risk-takers, not undertakers. Newt Gingrich conceded far too many defeats before the race in New York-23 had even begun, by settling for a candidate he could live with, instead of backing the one New York—and America—really needs.

The Momentum Of History
October 27, 2009

The hotly-contested 2009 races, especially the three-way congressional special election in New York, are the distant thunder of the storm approaching in 2010. The 2010 elections are not merely about gaining temporary political advantage for the Republican Party. The task ahead for American voters is nothing less than reversing the momentum of history. This will not be an easy task...and it will not be *simple.*

There is no question that the momentum of history has swung to the left, ever since the days of Wilson and Roosevelt. The New Deal promise of modest taxation, to pay crucial benefits to the most desperate among the poor, became first a lie, then a joke. No one on the Left even bothers pretending their agenda consists of selfless dedication to the poor any longer. It's all about desperate grabs for gigantic amounts of power over an increasingly impoverished and dominated middle class.

The madness of launching new trillion-dollar programs on top of a madly inflating deficit has become accepted as reasonable discourse. When Nancy Pelosi made her infamous comment that the constitutionality of individual health insurance mandates was not a "serious" question, she was committing a horrible offense against her office, but also providing an accurate description of the current atmosphere in Washington. We're twenty years past the point where such an outrageous statement could even shift the tracks beneath the Crazy Train of her political career.

Many factors combined to bring us to this moment. One of the most important is the blend of pragmatism and romanticism which characterizes the moderate American voter. They are easily excited by heady talk of "change" and "new ideas," but they don't want to be swept up into ideological crusades, or suffer any of that "change" within their own lives. They don't want to take risks with their jobs, or the financial future of their families, but they want to be *told* they're part of a bold new initiative that's changing the world.

The allure of New Deal liberalism does not lie in collective economics—most voters are not eager to view themselves as living off the government dole. The allure lies within collective *morality.* People love the idea of buying a slice of high-flying, big-spending government virtue for the low, low price of one little vote. After they cast that vote, they can go home and relax in front of the TV, while the latest out-of-control progressive spending program is quietly extracted from their paycheck...and their employers' bank account. For many voters, the punitive class warfare of liberal politics is one of its benefits, not part of its cost.

The leftward drift of American politics has continued through decades of prosperity, and the occasional sour little puddle of Carter malaise, because it has been possible for the Left to play its game without causing sudden or radical damage to the middle class it hates. The quality of American life continued to improve, even as a few more freedoms were clipped away, or another gigantic spending program was broken into millions of pieces, and piled carefully on our shoulders. It's no wonder that Barack Obama was able to sell people on "hope and change," even though he's never had an original thought in his life, and his domestic agenda is shrouded in dusty liberal cobwebs. His constituency *loves* to buy the same scratchy old record, year after year, as long as it comes with a flashy new album cover.

A truly transformational moment is upon us. The old game is over. The mad spending spree of 2009 has left America mortgaged to the hilt. The money is all gone. There are no more ways to pinch a few billion more out of the upper class, without destroying the middle class lifestyle. The Right has always been correct in its belief that tax-and-spend liberalism would not work. Every available dollar has been taxed and spent, and not *one single problem* the Left demanded the sacrifice of our wealth and freedom to address has been resolved. Not *one* of their programs has worked, and none of their cost estimates have been accurate, to within an order of magnitude. Tax-and-spend is over. The new coin of the realm will be *control*. A swarm of czars is already hard at work, minting these coins…and behind them, the momentum of history pushes a pendulum that has become a wrecking ball.

How do we reverse that terrible motion? We certainly won't do it by slipping Dede Scozzafava into a district that was Doug Hoffman's to win. We don't have time for twenty-year "big-tent" strategies that promise a 60% chance of reversing 70% of the damage Barack Obama has done in nine months. We also cannot afford to let any more socialists walk away with elections, just to teach the clueless GOP, and errant American voters, another painful lesson. We don't have enough blood left to endure those kinds of lessons.

I don't think the answer lies in confronting Republican candidates with non-negotiable lists of positions they must vow to uphold. The problem with this approach is that it focuses too much energy on compelling politicians, instead of persuading voters. There are places where the GOP falls down so badly that a third-party candidate makes sense, but we should also keep in mind that the Republican Party has money and influence that can be very useful to the conservative cause, and we won't get it by scowling at them and making throat-slitting gestures. The promising young conservative politicians of the moment combine a wonderful degree of confidence and determination with an affable, welcoming style. Doug Hoffman doesn't seem interested in burning the Republican house to the ground, despite the party's many offenses against him. The energetic captain of the *Millennium Palin* doesn't waste a lot of time talking about who she'd like to shove out the airlock.

If the Right can get the voters on board, most of the squishier politicians will begin sliding to starboard. The voters *can* be reached. A review of recent polls, the soaring ratings of Fox News, and the popularity of outspoken critics of the Left, such as Glenn Beck, tells us that people *know* something is terribly wrong. They don't see the Democrats' diagnoses as accurate, or their solutions as effective. They're waiting to hear a coherent explanation from the political leadership of the opposition. It's not enough to give Americans someone to applaud...they need someone to **vote for.**

How do you reverse the momentum of history? You can't do it by eking out a narrow win in a few congressional races, or even the presidency. You need the help of the American people, who have the power to correct much that is wrong with their country, very quickly... if they choose to use it. They should understand that inertia will guarantee the destruction of their lifestyle, as the economic doomsday machines cranked into high gear by Barack Obama complete terrible programs written seventy years ago. The days of purchasing easy grace, by supporting an avalanche of clever little spending programs funded by invisible taxes and antiseptic deficit spending, are over. The people who brought our country to this perilous hour must be stripped of the authority to decide what options are unthinkable, and which beliefs are mandatory.

The leader who emerges from the crucible of 2010, and begins the race for 2012, will be someone who relishes a job that is neither easy, nor simple.

The Stupid Party
November 2, 2009

*Author's Note: If you don't get the wisecrack about hot wires and petri dishes at the end of this piece, I strongly recommend you check out John Carpenter's magnificent remake of "The Thing" from 1982. This **was** written right after Halloween, you know. Alas, Doug Hoffman's campaign did not survive the Scozzafava treachery.*

New York Republicans got a rock in their trick-or-treat bags over the Halloween weekend, as Dede Scozzafava ripped off her million-dollar Republican mask and revealed herself to be a Democrat. It was never a very good disguise, but every previous attempt to peer beneath it was punished with stern lectures from Newt Gingrich and the rest of the party establishment. The bags of contributor money Republicans handed to the Scozzafava campaign would have been more usefully spent hiring detectives to trail ACORN operatives, and keep Democrat voter fraud down to manageable levels.

The Scozzafava campaign is the latest dreadful mistake from a party establishment enchanted by the mirage of the perfect moderate candidate. For Republican voters, it seems like *every* winter is the winter of their discontent. Many of the GOP's boneheaded mistakes come from exactly the same source as the Democrats' boneheaded mistakes: the tendency to believe the media action line about themselves. This produces arrogance in the Democrats, while the Republicans are like awkward, love-struck teenagers—terrified the slightest bit of confident self-expression will blow their chances with the cute moderate in the pink sweater seated beside them in homeroom class. They suffer beneath the same irony that crushes every awkward teenager, since confident self-expression is *exactly* what is needed to connect with the object of their affections…assuming they're not obsessing over someone they never had a chance with anyway.

Establishment mouthpieces trying to rationalize the Scozzafava debacle as a tactical maneuver, designed to win a liberal district by running a moderate candidate, can save their breath. The success of Doug Hoffman's insurgent candidacy blows that argument out of the water. Even if he suffers a narrow loss on Tuesday, Hoffman has certainly proven himself competitive. Just imagine what he could have done with, oh, say about $900,000 in Republican party funding!

As it stands, Hoffman has already crushed *one* of the Democrats in the race, and stands poised to claim victory over the other—and he did it with the help of all the conservative hobgoblins lurking within liberalism's nightmare closet. While Newt Gingrich was droning through the third hour of his Power Point presentation, explaining why running the Card Check-supporting wife of a union thug was a brilliant political maneuver, Sarah Palin roared up in her 4x4 and shouted the obvious truth: voting for actual conservatives is the only way to clear away the Obama malaise.

Every district presents different political challenges, and there are places where both parties are compelled to run candidates who deviate from their core philosophy. The degree of deviance is the issue…particularly for the Republicans, whose core philosophy runs counter to the collectivist momentum of the past century. The Democrats certainly have problems with their mavericks, but usually only when they attempt to implement the most extreme policies, such as trapping America in the nightmare of state-run medicine. As long as the growth of the State bubbles along at Clinton levels, the "Blue Dog" Democrats are content to sit quietly on their porches, ignoring the Republicans waiting for them to bark.

Meanwhile, the Republicans keep running "moderates" who prove to be very useful to the Democrats…which keeps the growth of the State bubbling along at Bush levels. The radical nature of the current Administration makes the idea of "moderate" compromise laughable. What's the moderate position on freedom-crushing trillion-dollar health care and environmentalist legislation? They're okay, as long as the Democrats pinky-swear to keep the cost under $800 billion? That's the kind of promise no politician could keep, even if it was made in earnest. A moderate Republican is someone who lives in a state of perpetual surprise as he ponders the monthly bills for nanny-state government. What's the point of electing people who are guaranteed to spend the rest of their political careers complaining about how they've been played for fools?

Too much of the Republicans' "Stupid Party" strategy is based on the mechanics of getting people with little elephants on their campaign signs elected. They view the election as the conclusion of a contest, when in fact it's only the beginning. A successful Republican Party doesn't have to be ideologically rigid, but it *should* insist on candidates who possess an intellectual foundation of conservative theory, and the ability to explain it at *least* as well as the thousands of people posting comments on conservative blogs.

Republican voters would be well-advised to ignore the people who engineered the Scozzafava debacle, and listen for the sound of Sarah Palin's monster truck instead. America needs conservatives more than it needs Republicans. Both the party, and the country, benefit when they are one and the same. Next Halloween, just to be on the safe side, we should test the blood of every "moderate" Republican with a hot wire and a petri dish, just to make sure we don't have another DIABLO on our hands.

How Do You Solve This Problem Without Sarah?
November 18, 2009

Newsweek advertised its cover story on the release of Sarah Palin's "Going Rogue" by asking, "How do you solve a problem like Sarah?" This headline was informed by the same journalistic standards that led the Washington Post to publish a book review by someone who admits she didn't read the book—and then prompted MSNBC to invite this person on the air as an expert on the book she didn't read. Newsweek apparently couldn't be bothered to watch "The Sound of Music" all the way through, because Maria is the *hero* of the piece. The nuns singing "How Do You Solve a Problem Like Maria?" are singing about suppressing the very spirit that will help Maria save her family from totalitarian oppression. Considering Palin's indestructible good cheer, if she runs for office again, I wouldn't be surprised if she used "How Do You Solve a Problem Like Maria?" as a campaign song…and thanked Newsweek for the suggestion.

The media has treated Palin's book like the mirrored scroll from "Kung Fu Panda": every reviewer sees themselves reflected in its pages. Imagine a mainstream news magazine trying to portray *any* liberal woman as a lightweight, by using a photo of her in running shorts to tease its review of her major new book. Running a book review by someone who admits to skipping the last third of the book is not an insult to Sarah Palin, who was not writing for an audience of lazy media hacks. It's an insult to the audience…including liberal readers of the Washington Post with the intellectual clarity to desire an understanding of those who eagerly devoured every single page. Palin is a phenomenon, and honest liberals would be well-advised to read her work and understand her appeal, just as conservatives should read "Dreams From My Father" to understand the mind of Bill Ayers.

The careless, sloppy disdain of the Left's reaction to "Going Rogue" is almost as strong an argument for Palin's politics as anything contained within its pages. The absolute lack of care and competence from the government that ran up a $12 trillion national debt is astonishing. Months of dithering over Afghanistan strategy, with American troops under fire, ends with a painfully unqualified Commander-in-Chief wailing that he wants a new set of options. The politicization of national defense ends in the absurd spectacle of a civilian trial for illegal enemy combatants…subcontracting national security to trial lawyers, and a randomly-selected pool of 12 people who never heard of 9/11.

The lunatic environmentalist movement, which is poised to push the American economy into a full-bore depression with its cap-and-trade bill, is headed by a man who admitted on national television that he thinks the Earth's core is hotter than the surface of a white dwarf star. The same elite that despises Sarah Palin as an ignorant chillbilly spent the last twenty years telling us this man is a genius.

The national debt is piling up like sales of Palin's book, and the elite don't understand how either of them got so huge. Taxpayers are trapped on a Willy Wonka boat, hurtling through psychedelic clouds of uncontrolled spending, while the President sits in the back and mumbles nonsense rhymes about imaginary jobs created in non-existent Congressional districts. The people lining up to buy Palin's book are not the authors of this careless, carnivorous government...but they are expected to pay for it. The assertion that someone who connects with them, and understands their beliefs, is unwelcome on the national stage is just the latest variation of "Shut up and pay your taxes." No one should accept that attitude from a government as incompetent as the journalists who fawn over it.

The argument over whether Sarah Palin is "qualified" for the presidency is the opposite of the question conservatives should be asking. What we need to know is whether any other aspiring candidate has the essential qualifications Palin brings to the table.

The tax-and-spend engine of collectivist government is locked into overdrive, and it's going to blow very soon—perhaps within the term of Barack Obama's successor, if dramatic steps are not taken. There's very little point in supporting a presidential candidate who won't take those dramatic steps, and that means we need someone who can connect with ordinary people, including moderates and independents, and *persuade* them to lend their support. Pandering to the uncommitted is tantamount to taking the bridge of a sinking ship, but refusing to touch the wheel. The challenges ahead require not just a victory, but a mandate, and you can't get a mandate by trying to appear inoffensive to moderates, in the hope they'll reluctantly bring up the rear of your campaign once you're already winning.

Most voters are not ideologues. They don't follow politics obsessively, and they probably haven't given much thought to a coherent philosophy of government...but they respond to one when they see it. It takes provocative energy to reach them through the media filter, and convince them to spare a little time from their busy lives to entertain reasoned arguments. Attempts to persuade them without inspiring them are like winning cases presented in dry whispers before an empty courtroom. A platform of small discounts on our $12 trillion government will not make enough of a difference to be worth the effort. There was never a *good* time for Democrat Lite politicians, but they have become a mistake we can no longer afford.

It's an ironic twist of democracy that small, passionate groups cannot get Presidents elected, without appeals to the broader electorate...but they *can* lock in outrageous spending programs, by savagely resisting attempts to cancel or reform them. The single-minded energy that repels voters is irresistible to politicians. The focused appetite of those on the receiving end of government billions will always be more influential than the diffuse annoyance of taxpayers…unless a reformist President continues to inspire, and persuade, after assuming the office. Maintaining that kind of connection with the voters requires conviction, courage, confidence, and boundless good cheer. It's a job for someone who can take a beating, and never lose faith in the American people…long after a sizable chunk of them have put that faith to the test.

I hope many candidates step forward with these qualifications, especially since Sarah Palin hasn't declared any intention to run for office again. Even if she does, it would be best to have a spirited competition between worthy nominees. Neither Republicans, nor the republic, have been well-served by "inevitable" candidates. Taming a berserk government will be a matter of politics, as much as policy, requiring both intelligent plans and the spirit to implement them. Some of the qualifications we should be looking for are difficult to quantify as bullet points on a resume. Those people standing in the freezing cold, happily awaiting the signature of an author who ignores every attempt to pronounce her dead, on a book the entire media establishment told them to ignore, might have an idea where to find what we need.

The question before conservatives is not whether Sarah Palin can win. The question is: at this desperate hour, what's the point of winning without someone like her?

What Democracy Is Not
December 23, 2009

I believe the current American government is far too large, and horribly corrupt. I often write critically of its actions. I don't hate the government, however. The defense of liberty is not a romance with anarchy. The federal government has vital functions to perform. Over the centuries, the American political class has produced men and women of eloquence, courage, and honor. I hate how far short our current crop of politicians falls from the standard set by the creators of this republic. I hate what the republic has been twisted into, and I implore my fellow citizens to stand up and put a stop to it, because it teeters on the precipice of becoming something much worse.

The American democracy was not created to dictate the destiny of its citizens. It has a duty to avoid interfering with our hopes and dreams, except where necessary to maintain order. The government should not be conscripting us into the service of its hopes and dreams, with thousand-page draft notices. A nation becomes great because of what its people achieve, not because of what they are required to do…or what they are forbidden to do.

The goal of representative democracy should not be sending the most aggressive team of brigands to Washington, to pillage the other states. The unseemly haste of Democrats to buy enough votes for their awful health-care bill, and push it through by Christmas, is reminiscent of a gang of thieves panicking at the sound of a burglar alarm going off, and racing to stuff pillowcases full of swag before the cops show up.

The suggestion by House Majority Whip Jim Clyburn, that every senator and representative should service their constituents by haggling over the highest price for their votes, is an insult to patriotism. The states should combine their strength in the federal union, for those limited number of tasks that only the central government can perform. The union was not meant to be a weapon for looting the states that aren't represented by ancient incumbents with powerful committee chairs.

The people of Nebraska did not send Ben Nelson to be first in line when the doors open on Washington's big Black Friday sale of federal goodies, waving his so-called "principles" like a credit card. The voters of the other states should not have to watch their representatives mope around like disappointed shoppers who missed the best deals. Firm adherence to clearly-stated principles is not merely a desirable trait for a member of Congress. It is **essential**. Voting for a political hack who lies about everything he believes in, and has no position without a price tag, is not an exercise in true democracy, any more than voting with a dart board and blindfold would be.

Sarah Palin described the revolting spectacle of the Senate health care bill on her Facebook page:

> The administration's promises of transparency and bipartisanship have been broken one by one. This entire process has been defined by midnight votes on weekends, closed-door meetings with industry lobbyists, and payoffs to politicians willing to sell their principles for sweetheart deals. Is it any wonder that Americans are so disillusioned with their leaders in Washington?

We reached the sorry moment Palin describes because our ruling class became disillusioned with *us*. When the government seizes control of something, it says that its citizens can no longer be trusted to manage it themselves. That's true of the federal government's legitimate responsibilities. National defense cannot be entrusted to irregular militias, no matter how patriotic and courageous their members. Health care is not something a free people can watch their government take away from them, ignoring the strident objections of a substantial majority. If we do, we are no longer free...and in the years to come, the ruling class will feel increasingly less pressure to pretend it serves the voters.

Transparency is not a gift to be promised in an election campaign, and withheld when opacity proves more convenient to the President. Bipartisanship is a compromise to meet the needs of all citizens, without exceeding the rules that constrain government. It is not a conspiracy to cobble together a coalition of dependents, and gain enough political strength to rewrite the rules.

Reckless deficit spending is not merely unwise financial policy. It is a damnable sin against democracy itself. Our nation was founded in defiance of the tyranny of taxation without representation. Levying monstrous taxes against generations unborn is an even more appalling example of that tyranny. Free men and women cannot be held responsible for the sins of their parents...and they cannot hold their children responsible for meeting their demands. Freedom does not carry the burdens of the past, or sustain itself by consuming the possibilities of the future. Liberty is meaningless in the absence of responsibility—you are not "free" unless you are accountable for your actions. An irresponsible democracy cannot survive for long.

Democracy is not about "rationing" goods and services through all-powerful Independent Medicare Death Panel Advisory Boards. Rationing means the people get what the government thinks they deserve. Those criteria will be determined with the same kind of back-room deals and midnight caucuses that put the Advisory Board in place. The government cannot control anything without rationing it. Rationing transforms your vote from a civic responsibility into a vital currency, which you must spend aggressively to survive.

Democracy is utterly incompatible with little rule-bending land mines hidden in gigantic bills, which only become public knowledge because they were spotted by a sharp-eyed staffer working for the opposition party. What is a half-written bill, largely unread by legislators, but an exercise in the same kind of arbitrary power that sent the Minutemen into the field against England? How does a responsible citizen assess the performance of his representatives, when their careers are spent voting on titanic hundred-billion-dollar bills with thousands of clauses? Responsibility drowns beneath huge bills sold with fraudulent accounting, based on promises no one takes seriously, with results no one could possibly predict.

What we have seen in the House and Senate during President Obama's first year is not the behavior of a responsible Congress, acting in the humble service of its constituents, and conducting the lawful business of a democratic republic. Congress gains its legitimacy from the laws that bind it, not the spectacular spending bills it passes in defiance of those laws. We started down this path when we began judging government by the way it responded to the demands of its citizens, instead of the faithful performance of its duties. It will take a lot of work to correct the situation. In undertaking that task, we will not be aspiring to a lofty ideal. We will be reclaiming our birthright. The Congress of Nancy Pelosi and Harry Reid has worked under cover of darkness to steal something incredibly precious, which the authors and signatories of the Constitution desperately wanted you to have.

Targeting the Tea Party
January 8, 2010

The Tea Party movement has grown with astonishing speed. Swaddled in discussion-board posts and nursed with e-mail over the past year, the movement is now a month away from speaking with a unified voice for the first time, at its first national convention in Nashville. The transition from demonstrations to conventions marks an evolution from expressing need to taking action...from describing what is *wrong* to declaring what would be *right*.

A concerted attempt to discredit and marginalize the Tea Party movement has developed with equally amazing speed. The dimmer bulbs in this pinball machine of contempt, such as Chris Matthews, have worked hard to make the derogatory, sexually tainted slang term "teabaggers" popular. The term spread to supposedly mainstream, "impartial" journalists with viral efficiency. It's hard to imagine a comparable grassroots movement, with a racial or collectivist agenda more agreeable to the Left, suffering this kind of crude insult. Mocking nicknames would never be slapped on a group of illegal aliens agitating for greater welfare benefits. That level of elite contempt is reserved for middle-class folks who object to *paying* for those benefits. The media covers Tea Parties with the same condescension they show to any unseemly spectacle of tax serfs refusing to "pay their fair share." To those who believe all virtue resides in the compassionate power of the State, resistance always equals greed.

The Tea Parties became impossible to dismiss after the massive demonstration in Washington, following the 9/11 commemoration. It therefore became necessary to slander them. The original strategy was to portray them as violent lunatics, a bit of intellectual crabgrass planted as far back as the infamous Defense Intelligence Estimate released by the politicized Department of Homeland Security last April. Even as Major Nidal Hasan was praising jihad in seminars and peppering al-Qaeda with Facebook friend requests, and the Underwear Bomber was singing the praises of the World Trade Center murderers, Janet Napolitano squeezed her eyes closed and finger-painted "right-wing extremists" as the hot new terrorist threat. The report came out a week before the big Tea Party protests on Tax Day.

The domestic terrorist smear didn't stick, so the race card was hauled from the bottom of the deck. Once again, MSNBC muppet Chris Matthews served up the fast-food version of this poison, with his deranged insistence that "every single teabagger in America is white." Remember: Matthews didn't write this script, he's just doing a clumsy job of reading it. Someone slipped him instructions to carefully insinuate the Tea Party movement is tinged with racism, and he responded by turning pink and screaming "They're all white!"

Ignoring this drivel based on the pathetic audience of MSNBC hosts would be a mistake. These cellar dwellers do the ground work for the media slander machine, sending toxic clouds of smoke upstairs for the more "respectable" journalists to notice after a discreet interval. After a few months of Chris Matthews confusing Tea Party footage with "Birth of a Nation," the NBC anchors who don't have to suffer wearing the MS Of Shame can start talking about the clouds of controversy swirling around the allegations that Tea Parties are suspected of reportedly harboring racist thoughts. Laughing at Matthews isn't enough. It's essential to laugh at anyone who even *thinks* about taking him seriously.

Not all of the Tea Party's enemies are on the Left. Some of them are nominally conservative elitists like David Brooks, who haven't thought elitism all the way through, and realized it leads inevitably to collectivism—because if the "educated class" is so magnificent, it makes sense for them to run the world, and resistance to their brilliant designs is stupid by definition. You can see the first glimmers of this truth in Brooks' dismissal of the Tea Parties as "a large, fractious confederation of Americans who are defined by what they are against." Being *against* things is reactionary and blockheaded, you know. Intelligence demands progress!

The Tea Party convention made a bold choice in selecting Sarah Palin as the keynote speaker for their convention. It was also very considerate of them—since the same people hate Palin and the Tea Parties, for the same reasons, their enemies can reduce their carbon footprint by carpooling to Nashville.

It has been suggested that Palin might not have been the most strategic choice for a keynote speaker, since she's not running for any office in 2010. I think she's perfect, because the Tea Party is looking for a *representative,* not a leader. They want a champion they can send into the field, carrying their banner. Some have criticized the Tea Parties as populist in nature, but populism is defined by pandering, rather than persuasion...and a movement that asks the author of America's best-selling political book to escort it into the American spotlight is definitely interested in persuasion.

The war against the Tea Party is an extension of the long war against the American middle class. The Left believes it will achieve final victory through socialized medicine, which will forever shackle the middle class as dependents of the State, and destroy the independence that makes them dangerous. The Tea Party says it has only *begun* to fight. Next month, the most sincerely middle-class major party candidate in recent history will take the stage on their behalf, and render two-thirds of David Brooks' analysis obsolete: the Tea Party will still be large, but it will no longer be quite so fractious, or defined only by what it opposes.

The Disconnected President
January 28, 2010

Author's Note: This is my analysis of President Obama's first State of the Union address. It was a novel experience to watch a SOTU carefully and take notes. I guess that officially makes me a political junkie. Actually, I gave up trying to take notes about halfway through, and started live-Twittering the address, which was a lot of fun.

Viewers of the State of the Union address last night were treated to the spectacle of a man completely disconnected from reality, insisting the country join him in celebrating his failures as rousing successes…or at least the best anyone could have expected to do, in the long shadow of George Bush. It wasn't a President honestly discussing the state of the union. It was a long, rambling exit interview from a deluded employee, who thinks he was called into the office to get a raise instead of a pink slip. It was the hurt and confusion of an academic who doesn't understand how his B+ term paper could have become such a disaster when implemented in the real world, and insists it will still work, if everyone pays closer attention to the extensive footnotes.

Beyond the fact-checkable whoppers fried up on the grill of desperate political necessity, the speech illustrated a disturbing ignorance of the way every facet of our economy and culture is **connected.** Barack Obama is a disconnected President, who lacks a basic understanding of the fantastically complex system he pretends to control. He's a vain and egotistical man frantically waving his arms in front of a symphony he can barely hear, and claiming to be the conductor.

It was surreal to watch a politician announce his top priority is job creation, then spend the next hour listing class-warfare enemies. I hope people making less than $250k per year start hiring like crazy, because everyone with a higher income just became a hated enemy of the state. Why, if they work for a large corporation, they shouldn't even have free speech rights!

It's painful to listen to someone who wants to add nationalized banks to his collection of state-run car companies wax poetic about the power of entrepreneurs, then list all the ways he's going to punish risk-taking and achievement. Anyone who successfully starts a business, and creates jobs through rising profits and expansion, will quickly become a member of the evil $250k Legion of Doom. The financial speculation he pounded with the poverty-stained cudgel of socialist rhetoric *provides the investment capital* for those small entrepreneurs. If no one has incentives to excel, and risk-taking is a felony offense, small businesses don't appear and grow. Entrepreneurship does not thrive in the thin soil of a command economy. Contrary to Democrat Party rhetoric, banks do not exist to give people credit cards they can pay off whenever they get around to it, or mortgages they "deserve" but cannot possibly afford.

Praise for the resilient spirit of the American people rings hollow, coming from a man who doesn't think they can be trusted to manage their own health care without government supervision. As Governor McDonnell explained in his splendid response, private property and free speech rights are inseparable components of liberty. Neither of them dissipates with rising income levels, or membership in private corporations disliked by the ruling political party. All of those targeted tax cuts and transfer payments promised in the State of the Union are links in the very chain of state control that strangles innovation and risk-taking. If a nation desires economic growth and technological development, it *must* celebrate achievement and respect individual wealth. The last thing America needs is another five thousand pages of tax law, telling us how we can avoid the tariffs our political class has leveled on activity it has declared *incorrect*. A "targeted tax cut" is actually a punitive fine, leveled at everyone who doesn't comply with the government's designs. We can only hope the Americans who work in the financial sector demonstrate resilience in the face of Barack Obama.

A politician who wants to swell the size of an already-titanic government has no business complaining about lobbyists and special interests, especially when he thinks "special interest" means "a powerful group that doesn't contribute money to my party." The party of George Soros, and the candidate who turned his campaign website into a Swiss bank account by disabling its basic identity checks, have nothing useful to say about keeping "foreign money" out of politics. Big Government always brings lobbyists. They're the only boom industry of the Obama economy. If you want to reduce the control of wealthy interests over our politics, you *must* reduce the size of government. As the sad fate of the McCain-Feingold regulations prove, you can't purge those interests through increasingly draconian and illogical rules on political speech. The acolytes of Big Government always pretend that "fighting special interests" means being more aggressive in designating their enemies as special interests.

This State of the Union speech was the midterm exam in a long, painful lesson about the interdependence of politics, culture, and the economy. The challenge facing a democracy is to maintain a government that secures freedom against anarchy, without following its worst instincts into tyranny. Government is force, and the larger its programs become, the more it becomes fixated on compliance. The belief that we can let the government control *some* portions of our lives and industry, while the rest remain vibrant and creative, is a childish fantasy that should have died for good last night, before the spectacle of a man who doesn't understand why his declared capitalist enemies aren't producing enough jobs to boost his approval ratings. When he urged Americans to begin removing the obstacles to their success, he was too disconnected to understand that process already began in Massachusetts last week.

Misunderstanding the Tea Party
February 9, 2010

The Tea Party movement is a political Andromeda Strain to the media, a baffling outbreak of viral unhappiness which has thus far defied every attempt at diagnosis. This is unsurprising, since the media has little interest in listening to what the Tea Party is actually saying. Instead, they attempt to stuff this remarkable grassroots movement into a variety of scary costumes, so they can be conveniently dismissed.

The most common of these costumes is a straitjacket. The media likes to view the Tea Party as a psychotic break with establishment reality. Writing in the *L.A. Times,* Gregory Rodriguez calls American distrust of government "neurotic—irrational, defensive, and born of emotional trauma." He prescribes a dose of past-life regression therapy, until we get back to "our national birth trauma, our violent revolt against our 'father', King George III, which gave us our independence in the first place." Wow, people named George cast really *long* shadows over history, don't they?

If the buckles on the straitjacket break, certain elements of the Left are quick to dress the Tea Party in white sheets. The tedious Joe Queenan, working for a*Guardian U.K.* that evidently couldn't afford to hire an American writer who has actually seen a Tea Party rally, describes the attendees as "smallish, grassroots, inbred" anti-intellectual pasty-white Nixon voters. He also can't stress enough how white these abhorrent, pasty-white, "ethnically monochromatic" white crackers are. Oh, and they're also a small fringe movement that likes to send tiny squads of loudmouths to intimidate rural Idaho congressmen…but they're also a vast, sinister, potentially violent mob, lurking in the deep red shadows of flyover country, where people have forgotten how to properly appreciate their massive central government.

If you can't quite buy the image of the Tea Party as a massive *Birth of a Nation* re-enactment, some liberals would like to conjure marionette strings leading from their awkwardly jerking limbs, up to puppet handles gripped in swollen feline paws. Lee Fang at Think Progress sees the helpless, mindless swarms of protesters as nothing but a Pampered Chef party for Republican "profiteers." The mainstream press retails the usual smear about anyone who protests high taxes or government spending as either unwitting tools, or paid operatives, of the fat cats who stand to rake in millions from their agenda. (Remember the feeble attempts to paint anyone who disagreed with ObamaCare as henchmen of the insurance industry? Joe Queenan would remind you they were *white* henchmen of the *white-owned* insurance industry.)

Of course, no leftist caricature of the Tea Party would be complete without a dunce cap. To paraphrase the exasperated alien villain of *Plan 9 From Outer Space,* these protesters are stupid, stupid, stupid! They're slaves of a woman Stephen Colbert assures us is "a f—-ing retard." Kurt Andersen of *New York Magazine* sees them as irrational hysterics, whipped into a frenzy by talk-radio hosts, threatening to unleash mere anarchy upon the nation by planting themselves ankle-deep in the blood-dimmed tide of mindless intransigence. They're too dense to realize the establishment they oppose is an eternal institution, their lives mere grains of sand against its trillion-dollar fortifications.

The Tea Party movement is not crazy, hateful, or stupid. Their rallies are disarmingly cheerful affairs, which most certainly do include women and minorities. The movement is still in the process of coalescing, and seeks inspiration and representation, rather than leadership. They know their country is rocketing down the wrong path, and while the current President has a heavy hand on the throttle, the course was set long before he entered politics.

If you seek madness, look for it in the President's delusional State of the Union speech, or the people who indulge his belief that another three or four trillion piled onto a $14 trillion national debt will get us at least halfway to utopia. If you want to taste hatred, sample the venom directed at Sarah Palin, the only person currently capable of building a bridge between the energy of the Tea Party, and the established resources of the GOP. If you would like stupidity illustrated, witness the spectacle of the Democrats passing off their oily mass of backroom deals and political payoffs as a rational plan for improving health care.

The lack of a comprehensive solution doesn't make criticism invalid. The point is that comprehensive solutions are *inherently* inadequate, compared to the creative power of free markets and private industry. Tea Party stalwarts are entirely rational in refusing to submit themselves as raw materials for the next big adventure in central planning. After several lifetimes of watching an increasingly huge federal government fail at almost everything it tries, while displaying increasingly less enthusiasm for the Constitutional duty of national defense that it actually excels at, the middle class demands the freedom and respect to get busy solving its own problems. They're understandably tired of watching every story in the evening news twisted into another reason the government needs more money, every market fluctuation offered as proof the private sector has too much freedom, and every change in the weather presented as a omen their standard of living is a mortal wound to the Earth.

Donald Luskin of the *Wall Street Journal* worries that the Tea Party could veer into destructive populism. Others fear they'll mutate into a third-party dead end that drains enough strength from the Republicans to ensure a continued plunge into the collectivist abyss. Both are real dangers—there are always predators hiding in the grass roots. I believe the Tea Party is not a populist revolt against Wall Street, but rather a firm indictment of centralized power in general. Big Business brings reduced costs and advanced products to consumers, and American prosperity would be impossible without the financial resources of major banks, from business loans to credit cards. However, when Big Business merges with Big Government, the result always ends up looking more like the latter. The temptation to purchase government power is great, and it has many aggressive salesmen. Risk-taking is an essential component of growth…but there is no such thing as *subsidized risk,* and no healthy gamble can be made by companies which have gained federal certification as Too Big To Fail.

The Tea Party movement is not simplistic. It's a revolt against the simplistic, and painfully inaccurate, notion that spending bills solve problems, and legislation is the only *real* form of action. It's a rising tide of indignation from people tired of being told they're ineligible to participate in the national discussion because of their race, class, religious belief, radio listening habits, or choice of cable news network. The idea that tagging a huge movement as "all-white" would serve as a devastating insult is deeply insulting to Americans of every skin color.

The Tea Party movement is young, and it could make a lot of mistakes…but it's amazing how much it's accomplished so far, just by clearing its throat. It's not surprising the Left is trying to dismiss them, instead of answering their questions…but they've come too far to be discarded as lunatics, hatemongers, or idiots. They're not a blank screen where the Left can project its neuroses and obsessions. They reject the narrative of a fading nation that should do the best it can to make amends for centuries of sins before it dies. They have not yet begin to fight, and theirs is the energy of a revolutionary spirit that can't *wait* to get back to building a future beyond the limited imagination of their detractors.

In Defense Of Gay Conservatives
February 23, 2010

Author's Note: Just before this essay was written, Michelle Malkin sold Hot Air to Salem Communications.

Bryan Fischer, host of the American Family Association's "Focal Point" radio talk show, is very upset about Hot Air's nose dive into the thundercloud of gay politics, and angry that it could happen with our new "Christian ownership" at Salem Communications slumped lifelessly in the pilot's seat:

> Wow. Just as soon as the "Hot Air" blog was purchased by the Christian conglomerate Salem Communications from conservative commentator Michelle Malkin, it has suddenly become an advocate for all things gay. What in the world is up with that?

> For background, GOPROUD is an organization dedicated to advancing special rights for homosexual behavior, and advocates the overthrow of the Defense of Marriage Act and the overthrow of the law banning homosexual service in the military.

> Not only was GOPROUD welcomed at CPAC, an event which is supposed to be the annual showcase for conservative values, the organization was allowed to sponsor the event, giving visibility and recognition to its effort to legitimize sexual deviancy.

Fischer presses his face to the passenger windows of Hot Air, and sees Green Room contributor Repurblican crouched on the wing, tearing pieces of conservative purity from the starboard engine:

> A Saturday post, from Repurblican, takes one of my new heroes, Ryan Sorba of California Young Americans for Freedom, to task for making the common sense statement at CPAC that homosexual sex cannot lead to reproduction. For this obviously correct observation, he was booed off the stage. And "Hot Air," now under Christian management, has made Sorba out to be the bad guy.

> Sorba showed the courage of his convictions by simply declaring the truth. Said Sorba, "Civil rights are grounded in natural rights, and natural rights are grounded in human nature…and the intelligible end of the reproductive act is reproduction…civil rights, when they conflict with natural rights, are contrary…" At this point, his remarks were drowned out by a chorus of vitriolic, angry boos. (View video of his remarks here.)

388

Consequently, Sorba said, "I'd like to condemn CPAC for bringing GOPRIDE (he meant "GOPROUD") to this event."

For speaking truth to power, "Hot Air" accused Sorba of "bombthrowing," and said his remarks represented a "gratuitous and public...slam on homosexuals."

The idea that Salem Communications has somehow enforced new pro-gay editorial standards on Hot Air is ridiculous. So is acting like a jerk in the name of ideological purity at CPAC. This kind of factional infighting is obviously unhelpful to overcoming the enormous challenges facing us in the next few elections. It would be tragic for the nation if we left it rolling towards the edge of the socialist cliff, while we spend our days tearing the mantle of "true conservatism" into a thousand pieces, and accusing each other of heresy. A certain degree of this conflict was inevitable, as different groups struggle for control of the resurgent Right, from David Frum squeaking that it's not too late to reach an understanding with our progressive masters, to Bryan Fischer advising his readers to "kiss off" Hot Air because some of our contributors dared to speak up in defense of GOPROUD.

I think my own credentials as a defender of traditional marriage are in order. They can be reviewed in detail here and here. I do not hold these beliefs out of animosity toward gay people, or disrespect for committed homosexual relationships. I believe in the positive value of the marriage tradition, and I reserve the right to celebrate that value without denigrating those who don't participate in it.

The gay-marriage movement is necessarily aggressive, because they seek a substantial change in society. I appreciate the strength of their conviction, and as long as they respect mine, we can have a civil discussion. The temptation to detonate conviction into anger is strong, and counter-productive. I'm no more impressed by Ryan Sorba's act than I was by Perez Hilton's.

It's remarkable how much the focus has shifted away from social issues, in the year since I began writing for Hot Air. Carrie Prejean's encounter with Perez Hilton was one of the hot topics back then. Now we stand in the shadow of a looming catastrophe which threatens the liberty and prosperity of our entire society. It's not surprising to see our focus shift toward the common menace. I don't feel traditional marriage is any less important than I did a year ago, but if GOPROUD wants to have that discussion later, after we wrestle down unsustainable government spending, and clear the danger of being thrown in jail for failure to purchase government-approved health insurance, that's fine by me.

I hope to reach something more than a temporary truce between the factions of the Right. The assertion that we are all captives of some agenda, which we must accept in full or reject utterly, is the language of identity politics, and of totalitarianism. The Fischer criticism of Hot Air demonstrates the foolishness of assuming that every member of an identity group is party to some kind of agenda. If there's a "Christian agenda," then either Salem Communications or Bryan Fischer was not invited to the meetings.

We can be united in our appreciation for liberty...and this requires respect for the individual, just as the embrace of collectivism ultimately brings contempt. You can't believe what I do about the transcendent rights of the individual, and the limitless potential of free men and women, while simultaneously assuming you can judge their innermost thoughts by their sexual preference, or the color of their skin. Rejecting gay conservatives because they disagree with me about marriage would be crawling back into the walled compound of my little tribe, and expecting them to do likewise. Each tribe would then resume shoving the wrecking ball of the State at the others, until someone gets flattened. That's not the game conservatives, or Americans, should be playing.

It's not going to be easy to hold the components of the Right together, especially as our ranks swell, and the dependents of State rally to its tattered banner of rage and despair. The constituencies of the Left have been fairly easy to buy off. Sometimes it was only necessary to buy their leadership off, and leave the common folk to suffer beneath failed programs they were told they have a moral duty to accept without question. No such arrangement will suffice for a conservative movement united by its rejection of the bloated and dying central government we inherited from the twentieth century...but still working to reconcile discordant visions of what should come next.

We can show each other a little grace and courtesy without abandoning our strongly-held beliefs...or at least refrain from trying to excommunicate each other. Leave the identity politics to the nitwits who look at Marco Rubio and see a coconut.

The Principle Of Repeal
April 2, 2010

Author's Note: It seems fitting to conclude this collection, and my first year as a blog author, with the essay that placed the Holy Grail of conservative authors into my astonished hands: a mention by Rush Limbaugh on his radio show. Naturally, I was away from the radio when this happened. I learned about it when I had an opportunity to check my email, and found a hundred messages and Tweets bearing congratulations. Luckily I was able to listen to Rush's podcast later, and hear it for myself. Thus concludes the fastest-moving year of my life...

The early battle cry of "Repeal and Replace!" has become stuck in a few Republican throats. The thinking among "top Republicans" is that outright repeal of ObamaCare might be impossible, leading to frustration among an energized base that demands nothing less. There is also some apprehension that an uncompromising push for repeal will alienate moderate and independent voters in otherwise winnable states.

Declaring repeal to be "impossible" is a self-fulfilling prophecy of American decline. A slapdash pile of graft and fraudulent cost projections, passed by a fantastically corrupt Congress that claims it couldn't hear the muffled screams of the outraged electorate through the thick doors of their smoke-filled rooms, instantly becomes an eternal component of our lives? That will only be true if we *make* it true...and even then, it won't be true for long.

One way or another, ObamaCare won't last far beyond the point where your kids go bankrupt trying to pay for it. The American entitlement state is the world's tallest, shakiest house of cards. We can find the strength and self-respect to repeal this garbage now, or weep in shame and confusion when it implodes, after years of increasing poverty and decreasing public health. I encourage wobbly Republican politicians to take a long look at their preschool-age children, grandchildren, nephews, or nieces during the Easter holiday. Make peace with ObamaCare now, and you give life to a system that has already declared war on those kids...and will utterly defeat them before they graduate high school.

It's true that the GOP cannot completely dedicate itself to the repeal of one piece of legislation for the next three years. Instead, they should dedicate themselves to slaying the blasphemous, rotting leviathan that gave birth to ObamaCare, and whose tentacles are visibly squeezing the life out of the American economy. Big Government is a parasite that is more than willing to kill its host. Ordinary people are beginning to see it for what it is. They understand that something is terribly *wrong* with their government. Now is the time to explain the origins of this leviathan, and put ObamaCare in its proper context...as the final, absurd contortions of a philosophy that acts in complete ignorance, and sometimes outright *contempt,* for what free people can achieve. Behold the toxic wonder of a bill that forces people to buy a product that it will also cause a shortage of.

In its final years, the Left can only communicate with the thundering stallions of American prosperity using curses and whips. It will answer every problem caused by the taxes and regulations of ObamaCare with more taxes and regulations, until the stallions of progress die beneath the lash, with the last impotent curses of angry and frightened liberals ringing in their ears.

Republicans, you *know* how this story ends. You've seen its miserable ending all over the world, from the ruins of Russia to the sick old men of Europe, dying from the fever of unsustainable entitlements and the chills of terminal demography...and too weak to protest as the shroud of fascism is drawn slowly over them. Repealing ObamaCare, and replacing it with *real and meaningful* health care reforms grounded in the fertile soil of the free market, should be the **beginning** of your commitment to guide your country away from this fate. To compromise with those who showed no interest in compromising their lust for power would be surrender. When you discover people trapped inside a burning car, you're not doing them any favors by feeding change into the parking meter.

As for those moderate and independent voters: the modern Democrat Party has *nothing* more to offer them. What "moderate" reforms could be applied to a multi-trillion dollar boondoggle, added to an already lethal national debt? No one who allows ObamaCare to survive beyond 2012 can call themselves an "independent." You won't be *allowed* to remain independent of State-controlled medicine. Sixteen thousand new IRS agents will be dropping by your house to explain this in more detail, if you press the issue.

If you're an independent who takes your vote seriously, you must understand by now that ObamaCare's failures will be addressed with further assaults on your independence, including massive taxes that will only accelerate the erosion of meaningful freedom. Moderate voters pride themselves on considering ideas from all sides of the political spectrum, and choosing wisely between them. When ObamaCare was signed, the political spectrum shifted violently into the infrared. If we still have it wrapped around our throats in 2013, there won't *be* any more ideas from the "right" for you to sagely consider. Your choices will be limited to various frequencies of hard-Left statism. Every serious moderate and independent voter is a Republican now...assuming the GOP has the wit and courage to *inspire* them, rather than pandering to them.

Politicians, of every party, tend to be slippery and undependable. That's one of the reasons I don't want them in charge of my life, or any industry I *choose* to do business with. A discerning voter looks for more than personal character in a politician, especially in high-stakes elections. They consider **principles** above all. It's not true that politicians are unprincipled—the worst of them are entirely dedicated to the principle of increasing their own wealth and power.

The Democrats made a fatal mistake in writing their principles of greed and control in red ink, across ObamaCare's thousands of shadowy pages. With the fiscally conservative Democrat exposed as a mirage, and the socially conservative Democrat a lie, the ears of our rapidly-growing independent population turn to the GOP. They're listening for the principles of faith in the common man, and humility before the creative power of freedom.

Speak, Republicans…and do not mumble.

Made in the USA
Lexington, KY
07 August 2010